You can teach grammar

Claudia Bertotto, Jimena del Azar-Pintaric and Margaret Hurley

You Can Teach Books, Inc.

You Can Teach Books, Inc.
Toronto, Ontario, Canada
www.youcanteachgrammar.com

© Copyright 2013 by You Can Teach Books, Inc. All rights reserved.

ISBN 978-0-9879003-3-3

Cover design by Sebastian Diaz Molaro

No part of this book may be reproduced in any form or by any electronic or mechanical means including information storage and retrieval systems, without permission in writing from the publisher. The only exception is by a reviewer, who may quote short excerpts in a review.

Image credits:
Images of flowers in Chapter 3; family in Chapter 5; musician, doctor and banker in Chapter 6; and appointment book in Chapter 11 are from Microsoft Word Clip Art. Used with permission of Microsoft.
World map image in Chapter 4 is from Wikimedia Commons. Used with permission.

Introduction

You Can Teach Grammar is for current and prospective teachers of English to speakers of other languages: it comprehensively describes the rules of English grammar and follows that up with practical examples of how to teach English grammar.

You Can Teach Grammar can function as a stand-alone text for the grammar portion of any English language teacher training course. With that as the main design, the text has a clear, direct ancillary use: as a reference work for English teachers in the field, providing both the technical rules of grammar and advice for effectively teaching specific grammatical forms.

The book covers all the parts of speech in depth. Each chapter contains multiple exercises for self-testing on the grammar topics. In addition, *In The Classroom* segments in each chapter address common issues related to teaching the grammar topics under discussion. Finally, each chapter ends with a full set of ideas for teaching the grammar in a classroom situation. The teaching ideas are oriented toward communicative teaching methods.

The field of English teaching is described with many different acronyms, including ESL (English as a second language), EFL (English as a foreign language), ESOL (English for speakers of other languages) and ESP (English for special purposes). Throughout this book, the term ESL is used as an all-encompassing term to refer to all categories of English language learning.

For more information on these and other resources for teaching grammar, please go to www.youcanteachgrammar.com

About the Authors

Claudia Bertotto is the Founder and Principal of Coventry House International and Ontesol.com. She is an ESL instructor and Trinity CertTESOL teacher trainer. She has over 30 years of teaching experience in England, Canada and Argentina.

Jimena del Azar-Pintaric is an ESL teacher in the Toronto public school system and Trinity CertTESOL teacher trainer at Coventry House International and Ontesol.com.

Margaret Hurley is an ESL instructor and Trinity CertTESOL teacher trainer at Coventry House International and Ontesol.com.

Table of contents

1 Parts of Speech 1
   1.1 Nouns 1
      1.1.1 Countability 1
      1.1.2 Concreteness 1
      1.1.3 Commonality 2
      1.1.4 Other characteristics 2
      Quiz 1: Nouns 2
   1.2 Pronouns 2
      1.2.1 Personal pronouns 2
      Table 1: Personal pronouns 3
      1.2.2 Reflexive and reciprocal pronouns 3
      Table 2: Reflexive and reciprocal pronouns 3
      1.2.3 Indefinite pronouns 3
      1.2.4 Relative pronouns 3
      1.2.5 Interrogative pronouns 3
      1.2.6 Demonstrative pronouns 4
      Quiz 2: Pronouns 4
   1.3 Adjectives 4
      1.3.1 Attributive or predicative 4
      1.3.2 Descriptive or limiting 4
      1.3.3 Gradable or non-gradable 4
      1.3.4 Other adjective forms 5
      Quiz 3: Adjectives 5
   1.4 Adverbs 5
      1.4.1 Adverb forms 5
      1.4.2 Adverb types 5
      Table 3: Adverb types 6
      Quiz 4: Adverbs 6
   1.5 Verbs 6
      1.5.1 Verb forms 6
      1.5.2 Main or auxiliary 7
      1.5.3 Dynamic or stative 7
      1.5.4 Transitive or intransitive 7
      1.5.5 Regular or irregular 7
      1.5.6 Other forms: Gerund and infinitive 8
      Quiz 5: Verbs 8
   1.6 Conjunctions 8
      1.6.1 Coordinating conjunctions 8
      1.6.2 Subordinating conjunctions 8
      1.6.3 Correlative conjunctions 8
      Quiz 6: Conjunctions 9
   1.7 Prepositions 9
      1.7.1 Preposition types 9
      Table 4: Preposition types (categorized by major function) 9
      1.7.2 Prepositional phrases 9
         1.7.2.1 Adjectival prepositional phrases 10
         1.7.2.2 Adverbial prepositional phrases 10
      Quiz 7: Prepositions 10
   1.8 Interjections 10
   1.9 Content words vs. function words 10
      *** In the classroom – Parts of speech *** 10
*** You can teach parts of speech *** 11

2 Parts of a sentence 13
2.1 Mandatory sentence elements 13
2.1.1 Subject and predicate 13
2.1.2 Clause 14
2.1.3 Phrase 14
Quiz 1: Mandatory sentence elements 15
*** In the classroom: Mandatory sentence elements *** 15
2.2 Optional sentence elements 15
2.2.1 Object 15
2.2.2 Complement 16
2.2.3 Adverbial 17
Quiz 2: Optional sentence elements 17
*** In the classroom: Optional sentence elements *** 17
2.3 Simple sentence structure 18
2.3.1 Subject + verb 18
2.3.2 Subject + verb + object(s) 18
2.3.3 Subject + verb + subject complement 19
2.3.4 Subject + verb + object + object complement 19
2.3.5 Subject + verb + (object) + adverbial 19
Quiz 3: Simple sentence structure 20
*** In the classroom: Simple sentence structure *** 20
2.3.6 Simple sentence structure expanded 21
Table 5: Simple sentence structure 21
2.4 Variations on subjects and objects 22
2.4.1 Cleft sentences 22
2.4.2 Preparatory *it* 22
2.4.2.1 Preparatory *it* in subject position 22
2.4.2.2 Preparatory *it* in object position 23
2.4.3 Non-referential *it* and *there* 23
2.4.3.1 Non-referential *it* 23
2.4.3.2 Non-referential *there* 23
Quiz 4: Variations on subject and object 24
*** In the classroom: It and there as subject and object 24
2.5 Sentence types 25
2.5.1 Declarative sentences 25
2.5.2 Interrogative sentences 25
2.5.3 Imperative sentences 27
2.5.4 Exclamatory sentences 27
Quiz 5: Sentence types 28
*** In the classroom: Sentence types *** 28
**** **You can teach parts of a sentence** **** 28

3 Nouns 31
3.1 Noun forms 31
3.2 Functions of nouns in a sentence 31
Quiz 1: Functions of a noun in a sentence 32
*** In the classroom: Functions of nouns *** 32
3.3 Noun placement 33
3.4 Noun types 34
Table 6: Noun types 34
3.4.1 Commonality 34
3.4.1.1 Common nouns 34
3.4.1.2 Proper nouns 35
3.4.2 Concreteness 35
3.4.2.1 Concrete nouns 35

      3.4.2.2   Abstract nouns 35
   Quiz 2: Commonality and concreteness 35
   *** In the classroom: Commonality and concreteness *** 35
   3.4.3   Countability 36
      3.4.3.1   Countable nouns 36
      3.4.3.2   Uncountable nouns 36
   Quiz 3: Countability 38
   *** In the classroom: Countability *** 38
   3.4.4   Inflection 38
      3.4.4.1   Number 39
   *** In the classroom: Number *** 39
   Table 7: Spelling rules for nouns with regular plurals 40
   Table 8: Spelling rules for certain nouns with Latin or Greek roots 40
      3.4.4.2   Gender 41
      3.4.4.3   Case 41
   Quiz 4: Inflection 43
  *** You can teach nouns *** 43

4 Pronouns 47
  4.1 Pronoun forms 47
    Table 9: Example pronoun forms by number, gender and case 48
  4.2 Pronoun types 48
    4.2.1   Personal pronouns 48
       4.2.1.1   Subjective pronouns 48
    Table 10: Subjective personal pronouns by person and number 48
       4.2.1.2   Objective pronouns 49
    Table 11: Subjective and objective personal pronouns 49
    Quiz 1: Subjective and objective pronouns 50
    *** In the classroom: Personal pronouns *** 50
       4.2.1.3   Possessive pronouns 52
    Table 12: Subjective and possessive personal pronouns 52
    Quiz 2: Personal pronouns and their forms 53
    *** In the classroom: Possessive pronouns *** 53
       4.2.1.4   Reflexive pronouns 53
    Table 13: Subjective and reflexive personal pronouns 54
    *** In the classroom: Reflexive pronouns *** 54
    4.2.2   Reciprocal pronouns 55
    *** In the classroom: Reciprocal pronouns *** 55
    4.2.3   Indefinite pronouns 55
       4.2.3.1   General indefinite pronouns 56
       4.2.3.2   Negative indefinite pronouns 56
       4.2.3.3   Quantifier indefinite pronouns 57
       4.2.3.4   Number in indefinite pronouns 57
       4.2.3.5   Affirmative, interrogative or negative uses of indefinite pronouns 58
       4.2.3.6   Summary of indefinite pronouns 60
    Table 14: Indefinite pronouns 60
    4.2.4   Relative pronouns 60
    4.2.5   Interrogative pronouns 61
    Table 15: Personal and non-personal reference of interrogative pronouns 61
    4.2.6   Demonstrative pronouns 63
    Quiz 3: Pronoun identification 64
    *** In the classroom: Common pronoun mistakes *** 64
    Quiz 4: Correct the errors 65
  *** You can teach pronouns *** 65

5 Adjectives 73

- 5.1 Adjective forms 73
  - 5.1.1 Suffixes and prefixes 73
  - 5.1.2 Compound adjectives 74
    - 5.1.2.1 One-word compound adjectives 74
    - 5.1.2.2 Multiple-word compound adjectives 74
    - 5.1.2.3 Hyphenated compound adjectives 75
  - *Quiz 1: Adjective forms* 75
  - **** In the classroom: Adjective forms **** 76
  - 5.1.3 Participial adjectives 77
  - Table 16: Examples of participial adjectives describing emotions 78
  - *Quiz 2: Participial adjectives* 79
  - **** In the classroom: Participial adjectives **** 79
- 5.2 Adjective types 80
  - Table 17: Limiting and descriptive adjectives 81
  - 5.2.1 Limiting adjectives 81
  - Table 18: Types of limiting adjectives 82
  - 5.2.2 Descriptive adjectives 82
    - 5.2.2.1 Qualifying adjectives 83
  - Table 19: Types of qualifying adjectives 83
    - 5.2.2.2 Classifying adjectives 83
  - Table 20: Types of classifying adjectives 84
    - 5.2.2.3 Intensifying adjectives 84
  - *Quiz 3: Limiting and descriptive adjectives* 85
  - *Quiz 4: Descriptive adjectives: qualifying or classifying* 85
  - **** In the classroom: Adjective types **** 85
- 5.3 Position of adjectives 86
  - 5.3.1 Attributive adjectives 87
  - 5.3.2 Predicative adjectives 87
  - *Quiz 5: Position of adjectives* 88
  - *Quiz 6: Categorization of adjectives* 88
- 5.4 Order of adjectives 88
  - Table 21: Limiting and descriptive adjectives, with specifying and intensifying adjectives 89
  - 5.4.1 Order of descriptive adjectives in attributive position 89
  - Table 22: Major descriptive adjective categories for purposes of adjective ordering ... 89
  - Table 23: Full set of adjective categories for purposes of adjective ordering 90
  - *Quiz 7: Order of adjectives* 90
  - **** In the classroom: Order of adjectives **** 90
- 5.5 Adjective or adverb 91
  - *Quiz 8: Adjective or adverb* 92
  - **** In the classroom: Adjective or adverb **** 92
- ***** You can teach adjectives ***** 92
  - Recognition activities for descriptive adjectives 92
  - Practising speaking, writing, reading and listening skills with adjectives 96

6 Determiners 99
  - Table 24: Determiners and the types of nouns they can modify 100
- 6.1 Structural classifications of determiners 100
  - Table 25: Predeterminers, central determiners and postdeterminers 101
  - *Quiz 1: Order of determiners* 101
  - **** In the classroom: Determiner structure **** 102
- 6.2 Functional classifications of determiners 102
  - 6.2.1 Definiteness 102
  - Table 26: Determiners of definiteness 103
  - **** In the classroom: Determiners of definiteness **** 103
  - 6.2.2 Magnitude 104

Table 27: Determiners of magnitude 104
Quiz 2: Functional classifications of determiners 104
*** In the classroom: Determiner functions *** 105

6.3   Quantifiers **105**
   6.3.1   Quantifier types 105
      6.3.1.1   Quantifying determiners 106
      6.3.1.2   Partitives 106
   6.3.2   Other quantifier phrases 107
Quiz 3: Subject / verb agreement with quantifiers 107
*** In the classroom: Quantifiers *** 107

6.4   Articles **107**
   6.4.1   Definite article 108
      6.4.1.1   Uniqueness 108
      6.4.1.2   Mutual understanding 108
      6.4.1.3   Explicit description 109
      6.4.1.4   Generic statements of fact 110
      6.4.1.5   Proper place names 110
   6.4.2   Indefinite article 111
      6.4.2.1   Not defined 112
      6.4.2.2   General idea 112
      6.4.2.3   Subject complements 113
      6.4.2.4   Replacement for the number "one" 113
Quiz 4: A versus AN 114
*** In the classroom: Indefinite article *** 114
   6.4.3   Zero article 114
Quiz 5: Correct the sentences (articles) 115
Quiz 6: Fill in the blanks (articles) 116
*** In the classroom: Articles *** 116
*** You can teach determiners *** **117**

7   Adverbs 125
Quiz 1: Adverbs modifying different parts of speech 125

7.1   Adverb forms **125**
***In the classroom: Identifying adverbs *** 126
Quiz 2: Adverbs or adjectives 127
*** In the classroom: Well or good? *** 127
   7.1.1   Spelling 128

7.2   Adverbials **128**
   7.2.1   Adverbial phrases 129
   7.2.2   Adverbial clauses 130
   7.2.3   Adverbs, adverbial particles and prepositions 130
Quiz 3: Adverb or preposition 131
*** In the classroom: Adverbs and prepositions *** 131

7.3   Adverbs and adverbials classified by meaning **131**
   7.3.1   Adverbs of manner 132
Quiz 4: Placement of adverbs of manner 133
   7.3.2   Adverbs of place 133
Quiz 5: Adverbials of place 134
   7.3.3   Adverbs of time 134
      7.3.3.1   Time-when 134
      7.3.3.2   Time-frequency 135
*** In the classroom: Adverbs of frequency and their meanings *** 135
Table 28: Adverbs of frequency and their meanings 136
      7.3.3.3   Time-duration 137
Quiz 6: Adverbs of time 140
*** In the classroom: For and since *** 140

  7.3.4 Adverbials of purpose 140
  **** *In the classroom: Order of adverbs and adverbial phrases* *** 141
  7.3.5 Adverbs of assertion 142
  7.3.6 Adverbs of degree... 142
  *** *In the classroom: Overuse of* very *** 144
    7.3.6.1 Adverbs of quantity 144
  Quiz 7: Adverb identification 145
  ****In the classroom: Very much* and *very* *** 145
 *** **You can teach adverbs** *** 145

8 Comparatives 151
8.1 Expressing equality and inequality 151
8.2 Gradability 152
  8.2.1 Gradability of adjectives 152
  Quiz 1: Gradability of adjectives 153
  8.2.2 Gradability of adverbs 153
  Quiz 2: Gradability of adverbs 154
8.3 Comparative and superlative forms 154
  8.3.1 One-syllable adjectives and adverbs 154
  Table 29: Comparative and superlative forms of one-syllable adjectives and adverbs .. 155
  Table 30: Comparative and superlative forms of one-syllable adjectives ending in vowel + consonant 155
  Table 31: Comparative and superlative forms of one-syllable adjectives: Exceptions .. 156
  Quiz 3: Correct the mistake 156
  *** *In the classroom: Spelling problems* *** 156
  *** *In the classroom: Older or elder* ***.. 157
  8.3.2 Adverbs greater than one syllable 157
  Table 32: Comparative and superlative forms of adverbs greater than one syllable 157
  8.3.3 Two-syllable adjectives 157
  Table 33: Comparative forms of two-syllable adjectives with stress on the first syllable 158
  Table 34: Two-syllable adjective types that always take the more/most form for comparative and superlative 158
  Table 35: Comparative and superlative forms of two-syllable adjectives ending in *–y* .. 158
  8.3.4 Three- (or more) syllable adjectives 158
  Table 36: Comparative and superlative forms of three- (or more) syllable adjectives 159
  8.3.5 Compound adjectives 159
  8.3.6 Adverbial phrases 159
  *** *In the classroom: Over-generalizing the rules* *** 159
  8.3.7 Irregular comparatives and superlatives 160
  Table 37: Irregular comparative and superlative forms 160
  *** *In the classroom: Irregular forms* *** 160
8.4 Comparative and superlative uses and structures 161
  Table 38: Uses of comparative adjectives and adverbs 161
  8.4.1 Comparing two nouns 161
  *** *In the classroom: Comparing one noun to another noun* *** 162
  8.4.2 Comparing one noun to a group or range 162
  8.4.3 Comparing verbs 163
  Quiz 4: Comparative constructions 164
  *** *In the classroom: Finishing the comparison* *** 164
  8.4.4 Adding comparative emphasis with adverbs 165
  Table 39: Adverbs used to emphasize comparatives 165
  Table 40: Adverbs used to emphasize superlative adjectives............................... 165
  Quiz 5: Intensifying adverbs 166
  *** *In the classroom: Advanced comparative constructions* *** 166
 *** **You can teach comparatives** *** 166

9 Prepositions ... 171
9.1 Preposition forms ... 171
9.1.1 Simple prepositions ... 171
Table 41: Simple prepositions ... 171
*** In the classroom: Prepositions vs. conjunctions *** ... 172
9.1.2 Complex prepositions ... 172
Quiz 1: Simple and complex prepositions ... 172
*** In the classroom: Mother tongue translation *** ... 173
9.2 Prepositional phrases ... 173
9.2.1 Structures of prepositional phrases ... 173
Quiz 2: Prepositional phrases ... 175
9.2.2 Functions of prepositional phrases ... 175
9.2.2.1 Adjectival prepositional phrases ... 175
9.2.2.2 Adverbial prepositional phrases ... 175
Quiz 3: Adjectival or adverbial prepositional phrase ... 176
***In the classroom: Order of prepositional phrases *** ... 176
9.3 Meanings of prepositions ... 176
*** In the classroom: In, on and at as prepositions of place *** ... 177
*** In the classroom: In, on and at as prepositions of time *** ... 178
Quiz 4: Correct the mistakes ... 179
***In the classroom: Focus on meanings of prepositions *** ... 180
9.4 Prepositional patterns ... 181
***In the classroom: Pronunciation of prepositions *** ... 182
*** You can teach prepositions *** ... 183

10 Conjunctions ... 189
*** In the classroom: Equivalence *** ... 189
10.1 Conjunction forms ... 189
10.1.1 Single-word conjunctions ... 189
Table 42: Single-word conjunctions ... 190
10.1.2 Conjunction phrases ... 190
Table 43: Conjunction phrases ... 190
10.1.3 Conjunction pairs ... 191
Table 44: Conjunction pairs ... 191
Quiz 1: Identifying conjunctions ... 191
*** In the classroom: Same word, different part of speech *** ... 191
10.2 Sentence types ... 192
10.2.1 Simple sentences ... 192
10.2.2 Compound sentences ... 192
10.2.3 Complex sentences ... 192
10.2.4 Compound complex sentences ... 193
10.3 Conjunction types ... 193
10.3.1 Coordinating conjunctions ... 193
10.3.2 Correlative conjunctions ... 194
10.3.3 Subordinating conjunctions ... 195
Quiz 2: Conjunction types ... 196
10.3.3.1 Complementizers ... 197
10.3.4 Other linkers and transition signals ... 197
*** In the classroom: Subordination *** ... 198
10.4 Punctuation ... 199
10.4.1 Linking nouns, verbs, adjectives and adverbs ... 199
10.4.2 Linking clauses ... 200
10.4.3 Punctuation for linkers and transitions signals ... 203
Quiz 3: Punctuation ... 204
*** In the classroom: Punctuation *** ... 204

*** You can teach conjunctions *** 205

11 Verbs 209
11.1 Verb forms 209
11.1.1 Non-finite forms 209
Table 45: Examples of non-finite verb forms 210
11.1.1.1 Base form 210
*** In the classroom: Base forms *** 210
11.1.1.2 Infinitive 211
11.1.1.3 Participle 211
11.1.1.4 Gerund 211
11.1.2 Finite forms 212
Table 46: Example finite verb forms, conjugated for person, number and tense 212
Quiz 1: Verb forms 213
*** In the classroom: Verb forms *** 213
11.2 Verb classifications 214
11.2.1 General classification 214
11.2.1.1 Main verbs 214
11.2.1.2 Auxiliary verbs 215
Quiz 2: Main and auxiliary verbs 216
*** In the classroom: Main and auxiliary verbs *** 216
11.2.2 Morphological classification 216
11.2.2.1 Regular verbs 217
Table 47: Spelling rules for regular verbs: simple past and past participle forms 217
Table 48: Spelling rules for regular and irregular verbs: present participle and gerund forms 217
11.2.2.2 Irregular verbs 217
Quiz 3: Spelling 218
*** In the classroom: Regular and irregular verbs *** 218
11.2.3 Semantic classification 218
11.2.3.1 Dynamic verbs 218
11.2.3.2 Stative verbs 219
Quiz 4: Dynamic and stative verbs 221
*** In the classroom: Dynamic and stative verbs *** 221
11.2.4 Syntactic classification 222
11.2.4.1 Intransitive verbs 222
11.2.4.2 Transitive verbs 222
Quiz 5: Transitive and intransitive verbs 226
In the classroom: Transitive and intransitive verbs 226
11.3 Mood 226
11.3.1 Indicative mood 227
11.3.2 Infinitive mood 227
11.3.3 Imperative mood 227
11.3.4 Subjunctive mood 228
Quiz 6: Mood 228
*** In the classroom: Mood *** 229
11.4 Verb phrases and phrasal verbs 229
11.4.1 Verb phrases 229
11.4.2 Phrasal verbs 231
11.4.2.1 Intransitive phrasal verbs 231
11.4.2.2 Transitive phrasal verbs 232
Quiz 7: Verb phrases and phrasal verbs 233
*** In the classroom: Verb phrases and phrasal verbs *** 233
*** You can teach verbs *** 233

12 Auxiliary and modal auxiliary verbs 237

12.1 Auxiliary verbs ... 237
12.1.1 Auxiliary verb *be* ... 237
12.1.2 Auxiliary verb *have* ... 238
12.1.3 Auxiliary verb *do* ... 238
*** In the classroom: Be, do and have as main verbs *** ... 239
Table 49: Examples of *be*, *do* and *have* as main and auxiliary verbs ... 239
Quiz 1: Auxiliary verbs or main verbs ... 240
12.2 Modal auxiliary verbs ... 240
*** In the classroom: Need and dare *** ... 241
12.2.1 Structure of modal auxiliary verbs ... 241
12.2.1.1 Similarities between auxiliary verbs and modal verbs ... 241
12.2.1.2 Differences between auxiliary verbs and modal verbs ... 242
Table 50: Summary of distinctions between auxiliary verbs and modal verbs ... 243
Quiz 2: Distinctions between auxiliary verbs and modal verbs ... 243
*** In the classroom: Simple present tense or base form? *** ... 243
12.2.2 Modal auxiliary verbs, semi-modals and modal phrases ... 244
*** In the classroom: Using more than one modal auxiliary verb *** ... 244
Quiz 3: Correct the errors ... 245
12.3 Modality ... 245
Table 51: Summary of modal verbs and associated modalities ... 246
12.3.1 Ability ... 246
Quiz 4: True or false ... 247
12.3.2 Advice / recommendation ... 247
*** In the classroom: Should, ought to and had better *** ... 248
12.3.3 Suggestion ... 249
Quiz 5: Modalities ... 250
12.3.4 Degrees of certainty: certainty, assumption, probability and possibility ... 250
12.3.4.1 Certainty ... 250
12.3.4.2 Assumption ... 250
*** In the classroom: Negative forms of modals *** ... 251
12.3.4.3 Probability ... 251
12.3.4.4 Possibility ... 251
12.3.5 Necessity / obligation / responsibility ... 252
12.3.5.1 Must, will, be to, be supposed to, have (got) to ... 252
12.3.5.2 Shall, should, and ought to ... 253
12.3.5.3 Need, needn't and don't need to ... 253
Quiz 6: Modal verbs of necessity ... 254
12.3.6 Requests ... 254
*** In the classroom: Answers to requests *** ... 254
12.3.7 Offers ... 255
12.3.8 Permission/prohibition ... 255
*** In the classroom: Can I? *** ... 256
Quiz 7: Defining modalities ... 256
12.3.9 Preference ... 256
12.3.10 Promises ... 257
12.3.11 Non-modal meanings ... 257
*** In the classroom: pronunciation of auxiliary verbs *** ... 258
*** You can teach modal auxiliary verbs *** ... 259

13 Gerunds and infinitives ... 265
Quiz 1: Gerunds and infinitives ... 266
*** In the classroom: Gerunds and infinitives *** ... 266
13.1 Functions of gerunds in a sentence ... 266
Quiz 2: Functions of gerunds ... 269
13.2 Gerundial forms ... 269
Quiz 3: Gerundial forms ... 270

13.3		Other uses of gerunds	270
	13.3.1	After certain words or expressions	270
	13.3.2	After possessives	270
	13.3.3	As nouns related to leisure, hobbies or jobs	270

*** In the classroom: Gerund and present participle *** 271
Quiz 4: Gerund or present participle? 272
*** In the classroom: –ing form after verbs of perception *** 272

13.4	Functions of infinitives in a sentence	272

Quiz 5: Functions of infinitives 274

13.5	Infinitival forms	274

Quiz 6: To-infinitive or bare infinitive? 276

13.6		Other uses of infinitives	276
	13.6.1	Acting as adverbs	276
	13.6.2	Acting as adjectives	277
	13.6.3	After wh- words in noun clauses	277

Quiz 7: Functions of gerunds and infinitives 278
*** In the classroom: Ellipsis of the infinitive phrase *** 278

13.7			Verbs followed by gerunds *or* infinitives	278
	13.7.1		No change in meaning	278
	13.7.2		Little difference in meaning	279
		13.7.2.1	Considering the do-er of the actions	279
		13.7.2.2	Particular habits vs. general enjoyment	280
		13.7.2.3	Progress versus completion	280
	13.7.3		Change in meaning	281
		13.7.3.1	Time of the action: remember, forget, stop and regret	281
		13.7.3.2	Intention or involvement: *mean*	282

Quiz 8: Choose the correct form 283
*** In the classroom: Gerund or infinitive after certain verbs *** 283
*** You can teach gerunds and infinitives *** 283

14 Tenses 289

Tense (time) 289
Quiz 1: Tense (time) 290
*** In the classroom: Presenting time *** 290
Aspect 291
Table 52: Grammatical aspects of verbs 292
*** In the classroom: Aspect *** 292

14.1 Forms of tenses 293

Table 53: Forms of tenses in affirmative statements 293
Table 54: Forms of tenses in negative statements 293
Table 55: Forms of tenses in affirmative or negative interrogatives 294
Quiz 2: Forms 294
Table 56: Examples of tenses in active and passive voice 294

14.2 Present tenses 295

14.2.1 Present simple 295
Table 57: Forms of the present simple tense 295
Table 58: Simple present (finite) forms of the verb *be* 296
*** In the classroom: Present simple *** 298
14.2.2 Present progressive 299
Table 59: Forms of the present progressive tense 299
*** In the classroom: Present progressive *** 301
14.2.3 Present perfect 301
Table 60: Forms of the present perfect tense 302
*** In the classroom: Present perfect *** 304
14.2.4 Present perfect progressive 304

- Table 61: Forms of the present perfect progressive tense 305
  - *** *In the classroom: Present perfect progressive* *** 307
  - *Quiz 3: Present tenses* 307
- **14.3 Past tenses** 307
  - 14.3.1 Past simple 307
  - Table 62: Forms of the past simple tense 308
  - Table 63: Simple past (finite) forms of the verb *be* 308
  - *** *In the classroom: Past simple* *** 310
  - 14.3.2 Past progressive 310
  - Table 64: Forms of the past progressive tense 311
  - *** *In the classroom: Past progressive* *** 313
  - 14.3.3 Past perfect 313
  - Table 65: Forms of the past perfect tense 314
  - *** *In the classroom: Past perfect* *** 315
  - 14.3.4 Past perfect progressive 316
  - Table 66: Forms of the past perfect progressive tense 316
  - *** *In the classroom: Past perfect progressive* *** 318
  - *Quiz 4: Past tenses* 318
- **14.4 Future tenses** 318
  - 14.4.1 Future simple 319
  - Table 67: Forms of the future simple tense 319
  - *** *In the classroom: Future simple* *** 321
  - 14.4.2 Future progressive 321
  - Table 68: Forms of the future progressive tense 321
  - *** *In the classroom: Future progressive* *** 323
  - 14.4.3 Future perfect 323
  - Table 69: Forms of the future perfect tense 324
  - *** *In the classroom: Future perfect* *** 325
  - 14.4.4 Future perfect progressive 325
  - Table 70: Forms of the future perfect progressive tense 326
  - *** *In the classroom: Future perfect progressive* *** 327
  - *Quiz 5: Future tenses* 328
- **14.5 Tenses tree** 329
- *** ***You can teach tenses*** *** 330

15 Interjections 337
- **15.1 Interjection forms** 337
- **15.2 Interjection placement** 338
  - *** *In the classroom: Interjections* *** 339
  - *Quiz: Defining interjections* 339
- *** ***You can teach interjections*** *** 339

Appendices 343
- Appendix I: Irregular verbs 344
- Appendix II: Ditransitive verbs 346
- Appendix III: Transitive complex verbs 347
- Appendix IV: Ergative verbs 348
- Appendix V: Phrasal prepositional verbs 349
- Appendix VI: Intransitive phrasal verbs 349
- Appendix VII: Separable transitive phrasal verbs 350
- Appendix VIII: Inseparable transitive phrasal verbs 350

Answer key 351
Bibliography 365
Index 371

You can teach grammar

1 Parts of Speech

The first step in studying grammar is to understand the functions and uses of words in a sentence. Words follow a certain order in a sentence for intelligible communication. Words are classified in categories depending on their function, meaning, and position in a sentence. These categories of words are known as the parts of speech.

It is not always obvious which category a word belongs in. Words that function as nouns in one sentence, for example, may function as verbs in another.

There are eight main parts of speech: **nouns, pronouns, adjectives, adverbs, verbs, conjunctions, prepositions** and **interjections**. Each of these categories is discussed in detail in later chapters. This chapter gives an overview of the parts of speech. Some of the descriptions in this chapter refer to clauses and to the subject and object of a sentence; subjects, objects and clauses are described in more detail in Chapter 2.

1.1 Nouns

Nouns are words which name people, animals, things, places, abstract ideas, feelings, substances or qualities. They can be classified as: common or proper; concrete or abstract; countable (singular or plural) or uncountable. Nouns may also be collective, compound or possessive. The highlighted words below are all nouns.

> What a lovely **baby**!
> The **pigs** are covered in **dirt**.
> **Sue** needs to accept her **brother's proposal**.

1.1.1 Countability

For learners of English, the countability of a noun is a fundamental concept. Nouns in English generally only change form for number, which is related to countability. (A few nouns may change form for gender.) Singular countable nouns and uncountable nouns take the same form, and are accompanied by the same verb form. Plural countable nouns take a different form (most commonly, the addition of an –s) and require a distinct verb form.

If a noun can be differentiated into discrete occurrences, then it is countable. Countable nouns may be singular or plural. If it cannot be seen as existing in meaningful individual units, it is uncountable. For example, **table** is a countable noun; it is possible to differentiate individual occurrences of **table** and count individual tables. On the other hand, **water** is not countable in this way. Individual occurrences of **water** can only be differentiated by dividing **water** into units that can be counted: drops, glasses, litres or jugs, for example.

1.1.2 Concreteness

A noun's concreteness can be one of two types: concrete or abstract. Nouns that name people, places, animals or substances are concrete nouns. They represent things that can be experienced with the five senses. Nouns that name concepts, feelings or qualities are abstract nouns. They are things that are perceived intellectually, rather than physically.

1.1.3 Commonality

A noun's commonality can be one of two types: common or proper. A proper noun gives a specific, known, named occurrence of a noun. In written form, a proper noun always begins with a capital (upper case) letter. People's names, company names, country names, days of the week, and months of the year are proper nouns. The vast majority of nouns are common nouns. Common nouns name things in a general sense.

1.1.4 Other characteristics

Nouns are fundamental to sentences in English, and are the foundation upon which other parts of speech rest. Adjectives work solely to describe and define nouns. The number (whether it is singular, plural or uncountable) and case (whether it is a subject, object or possession) of nouns dictate the forms that verbs can take. When nouns are in possessive form, they take on the role of other parts of speech as well, either working as adjectives or as pronouns. Sometimes, two nouns may be joined together into a single word, forming a new noun, called a compound noun (like **basketball**). Collective nouns are ones which are singular in form, but which name a group of people or things (like **audience**).

Other parts of speech may take on the function of nouns. In particular, verbs in gerund (*–ing*) form and to-infinitive form usually take the role of a noun in sentences. *(See 13 Gerunds and infinitives)*

Quiz 1: Nouns

Identify the types of nouns in the example sentences in section 1.1.

1.2 Pronouns

Pronouns replace nouns. They are used to reduce repetition. They can be personal (subjective or objective or possessive), reflexive, reciprocal, indefinite, interrogative, relative or demonstrative. The highlighted words below are all pronouns.

> **We** are all in **this** together.
> Stuart scared **himself**.
> Mike told **me** that **somebody** called **him** last night.
> I wish **everyone** loved **one another.**
> **What** is the name of the man **who** starred in the show?
> I forgot **mine**; can **you** lend **me yours**?

1.2.1 Personal pronouns

Personal pronouns replace the names or possessions of known people or things.

> Mr. Owen is talking to Jane. **He** looks angry.

In the example above, the pronoun **He** replaces the proper noun *Mr. Owen*, eliminating the need to repeat the noun *Mr. Owen*. Personal pronouns can be further categorized based on their function.

Table 1: Personal pronouns

Subjective pronouns replace nouns in the subject position	I	you	he	she	it	we	they
Objective pronouns replace nouns in the object position	me	you	him	her	it	us	them
Possessive pronouns replace nouns which name a possession	mine	yours	his	hers	its*	ours	theirs

* *its* is almost never used as a pronoun

1.2.2 Reflexive and reciprocal pronouns

Reflexive and reciprocal pronouns are types of personal objective pronouns. They are used in cases where the subject and object are the same, or when the subject and object are performing some action mutually.

You should take better care of **yourself**.
We must look after **each other**.

Table 2: Reflexive and reciprocal pronouns

Reflexive pronouns replace nouns in the object position when the subject and object are the same	myself	yourself	himself	herself	itself	ourselves	themselves
Reciprocal pronouns replace plural nouns in the object position when the action is performed on both subject and object	-	-	-	-	-	each other	one another

1.2.3 Indefinite pronouns

Indefinite pronouns stand in for unnamed, unknown or undefined people or things. They may function in both the subject and object positions. Most pronouns replace nouns that are known, usually because they are already mentioned. Indefinite pronouns do not need any other reference. They can replace known nouns or unidentified ones. The major indefinite pronouns are **anybody, anyone, anything, everybody, everyone, everything, nobody, no one, nothing, somebody, someone, something, all, any, both, neither** and **some**.

1.2.4 Relative pronouns

Relative pronouns are ones which sit at the head of a relative clause. *(See 2.1.2 Clause and 4.2.4 Relative pronouns)* Relative clauses give more information about a noun in the main clause; relative pronouns replace that noun in the relative clause. The relative pronouns are **that, which, who** and **whom**.

1.2.5 Interrogative pronouns

Interrogative pronouns are used in questions to substitute for the thing that the question is about. Interrogatives are, by definition, unknown, so interrogative pronouns are standing in for unknown people or things. They may function as the subject or object of a question. The interrogative pronouns are **what**, **which**, **who**, **whom** and **whose**. The interrogative pronoun **whose** is also a possessive pronoun.

1.2.6 Demonstrative pronouns

The four demonstratives are **this**, **that**, **these** and **those**. They may replace nouns naming people or things. They carry a sense of proximity, and are influenced by grammatical number. **This** and **that** replace singular or uncountable nouns; **these** and **those** replace plural countable nouns.

Quiz 2: Pronouns

Identify the types of pronouns highlighted in the example sentences in section 1.2.

1.3 Adjectives

Adjectives modify nouns. They may also modify pronouns. They present characteristics that help describe and distinguish places, people and things; or they simply identify or quantify them. Adjectives can be attributive or predicative; descriptive or limiting; gradable or non-gradable. Their forms may be compound or participial. The highlighted words below are all adjectives.

> Mr. Owen, **a handsome middle-aged** man, strolled along **the** shore very early in **the** morning. Reluctantly, he went back to **his** house in **the** city where **his** wife and **their three** children were waiting for him. When they saw him, they were **shocked**. With **a** frown and in **a no-nonsense** tone of voice, his **oldest** child said, "I knew something **bad** would happen. You look **terrible**. What happened?"

Determiners – including articles (*the, a, an*), quantifiers (*two, some, few*), possessives (*my, your, his*), and others – modify nouns, and are therefore adjectives.

1.3.1 Attributive or predicative

If an adjective is placed directly next to the noun it is modifying, it is an attributive adjective. An attributive adjective may premodify (be placed before) or postmodify (be placed right after) a noun. The vast majority of attributive adjectives premodify nouns. If an adjective modifies a noun after a linking verb, then it is a predicative adjective. Linking verbs are a type of stative verb that indicate state or condition (such as *appear*, *seem*, and *be*) or ones that indicate physical or emotional senses (such as *see, smell*, or *sound*).

1.3.2 Descriptive or limiting

The vast majority of adjectives are descriptive. They directly describe some characteristics of the nouns they modify. These characteristics include size, shape, colour, opinion, condition, origin and purpose. Limiting adjectives are ones that, rather than describe, put some kind of limit on the nouns they modify. Limiting adjectives include articles, cardinal numbers, ordinal numbers, demonstratives and possessives.

1.3.3 Gradable or non-gradable

Some descriptive adjectives may be modified to indicate relative degree. Adjectives that can be modified in this way are gradable. These adjectives may take a comparative or superlative form, showing a higher or lower intensity of the adjective, compared to some other noun or some other adjective. In the previous sentence, **higher** and **lower** are the comparative forms of the gradable adjectives **high** and **low**. Other adjectives cannot take comparative or superlative forms; they are non-gradable. In the previous sentence, the adjectives **comparative** and **superlative** are non-gradable.

1.3.4 Other adjective forms

In addition to standard adjective forms, it is possible to create adjectives through other constructions. A compound adjective is formed from two or more words, which work together as a unit to modify a noun. Examples of compound adjectives include **long-legged** and **top-notch**. Adjectives are often derived from verbs. The participial forms of verbs (both past and present participle) may be used as adjectives. Examples of participial adjectives are **excited** and **boring**.

Quiz 3: Adjectives

Identify the types of adjectives highlighted in the example sentences in section 1.3. Identify which noun or pronoun each adjective is modifying.

1.4 Adverbs

Adverbs can modify verbs, adjectives and other adverbs. They may also modify entire clauses or sentences. They can indicate manner, place, time, purpose, assertion and degree. The highlighted words and phrases below are adverbs.

>He drives **carelessly**.
>**Unfortunately**, we do not accept credit cards.
>I **always** get up **early**.
>He is a **very** nice man.
>I am not going **there today**.
>She is studying **to be a doctor**.
>**Frankly**, I think it's ridiculous, but I won't say anything.

1.4.1 Adverb forms

Adverbs can take several forms. The most common, and easiest to detect, is the addition of an *–ly* ending to an adjective. Other than this generalization, it is difficult to identify an adverb simply by its form. The function is the true identifier. Adverbs may be single words, or they may be entire phrases or clauses (called adverbials).

1.4.2 Adverb types

There are several broad types of adverbs. The specific categorization of adverbs varies, but the main groupings will usually include: manner; place; time; purpose; and degree. There are three adverbs of assertion: **yes**, **no** and **not**.

Table 3: Adverb types

Type	Function
Adverbs and adverbials of **manner**	describe how an action is executed; most adverbs which take the form of an adjective plus an –ly ending are adverbs of manner (examples: **gracefully, happily, with gusto**)
Adverbs and adverbials of **place**	describe where an action takes place; used to indicate location and to give directions (examples: **here, upstairs, to the right**)
Adverbs and adverbials of **time**	describe the timing of an action in several ways; can indicate the precise time, the frequency, or the duration of an action (examples: **now, annually, until 5:00**)
Adverbs and adverbials of **purpose**	describe why an action occurs, indicating the intention, cause or reason; they take the form of an adverbial phrase or clause (examples: **for exercise, to get a better deal**)
Adverbs and adverbials of **degree**	describe the extent or quantity of adjectives, other adverbs and, occasionally, verbs; also known as intensifiers (examples: **extremely, tenfold, to the limit**)

Quiz 4: Adverbs

Identify the types of adverbs highlighted in the example sentences in section 1.4. Identify the verb, adjective, adverb, clause or sentence that each adverb is modifying.

1.5 Verbs

Verbs describe the action the subject of a sentence or clause is performing, or the state the subject is in. Verbs may change form for tense, aspect and mood. *(See 14 Tenses and 11.3 Mood)* Verbs can be classified as: main verbs or auxiliary verbs; dynamic or stative; transitive or intransitive; and regular or irregular. A single verb may be composed of a single word or it may be a phrase. The highlighted words below are all verbs.

> After her workouts, Mary **stretches**.
> That guy always **stretches** the truth.
> We **ran into** Peter at the concert last night.
> They **will be flying** to Portugal tomorrow night.
> **Are** you sure?

1.5.1 Verb forms

Verbs are generally found in the dictionary in their base forms, though they are not always used in base form. The form of the verb may change for tense, aspect and mood. The simple tenses – past, present and future – require basic changes to the form of the verb. Simple present requires either the addition of an *–s* or no change from the base form. Simple past usually adds *–ed* to the base form. The future tense usually combines the modal auxiliary verb **will** with the base form. Further refinement of time reference – known as aspect – includes the progressive and perfective verb forms. The progressive aspect is composed of the auxiliary verb **be** combined with a verb in its present participle (*–ing*) form. The perfective aspects are composed of the auxiliaries **has**, **have** or **had** combined with a verb in its past participle form (for regular verbs, the *–ed* form).

The grammatical moods of verbs include the indicative mood (used for simple, positive statements) and the interrogative mood (used for asking questions). The specific verb forms used for different grammatical moods is a result of a combination of mood, tense and aspect. *(See 14 Tenses and 11.3 Mood)*

Verbs may be combined with other words to create entirely new verbs, with a meaning that is distinct from the original verb. These are known as phrasal verbs. For example, the verb **count**, when combined with *on*, creates an entirely new verb, **count on**, with a meaning that is different from that of the original verb.

1.5.2 Main or auxiliary

Most verbs indicate the main action or condition of the subject in a sentence. When a verb is performing this function, it is a main verb. **Eat**, **shake**, **seem** and **become** are examples of main verbs. Some verbs work together with the main verb to allow a change in aspect or to add some meaning; they do not stand alone. These are auxiliary verbs. Auxiliary verbs can be further defined as (standard) auxiliary verbs (also known as helping verbs) or modal auxiliary verbs. **Do**, **be** and **have** are auxiliary verbs. Examples of modal auxiliary verbs are **could**, **will**, **might** and **shall**.

Three verbs can be either main verbs or auxiliary verbs, depending on the context: **do**, **be** and **have**.

1.5.3 Dynamic or stative

Most verbs indicate an action. These are known as dynamic verbs; they are also known as action verbs. **Eat** and **shake** are examples of dynamic verbs. Other verbs do not indicate action on the part of the subject of the sentence; they are used to show the state or condition of the subject. These are known as stative verbs. Stative verbs are also known as state verbs. **Seem** and **dislike** are examples of stative verbs.

1.5.4 Transitive or intransitive

Verbs give information about the subject of a sentence. Some verbs can connect two nouns and apply to both of them. One of these nouns is the subject, the other is the object of the verb. When a verb relates one noun to another, it can be imagined that the information transits – it travels – through the verb, from one noun to another. Verbs that allow this transit of information are known as transitive verbs. **Like** and **take** are examples of transitive verbs. In the sentence *We **like** chocolate cake*, the verb is acting on both the subject, *We*, and the object, *chocolate cake*.

Other verbs cannot work in this way. They can only apply to a subject and cannot take an object. These are intransitive verbs. **Sleep** and **snore** are examples of intransitive verbs.

Some verbs can be either transitive or intransitive. In the sentence *The new puppies can't **see***, the verb is intransitive. In *I can **see** the ocean*, the verb is transitive.

1.5.5 Regular or irregular

There are general rules for changes in form for tense and aspect. If a verb conforms to this general set of rules, it is a regular verb. If it is an exception to these rules of form, then it is an irregular verb. One of the rules of form is that a verb in simple past tense will add *–ed* to its base form. The verb **walk** conforms to this rule; the simple past tense form of **walk** is **walked**. It is a regular verb. The simple past tense form of the verb **eat** is **ate**. It does not conform to this rule. It is an irregular verb.

1.5.6 Other forms: Gerund and infinitive

Gerunds and infinitives are forms of verbs that act as other parts of speech. They are formed from verbs, but are used in sentences together with other verbs to act as nouns or adverbs. Gerunds take the same form as present participles (*-ing* form). Infinitives are composed of the base form of the verb, plus the particle *to*.

> Do you enjoy **swimming**?
> (gerund **swimming** functioning as a noun: direct object of *enjoy*)
> **Swimming** is not allowed.
> (gerund **swimming** functioning as a noun: subject of the sentence)
> I've decided **to accept** the offer.
> (infinitive **to accept** functioning as a noun: direct object of *decided*)
> She left home **to start** her career.
> (infinitive **to start** functioning as an adverb: describing purpose of *left*)

Quiz 5: Verbs

Identify the types and forms of the verbs highlighted in the example sentences in section 1.5.

1.6 Conjunctions

Conjunctions connect words, phrases, clauses or sentences. Conjunctions may be classified as coordinating, subordinating or correlative. The highlighted words below are all conjunctions.

> He stumbled **and** fell down **because** he was drunk.
> I do not know **whether** to stay in this city **or** move to Denver.

Conjunctions connect separate ideas in a sentence. They connect – but do not modify – words, phrases and clauses.

1.6.1 Coordinating conjunctions

Coordinating conjunctions connect similar things, in a roughly equivalent sense. The main coordinating conjunctions are **and**, **but**, **nor**, **or** and **yet**. The conjunctions **for** and **so** may also be classified as coordinating conjunctions, but this categorization is less clear.

1.6.2 Subordinating conjunctions

Subordinating conjunctions indicate that one idea is dependent upon – or subordinate to – another. Some of the main subordinating conjunctions are **after**, **because**, **before**, **if**, **since**, **unless** and **until**.

1.6.3 Correlative conjunctions

Correlative conjunctions are pairs of words that work together to show a relationship between two roughly equal elements of a sentence. The main correlative conjunctions are **as...so, both...and, either...or, if...then, neither...nor, no sooner...than, not...but** and **whether...or**.

Quiz 6: Conjunctions
Identify the types of conjunctions highlighted in the example sentences in section 1.6. Identify the words, phrases or clauses that are connected with the conjunctions.

1.7 Prepositions

Prepositions connect certain parts of speech (nouns, verbs, adjectives, adverbs) to another part of a sentence, showing some kind of relationship between them. They are generally followed by a noun (or noun equivalent) to form adjective or adverb equivalents. When they form adjective equivalents, they describe a noun or noun phrase in some way. When they are adverb equivalents, they show relationships such as direction, time, place, purpose, cause, and manner. The highlighted words below are all prepositions.

> He was born **in** Paris **on** October 26th.
> Ellen ran her hands **over** the rough surface.
> What is that building **with** a green roof?
> You should turn **at** the next intersection.
> Kathleen met the Queen **of** England.
> I usually go there **for** a haircut.
> Stevie gave his speech **in** a loud voice.

1.7.1 Preposition types

There are fairly few prepositions, but they have many complexities. They may be viewed from several perspectives. The most common categorization of prepositions is one which separates simple (one-word) prepositions according to their major functions. The most common of these are prepositions of place, time and direction. Other such categories include possession, manner, purpose and degree.

Table 4: Preposition types (categorized by major function)

Type	Function
Prepositions of **place**	indicate the location of a thing or an action (examples: **above**, **at**, **below**, **beside**, **between**, **in**, **near**, **on** and **under**)
Prepositions of **time**	indicate the timing of an event or action; may show precise time, duration or frequency (examples: **after**, **at**, **before**, **during**, **from**, **on**, **since** and **until**)
Prepositions of **direction / movement**	indicate the progress of an action (examples: **across**, **around**, **at**, **by**, **down**, **into**, **off**, **onto** and **over**)

1.7.2 Prepositional phrases

Prepositions take their name from the idea that they are "pre" positioned; they are positioned before something. They are usually, therefore, at the beginning of a phrase. These phrases are called prepositional phrases. Prepositional phrases act as a single unit to modify some other part of a sentence, usually in the same way as an adverb or an adjective. In a prepositional phrase, the word or phrase that follows the preposition is known as the object of the preposition.

1.7.2.1 Adjectival prepositional phrases

When a prepositional phrase (a preposition plus its object) works as one entity to describe a noun or a noun phrase, it is doing the work of an adjective. It is therefore known as an adjectival prepositional phrase. In the song lyric *The look of love is in your eyes*, the adjectival prepositional phrase *of love* is describing the noun phrase *The look*. The head of the prepositional phrase is the preposition **of**. The object of the preposition is the noun *love*.

1.7.2.2 Adverbial prepositional phrases

When a prepositional phrase (a preposition plus its object) works as one entity to describe a verb, an adjective, an adverb or a clause, it is doing the work of an adverb. It is therefore known as an adverbial prepositional phrase. In the song lyric *We can't go on with suspicious minds*, the adverbial prepositional phrase *with suspicious minds* is modifying the phrasal verb *go on*. It is working as an adverbial of manner. The head of the prepositional phrase is the preposition **with**. The object of the preposition is the noun phrase *suspicious minds*.

Quiz 7: Prepositions

Identify the types of prepositions highlighted in the example sentences in section 1.7. Identify the entire prepositional phrase. Identify whether the prepositional phrase is acting as an adjective or an adverb. Identify the noun or verb that the prepositional phrase is modifying.

1.8 Interjections

Interjections are words or phrases that add emotion to a sentence. In writing, they are often followed by an exclamation mark. Spoken interjections carry much of their meaning through intonation. It is not necessary to connect interjections to other parts of speech through grammatical means. They stand alone and carry their own meanings. The highlighted words below are all interjections.

> **Ouch!** It hurt.
> **Oh my!** I missed it again.
> **Hmm,** I'm not sure about that.

1.9 Content words vs. function words

The parts of speech that carry the most meaning are known as content words. Nouns, verbs, adjectives and adverbs are content words. Knowing only content words is sufficient for intelligible rudimentary communication. The other parts of speech (pronouns, conjunctions, prepositions and interjections) are function words. They add nuance and facilitate clear structure of language for more complete and precise communication.

**** In the classroom – Parts of speech ****

When teaching beginner students, content words are taught first, while function words are usually taught as part of a structure. Pictionary, memory games, and word bingo are a few examples of memorable activities for teaching or practising content words.

Identifying content and function words is important when considering mistakes made by students. When students make mistakes with content words, the message they want to communicate is almost always hindered or lost; however, if a mistake is made with a function word, the message is usually conveyed in spite of the incorrect grammar of the structure used.

> ~~Mary **lives** ice cream~~.
> Mary **likes** ice cream.

The first sentence does not make sense because the verb is incorrect. A simple mistake with a content word affects communication.

> ~~Mary was born **on** December~~.
> Mary was born **in** December.

In spite of its structural problem (incorrect preposition), the basic message in the first sentence is clear, and communication is not significantly hindered.

Another important use of identifying content and function words is that of stress in a sentence. Content words almost always carry the pronunciation stress in sentences. When students can identify the content words, they will be able to say sentences with better stress and intonation. Compare the following examples:

> **THE** cat wants **TO** go.

> The **CAT WANTS** to **GO**.

*** *You can teach parts of speech* ***

Following are some ideas to help students identify the different parts of speech and learn their correct usage. Subsequent chapters will contain more tailored teaching suggestions for each part of speech.

Word bags

Decide which parts of speech you want your students to practise. Assign a different bag for each part of speech and color code it. If you want your students to work with all parts of speech, you will then have eight different bags. Now, prepare cue cards with varied examples of the part(s) of speech you are teaching. Make sure that the examples show different types of each part of speech; for example, if the bag contains nouns, write cue cards with examples of a variety of noun types (proper, common, abstract, concrete, countable, uncountable or possessive).

Divide the class into groups, distribute the bags and have students identify the part of speech in each bag by reading the cue cards for each bag. Then, ask the group to further categorize the cards in the bag. Once they have them categorized, get the group to think of more examples in each category (concrete nouns, for example).

To make the activity more challenging, you can get the students to create grammatically correct sentences with the words in the different bags. The level of difficulty of the words will depend on the level of the students.

Magazine cut outs
Distribute magazines to the class. In pairs or small groups, each working at their own desk or table, have students cut out pictures and place them on their table. Each group should cut out at least five different pictures. Then, the pairs change tables – and magazines. The new group has to find words in the magazines that represent or describe the pictures. They have to identify the types of the words they cut out and must then create a sentence using those words.

        For example:
        Picture: a woman, walking, wearing a long dress
        Words: glamorous (adjective) – red (adjective) – woman (noun)
        Sentence: This woman is wearing a glamorous red dress.

2 Parts of a sentence

Clear communication depends on understanding the relationships among words. The proper placement of words in a sentence is fundamental to defining those relationships. This structuring varies among languages. A requirement in one language (for example, in English, the presence of a subject) is optional in others (many languages permit, but do not require, a subject). This chapter provides an overview of the fundamental elements of English sentences. The focus of this chapter is on simple sentences. Complex sentences are described in more detail on the *You Can Teach Grammar* companion web site.

2.1 Mandatory sentence elements

The parts of speech discussed in Chapter 1 are the building blocks necessary for creating sentences. There is a direct relationship between some of those elements and the parts of a sentence. Every sentence must have a **subject** and **predicate**. A subject may be a noun (or noun equivalent), a noun phrase or a pronoun. A predicate must contain at least one verb. A sentence will always contain at least one **clause**. The individual parts of a sentence may consist of a word, a clause or a **phrase**. In writing, a sentence always begins with a capital (upper case) letter in its first word, and is always completed with a punctuation mark. The most common punctuation mark for a sentence ending is a period (also known as a full stop). Sentences may also end with a question mark (?) or an exclamation mark (!). Other (optional) basic elements of a sentence are the **object**, the **complement** and the **adverbial**.

2.1.1 Subject and predicate

A sentence is a set of grammatically related words. It always contains a subject and a predicate. The subject of a sentence is the thing – the *'what'* or the *'who'* – to which the predicate refers. The predicate is the part of the sentence that is giving information about the subject. The predicate is generally introduced by a verb, which constitutes the head of the predicate. It is *'what is being said'* about the subject. The subject of a sentence must be a noun or noun equivalent (pronoun, noun phrase or other structure that acts as a noun). The following are examples of simple sentences. In each example, the subject is highlighted in bold and the predicate is shown in italics. The head of the predicate – the verb – is underlined.

> **You** *<u>can go</u> now*.
> **Mary** *<u>has finished</u> her task*.
> **The boy** *<u>is</u> outside*.
> **It** *<u>rained</u> heavily last night*.
> **Eating out** *<u>is</u> expensive*.

These simple sentences have subjects and predicates that are easily identified. Note the subject in the third sentence. It is not a single noun, but a two-word combination: a noun phrase. Subjects are not restricted to single words, and can become quite complex. The subject in the fifth example (*eating out*) is formed from a verb, but it is not acting as a verb here. These verb-based noun equivalents are discussed in more detail in Chapter 13 Gerunds and infinitives.

A subject may be composed of a phrase or a clause. For example:

Subject
(who/what is being referenced)
You and all your friends
Mary, whom you've already met,
The boy in the blue suit

Predicate
(what is being said about the subject)
can go now.
has finished her task.
is outside.

2.1.2 Clause

A clause is formed by a subject and a verb. It is part of a sentence. Every sentence has at least one clause, and a clause can be an entire sentence. Simple sentences contain a single clause. The following example is a simple sentence. The verb (head of the predicate) is highlighted.

Freddy **watched** TV all day.
<subject>   <--------predicate-------->
<----------------------clause------------------>

Compound and complex sentences have more than one clause. The following example sentence has two clauses, connected by the conjunction *because*. (Clauses are discussed in more detail on the *You Can Teach Grammar* companion web site.)

Freddy   **watched** TV all day   because   he   **was** very tired.
<subject 1> <-------predicate 1------> <conjunction> <subject 2> <--predicate 2-->
<----------------------clause------------------>   <-----------------------------clause---------------------------->

2.1.3 Phrase

A phrase is a set of grammatically related words. A phrase may contain a noun or a verb, but they are not requirements. A phrase is different from a clause or a sentence in that it does not have both subject and predicate. The following are phrases:

at the corner
the **man** of the year
really **pretty**
running around wildly
going to school
to **bake** a cake
very **well**
beautifully **written**

Each phrase has a head (also called a nucleus) that defines what type of phrase it is. The heads of the example phrases above are highlighted. A phrase may function as a noun, a verb, an adjective or an adverb. These multi-word versions of the parts of speech function in the same way, grammatically, as the single-word versions. Their placement in a sentence is also the same. A noun phrase (*the man of the year*) functions in the same way as a single-word noun (*Harry*), for example.

She gave the award to **Harry**.
She gave the award to **the man of the year**.

Quiz 1: Mandatory sentence elements
Identify the subject in each sentence. Identify whether the underlined section in each sentence is a phrase or a clause.

1- He told me he would come.
2- Arriving home, he found out he had lost his keys.
3- He told me he would come by 7 p.m.
4- My closest friend will get married soon after graduation.
5- Although he was exhausted, he managed to finish the assignment.
6- Eating in restaurants is very expensive these days.
7- He came home directly after school.
8- He came home directly after he finished school.
9- He wants to come to the party.
10- I have been studying for the test since last week.
11- I have been studying for the test since I left my job.
12- Do you know her pretty well?
13- I do not know how I will get there.
14- Injured in the war, he could never work again.

*** In the classroom: Mandatory sentence elements ***

In the ESL classroom, the most fundamental grammatical structure for students to comprehend is that of subject + predicate. Students must understand that all English sentences require, at very least, a subject and a verb. This concept is taught and reinforced frequently at lower levels. It may be necessary for teachers to review this concept even through high intermediate levels, especially for any student whose first language does not require an explicit subject in all sentences.

2.2 Optional sentence elements

Beyond the basic elements of subject and predicate, there are three additional common parts of a sentence: the **object**, the **complement** and the **adverbial**. An object may be classified as direct or indirect. A complement may be a subject complement or an object complement. Objects and complements are always found in the predicate.

2.2.1 Object

An object in a sentence is usually represented by a noun, pronoun or noun phrase. Some other types of phrases and clauses may also be objects. An object is the thing upon which a transitive verb is acting. It is the "receiver" of the action of a transitive verb. Intransitive verbs do not take objects.

It is possible for a transitive verb to have more than one object. If there is one object, then it is a direct object. A direct object is the direct recipient of the action of a dynamic verb. If there are two objects, then one is the direct object, the other is the indirect object. The indirect object is the recipient of the direct object in some way. *(See 2.3.2 Subject + verb + object(s))*

```
Dr. Edmunds      teaches                          computer science.
                 <dynamic transitive verb>        <----direct object---->
<---subject--->  <------------------------------predicate------------------------------>

Dr. Edmunds      teaches                    us                      computer science.
                 <dynamic transitive verb>  <indirect object>       <----direct object---->
<---subject--->  <--------------------------------------predicate-------------------------------------->
```

For a small group of verbs (including *owe*, *pay*, *promise*, *refuse*, *show*, *teach*, *tell* and *write*), the direct object may be elided if it is understood, leaving the indirect object as the only explicitly stated object.

```
Dr. Edmunds      teaches                    us.
<---subject--->  <dynamic transitive verb>  <indirect object>
```

2.2.2 Complement

A complement may be a noun, noun phrase, pronoun, adjective, adjective phrase, clause or prepositional phrase. Certain types of verb phrases may also function as complements. A complement further describes the state or condition of the subject or object. The term "complement" is derived from the idea that it "completes" the subject or object by providing a more thorough description. Dynamic verbs do not take complements; they take objects. The stative verbs known as linking verbs take complements. Linking verbs – also known as copular verbs or copulative verbs – include verbs describing a sense *(feel, taste, look)* or condition *(seem, become, be)*. *(See 11.2.3.2.1 Linking verbs)*

A subject complement follows a linking verb. It describes the end state of the subject.

```
The CEO        is                a licensed engineer.
               <linking verb>    <subject complement-noun phrase>
<-subject->    <--------------------------predicate-------------------------->

These shoes    feel              uncomfortable.
               <linking verb>    <subject complement-adjective>
<---subject---> <--------------------------predicate-------------------------->
```

The structure for object complements is different. Object complements describe the end state of a direct object. Dynamic verbs that describe assigning or changing states *(name, appoint, call, paint, make)* or making judgments *(consider, rule, judge, think, deem)* are the types with direct objects that may take a complement. The majority of verbs do not fall in this category.

```
He         called                      the waiter          a bad name.
           <dynamic transitive verb>   <direct object>     <object complement-noun phrase>
<subject>  <--------------------------------------predicate-------------------------------------->

The toy    made                        the dog             happy.
           <dynamic transitive verb>   <direct object>     <object complement-adjective>
<subject>  <--------------------------------------predicate-------------------------------------->
```

2.2.3 Adverbial

An adverbial may be a single word (an adverb), a phrase or a clause. It serves the function of an adverb, so it may describe a verb, an adjective, another adverbial, or an entire clause. Its position in a sentence depends on which part of the sentence it is describing.

Dr. Edmunds teaches comprehensively.
<----subject----> <-verb-> <adverbial describing verb>

That was funny in its own way.
<subject> <verb> <adjective> <adverbial describing adjective>

Dr. Edmunds teaches quite comprehensively.
<----subject----> <-verb-> <adverbial describing adverbial> <adverbial describing verb>

Honestly, that was funny.
<adverbial describing entire clause> <-----clause----->

Adverbials can be characterized by their function. The most common such categories are time, place, manner and degree. In the examples above, all the adverbials except *quite* are adverbials of manner. *Quite* is an adverbial of degree.

Quiz 2: Optional sentence elements

What part of a sentence is the underlined portion: subject, predicate, verb, direct object, indirect object, subject complement, object complement or adverbial?

1. My sweater is different from yours.
2. I found my jacket.
3. They looked tired.
4. His peers acknowledge his efforts.
5. The man at the corner sells popcorn.
6. What does she like to eat?
7. We saw the building we are going to move into.
8. Would you mind meeting him before noon?
9. He drove carefully.
10. We painted the room purple.
11. He told me to mind my own business.
12. They will go to the port.
13. They gave the judge all the documents.

**** In the classroom: Optional sentence elements ****

A common area of confusion is the distinction between objects and complements. Much of the time, knowledge of whether a sentence element is classified as one or the other is not necessary for correct grammatical structure. The greatest confusion comes in knowing whether an adjective or an adverb is the appropriate follow-on to a particular verb. A common error is to follow a linking verb with an adverb. This is generally not the intended meaning, and in these cases, an adjective is almost always preferred, as subject complement.

In the sentence *Sharon feels badly*, the choice of the adverb *badly* probably does not convey the intention, as it means that Sharon's capacity or ability to feel is substandard; *badly* is modifying the verb *feel*. If the intended meaning is that Sharon is in some way dissatisfied or unhappy, then the adjective *bad* is the correct choice; it is the subject complement. In the sentence *Sharon feels bad*, the adjective *bad* is describing the subject, *Sharon*.

2.3 Simple sentence structure

Word order is fundamental to correct English grammar. This section describes the basic constituents and word order of simple sentences. (Complex and compound sentence structures are covered on the *You Can Teach Grammar* companion web site.)

2.3.1 Subject + verb

Nouns and verbs are the two main elements of a sentence. The shortest possible sentences in English contain at least one noun (or pronoun) – which is the subject – and one verb, which constitutes the entire predicate.

> Mary laughs.
> He cried.

This structure is possible for intransitive dynamic verbs only.

2.3.2 Subject + verb + object(s)

After subject and verb, the third most common element in sentences is the object. This is the "receiver" of the action of the verb. When there is only one object in the sentence, it is the direct object.

> Mary   eats   ice cream.
> *<subject>*   *<verb>*   *<direct object>*

Sometimes there are two objects in a sentence. When this is the case, one of them is the direct object and the other is the indirect object. The direct object, as the name implies, is the direct recipient of the action of the verb. The indirect object "receives" the direct object in some way.

> Mary   gave   Tom   a gift.
> *<subject>*   *<verb>*   *<indirect object>*   *<direct object>*

One way of identifying an indirect object is to try to invert the order of the two objects. When this is done, the indirect object requires a preposition in front of it.

> Mary   gave   a gift   to Tom.
> *<subject>*   *<verb>*   *<direct object>*   *<indirect object>*
>   *(introduced by a preposition)*

2.3.3 Subject + verb + subject complement

A linking (or copular) verb always requires another word after it.

~~Mary is~~.
~~He became~~.

After verbs that denote the state or condition of the subject, a subject complement is necessary. A subject complement describes, or completes, the subject of a sentence. Subject complements are usually nouns or adjectives (or their equivalents). They are also called subjective complements.

Mary	is	my sister.
<subject>	<linking verb>	<subject complement> (noun phrase)
Mary	seems	happy.
<subject>	<linking verb>	<subject complement> (adjective)

2.3.4 Subject + verb + object + object complement

When a sentence includes an object, an object complement may sometimes follow it. This object complement can be a noun (or noun equivalent) or an adjective which describes what an object has become, or that gives it another name. It is also called an objective complement. There is a small group of verbs whose objects can take an object complement.

The barking dogs	made	me	nervous.
<--------subject-------->	<verb>	<direct object>	<object complement> (adjective)
The committee	appointed	Tom	chairman.
<-----subject------>	<---verb--->	<direct object>	<object complement> (noun)

2.3.5 Subject + verb + (object) + adverbial

An adverbial is a single word (an adverb) or a group of words (a phrase or clause) that take on the function of an adverb; it can modify a verb, an adjective, another adverb, or an entire clause or sentence. Adverbials may be placed in many spots in a sentence. In this sense, they are much more flexible than subjects, objects and verbs. In simple sentences, adverbials are typically found at the end of the sentence. In these cases, they function to modify the main verb or to modify the entire sentence.

He sings every song **well**. (adverb modifying the verb *sings*)
He will arrive **within the next hour.** (adverbial modifying the entire sentence)

An adverbial may also be placed before the word, phrase or sentence it is modifying.

It is **terribly** hot. (adverb modifying the adjective *hot*)

We **always** order the extra-large pizza. (adverb modifying the verb *order*)

Uncharacteristically, George didn't say a word. (adverb modifying the sentence)

Quiz 3: Simple sentence structure

A) Identify every part of the following two sentences in the spaces provided.

1- I have given this exercise to hundreds of people.
   a- I _____
   b- have given this exercise to hundreds of people _____
   c- have given _____
   d- this exercise _____
   e- to hundreds of people _____

2- He ate the pizza in a hurry.
   a- He _____
   b- ate the pizza in a hurry _____
   c- ate _____
   d- the pizza _____
   e- in a hurry _____

B) Identify the pattern in each of the following sentences by entering the parts of the sentence in the appropriate boxes. The verb may be a verb phrase.

1.) The children seem awfully quiet tonight.						
Subject	Verb	Direct Object	Subject Complement	Indirect Object	Object Complement	Adverbial

2.) Could you lend me that magazine when you're done?						
Subject	Verb	Direct Object	Subject Complement	Indirect Object	Object Complement	Adverbial

3.) I find the hamburgers at this restaurant overcooked most of the time.						
Subject	Verb	Direct Object	Subject Complement	Indirect Object	Object Complement	Adverbial

4.) Jim's tools don't work on 220-volt power sources.						
Subject	Verb	Direct Object	Subject Complement	Indirect Object	Object Complement	Adverbial

*** In the classroom: Simple sentence structure ***

These basic structures are staples of beginner- and intermediate-level ESL classes. They will very likely need to be reinforced with frequency, right up through the intermediate level. The particular difficulties that students may have with the structure will vary depending on the structural rules of their first language. The better-acquainted students are with these fundamentals, the more easily they will be able to comprehend more advanced concepts, which will be variations of these standards. Among the most common elements to reinforce will be the requirement for a subject in every sentence, and the distinctions between objects, complements and adverbials, particularly in the roles they perform.

2.3.6 Simple sentence structure expanded

A general principle of English sentence organization is to keep what is familiar or known at the beginning of a sentence. New information is stressed, or given special importance, by being placed at the end of the sentence. This is known as end focus. The following chart depicts ordering of elements in a sentence. It corresponds to the basic structures given in preceding sections, with an expansion of detail for adverbials. This order is common, but not fixed. The principle of end focus, for example, may cause a shift in the order of sentence elements.

Bearing these considerations in mind, here is an overview – with examples – of the correct ordering of simple sentences in English. The shaded boxes represent elements that are optional. If all elements (including all the optional ones) are included in a single sentence, very often the word order will change (especially adverbials of manner).

Table 5: Simple sentence structure

Subject	Stative verb	Adverbial of place (locative complement)	Adverbial of time
Mary	was	in Toronto	last week.

Subject	Stative linking verb	Subject Complement	Adverbial of place	Adverbial of time
She	will be	a lawyer	in New York	after her exams.

Subject	Stative linking verb	Subject Complement	Adverbial of manner	Adverbial of place	Adverbial of time
That style	became	popular	quickly	in Europe	at that time.

Subject	Dynamic verb	Direct Object	Adverbial of place	Adverbial of time
Martin	caused	an accident	on his street	yesterday.

Subject	Dynamic verb	Direct Object	Adverbial of manner	Adverbial of place	Adverbial of time
We	devoured	the dessert	hungrily	at the table	last night.

Subject	Dynamic verb	Indirect Object	Direct Object	Adverbial of manner	Adverbial of place	Adverbial of time
Mark	offered	us	some wine	cheerfully	in the den	while we waited.

Subject	Dynamic verb	Direct Object	Object Complement	Adverbial of manner	Adverbial of place	Adverbial of time
The board	elected	Sue	manager	unanimously	in New York	last month.

Subject	Dynamic verb	Adverbial of manner	Adverbial of place	Adverbial of time
The ferry	arrived	smoothly	at the port	on schedule.

2.4 Variations on subjects and objects

English requires a subject in virtually every sentence. Subjects (and objects) can be fairly complicated phrases or clauses. In these cases, the placement of the full subject at the beginning of the sentence might give an unintended emphasis. Or, the subject might be an ephemeral reference. In these cases – which are frequent – substitutes may be used. The words **it** and **there** are common substitutes as subject or object.

2.4.1 Cleft sentences

The standard ordering of English sentences does not always allow the intended emphasis. A common variation of the standard structure is one that splits (or cleaves – hence the adjective "cleft") a sentence, allowing non-standard placement of the subject or object. Consider the following sentence:

> The military man told Caroline that her home was safe.

The subject is *The military man*. The main verb is *told*. The principle of end focus suggests that the new, or more important, information is *told Caroline that her home was safe*. If the more important information is that the person who convinced Caroline was *the military man* (and not someone else), then that emphasis can be achieved by placing *the military man* in the predicate, after a verb.

Cleft sentences use *be* as the main verb. Since they shift the ostensible subject into the predicate, then something else must be used to occupy the subject position. A common substitute in the subject position is *it*.

> It was the military man who told Caroline that her home was safe.

Other common structures for cleft sentences use phrases (such as *the thing that...*, or *the reason...*) or *what*-clauses in the subject position, preceding the verb *be*.

> What the military man told Caroline was that her home was safe.

2.4.2 Preparatory *it*

In cleft sentences and other structures, an entire clause can be the subject or object in a sentence. In such cases, the clause is performing the function of a noun. Certain verb forms may also function as nouns: gerunds (verbs in *–ing* form), gerund phrases, infinitives (verbs in base form, preceded by the particle *to*) and infinitive phrases. *(See 11.1.1 Non-finite forms and 13 Gerunds and infinitives)* Subjects or objects that are composed of clauses, gerund phrases or infinitive phrases are often simplified to the single pronoun **it**. This usage is known as the preparatory *it*. It is also known as the anticipatory *it*.

2.4.2.1 Preparatory *it* in subject position

Clauses, gerund phrases and infinitive phrases may be the subjects of sentences.

> *To be honest at all times* is important. (infinitive phrase as subject)
> *Meeting you* was great. (gerund phrase as subject)

> *That he can't be present for today's meeting* is true. (*that*-clause as subject)

The example sentences above are permissible, but are not the preferred structures. Sentence subjects that are clauses, gerund phrases or infinitive phrases have a high (often the highest) information value in the sentence. As a result – because of the principle of end focus – it is preferable to place them toward the end of a sentence, in the predicate. But, English usually requires a subject at the beginning of the sentence. These dual requirements are accommodated by using the preparatory *it* as the subject, and putting the clause or phrase at the end. These phrases or clauses are sometimes called postponed subjects.

> **It** is important *to be honest at all times*.
> **It** was great *meeting you*.
> **It** is true *that he can't be present for today's meeting*.

2.4.2.2 Preparatory *it* in object position

The preparatory *it* can also be found in the object position. In these sentences, the phrase or clause that functions as an object is moved to the end of the sentence in accordance with the principle of end focus. When the clause or phrase is moved to the end of the sentence, then the anticipatory *it* fills the object position following the verb.

> They've made **it** a difficult process *to join the club*.
> She found **it** incredible *being on top of Mount Everest*.

2.4.3 Non-referential *it* and *there*

A sentence may include the words **there** or **it** as the subject without replacing any word or phrase, or without any obvious reference (such as a postponed subject). These uses are known as non-referential *it* and *there*. They are used to fill the subject position. Though they are confined to particular uses, they occur quite frequently.

> **It**'s cold here.
> **There** are two books on the table.

2.4.3.1 Non-referential *it*

Non-referential *it* is used to express time, distance and weather. It is used to make comments about surroundings or the environment.

Time:	**It**'s twenty past eleven already.
Distance:	**It**'s quite far to Miami.
Weather:	**It** seems chilly today.
Surroundings / environment:	**It** feels tense in that room.

In the four examples above, it is not explicitly clear what **it** is referring to. The presence of **it** is necessary to fulfill the requirement for a subject in English sentences. This non-referential subject is also called an empty subject or a dummy subject.

2.4.3.2 Non-referential *there*

Non-referential *there* is more general in its usage. The non-referential uses of *there* fall into four main functional categories:

– to present or introduce a new topic (usually expanded upon immediately after)
>   **There**'s a fast way to get there; just take the road through the park.
– to introduce the logical subject and where it is located
>   **There** is a dirty mug on the counter.
– to emphasize the existence of something
>   **There** are always ethical choices.
– to list a number of options
>   For your dessert, **there**'s a selection of pies, cakes and ice cream.

Quiz 4: Variations on subject and object

A- Restate each of the following sentences by shifting the subject to the predicate.
1. Cleaning the house is time-consuming.
2. Andy should have won the race.
3. To sleep for a full eight hours seems impossible.
4. What I wanted to show you was the new shopping centre.

B- Restate each of the following sentences by shifting the direct object to the end of the sentence.
1. We always find being here so peaceful.
2. The summers here make staying outdoors imperative.

C- Insert non-referential it *or* there *as appropriate.*
1. I think _____ is a thunderstorm coming.
2. _____ 's late.
3. _____ are two certainties in life: death and taxes.
4. _____ seems a little dark.

*** In the classroom: It *and* there *as subject and object*

When translating, sentences with a preparatory *it* may be impossible to match with an equivalent version in another language. These structures represent special challenges for ESL students whose native language allows affirmative sentences without an explicit subject. (English does not.) In these cases, the most common error is to begin a sentence with a verb, omitting the necessary subject. This error may be hard to detect if the main verb is *is*, since contraction may make *it is* sound very similar to simply *is*.

>   ~~Is cold out today~~.
>   It's cold out today.

Non-referential *there* can be slightly more difficult for ESL students to master since it also requires the verb *be* to have agreement in number with the subject complement. This particular error may be reinforced by the native English-speaking community. Your students will hear "real world" English speakers make errors in subject/verb agreement in combination with the non-referential *there*. **There's** is almost invariably used, regardless of whether "there is" one thing or "there is" two things under discussion. The main culprit in this usage is the contraction of *there is* to *there's*. **There are** does not contract nearly as easily, and is therefore sublimated to the simpler *there's*.

~~There's~~ hundreds of opportunities at that company.
There are hundreds of opportunities at that company.

2.5 Sentence types

There are four main sentence types: declarative, interrogative, imperative and exclamatory. Each type has its own grammatical structure. Declarative sentences follow the patterns laid out earlier in this chapter. *(See 2.3 Simple sentence structure)* Interrogative, imperative and exclamatory sentences use different patterns.

2.5.1 Declarative sentences

Declarative sentences make statements or assertions. They can be classified as affirmative or negative. Affirmative sentences assert that what is being said is true.

> We like coffee.
> They have been to Europe.

Negative declarative sentences deny the truth of a statement. This negation is achieved by attaching the particle *not* to an auxiliary verb – or to the verb *be* when it is the main verb. If the affirmative sentence form already contains an auxiliary, then *not* is attached to that auxiliary. If the affirmative sentence does not contain an auxiliary, then the auxiliary *do* must also be added, together with *not*.

> We *like* coffee. We **do not** *like* tea.
> They *have been* to Europe. They *have* **not** *been* to Asia.
> She *is* aware of that. She *is* **not** aware of this.
> That computer *does* graphics. This computer **does not** do graphics.

In conversational English, the particle *not* is contracted to the auxiliary verb (or main *be* verb).

> We **don't** like tea.
> They **haven't** been to Asia.
> She **isn't** aware of this.
> This computer **doesn't** do graphics.

British English also allows attaching the particle *not* to *have* when it is the main verb. American English generally negates the main verb *have* with *do not*.

> I **haven't** a clue.
> I **don't** *have* a clue.

Negative adverbs like *never*, *seldom*, *rarely* and *hardly ever* can also convey a negative meaning in a sentence.

> Guadalupe **never** cries.

2.5.2 Interrogative sentences

Interrogative sentences ask questions. In writing, they are always completed with a question mark. In most questions, the subject of the sentence is preceded by an auxiliary. Other features of interrogative sentence structure depend on the type of question.

Yes / No questions: *auxiliary + subject + verb (+ object or adverbial)*

Some questions can only be answered with either *yes* or *no*. These sentences begin with an auxiliary.

Do	you	like	coffee?
<auxiliary>	*<subject>*	*<verb>*	*<object>*

Will	you	return	by Monday?
<auxiliary>	*<subject>*	*<verb>*	*<--adverbial-->*

Alternative questions: *auxiliary + subject + verb + choice 1 + or + choice 2*

Alternative questions expect an answer which is a choice from a given list. The choices are given in the question, separated by the conjunction *or*.

Do	you	like	coffee	or	tea?
<auxiliary>	*<subject>*	*<verb>*	*<choice 1>*	*<or>*	*<choice 2>*

Will	you	arrive	early	or	late?
<auxiliary>	*<subject>*	*<verb>*	*<choice 1>*	*<or>*	*<choice 2>*

Wh-questions: *interrogative + auxiliary + subject + verb*

Wh-questions allow for a wide range of possible answers. They are introduced by interrogatives (pronouns, adverbs or adjectives). Interrogative pronouns are usually the object of the verb.

Whom*	did	you	see?
<interrogative pronoun>	*<auxiliary>*	*<subject>*	*<verb>*

* Although the object form *whom* is correct, usage of the subject form *who* is very common, even when the pronoun is the object of the verb.

When	will	you	come?
<interrogative adverb>	*<auxiliary>*	*<subject>*	*<verb>*

The interrogative pronouns *who* or *what* can fill the subject position in an interrogative sentence.

Who	saw	you?
<subject>	*<verb>*	*<object>*

What	happened?
<subject>	*<verb>*

Tag questions: *declarative structure + , + auxiliary + subject*

A tag question is an add-on to a declarative sentence. It seeks affirmation or denial of the declarative sentence. If the declarative statement is positive, then the tag question is usually posed as a negative. If the declarative statement is negative, then the tag question is usually posed as a positive. In writing, the tag question is separated from the declarative statement by a comma.

She is coming soon,	isn't	she?
<declarative statement + , > (positive form)	<auxiliary> (negative form)	<subject>

You didn't buy that,	did	you?
<declarative statement + , > (negative form)	<auxiliary> (positive form)	<subject>

Negative questions: particle* not *added to auxiliary

Negative questions are variations on yes/no questions and wh-questions. They seek the same response as their positive counterparts. The distinction is not in the actual response, but in the questioner's expectation.

Don't you enjoy going to the movies?
Why **doesn't** she join us for dinner?

Negative questions are usually posed with the particle *not* contracted to the auxiliary verb. When *not* stands alone, it follows the subject.

Do you **not** enjoy going to the movies?
Why **does** she **not** join us for dinner?

There is no widely-accepted contracted form of *am not*. The contracted form **aren't** is used. When the particle *not* stands alone, then **am** is used.

Aren't I lucky?
Am I **not** a man?

2.5.3 Imperative sentences

Imperative sentences are used to give commands, orders, directions or instructions. They assume the subject *you*, and do not include an explicit subject. They can be classified as affirmative or negative. Imperative affirmative sentences are introduced by the verb in its base form. Imperative negative sentences are introduced by the negative auxiliary verb *do not* (or *don't*).

Eat it up!
Don't bring that home, please.

2.5.4 Exclamatory sentences

Exclamatory sentences are a variation of declarative sentences. This type of sentence shows emotion and it usually ends with an exclamation mark (!). Declarative sentences that begin with *how* and *what* are generally exclamatory.

How beautiful she is!
What a day we had!

Quiz 5: Sentence types

Identify the type of each of the following sentences.
1. What a wonderful sight!
2. They haven't arrived yet.
3. Did you ever tell him about the situation?
4. How long did you say it was?
5. I am a fool, aren't I?
6. Add two eggs and mix well.
7. Are you coming with us or taking the bus?
8. You will get that promotion.
9. Don't you like it?
10. That's it.

*** In the classroom: Sentence types ***

The basic structures of declarative and interrogative sentences take up much of the grammatical instruction of the beginner and low intermediate levels. Interrogative sentences and negative declaratives usually take some time to master, especially when they are different from a student's native language. The difficulty that seems to persist the longest – often all the way up through to advanced levels – is the correct mode of responding to negative interrogatives. Unlike English, many languages expect a different answer to a negative interrogative than to an affirmative one. This thinking is difficult for students to shake.

Take as an example the case where the true situation is that Jerry is happy. In English, it doesn't matter how the question is asked: the answer is the same.

        Is Jerry happy?   Correct answer: Yes.
        Isn't Jerry happy?   Correct answer: Yes.

In many languages, the correct answer to the negative question would be, "No (he *is* happy)."

*** You can teach parts of a sentence ***

Following are ideas to help students internalize correct sentence structure. These exercises are appropriate for teaching and review of sentence structure concepts for beginner and low intermediate levels. Subsequent chapters will contain more tailored teaching suggestions for specific grammar points within sentences.

Is this a sentence?

Give students cue cards, some with full sentences (showing subject and predicate very clearly) and some with broken sentences (sentences that are not complete). Students must identify which ones are full sentences and which are not. They then have to create full sentences from the broken sentences.

Example:
Card 1: Mario likes ice cream very much. (full sentence)
Students should identify subject *Mario* and predicate *likes ice cream very much*.
Card 2: not eat much (not a sentence)
Students can come up with something like this to make it a simple full sentence: *Pam does not eat much ice cream.*

Identifying sentence types

Provide students with a short paragraph. Have them code sentences according to the sentence type (declarative, interrogative, imperative, exclamatory). Make sure the text has a variety of sentence types.

Get silly!

Divide the class into groups. Have groups work together to create sentences that are grammatically correct but that are silly. The teacher can assess students' comprehension of structure while the students have fun thinking of silly sentences. Example output: *The upset ant danced all night.*

3 Nouns

Nouns are words that name people, animals, things, places, abstract ideas, feelings, substances or qualities. The following are examples of nouns.

>man *(person)*
>lion *(animal)*
>table *(thing)*
>beauty *(abstract idea)*
>happiness *(feeling)*
>park *(place)*
>iron *(substance)*
>stubbornness *(quality)*

If parts of speech are considered the building blocks of a sentence, nouns would be the cornerstone. They are the most substantive elements of communication. Without a noun (or noun equivalent) it is almost impossible to build a sentence in English.

3.1 Noun forms

Nouns do not have a distinct form that immediately identifies them as nouns. There are, however, some word endings which indicate that a word is probably a noun.

-ence:	confidence, silence	*-dom:*	freedom, kingdom
-ment:	disappointment, equipment	*-ture:*	fixture, signature
-ion:	communion, complexion	*-tion:*	action, education
-ance:	abundance, distance	*-ery:*	archery, lottery
-er:	manager, teacher	*-ness:*	friendliness, happiness
-an/-ian:	artisan, politician	*-or:*	creator, spectator
-sion:	collision, television	*-ity:*	opportunity, invisibility
-ation:	probation, information	*-hood:*	childhood, neighbourhood
-ice:	advice, malice	*-ship:*	membership, partnership
-ology:	geology, technology	*-ist:*	socialist, scientist
-ism:	capitalism, Buddhism	*-graph:*	autograph, paragraph
-ency:	tendency, presidency	*-ancy:*	vagrancy, pregnancy

Some nouns are formed from verbs. Nouns formed by adding the ending *–ing* to the base form of a verb are known as gerunds. *(See 13 Gerunds and infinitives)*

Compound nouns are nouns formed from two words, (for example, *classroom*, *basketball* and *woodworm*), or less commonly, three or more words (*son-in-law*). Sometimes compounds are spelled with a hyphen, and sometimes not (*sight-seeing*, *sunbathing*).

3.2 Functions of nouns in a sentence

Nouns can have different functions in a sentence. They can be found in the subject or predicate of a sentence. They are frequently accompanied by modifiers, forming a noun phrase: the **dog**; an English **teacher**; an absolute **coincidence**. Examples of the different functions of nouns or noun phrases are given in the sentences below.

Subject of a sentence

    The **dog** is eating.
    <subject> <predicate>

    Sam will come soon.
    <subject> <-----predicate----->

Object of the main verb

    Carol likes **coffee**.
    <subject> <verb> <direct object>

    Judd gave **Sue** his **book**.
    <subject> < verb> <indirect object> <direct object>

Subject complement of linking verbs such as *be, seem, become,* and *appear*

    He became an English **teacher**.
    <subject> <--verb--> <-subject complement->

    These are **cups**.
    <subject> <verb> <subject complement>

Object complement

    They appointed Mr. Smith **president**.
    <subject> <--- verb---> <direct object> <object complement>

Appositive (a noun or noun phrase which gives further information on another noun phrase which immediately precedes it, separated by commas)

    My uncle, the **artist**, practises yoga every day.
    <-subject-> <appositive> <-------------predicate-------------->

Quiz 1: Functions of a noun in a sentence

Identify the functions of the nouns underlined in the following sentences.

1. We named the baby <u>Alec</u> after his grandfather.
2. When you buy something from a shop, you are making a <u>contract</u>.
3. Janice and Boris are antique <u>dealers</u>.
4. The <u>tower</u> was built in 1989.
5. Lucerne, a magnificent <u>city</u>, is located on Lake Lucerne.

**** In the classroom: Functions of nouns ****

When students understand sentence structure and have appropriate vocabulary, they can generally pick out the nouns. One fundamental point of confusion is that in English, many words that are nouns can also function as verbs. For example: *The book is on the table* vs. *I want to book a table for two at The Ritz.*

In addition to an understanding of structural rules, word stress can be a significant differentiator in these cases, as the distinction between nouns and verbs is often a matter of shifting the stress. For example: *REC*ord (noun) vs. re*CORD* (verb).

3.3 Noun placement

Nouns can be preceded by determiners. *(See 6 Determiners)* Singular countable nouns always require a determiner (for example, *a*, *an*, *the*, *another*, *every*, *some*, *my*, *this*).

>*an* **egg**
>*every* **person**
>*that* **man**
>*your* **pen**

Plural nouns are not preceded by a determiner when they refer to things or people in general.

>**The people** in my neighbourhood are generous. (specific people)
>**People** are becoming more aware of the situation. (people in general)

Nouns come after descriptive adjectives. *(See 5.2.2 Descriptive adjectives)*

>A *blue* **car** is parked outside.
>His *narrow, bright* **eyes** scared me.

A noun can follow a preposition as the object of the preposition. (A preposition followed by a noun or pronoun is called a prepositional phrase. The preposition introduces the phrase and the noun is the object of that preposition.)

>He lived *in* **Paris** *for* **months.**

A noun can be placed before another noun to describe or define it; the noun that precedes another noun is functioning as an adjective.

>The ***kitchen*** **walls** are painted blue.
>(noun *kitchen* functioning as an adjective describing the noun *walls*)

3.4 Noun types

The following table gives a complete rendition of the characteristics of nouns. Each of the characteristics is explained in further detail below.

Table 6: Noun types

Nouns	Commonality	Concreteness	Countability	Number	Case
	Common	Concrete	Countable	Singular	Subjective *
					Objective **
					Possessive ***
				Plural	Subjective
					Objective
					Possessive
			Uncountable		Subjective
					Objective
					Possessive
		Abstract	Countable	Singular	Subjective
					Objective
					Possessive
				Plural	Subjective
					Objective
					Possessive
			Uncountable		Subjective
					Objective
					Possessive
	Proper	Concrete	Countable	Singular	Subjective
					Objective
					Possessive
				Plural	Subjective
					Objective
					Possessive
		Abstract	Countable	Singular	Subjective
					Objective
					Possessive
				Plural	Subjective
					Objective
					Possessive

* Subjective case is also called nominative case
** Objective case is also called accusative case
*** Possessive case is also called genitive case

3.4.1 Commonality

A noun's commonality is one of two types: common or proper.

3.4.1.1 Common nouns

Common nouns are nouns referring to a person, creature, place or thing in the general sense: *man*, *car*, and *park*, for example. They are only capitalized when they occur at the beginning of the sentence. The majority of nouns are common nouns.

3.4.1.2 Proper nouns

Proper nouns name a specific person, place or thing: *John*, *Paris*, and *Buddhist*, for example. They are always capitalized. Some other nouns such as days of the week, months of the year, institutions and organizations are also proper nouns, and are therefore capitalized. Following are examples of common and proper nouns of similar meaning.

Common	**Proper**
house	The White House
computer	Hewlett Packard
soldier	Mark Smith
deer	Bambi

3.4.2 Concreteness

A noun's concreteness may be one of two types: concrete or abstract.

3.4.2.1 Concrete nouns

Concrete nouns are those that refer to things that exist physically and can be experienced with at least one of the five senses.

3.4.2.2 Abstract nouns

Abstract nouns refer to ideas or concepts, or anything that cannot be perceived through the five physical senses: *beauty*, *childhood* and *loneliness*, for example. Abstract nouns are perceived intellectually, not physically. Following are examples of concrete and abstract nouns of similar meaning.

Concrete	**Abstract**
house	shelter
computer	calculation
soldier	bravery
deer	gentleness

Quiz 2: Commonality and concreteness

Identify the types (common/proper; concrete/abstract) of the underlined nouns in the following sentences.

1. Hello! This is Philip, the estate agent.
2. The hairdryer I bought yesterday was faulty.
3. The law is on his side.
4. They are agents from the National Revenue Service.
5. Ainsley had a smile on her face.

*** *In the classroom: Commonality and concreteness* ***

Compared to abstract nouns, concrete nouns are easier to teach and easier for ESL beginner students to identify. The teacher can use realia (real objects), pictures, or drawings to show the meanings of concrete nouns. When teaching abstract nouns, the teacher has to make sure that the level of complexity is appropriate for students' level of English. Abstract, collective and some other types of nouns are more difficult for beginner students. Their meanings are not easily conveyed through showing objects or drawing pictures. Abstract nouns may need to be described through definitions, situational sentences, synonyms or antonyms. These techniques often result in confusion for beginner students. Mother tongue translation or the use of a bilingual dictionary may help in these cases.

3.4.3 Countability

A noun's countability may be one of two types: countable or uncountable.

3.4.3.1 Countable nouns

Countable nouns are nouns that can be differentiated into distinct individual occurrences. They have both singular and plural forms. *(See 3.4.4.1 Number)* These nouns may have articles and numbers placed in front of them in sentences.

Singular form (refers to one thing or person):

> a **table**
> another **boy**

Plural form (refers to more than one thing or person):

> two **tables**
> those **boys**

3.4.3.2 Uncountable nouns

If a noun cannot be differentiated into discrete individual units, it is uncountable. Uncountable nouns have only one form. They do not have a plural form. They refer to substances, concepts or abstract ideas which cannot be counted. They are also known as mass nouns and non-count nouns.

Some grammarians classify uncountable nouns in groups such as: food and beverages; materials; activities, subjects and languages; concepts; feelings; natural phenomena; and groups. This is done in order to facilitate the teaching of this kind of noun. There are no grammatical differences among these classifications.

Food and beverages:	milk, sugar, bread, water
Materials:	air, gas, plaster, brick
Activities, subjects and languages:	rollerblading, math, French
Concepts:	help, news, knowledge
Feelings:	happiness, guilt, love
Natural phenomena:	rain, weather, hail, lightning
Groups:	furniture, equipment, money

Following are examples of countable and uncountable nouns of similar meaning.

Countable	Uncountable
house	wallpaper
computer	software
soldier	humanity
deer	venison

Uncountable nouns cannot be used with the indefinite articles *a* and *an*, or with numbers. However, we can refer to quantity by using words and phrases like *some*, *a piece of* ... or *a bit of* .... These expressions are called partitives. *(See 6.3.1.2 Partitives)*

a piece of news	a loaf of bread
a carton of milk	a cup of coffee
a packet of sugar	a bit of land
a lot of homework	a work of art
an act of violence	a piece of advice
a grain of sand	a drop of water
a speck of dust	a strand of hair

Some uncountable nouns that are in the food and beverage category can be used in a countable way when referring to types of food or drink.

I enjoy **wine** with my meals in the summer. (uncountable)
Canada produces different **wines** in the Niagara region. (countable)

Sometimes uncountable nouns can be used as countable nouns, but with a change of meaning.

There is too much **noise** in the room. (uncountable)
I heard *a* **noise** downstairs. (countable)

It is not good to read with little **light**. (uncountable)
The **lights** in the room need changing. (countable)

There isn't much **room** in my car. (uncountable)
The house has *five* big **rooms.** (countable)

There are other nouns that follow a similar pattern, including *glass*, *iron*, *time*, *hair*, *work*, *paper*, *chicken*, *fish* and *lamb*.

Many uncountable nouns can be treated as countable when they are refined with descriptive adjectives, clauses or prepositional phrases which render them seemingly definite or unique. Whether to treat these nouns as countable or uncountable becomes a style choice.

The children felt **freedom** unlike anything in their experience. (uncountable)
The children felt *a* **freedom** unlike anything in their experience. (countable)

Quiz 3: Countability

Identify the type (countable or uncountable) of the highlighted nouns in the following sentences. Be sure to consider the context in determining countability.

1. Basic **understanding** of the **topic** is typical at his **age**.
2. What about **accommodation**? Do you know where to stay for the two **weeks**?
3. Are you willing to give him any **advice** on this **matter**?
4. That's too much **mayonnaise** for my **taste**.

*** In the classroom: Countability ***

Many seemingly uncountable nouns are used in everyday English in plural form. In these cases, the necessary partitive is implied or understood, but not explicitly stated. For example:

How many **sugars** do you want?	=	How many *spoonfuls of* **sugar** do you want?
I'd like two **waters**, please.	=	I'd like two *glasses of* **water**, please.

Students will encounter examples like these (especially pertaining to food and drink) quite often and will question the grammar rules and their own comprehension as a result.

There are other, less common, examples; these should be handled with care in the classroom. A great many seemingly uncountable nouns can be stated in the plural, omitting the implied partitive. These constructions are possible, but far less common. Save them for advanced learners.

Such **joys** should be treasured.	=	Such *feelings of* **joy** should be treasured.

Cases where the choice is a stylistic one should be reserved for advanced students. Until students have a strong grasp of countability, keep the delineation between countable and uncountable nouns clear for students.

Another confusing matter for ESL students is that many uncountable nouns in English are countable in their own languages. Therefore it is not unusual to hear ESL students saying, for example, ~~advices~~ instead of *advice*. Some other common examples are *bread*, *furniture*, *luggage*, *information*, *knowledge* and *travel*.

3.4.4 Inflection

Nouns in English have inflection; they may change their forms slightly according to how they are used in a sentence. There are three types of inflection possible for nouns: number, gender and case.

3.4.4.1 Number

Number is the most common type of inflection. It occurs when a noun is countable, and indicates whether a countable noun is singular or plural. Uncountable nouns do not have any inflection for number. The most common inflection for number is the addition of an –s at the end of the word to indicate plural number.

>cat (singular)
>cat**s** (plural)

The number (singular, plural or uncountable) of a noun has a direct effect on the form of the verb associated with it in a sentence. Singular and uncountable nouns require verbs to be in one form; plural nouns may require verbs in a different form. This matching of the forms of nouns and verbs is known as subject/verb agreement.

Not every noun which ends in –s is in the plural form. Some nouns which end in –s are uncountable nouns. They are followed by a verb in the singular form.

>The **news** *is* good.

Other examples of this case are: *physics*, *athletics*, *statistics*, *measles* and *mumps*.

The following nouns refer to single items that have two parts. They are considered plural nouns. They can be used with the phrase *a pair of* to make the reference singular.

>scissors   scales   glasses   pajamas
>shorts   pants   trousers   tights

>The **scissors** I bought *are* sharp. (*scissors*: plural)
>There *is* a pair of **scissors** on the table. (*pair*: singular)
>I gave away *two pairs of* **pants** last winter. (*two pairs*: plural)

*** *In the classroom: Number* ***

Plurals

To form the plural of most nouns in English, an –s is added to the end of the word. However, not all nouns in the plural form end in –s. This makes spelling of plural nouns difficult for ESL students. When teaching or reviewing nouns, make sure that students get enough practice in spelling all forms.

The addition of –s has some variation depending on the ending of the base noun.

Table 7: Spelling rules for nouns with regular plurals

Characteristics of base form noun	Rules for forming plural
ending in –*ch*, –*s*, –*sh*, –*ss* or –*x*: **watch, bus, wish, glass, box**	add –*es*: watch**es**, bus**es**, wish**es**, glass**es**, box**es**
(some nouns) ending in –*o*: **potato, hero**	add –*es*: *potato***es**, *hero***es**
ending in consonant + –*y*: **lady, party**	drop the –*y* and add –*ies*: lad**ies**, part**ies**
(most nouns) ending in –*f* or –*fe*: **loaf, knife**	drop the –*f* or –*fe* and add –*ves*: *loa***ves**, *kni***ves**
all other nouns: **snake, chair, piano, pen**	add –*s*: snake**s**, chair**s**, piano**s**, pen**s**

Some nouns have irregular plurals. Here are some of the most common of these.

man	⇒	men	foot	⇒	feet
woman	⇒	women	mouse	⇒	mice
child	⇒	children	sheep	⇒	sheep
person	⇒	people	deer	⇒	deer
tooth	⇒	teeth	fish	⇒	fish

Some nouns from Latin or Greek origin follow different rules in their plural forms.

Table 8: Spelling rules for certain nouns with Latin or Greek roots

Characteristics of base form noun	Rules for forming plural
ending in –*us*: **syllabus, nucleus**	change –*us* to –*i*: syllab**i**, nucle**i**
ending in –*is*: **crisis, thesis**	change –*is* to –*es*: cris**es**, thes**es**
ending in –*on*: **phenomenon, criterion**	change –*on* to –*a*: phenomen**a**, criteri**a**

Collective nouns

Collective nouns refer to a group of things, people or animals. Common examples are **class, committee, group, herd, company, audience, team, family** and **flock**.

Nouns that refer to a group of people or things can be treated as singular or plural. They are generally treated as singular because they are seen as a unit or in an impersonal way (can be replaced by *it*). However, collective nouns can also be treated as plural when thought of as a group of people or things, or in a more personal way (can be replaced by *they*).

My *family* **is** big. (*family* seen as a unit)
My *family* **are** coming to my wedding in June. (*family* seen as a collection of individuals: my mother and my father and my sister)

The conventions for the classification of collective nouns are among the most significant grammatical differences between British and American English. In general, collective nouns are treated as plural in British English and as singular in American English.

British	American
The *audience* **were** amazed.	The *audience* **was** amazed.
Microsoft **refuse** to reveal the secret.	*Microsoft* **refuses** to reveal the secret.
New Zealand **have** won the trophy.	*New Zealand* **has** won the trophy.

There are some exceptions in American English. *Police* is treated as plural. Team, group or company names that are in plural form are treated as plural.

> *Police* **say** they don't have a suspect.
> *The New York Yankees* **have** won the last six games.

The way to teach this usage will depend on the student base. Neither is "wrong" - the usage must be appropriate for the circumstance.

3.4.4.2 Gender

Gender is another type of inflection. A few nouns change form based on gender. The vast majority of nouns in English are neuter, which means that they make no reference to the gender (sex) of the noun. The other possible genders are masculine and feminine.

Masculine gender applies to some nouns which stand for explicitly male humans or animals, including *man*, *boy*, *father*, *brother* and *male*. Feminine gender applies to some nouns which stand for explicitly female humans or animals, including *woman*, *girl*, *mother*, *sister* and *female*. Some nouns naming professions have masculine and feminine forms (for example, *waiter/waitress*, *actor/actress* and *executor/executrix*). Neuter gender covers nouns which do not have distinctions of sex (almost all nouns) and often includes some which do have a natural sex distinction; animals are very often referred to in the neuter gender.

Gender is a little-used element of English grammar. It is rarely manifest in nouns, and never in adjectives or adverbs. Its main occurrence is in some pronouns. *(See 4.1 Pronoun forms)*

3.4.4.3 Case

Both nouns and pronouns may be inflected for case. There are three grammatical cases: subjective (also called nominative), objective (also called accusative) and possessive (also called genitive).

When a noun is the subject of a sentence, it is in subjective case. When a noun is a direct object, an indirect object or the object of a preposition, it is in objective case. Nouns do not have inflection for subjective and objective case; they look the same in either case. (Pronouns do have this inflection. *See 4.2.1 Personal pronouns*)

Mary	ate	all the **food**.
<noun in subjective case>	< verb >	<noun in objective case>
The **food**	satisfied	**Mary**.
<noun in subjective case>	< verb >	<noun in objective case>

A noun in possessive case demonstrates that the noun is the possessor (or associate or controller or owner) of another noun. Nouns *do* have inflection for possessive case. Possessive case for a noun is shown by some combination of an apostrophe and an –s at the end of the noun. A noun in possessive case is usually followed by another noun (which is the possession).

    Mary's   *food*   was delicious.
    <noun in possessive case>   < noun in subjective case >   <---predicate--->
    (noun is the possessor of the following noun)

Possessive case for singular and uncountable nouns is formed by adding an apostrophe and an –s, as in:

    Greta**'s** house
    James**'s** bicycle
    my boss**'s** laptop

Some style guides consider it unnecessary to add an –s to a noun that already has an –s at the end, and prefer just adding an apostrophe.

    James' bicycle

Plural nouns ending in –s form the possessive case by adding only an apostrophe:

    the girls' house (more than one girl)
    the Blacks' cabin (the Black family; more than one Black)

Irregular plural nouns add an apostrophe and an –s:

    the children**'s** toys
    the women**'s** changing room

When there are multiple named possessors, the placement of the apostrophe and –s signifies the ownership and the respective possessions. When the apostrophe is placed only after the last noun, the possessive implies that possession applies to the whole list as a unit, not just the last noun on the list.

    Martin and Carol**'s** house is on Yonge Street.

In this example, the house belongs to both Martin and Carol.

When the apostrophe and –s are placed after each of the elements of the phrase, the possessive implies that the nouns are acting separately. There is separate ownership of different instances of the following noun.

    Martin**'s** and Carol**'s** children go to Denby High School.

In this example, it is implied that Martin has children and, separately, Carol has children, and the different sets of children go to the same school.

The possessive case is commonly used with expressions related to time, money and holidays.

>two weeks' notice
>a month's salary
>New Year's Day
>Mother's Day

When the noun which shows possession is an inanimate noun, the preposition *of* is generally used to express possession. The noun may also be used as an attributive adjective. *(See 3.3 Noun placement)*

>the walls of the kitchen   OR   the kitchen walls
>NOT ~~the kitchen's walls~~

Quiz 4: Inflection

Identify any nouns which show inflection for number, gender or case. Identify any collective nouns.

>Come on and hear! Come on and hear! Alexander's ragtime band!
>Come on and hear! Come on and hear! It's the best band in the land!
>They can play a bugle call like you never heard before
>So natural that you want to go to war
>Source: Alexander's Ragtime Band by Irving Berlin, 1911
>
>I'm a Yankee doodle dandy,
>Yankee doodle do or die.
>A real live nephew of my Uncle Sam,
>Born on the 4th of July.
>I've got a Yankee doodle sweetheart,
>She's my Yankee doodle joy.
>Yankee doodle came to London,
>Just to ride the ponies.
>I am a Yankee doodle boy.
>Source: The Yankee Doodle Boy by George M. Cohan, 1904

**** You can teach nouns ****

Classroom focus on nouns is usually necessary at beginner and low intermediate levels; it becomes less of a focus as students progress. It is best to present or review nouns in thematic units. This will help students remember their meanings and use better. For example: foods that you like or dislike; objects in an office/in the classroom; articles of clothing for winter/summer.

The following functions and structures are appropriate for beginner levels and can be used to develop all the major language skills (listening, speaking, reading, writing). The teacher can create situations or dialogues where these structures and nouns can be heard or read and therefore integrate the theme and grammatical topic to reading, listening and speaking skills.

GRAMMAR:	Countable and uncountable nouns
FUNCTION:	Discussing likes and dislikes
STRUCTURE:	I like.. / I don't like.. I love.. / I hate..
Description:	Present students with the appropriate structure and topics for discussion of likes and dislikes. Ensure that the possible topics include a targeted mixture of countable and uncountable nouns. Possible topics include food (apples, ice cream) or leisure activities (tennis, shopping)

GRAMMAR:	Using much / many with countable and uncountable nouns
FUNCTION:	Asking and talking about quantity
STRUCTURE:	How much + uncountable noun …? How many + countable nouns..?
Description:	Set up a situation in which students ask and answer questions about quantity. Common topics include making a grocery list or describing ingredients needed for a recipe.

GRAMMAR:	Subject/verb agreement with singular and plural nouns; non-referential *there*; indefinite articles *a* and *an*; prepositions of place
FUNCTION:	Talking about where things are in a room / describing a room
STRUCTURE:	There is (a/an) + noun in the living room / There are + plural noun + in the kitchen/on the shelves
Description:	Provide students with a pictures of a room and get them to describe the placement of articles in the room; or ask them to describe a room that they know or the room they are in.

GRAMMAR:	Possessive nouns; subject/verb agreement with the verb *have*
FUNCTION:	Talking about possessions
STRUCTURE:	subject + have / has (or don't / doesn't have) – 's + noun
Description:	Provide students with pictures or videos showing people with possession or ownership. Get students to ask and answer questions about ownership. Possible topics include simple objects, pets, vehicles, living quarters.

GRAMMAR:	Singular nouns ending in –*s*; definite and indefinite articles; subject/verb agreement with the verb *have*
FUNCTION:	Talking about health problems
STRUCTURE:	I have a headache / She has the measles
Description:	Get students to role play a visit to a doctor's office or a pharmacy.

More ideas to practice nouns

Word building: Students complete a list of nouns that corresponds to the verbs in a chart. (The following is just an example. The same can be done with any family of words.) The vocabulary and the complexity of the transformation may be adjusted to make this exercise suitable for different levels.

Verb	Noun
to burgle	
to rob	
to smuggle	
to mug	

Gap filling activities: Choose a paragraph and delete all nouns. Students must provide the missing words. Depending on the level, hints may be given: a drawing of the noun, a synonym, an antonym or a definition. See an example below:

Pat loves _____ . It is something that she does every weekend.

Her favourite _____ are _____ .

Answers: gardening – flowers – roses
Source of images: Microsoft Word Clip Art. Used with permission of Microsoft.

Collocations: Some nouns and noun phrases are always attached to specific verbs. Give students a list of verbs and a list of nouns to match with them. See an example below:

Verbs	Noun phrases
to do	the bed every morning
	a favour for a friend
to make	sure that you arrive on time
	business
	friends with different people

Collocations need review beyond the beginner level. Verb and phrase choices may be adjusted to fit various levels.

Identifying nouns in the classroom: This can be done in pairs or groups. Students write the names of the objects in the classroom on colourful cards and stick them to the objects. The same can be done on pictures of objects.

Noun brainstorming: Restricting the choices to nouns that begin with a certain letter of the alphabet, students write down as many nouns as they can think of. The list of nouns can be more directed toward a specific topic, such as: places to go on vacation; places that are very hot / cold; family members; weird / interesting / boring / dangerous jobs. Give a short time limit (one or two minutes) for creating the list.

Crossword puzzles: Giving students crossword puzzles with definitions appropriate to their level (even pictures) can be a helpful and fun way to review nouns. Because of the nature of crossword puzzles, it also helps students to focus on spelling. Crossword puzzles created by the teacher based on what the students have learned are more effective than those found in magazines and newspapers, not only because the latter are usually more difficult, but also because a teacher can focus on the words known to pose problems or difficulties for the students. There are many free software programs that allow self-generation of crossword puzzles.

Games such as anagrams, hangman, Junior Scrabble®, and Boggle® can also help students review nouns they have learned and focus on their spellings and meanings.

4 Pronouns

Pronouns replace nouns, noun phrases or other pronouns. The following words are examples of pronouns:

I	**themselves**
something	**which**
him	**this**
whose	**one**

Pronouns are mainly used with anaphoric reference; they refer back to previously-mentioned nouns or noun phrases so as to avoid repetition. These previously-mentioned nouns are known as antecedents.

The repetition of nouns in the second and third clauses below makes the sentence awkward:

> <u>Matthew</u> wants to visit <u>the nice girl</u> that <u>Matthew</u> met at the party last night, but <u>Matthew</u> does not know where <u>the nice girl</u> lives.

A more fluent way to express the ideas in the example above is to replace the nouns and noun phrases in those clauses with their corresponding pronouns.

> <u>Matthew</u> wants to visit <u>the nice girl</u> that **he** met at the party last night, but **he** does not know where **she** lives.

4.1 Pronoun forms

Pronouns can change form (have inflection) based on certain characteristics: person, number and gender. The position of the speaker relative to others is clarified by the grammatical "person" that is used in the sentence. The grammatical persons are: first person (the speaker or writer); second person (the listener or reader); and third person (other than the speaker or writer). Some pronouns can distinguish between one (singular) and more than one (plural). This is known as grammatical number. Some pronouns have inflection for feminine gender, masculine gender and neuter gender.

Pronouns can perform different functions in a sentence. Their forms may change based on function. This differentiation of function is known as grammatical case. When a pronoun is acting as the subject of a sentence or finite clause (or as a subject complement), it is in its subjective case. When a pronoun is acting as an object of a verb or the object of a preposition, it is in its objective case. When a pronoun is substituting for a possession (whether subject or object), it is in its possessive case.

The following table gives a few basic examples of change of form for pronouns based on these factors.

Table 9: Example pronoun forms by number, gender and case

Person	Number	Gender	Case	Pronoun
first person	singular	n/a	subjective	I
first person	plural	n/a	possessive	**ours**
third person	singular	masculine	objective	**him**

4.2 Pronoun types

Pronouns are classified by type, reflecting their different functions in a sentence. There is not total agreement among grammarians about these classifications; the following list gives the types of pronouns recognized in the majority of grammar texts.

- personal
    - subjective
    - objective
    - possessive
    - reflexive
- reciprocal
- indefinite
- relative
- interrogative
- demonstrative

4.2.1 Personal pronouns

The personal pronouns have distinct forms for grammatical person, number, gender and case. Personal pronouns also have a reflexive form. *(See 4.2.1.4 Reflexive pronouns)*

4.2.1.1 Subjective pronouns

Subjective pronouns function mainly as subjects of sentences or subjects of finite clauses. They are also known as nominative pronouns.

```
We                      wonder    whether        she knows about it.
<subject of the sentence>  <-verb->  <conjunction>  <subject of finite clause>
                        <--------------------- predicate --------------------->
```

The table below lists the subjective personal pronouns. The third person singular form has inflection for gender: **he** (masculine), **she** (feminine) and **it** (neuter). All other forms are strictly neuter.

Table 10: Subjective personal pronouns by person and number

	Singular	Plural
first person	I	we
second person	you	you
third person	he / she / it	they

Subjective personal pronouns can also be found as subject complement in very formal English. Subject complements are in subjective case, and so are generally considered to be correct when in subjective form. This usage has changed significantly, and it is now the norm to use the objective form as subject complement after the linking verb *be. (See 4.2.1.2 Objective pronouns)*

> Who is it? It is **I**. (Although correct, this form is not often used)
> Who is it? It's **me**. (More common usage, accepted in all but the most formal contexts)

4.2.1.2 Objective pronouns

An objective pronoun can function as the object of the main verb or the object of a preposition. Objective pronouns are sometimes used as subject complement. They are also known as accusative pronouns. The personal pronouns in their objective form are shown in the table below, next to their subjective counterparts.

Table 11: Subjective and objective personal pronouns

Person and number	Subjective	Objective
first person singular	I	me
second person singular	you	you
third person singular	he / she / it	him / her / it
first person plural	we	us
second person plural	you	you
third person plural	they	them

Personal pronouns in their objective forms can be found in the following positions:

Direct object of the main verb

> Suzanne   rejected   **them**.
> < subject >   < verb >   <direct object of main verb rejected>

Indirect object of the main verb (Objective pronouns used as indirect objects are also said to be in dative case.)

> Can you   tell   **me**   the way to go?
> < auxiliary + subject >   < verb>   <indirect object of tell>   <--direct object-->

Object of a preposition

> I   am looking forward   to **it**.
> <subject>   <--- verb + adverbial---->   <object of the preposition to>

> They   would consider anybody   except **him**.
> <subject>   <--- verb + object of verb --->   <object of the preposition except>

Quiz 1: Subjective and objective pronouns

Fill in the blanks with the correct personal pronouns and identify the antecedent. Identify whether each pronoun is subjective or objective.

1. Did you talk to the Joneses? Would you like to invite _____ to the meeting?
2. The cartons of milk are on the counter, ready for you to put _____ away in the fridge.
3. Maria said _____ would never be able to accept that Paul did not love _____.
4. Caroline is here with the little puppy. Please tell _____ to wash _____ with this shampoo for pets.
5. Harry has been away for 5 months. I am so looking forward to seeing _____ after such a long time.
6. "Farah, I've chosen to watch this movie. Would _____ like to watch _____ with _____?"
7. _____, (your name here), agree to the terms on this contract.

*** In the classroom: Personal pronouns ***

Problems related to personal pronoun use often come up in the classroom: confusion over whether to use the subjective or objective form; the many ways of using the personal pronoun **it**; and confusion that results from different structures for pronoun use in students' natives languages. The following sections address some of these problems.

Omission of a personal subjective pronoun

English requires an explicitly stated subject. This is not true in every language. In the romance languages (Spanish, Portuguese and Italian, for example), the subject may be implied or inferred. A common mistake made by learners who are speakers of these languages is that they omit the subjective pronoun.

> Teacher: "What does Peter do?"
> Student: "~~Is an accountant~~." (instead of "**He** is an accountant.")

Double subject

Another common mistake related to the structure of students' mother tongue is repetition of the subject. A personal subjective pronoun is unnecessarily inserted after a noun phrase functioning as subject.

> *Joan* ~~she~~ is a nurse.
> *The doctor* ~~he~~ warned me about the medication's side effects.

Subjective or objective?

Objective pronouns cannot be placed in the subject of a sentence. Subjective pronouns cannot be placed in the predicate of a sentence. These errors are also somewhat common among native English speakers, so students may hear them often and be confused.

> ~~**Me** and my friends ate at that restaurant on Saturday.~~
> My friends and **I** ate at that restaurant on Saturday.

~~It was good enough for I and Bobby McGee.~~
It was good enough for **me** and Bobby McGee.

Grammatical number agreement

Knowledge of the appropriate grammatical number is necessary when choosing the correct pronouns to substitute for nouns. Collective nouns and plural nouns in particular can have grammatical number reference which is not only confusing to ESL students, but also to native speakers of English.

Collective nouns

Nouns such as *family, committee* and *audience* may have a singular or plural reference depending on how the speaker or writer sees the collective noun: as a single unit, or as many individuals belonging to a group. *(See 3.4.4.1 Number)* Singular pronouns are almost exclusively used for collective nouns in American English. *Police* is an exception.

The committee didn't understand what awaited **it**.
(Treats *the committee* as one entity)

The committee didn't understand what awaited **them**.
(Treats *the committee* as many individual, countable members)

Plural nouns

Several items which are composed of two easily identifiable parts have plural names in English. Examples include *shorts*, *scissors* and *glasses*. The pronouns for these items must be plural.

Have you seen *the scissors*? I can't find **them**.

Plural nouns treated as singular

Some academic subjects (mathematics, physics), games (athletics, darts) and illnesses (measles, mumps, shingles) appear to be plural because they end in –s. But they are singular, and take singular verbs and are replaced by the singular pronoun **it**.

Darts is not a difficult game. I learned to play **it** yesterday.

Personal alternatives to **it**

English does not have a gender-neutral, third-person, singular *personal* pronoun (in the sense of replacing a named *person*). **It** works for non-personal reference, but for personal reference, alternatives are necessary. The propriety of using the pronouns **he** and **him** to refer to an antecedent with personal reference but whose gender is unspecified has been an argument that native speakers of English have had for decades.

In *Any athlete knows that* **he** *must eat nutritious food*, the choice of the personal subjective pronoun **he** to refer to the antecedent *any athlete* does not necessarily mean that the unspecified athlete is male. The masculine pronoun **he** has long been a stand-in for a neuter third-person singular personal pronoun. This use of the impersonal pronoun **he** is considered sexist by many, but proper for some others in writing and formal English.

There have been different attempts to compensate for the absence of a gender-neutral pronoun, including:
- using **he or she**, **s/he**, or **he/she** in writing (*Any athlete knows that he or she must eat nutritious food.*)
- using the gender-neutral plural pronouns **they** or **them** as singular pronouns (*Any athlete knows that they must eat nutritious food.*)
- using passive voice sentences which eliminate the subject (*Nutritious food must be eaten.*)
- using nouns in the plural as antecedents replaced by plural pronouns (*Athletes know that they must eat nutritious food.*)
- using the impersonal **you** or **one** when applicable (*As an athlete, you must eat nutritious food.*)

4.2.1.3 Possessive pronouns

Possessive pronouns are used in place of nouns in possessive form. They indicate the ownership or control of something. They are also known as genitive pronouns. The possessive forms of the personal pronouns are shown in the table below.

Table 12: Subjective and possessive personal pronouns

Person	Subjective	Possessive
first person singular	I	mine
second person singular	you	yours
third person singular	he / she / it	his / hers
first person plural	we	ours
second person plural	you	yours
third person plural	they	theirs

Possessive pronouns can function as:

Subject of a clause or sentence

>Her husband works in a bank. **Mine** is unemployed.
>(**Mine**, standing in for *my husband*, is the subject of the second sentence.)

Direct object of the main verb

>I want you to read these two essays. One was written by Peter and the other one by Carol. Read **hers** first.
>(**hers** stands in for *Carol's essay* and is the direct object of the main verb *read*.)

Indirect object of the main verb

>Among all the projects, I gave **mine** high priority.
>(**mine** stands in for *my project* and is the indirect object of the main verb *gave*; the direct object is the noun phrase *high priority*)

<u>Object of a preposition</u>

> Do not talk to Joan's mother; talk to **mine**!
> (**mine** stands in for *my mother* and is the object of the preposition *to*.)

<u>Subject complement</u>

> Whose pen is that? It's **hers**.
> (**hers** stands in for the noun phrase *her pen* and is the complement of the subject *it*.)

Quiz 2: Personal pronouns and their forms

Complete the following table with the correct forms of personal pronouns.

Person/Number/Gender	Subjective (Nominative)	Objective (Accusative)	Possessive (Genitive)
first person singular neuter			
second personal singular neuter			
third personal singular masculine			
third personal singular feminine			
third personal singular neuter			
first person plural neuter			
second person plural neuter			
third person plural neuter			

**** In the classroom: Possessive pronouns ****

Two areas of frequent confusion regarding the use of possessive pronouns are: using an objective pronoun when a possessive pronoun is correct; and confusion of possessive pronouns with their similar adjective counterparts, possessive determiners.

When it is indicating possession, a noun phrase with the structure *(a/an/some) + noun + of* is followed by a possessive pronoun or a noun in the possessive case. Objective pronouns are often erroneously used in these structures.

> ~~A friend of him called to say that Martin will be late.~~
> A friend of **his** called to say that Martin will be late.
> A friend of **Martin's** called to say that he will be late.

Possessive pronouns are often confused with the possessive determiners *my, your, his, her, its, our, your, their. (See 6.2.1 Definiteness)*

Pronoun	**Determiner**
This is **mine**.	This is **my** book.
Where is **yours**?	Where is **your** tape?

4.2.1.4 Reflexive pronouns

Reflexive pronouns are personal pronouns characterized by the ending *-self* (singular) or *-selves* (plural). They are mainly used when the object of the main verb or object of a preposition has the same reference – is, in fact, the same – as the subject of the clause or sentence.

Freddie will let **himself** in. (Freddie will let Freddie in.)

Each reflexive pronoun has a subjective pronoun counterpart; thus, there are reflexive pronouns for each of the three different persons in singular and plural form, and some of them carry inflection for gender.

The reflexive forms of the personal pronouns are shown in the table below.

Table 13: Subjective and reflexive personal pronouns

Person	Subjective	Reflexive
first person singular	I	myself
second person singular	you	yourself
third person singular	he / she / it	himself / herself / itself
first person plural	we	ourselves
second person plural	you	yourselves
third person plural	they	themselves

Reflexive pronouns can only function in object position: as direct or indirect object of a verb, or as object of a preposition.

> Giuseppe taught **himself** how to make puppets. (direct object of *taught*)
> (You) Buy **yourself** a new coat. (indirect object of *buy*)
> Dan is always talking about **himself**. (object of preposition *about*)

Reflexive pronouns are typically used with reflexive verbs such as *blame, cut, help, hurt, introduce, kill, prepare* and *teach*.

*** In the classroom: Reflexive pronouns ***

Reflexive pronouns always refer to the subject of the sentence. Personal objective pronouns may or may not refer to the sentence's subject. Students may be confused about whether to use a reflexive or an objective pronoun in the object position in a sentence. There is a difference in meaning between the use of the objective pronoun and reflexive pronoun in the following sentences.

> Peter   saw   **him**   in the mirror.
> <subject>   <verb>   <direct object>   <remainder of the predicate>
>   *(objective pronoun; not Peter, but another person – he saw somebody else)*

> Peter   saw   **himself**   in the mirror.
> <subject>   <verb>   <direct object>   <remainder of the predicate>
>   *(reflexive pronoun; this is the subject, Peter – he saw his own reflection)*

Students may see reflexive pronouns in different contexts and question their correct usage. Aside from their main use in the object position, reflexive pronouns may also be used in apposition (as a grammatical parallel), as a way of intensifying a subject.

> The city **itself** was so dirty that we left soon.

This intensifying use of reflexive pronouns can also emphasize that someone does something alone, without any help. These reflexive pronouns are placed at the end of the sentence. The preposition *by* can be inserted in these cases without a change in meaning.

> Lainie is only two years old and she can tie her shoes **herself.**
> Lainie is only two years old and she can tie her shoes *by* **herself**.

Incorrect use of reflexive pronouns as objects is common in cases where the speaker is attempting to sound polite or deferential. It is particularly common in questions.

> ~~How about yourself?~~   How about you?

4.2.2 Reciprocal pronouns

Reciprocal pronouns show that the action expressed by the main verb in the sentence is reciprocated by the subjects. The subject cannot be singular; reciprocity requires a plural subject. The reciprocal pronouns are the phrases **each other** and **one another**. Because these pronouns are phrases, they are also known as pronominal phrases.

> Scott and Amber talked to **each other** for the first time after their divorce. (Scott talked to Amber and Amber talked to Scott.)

Each other is generally used to refer to two or more people. **One another** is generally used to refer to more than two people. However, **each other** and **one another** are synonymous and can be used interchangeably. **One another** may seem more formal, and is less common in spoken English.

*** In the classroom: Reciprocal pronouns ***

When a sentence has a plural subject (for example, *John and the kids* or *We*), it is not always clear whether to choose the plural reflexive pronouns (*yourselves, ourselves, themselves*) or one of the reciprocal pronominal phrases *each other* and *one another*. The distinction is the direction of the action. If any do-er of the action receives the action from himself, then the reflexive pronoun is needed. If the do-ers of the action only perform the action on the other members of the plural subject, then a reciprocal pronominal phrase is needed. There is a difference in meaning between the use of the reflexive pronoun *themselves* and the reciprocal pronoun *each other* in the following sentences.

> John and the kids gave **themselves** a fright.
> (The subject *John and the kids* scared all members of the group. John scared John and John scared the kids; the kids scared John and the kids scared the kids.)

> We are looking at **each other**.
> (In this case, the members of the plural subject *We* are facing each other and looking in everybody's eyes except their own).

4.2.3 Indefinite pronouns

Indefinite pronouns refer to people, places or things without identifying them or referring to any specific antecedent. Some indefinite pronouns replace singular nouns, some replace plural or uncountable nouns. They may also indicate absence of something (negation). Indefinite pronouns are always gender-neutral. They may have personal reference (referring to people) or non-personal reference (referring to things). They may also convey possession.

The following is a list of indefinite pronouns:

anybody	**anyone**	**anything**
everybody	**everyone**	**everything**
nobody	**no one**	**nothing**
somebody	**someone**	**something**

The following words usually function as determiners *(See 6 Determiners)*, but may sometimes function as indefinite pronouns:

all	**both**	**neither**	**several**
another	**each**	**none**	**some**
any	**either**	**one**	

few (a few / fewer / fewest)	**many (more / most)**
little (a little / less / least)	**much (more / most)**

The pronouns **you** and **they** can also express indefiniteness. *(See 4.2.3.1 General indefinite pronouns)*

4.2.3.1 General indefinite pronouns

Pronouns usually substitute for a noun (or a noun phrase) which has already been mentioned (anaphoric reference), or that will be mentioned later in the sentence (cataphoric reference). However, some indefinite pronouns refer to people or things which are not mentioned or referenced anywhere else in the sentence. The following indefinite pronouns belong to this category:

anybody	**everything**	**some**
anything	**one**	**somebody**
all	**nobody**	**something**
everybody	**nothing**	

> **Everything** is fine; don't worry.
> **Someone** is at the door.
> **One** never knows when trouble may come.

You and **they** are sometimes used in this way as well. This is not the primary use of these pronouns, but they can be used to substitute for undefined, unknown or unnamed subjects or objects.

> **They** say it is the worst crisis ever.
> **You** can't judge a book by its cover.

4.2.3.2 Negative indefinite pronouns

Negative indefinite pronouns have negative reference and indicate an absence or a quantity of zero. The pronouns that belong to this category are:

neither	**nobody**	**nothing**
no one	**none**	

Nothing, nobody and **no one** are used in negative sentences instead of *not ...any* with the verb in its affirmative form. When the verb is negative, the *any–* family of pronouns is used. *(See 4.2.3.5 Affirmative, interrogative or negative uses of indefinite pronouns)*

> I *can* see **nothing**.
> I ~~can't see nothing~~
> I *can't* see **anything.**

Using a negative indefinite pronoun together with a negative verb is called a double negative construction. *(See In the classroom: Double negative after section 4.2.6)*

None refers to more than two people or things. **Neither** refers to two people or things.

> **Neither** accepted the resolution.
> (There are two people involved; zero people out of the two accepted the resolution.)

4.2.3.3 Quantifier indefinite pronouns

Indefinite pronouns can express quantity. They can refer to countable or uncountable quantity. The pronouns in this category are also called quantifiers.

all	**either**	**much**	**other**
another	**enough**	**neither**	**others**
any	**few**	**none**	**several**
both	**little**	**one**	**some**
each	**many**		

> **Many** are called, but **few** are chosen.
> These are delicious; may I have **another**?
> **Some** say it's true, but **others** disagree.

4.2.3.4 Number in indefinite pronouns

Some indefinite pronouns take singular verbs, some take plural verbs, and some can take either, depending on context. The question of number in relation to indefinite pronouns is particularly troublesome, as an indefinite pronoun that is replacing a plural noun may be treated as a singular pronoun and take a singular verb form.

All the indefinite pronouns in the *–body –one –thing* series take a singular verb, even when they are replacing a plural noun or noun phrase.

> **Everyone** *is* tired.
> *Does* **anyone** like the idea?

Other indefinite pronouns that only take a singular verb form are:

another	either	neither	one
each	little (a little / less / least)		

Neither *likes* to be patronized.
Less *is* known about the oceans than about space.

Neither and **either** refer to zero or one out of a total of two people or things, and therefore are singular references. **Each** is also a singular reference to members of a group of two or more.

Indefinite pronouns that only take a plural verb form are:

both	many (more / most)	several
few (a few / fewer / fewest)		others

Few *are* as energetic as she.

A few indefinite pronouns may take either singular or plural verb forms, depending on context.

all	enough	some
any	none	

All *is* well.
(**All** in this context is the same as 'everything' and is treated as singular.)

All *are* present and accounted for.
(Within a known group, 100% of the unnamed, unidentified members are accounted for and **all** effectively replaces *all members* and is treated as plural.)

4.2.3.5 Affirmative, interrogative or negative uses of indefinite pronouns

The indefinite pronouns ending in *–body*, *–thing*, and *–one* have different uses depending on whether the sentences are affirmative, interrogative or negative.

Somebody, **something** and **someone** are normally used in affirmative sentences.

He's got **something** in mind.
Somebody is at the door.

They can be used in interrogative sentences when the speaker is expecting a positive answer, or when the speaker is making an offer.

Would you like **something** to eat?
(The speaker is making an offer.)

Is there **somebody** at the door?
(The speaker is fairly sure that the answer is yes.)

Anything, **anybody** and **anyone** are mainly used in interrogative and negative sentences.

Is there **anything** that we can do for you?
There isn't **anybody** at home.

When these pronouns are used with a negative reference, the verb in the sentence must take negative form.

The baby *won't eat* **anything** chewy.

Anything, **anybody** and **anyone** can also express negation when used with negative words such as *without, never, seldom, and rarely*.

I *rarely* meet **anybody** on my way to work.

Anything, **anybody** and **anyone** can also be used in affirmative sentences, but with a somewhat different meaning from the **something, somebody** and **someone** described above. The *any–* series suggest that there is an indifference. The *some–* series suggests that it is not known.

Please give this to **anyone**. (It doesn't matter who – just get rid of it.)
Please give this to **someone**. (The giver has some choice in the matter, but it is not known whom the giver will choose.)

4.2.3.6 Summary of indefinite pronouns

Table 14: Indefinite pronouns

	Requiring a singular verb	Requiring a plural verb	Giving a personal reference	Giving a non-personal reference	Possessive form (if applicable)	Reflexive form (if applicable)
General indefinite pronouns	somebody someone something anybody anyone anything everybody everyone everything		anybody anyone everybody everyone somebody someone	anything everything something	anybody's anyone's everybody's everyone's somebody's someone's	
Negative indefinite pronouns	none no one nobody nothing neither	none	neither no one nobody none	neither none nothing	nobody's no-one's	
Quantifier indefinite pronouns	all another any each either enough little (a little / less / least) much (more / most) one other some	all any both enough few (a few / fewer / fewest) many (more / most) others several some	all another any each either enough few (a few / fewer / fewest) many (more / most) one other others some	all another any each either enough few (a few / fewer / fewest) little (a little / less / least) many (more / most) much (more / most) one other others some	one's other's others'	oneself

4.2.4 Relative pronouns

Relative pronouns join main clauses with subordinate adjectival clauses (also called relative clauses). These pronouns always refer to and describe a noun in the main clause. (For more on relative clauses, see the *You Can Teach Grammar* companion web site.)

The four relative pronouns are **that**, **who**, **whom** and **which**.

Relative pronouns take subjective case when they function as the subject of the relative clause, and objective case when they function as the object of the verb in a relative clause or an object of a preposition.

I saw *the man* **who** sold us the boat.
(**who** (relative pronoun in subjective case) is the subject of the relative clause *who sold us the boat* and refers to the noun phrase *the man* in the main clause *I saw the man*)

The lady **whom** we met at the party is the CEO of MegaStore.
(**whom** (relative pronoun in objective case) is the direct object of the verb *met* in the relative clause *whom we met at the party*, and refers to the noun phrase *the lady* in the main clause *the lady is the CEO of MegaStore*)

When a relative pronoun is the object of a verb in the relative clause, the relative pronoun can be omitted.

The *lady* we met at the party is the CEO of MegaStore.

The relative pronouns **that**, **who** and **whom** can be used to refer to people (personal reference), while **that** and **which** are used to refer to things (non-personal reference).

4.2.5 Interrogative pronouns

Interrogative pronouns are part of the wh-words family. They are used in questions to substitute for the noun or pronoun being asked about. The following wh-words can function as interrogative pronouns.

what **which** **who** **whom** **whose**

Like some other pronouns, interrogative pronouns can indicate grammatical case (subjective, objective and possessive), and they can have personal and non-personal reference.

Table 15: **Personal and non-personal reference of interrogative pronouns**

Personal reference	Non- personal reference
who	what
whom	which*
whose	
which*	

*****which** can have personal or non-personal reference depending on definiteness.

The placement of the subject and object in interrogative sentences is different than the placement in declarative sentences. *(See 2.5.2 Interrogative sentences)* To determine an interrogative pronoun's function, it can help to re-phrase the sentence in its declarative form. Each of the examples below is paired with its declarative equivalent, in order to illustrate the interrogative pronouns' functions. Interrogative pronouns can function as:

Subject of the question (subjective case)

Who	is helping	Mom	in the kitchen?
<subject >	*<verb >*	*<direct object>*	*<adverbial>*

The twins	are helping	Mom	in the kitchen.
<subject >	*<verb >*	*<direct object>*	*<adverbial>*

Direct object (objective case)

Whom	did	the director	choose	for the play?
<direct object>	<auxiliary>	<subject>	<verb>	<adverbial>

The director		chose	*Joanna*	for the play.
<subject>		<verb>	<direct object>	<adverbial>

Object of a preposition (objective case)

What	are	they	looking	at?
<object of prepositon>	<auxiliary>	<subject>	<verb>	<preposition>

They		are looking	at	*the sea*.
<subject>		<verb>	<preposition>	<object of preposition>

Subject complement (subjective case)

What	is	her name?
<subject complement>	<stative verb>	<subject>

Her name	is	Maria.
<subject>	<stative verb>	<subject complement>

Which	is	your coat?
<subject complement>	<stative verb>	<subject>

Mine (my coat)	is	the blue one.
<subject>	<stative verb>	<subject complement>

Whose is the only interrogative pronoun that carries possessive case. It is used to ask about possession.

Whose	is	that house?
<possessive pronoun> (subject complement)	<stative verb>	<subject>

That house	is	*the Brauns'*.
<subject>	<stative verb>	<possessive noun> (subject complement)

The direction of the action is important in the structure of interrogatives. When an interrogative pronoun functions as direct object of the main verb (its declarative equivalent is *receiving* the action of the main verb), the interrogative pronoun is followed by an auxiliary or modal verb, followed by the subject (the do-er of the action of the main verb) and, finally, the verb.

interrogative pronoun + auxiliary/modal + subject + main verb + ?

Whom	*did*	he	call?
<direct object>	<auxiliary>	<subject>	<main verb>

He		called	Peter.
<subject>		<main verb>	<direct object>

What	*does*	John	need?
<direct object>	<auxiliary>	<subject>	<main verb>

John	needs	more information.
<subject>	<main verb>	<direct object>

When an interrogative pronoun functions as the subject of the main verb (its declarative equivalent is the do-er of the action of the main verb), the pronoun does not need an auxiliary.

Who	called	Peter?
<subject>	<main verb>	<direct object>

John	called	Peter.
<subject>	<main verb>	<direct object>

What	caused	the accident?
<subject>	<main verb>	<direct object>

Bad weather	caused	the accident.
<subject>	<main verb>	<direct object>

4.2.6 Demonstrative pronouns

Demonstrative pronouns point out people, places or things. They replace nouns that are understood from the context. The four demonstrative pronouns are **this**, **that**, **these** and **those**.

Demonstrative pronouns indicate grammatical number and have a reference to proximity. A sense of physical distance or distance in time can be conveyed by choosing **this**, **that**, **these** or **those**.

> **This** is not the book I was looking for.
> (The book is close by: sense of physical distance.)
>
> **That** was a great time.
> (Referring to a time in the past: sense of distance in time.)

Demonstrative pronouns must agree in number with the nouns they replace and have concord with the verb in the sentence when functioning as subjects.

I do not like black *socks*, but **these** are nice.
(**these** replaces the plural noun *socks* and agrees in number with *are*, the form of the verb *be* used for plural subjects)

	Proximity: Near	Proximity: Far
Number: Singular	**this**	**that**
Number: Plural	**these**	**those**

Quiz 3: Pronoun identification

Identify type (personal, indefinite, etc.), case (subjective, objective, possessive) and function (subject of sentence, direct object, etc.) of the underlined pronouns below.

1. Something is burning. Can you go check in the kitchen?
2. Show me those over there, please.
3. They wrote the letter, which described their situation.
4. This is the girl that I saw at the beach.
5. Praising oneself is not always recommended during a job interview.
6. Manuel and Parisa talk to each other every day.
7. What do you want to do during your holiday?
8. A friend of his lent us a tent for the camping trip.

*** In the classroom: Common pronoun mistakes ***

Problems with pronouns are very common among ESL students and even native speakers of the English language. The proper use and placement of pronouns is a common point of frustration for students, especially when they are trying to equate structures to the ones they know from their native languages. The following are typical pronoun problems for ESL students.

Cataphoric and anaphoric reference

A common point of confusion, more obviously noticed in writing, is that a pronoun is placed very far from the noun it refers to. This loss of clarity is particularly pronounced when the pronoun's reference is cataphoric (replacing a noun that is given *after* the pronoun).

> While looking at **him**, and almost reeling from the weight of all these extraordinary and profound emotions, Marian lifted *the baby* from the cot. (The pronoun **him** refers to *the baby* in the last clause of this compound-complex sentence.)

A clearer way of saying this is:

> While looking at *her baby*, and almost reeling from the weight of all these extraordinary and profound emotions, Marian lifted **him** from the cot.

Omission of antecedent

This can be a confusing point for students, particularly because there are cases (non-referential *it*, for example) when English does not need an antecedent.

I visited a farm and I liked **them** because **they** do not use harmful pesticides. (The antecedent of the pronouns **them** or **they** are not mentioned. Therefore, it is not clear who **they** are.)

A clearer way of saying this is:

I visited a farm and I liked *the owners* (antecedent) because **they** do not use harmful pesticides.

Ambiguity of antecedent

With multiple possibilities of antecedent, it is easy for pronoun use to be ambiguous.

Juan told Luc that **he** was not invited to the party.
(It is unclear if the intended antecedent of the pronoun **he** is Juan or Luc. Is it Juan or is it Luc who was not invited to the party?)

A clearer way of conveying this could be:

Luc was not invited to the party, and Juan told him so.
    or,
Juan told Luc that Luc was not invited to the party.
    or, in a written context,
Juan told Luc that he (Luc) was not invited to the party.

Double negative

It is incorrect to use a negative pronoun in combination with any other negative word in a sentence. The following are typical mistakes of double negatives:

~~I do not like nobody.~~
~~He doesn't have no money.~~

The correct versions would be:
I *do not* like *any*body. –OR – I like *no*body.
He *doesn't* have *any* money. –OR – He has *no* money.

Quiz 4: Correct the errors

Identify the mistakes in the following sentences and explain why they are incorrect.

1. Every morning Nicholas shaved him before he went to work.
2. He doesn't know nothing.
3. A friend of me is coming later.
4. That boy which you can see over there is Marietta's son.
5. The two apple cakes we cooked were not good. None had enough apples.

**** You can teach pronouns ****

The following are ideas to help ESL students learn and practise using the different types of pronouns. Each of the suggested activities below addresses a specific subset of pronoun use, and includes, when possible, the communicative function of the use of pronouns. As pronouns are hard to define in context, it is not as simple to create communicative activities specifically developed for pronouns as it is for other grammatical topics.

Introductions

TYPE OF PRONOUN:	Personal subjective pronouns (I, you, he, she) and demonstrative pronoun (this)		
TOPIC:	Introducing oneself and others		
SKILL:	Speaking	LEVEL:	Beginner
TYPE OF ACTIVITY:	Role play with activity cards		

The purpose of this simple activity is to practice how to introduce oneself and others. It is one of the first role play activities true beginner students will be exposed to. At first, students can practice the following guided role-play activity with their real names. To provide students with further practice using the pronouns, use name tags, cue cards or pictures to play different roles in this simple conversation. Write this guided dialogue on the board or give out handouts.

> A: Hello. I am (say your name) _____. What is your name?
> B: Hi. I am (say your name) _____.
> A: Nice to meet you. (introduce C) This is (say C's name) _____.
> (He/She) is my friend.
> B: Nice to meet you, (name).
> C: Nice to meet you, too.
>
> Expected performance:
> A: Hello. I am Maria. What is your name?
> B: Hi. I am Paolo.
> A: Nice to meet you. This is Joseph. He is my friend.
> B: Nice to meet you, Joseph.
> C: Nice to meet you, too.

Asking and talking about origins

TYPE OF PRONOUN:	Personal subjective pronouns (I, you, he, she, they); demonstrative pronouns (this, these)		
TOPIC:	Asking and talking about origin (countries)		
SKILLS:	Listening, speaking and writing	LEVEL:	Beginner
TYPE OF ACTIVITY:	Listening comprehension matching activity; writing sentences		

Students will have the following material for this activity:

- a handout with a map of the world for each student, or every two students
- a set of cards with names of people
- a set of cards with names of countries or cities

Instructions: tell students that you will read aloud some information about the people whose names are on the cards. Students will have to find the people's countries on the map, and place the corresponding name and country cards on the map. You may need to read the text twice or more. (See sample text below.)

Example of text:
I have lots of friends. They are from different countries. Mariana is from Brazil. Pedro is from Spain. Matt and Lorna are from England. Maiko is from Japan and Gabrielle is from France. Where am I from? I am from the USA. And you, where are you from?

Map of the world handout:

Listening comprehension feedback: To have the students use the personal pronouns to talk about where the people are from, ask the students the following questions:

    T: Where is Marianna from?   S: <u>She</u> is from Brazil.
    T: Where am I from?   S: <u>You</u> are from the USA.

To have the students practice the demonstrative pronouns, ask them the following questions while pointing at the name cards.

    T: Who's this?   S: <u>This</u> is Mariana. <u>She</u> is from Brazil.
    T: Who are they?   S: <u>They</u> are Matt and Lorna. <u>They</u> are from England.

After the answers are checked orally, students will write complete sentences like the ones said in the oral practice.

Name and country cards should be cut out and jumbled to make the listening activity more meaningful.

Mariana	**Spain**
Pedro	**the USA**
Matt and Lorna	**France**
Maiko	**Brazil**
Gabrielle	**Japan**
You	**England**
I	**?**

Identifying people

TYPE OF PRONOUN:	Demonstrative pronouns (this, that, these, those)		
TOPIC:	Identifying people		
SKILL:	Speaking	LEVEL:	Beginner
TYPE OF ACTIVITY:	Asking questions about people in photos		

Ask students to bring pictures of their family or friends. Have them ask one another who the people in the photos are.

Expected performance:

> Who is this? That is my uncle.
> Are these your parents? Yes, they are. This is my mom, Cara, and that is my dad, Manuel.
> Who are these people in the photo? Those are my cousins.

Asking about possessions

TYPE OF PRONOUN:	Possessive pronouns (mine, hers, yours, etc), possessive interrogative pronoun *whose*, possessive nouns (Mary's)		
TOPIC:	Identifying possessions		
SKILL:	Speaking	LEVEL:	Beginner
TYPE OF ACTIVITY:	Asking and answering questions		

Have the students put some of their belongings in a bag without the others noticing what the objects are. Then one student picks out one object from the bag and asks:

> A: Whose is this key ring? Is it (yours/Peter's)?
> B: (Peter): No, it isn't mine. Is it (John's)?
> C: (John): No, it isn't mine. Is it (yours)?
> D: Yes, it is mine.

Find the mistakes

TYPE OF PRONOUN:	Various pronouns		
TOPIC:	Varies with reading material		
SKILL:	Integrated (listening, speaking, reading and writing)	LEVEL:	Low intermediate + (depending on text)
TYPE OF ACTIVITY:	Find and correct mistakes in a story		

Provide students with a short and simple story. One or two paragraphs will be enough. Any story from the textbook or any source can be useful for this activity, or even one made up by the teacher. Once the story is chosen or written, substitute the pronouns in the story with incorrect pronouns. For example, write a possessive pronoun (mine) instead of an objective pronoun (me). One positive feature of an activity like this is that the teacher decides what type of pronoun to review depending on the level.

Once students read the text with the mistakes chosen by the teacher, pair them up to find the mistakes and discuss the rules. Then, they rewrite the story with the correct pronouns and any other necessary changes, and read it aloud to the rest of the class.

The following is a sample of this type of activity. The example below also has a case of a possessive determiner and a verb form change. The mistakes are underlined and the correct answers are in parentheses.

Jane and Helen visited her (their) grandmother in Moncton last weekend. Although he (they) arrived there by 9 a.m., they had told him (her) that they would arrive much later. Their grandmother is a person which (who) does not like to wait for nobody (anybody), because they (she) get (gets) very nervous.......

Guessing game – "I spy"

TYPE OF PRONOUN:	Indefinite pronouns (somebody / something, in questions when a positive answer is expected); personal subjective pronouns; relative pronouns (who, which)		
TOPIC:	Identifying objects		
SKILLS:	Speaking, spelling	LEVEL:	Low intermediate +
TYPE OF ACTIVITY:	Guessing game "I spy...."		

This is a very popular game where other parts of speech can be practised or reviewed. Student A chooses somebody or something in the classroom (or from a picture) without saying who or what has been chosen. The students in the class guess who or what Student A has chosen by asking yes/no questions. Example:

A: I spy with my little eye <u>something</u> beginning with "c".
B: Is it <u>something</u> called "cup"?
A: No.
B: Is it <u>something which</u> has two handles?
A: No.
B: Is it <u>something</u> furry?
A: Yes. It is a cat.

Hot potato

TYPE OF PRONOUN:	Any type		
TOPIC:	Various		
SKILL:	Speaking	LEVEL:	Beginner + (depending on vocabulary)
TYPE OF ACTIVITY:	Hot potato game (aid: soft ball)		

Choose any type of pronoun, and announce a pronoun of that type as you throw a soft ball to a student. The student who catches the ball has to make a correct sentence with this pronoun. Then the student throws the ball back to you so that you can choose another pronoun. Then throw the ball to another student. An alternative is that each student who comes up with a correct sentence chooses a new pronoun and throws the ball to a classmate.

Substitution exercise

TYPE OF PRONOUN:	Personal subjective, personal objective (along with some possessive determiners)		
TOPIC:	Various		
SKILLS:	Reading and writing	LEVEL:	Low intermediate
TYPE OF ACTIVITY:	Substitution written exercise		

Provide students with a short descriptive or narrative paragraph containing no pronouns, only nouns or noun phrases. The purpose of the activity is for students to re-write the paragraph, substituting the correct pronouns for repeated nouns in the appropriate places.

> *Frank decided to take a week off work after all Frank had worked in the last year. Frank saw an article on Brussels that really caught Frank's attention, so Frank thought Brussels would be the best option for a short vacation. Brussels is the capital city of Belgium. Brussels is a modern city that is rich in old medieval buildings.*
>
> *Before the trip, Frank read all about Brussels and Brussels' historical buildings. Frank's friends lent Frank some books on Belgium, as Frank's friends had already been there. Frank planned to see as much as possible in one week. Frank started sightseeing the numerous 15th and 17th century buildings around the city. Frank could not believe what Frank was seeing: one thousand years of history in one place! How fascinating. Something Frank would never forget.*

Extension: To have students practise tense structure as well, the teacher can find or write a paragraph which mainly contains the simple present tense and ask students to re-write the text in the first person if the text is written in the third person, or vice versa. For example:

> *Jeannette gets up very early every morning. Jeanette doesn't like to get up early, though. Jeanette starts Jeanette's day with yoga. Then, Jeannette has a healthy breakfast.*

Students can now re-write the above paragraph using the first person and making the necessary verbs changes.

> *<u>I</u> get up very early every morning. <u>I</u> <u>don't</u> like **it**, though. <u>I</u> <u>start</u> **my** day with yoga. Then, <u>I</u> <u>have</u> a healthy breakfast.*

Note-taking and re-telling

TYPE OF PRONOUN:	Any type		
TOPIC:	Various		
SKILLS:	Reading aloud (for pronunciation), listening and speaking	LEVEL:	Low intermediate / Intermediate
TYPE OF ACTIVITY:	Note taking, retelling		

Find a short paragraph that is simple to understand. Have one student read it aloud while the rest of the class listens to it and takes notes of important facts in the story. Then ask the listeners to retell the story they heard. In the reproduction of the story, the students will be practicing different types of pronouns.

Create a story

TYPE OF PRONOUN:	Any type		
TOPIC:	Various		
SKILLS:	Speaking, writing	LEVEL:	Low intermediate +
TYPE OF ACTIVITY:	Creating a story		

Bring cards with varied types of pronouns, and distribute them on a desk. Write on the board the names of the different types of pronouns you are planning to teach or review. (Example: personal subjective pronouns; indefinite pronouns; relative pronouns, etc). Ask your students to come to the front and pick up a card from the desk and stick it on the board under the corresponding type of pronoun. Once the board work is complete and the students can see a great variety of pronouns, ask them to choose at least ten of those words, and in pairs write a story using those words. Students then present their stories to the rest of the class. (Other parts of speech such as nouns, adjectives and verbs are being practised in this activity.)

Story details

TYPE OF PRONOUN:	Any type		
TOPIC:	Various		
SKILLS:	Reading, speaking	LEVEL:	Intermediate +
TYPE OF ACTIVITY:	Reading for details; collaborative work		

Choose a newspaper article on a theme that might interest students. (A text from an ESL book can serve the same purpose). Give the students between two and five minutes (depending on the length and difficulty of the article) to underline all the pronouns in the text. Check that all pronouns in the article have been found. Then, pair the students up and have them find the nouns that those pronouns are referring to (cataphoric and anaphoric reference, and non-referential uses). Each pair presents its findings to the rest of the class.

Gap-filling and retelling

TYPE OF PRONOUN:	Any type		
TOPIC:	Various		
SKILLS:	Reading, writing and speaking	LEVEL:	High beginner – low intermediate
TYPE OF ACTIVITY:	Gap filling; re-telling		

Students fill in the blanks in a paragraph like the one in the example below. Have them check their answers in pairs and then ask them to retell the story in their own words. To guide high beginner students in identifying the pronouns, list all the pronouns, plus one extra, at the beginning of the activity. At a higher level (low intermediate and up), after they fill in the gaps, they can work in pairs to find the antecedents that the pronouns in the text are referring to.

Complete the blanks with one of the pronouns on the list. There is one extra pronoun.

I (x3)　　her (x2)　　me (x2)　　she　　myself　　everyone　　them　　it (x3)　　that someone　　they　　you　　who/that

Hi dear friends,
____ wouldn't believe what I did last weekend! Listen!
____ was invited to a BBQ party at Paulette's house and _____ had asked _____ to make a special dressing that my mother puts on meat: chimichurri. I told _____ to count on _____, although I had to call my mom and ask _____ for the recipe.
My mom was not at home, so _____ decided to go ahead and make ____ by _____. I thought _____ would not be a difficult thing to do. _____ had seen my mom cook this dressing many times. So I got the ingredients and put _____ in a mixer, then in a jar, and off I rushed to the party because I was late.
When the meat was ready and _____ was at the table, Paulette asked _____ if I had brought the chimichurri. Of course, I had. So, I brought the jar to the table, but the lid was stuck and I couldn't open _____. There were these two ladies _____ were wearing beautiful light summer dresses sitting next to me. _____ offered their help but I refused. Then _____ suggested using a knife to remove the stuck lid. I followed his advice with such bad luck that the lid broke and the oily stuff spilled out of the container all over their beautiful dresses. What a shame!

Answer key: you - I - she - me - her - that - her - I - it - myself - it - I - them - everyone - me - it - who/that - they - someone

5 Adjectives

Adjectives modify and describe nouns, pronouns and clauses. They provide more information about the noun, pronoun or clause. The additional information that adjectives provide falls into two major categories: descriptive and limiting. The majority of adjectives are descriptive adjectives. Limiting adjectives set some kind of range on a noun and include words such as **all**, **my** and **the**.

Adjectives modifying nouns:

        a **wonderful** picture   an **early** train

Adjectives modifying pronouns:

        someone **healthy**   it is **pretty**

Adjectives modifying clauses:

        It is **probable** *that he won't come.*
        I'm not **sure** *whether he'll succeed.*

5.1 Adjective forms

In English, the vast majority of adjectives fall into the category of descriptive adjectives. *(See 5.2.2 Descriptive adjectives)* Descriptive adjectives do not change form (have inflection) for different types of nouns. They do not have singular and plural forms, nor do they have feminine and masculine forms, as they do in some other languages.

        a **beautiful** girl   some **beautiful** girls
        a **tall** woman   a **tall** man

A relatively small group of adjectives fall into the category of limiting adjectives. *(See 5.2.1 Limiting adjectives)* A few limiting adjectives indicate number or countability. These include: **a/an**, **this**, **that**, **these**, **those**, **some**, **few**, **another**, **both**, **each**, **either**, **neither**, **many**, **much** and all cardinal numbers.

        this cake   **these** cakes

5.1.1 Suffixes and prefixes

Although most adjectives do not have any special form, some suffixes (word endings) are associated with descriptive adjectives.

Always associated with adjectives:
–*able*: adorable, comfortable
–*ible*: impossible, feasible
–*ous*: courageous, fatuous
–*less*: helpless, restless
–*ish*: childish, bluish

Often associated with adjectives:
–*al*: unusual, practical
–*ate*: delicate, desperate
–*an/ian*: American, vegetarian
–*ant*: exuberant, elegant
–*ent*: innocent, different
–*ful*: doubtful, delightful
–*ic*: nostalgic, enthusiastic
–*ive*: inquisitive, cooperative
–*ory*: compulsory, obligatory
–*some*: troublesome, loathsome
–*en*: wooden, golden
–*y*: cloudy, sleepy

Likewise, some prefixes (word beginnings) are associated with adjectives. These prefixes, when placed before an existing adjective, create an adjective with a meaning that is the opposite of the original adjective.

dis–: disrespectful   *il–*: illegal   *im–*: immature   *in–*: informal
ir–: irrelevant   *mis–*: misplaced   *non–*: nonexistent *un–*: unfaithful

5.1.2 Compound adjectives

Adjectives can be formed by combining words (compounding). These compound adjectives may be melded together as one word, left as separate words, or hyphenated. There is not always complete agreement on when and whether to express a compound adjective in writing using a single word, separate words or hyphens. While some compounds are set, many others are subject to style preference.

5.1.2.1 One-word compound adjectives

These are generally recognized as single words and behave in the same manner as non-compound, single-word adjectives.

a **coolheaded** man   **heartfelt** gestures   an **underachieving** team

5.1.2.2 Multiple-word compound adjectives

It is possible to use multiple words to form a single descriptor that modifies a noun, pronoun or clause. In some cases, these words remain separate, though they are clearly working together to form a single idea. In general, if the compound consists of more than two adjectives, it is hyphenated.

a **late night** meal   it is **first rate**   a **senior management** decision

The choice of when and whether to keep a multiple-word adjective as separate words or to hyphenate it is usually a matter of clarity and of style. When the compound adjective contains a noun, it is not always clear which noun is being modified. If it is unclear, then the use of a hyphen clarifies.

5.1.2.3 Hyphenated compound adjectives

In a majority of cases, compound adjectives are expressed in writing with the aid of hyphens. The main benefit of the hyphen is the addition of clarity. A good rule of thumb is to hyphenate multiple-word adjectives when they occur immediately before a noun in a sentence. Here are some examples:

> a **mind-blowing** experience **spine-tingling** music
> a **well-dressed** model a **thunder-struck** teenager
> a **multiple-word** adjective a **first-rate** restaurant

When they occur after the noun (usually separated from the noun by a linking verb), hyphens are generally not necessary (compare *a **first-rate** restaurant* and *it is **first rate***).

There are many basic structures for forming hyphenated compound adjectives. Here are some of the most common.

(noun or adverb) + participle
This is a variation of participial adjectives. *(See 5.1.3 Participial adjectives)*

> a **heart-stopping** moment a **poorly-sewn** patch

adjective + noun + -ed
These adjectives should not be confused with participial adjectives.

> a **blue-eyed** girl a **short-tempered** man

number + (age or time)

> a **three-hour** trip a **six-year-old** boy

combined structures
These adjectives are formed from various parts of speech and work together as a unit to describe a noun or noun phrase.

> **one-of-a-kind** show a **must-see** exhibition
> an **up-and-coming** athlete a **part-time** job

Quiz 1: Adjective forms

A. *Transform the following words into their adjective forms. More than one form may be possible.*

	Adjective form		Adjective form
1) satisfaction	1)	6) envy	6)
2) humour	2)	7) waste	7)
3) degrade	3)	8) spirit	8)
4) religion	4)	9) shine	9)
5) radiate	5)	10) hate	10)

B. *Identify the part of speech of each of the highlighted words.*

1) Susan plans to study **Italian** next year.
2) That method is **wasteful**.
3) Dad just taught me a **magic** trick.
4) The **cowardly** lion makes me laugh.
5) That style should appeal to the **creative** among us.

**** In the classroom: Adjective forms ****

Adjectives can sometimes be difficult for ESL students to identify, as these words can have different forms and positions in a sentence. For this reason, it is important that teachers present the topic of adjectives from both semantic (related to meaning) and syntactic (related to structure) points of view. Teaching adjectives thematically will help students understand meaning and form more easily.

Adjective suffixes and prefixes

Nouns and verbs can be converted to adjectives by adding a suffix (dirt ⇨ dirt**y**; attract ⇨ attract**ive**). Likewise, by adding a prefix to an adjective, it is converted into a word with the opposite meaning (happy ⇨ **un**happy). There is no easy way of knowing which suffix or prefix should be used with a given word. Although there are some suffixes or endings that are directly connected to the formation of adjectives, not all words ending with those syllables are adjectives.

The list given in section 5.1.1 shows some suffixes connected to the forms of adjectives (for example, words ending in *–ive*, such as *inquisitive* and *cooperative*). ESL students might then think that all words ending in *–ive* are adjectives. That is not the case. One example is the word *detective*. It is a noun ending in *–ive*. Another example is *fugitive*. This word can function as a noun as well as an adjective, without a change of form. These words that can be used, unchanged, in different parts of speech are more troublesome for ESL students to identify or use.

Another example of word endings is the case of the suffix *–al*. Words like *natural, pastoral, practical* and *usual* are adjectives. The same is not true for words like *denial* and *refusal,* which both end in the suffix *–al*, forming a noun from a verb.

Suffixes that end in *-ly* could also be a problem for ESL students. As a general rule, adverbs of manner end with the syllable *–ly*. The adjectives *lovely* and *friendly* can be confused with adverbs if students assume that all words ending in *–ly* are adverbs. The easiest rule of thumb here is that a noun + *-ly* creates an adjective: *heavenly, woolly, worldly*. When *–ly* is added to an adjective, it creates an adverb: *brazenly, frighteningly, coldly*.

In spite of these difficulties, there are some suffixes that are only connected with adjectives. *(See 5.1.1 Suffixes and prefixes)* Identifying these suffixes can be very helpful for ESL students. (Note: *-ful* is mostly connected to adjectives. There are a few exceptions with nouns connected to quantity: *armful, teaspoonful*.)

This problem of identifying adjectives according to their form is not restricted to suffixes. Adjectives can form their negative meanings by adding certain prefixes such as *im-, il-, dis-* and *in-*. However, not all the words which begin with the prefixes *dis-* or *un-* are adjectives expressing a negative meaning. There are verbs and nouns which use the same prefixes. See the following examples:

>agree (v.) ≠ **dis**agree (v.)
>agreement (n.) ≠ **dis**agreement (n.)
>wrap (v.) ≠ **un**wrap (v.)

The prefix *in-* can be particularly confusing for students; for example, *internal* does not have a negative connotation. Its opposite counterpart is *external.*

Same form, different part of speech

In English, words can function as different parts of speech without any change in form. For example, the word *clean* can be a verb and an adjective. *Clockwise* can be an adverb and an adjective.

>You should *clean* your room. (v.)
>You room should be **clean**. (adj.)
>
>Move your hands *clockwise*. (adv.)
>It is not difficult; just think of a **clockwise** movement. (adj.)

When students encounter these problems, their knowledge of sentence structure and the function of adjectives could help them clarify their doubts.

Pluralization of adjectives

Attempting to make adjectives plural is a common error for learners whose native language has plural forms of adjectives.

>the *greens* cars
>The cars are *greens*.

In order to prevent this common error, introduce different examples with singular and plural nouns when teaching adjectives to lower level students.

5.1.3 Participial adjectives

Participial adjectives are past participle (usually ending with *-ed*) or present participle (*-ing*) forms of verbs which function as adjectives, modifying the same words that other descriptive adjectives do, in the same way that other descriptive adjectives do. They can be placed before nouns or after linking verbs.

>Can you send me your recipe for **stuffed** peppers?
>Charles is a **loving** husband.
>We're **exhausted**.
>The performance was **shocking**!

Many participial adjectives ending in *–ed* describe people's emotions. They reflect the emotional state of the receiver of the action in the participial verb. When they end in *–ing*, they describe the cause or source of the feeling: a thing, person or situation. They reflect the condition of the creator of the action.

He was **bored.** / He was **amazed.** (Describes how *he* felt; *his* emotional state.)
The film was **boring.** / The film was **amazing.** (Describes the cause or source of the feeling: in this case, the film.)

Here are more examples of participial adjectives describing emotions.

Table 16: Examples of participial adjectives describing emotions

Emotion / feeling	Base form of verb	Describing the receiver of the emotion (past participle)	Describing the cause of the feeling or emotion (present participle)
amusement	amuse	amused	amusing
confusion	confuse	confused	confusing
embarrassment	embarrass	embarrassed	embarrassing
exhaustion	exhaust	exhausted	exhausting
forgiveness	forgive	forgiven	forgiving
fright	frighten	frightened	frightening
hurt	hurt	hurt	hurting

In addition to emotions, past participial adjectives can reflect the condition or state of the receiver of the action.

an **electrified** rail   **painted** walls   some **buttered** toast

Irregular past participial adjectives function in the same way as regular past participial adjectives ending in *–ed*.

the **written** word   **lost** time   a **torn** page

To differentiate participial adjectives from verbs in the past or present participle, an analysis of the function of the participial verb in its context is necessary. Past participles are used in verb phrases for the passive voice construction (*be*-verb + past participle) or perfective aspect (*has* or *had* + past participle). Present participles are used in verb phrases for progressive aspect. *(See 14 Tenses)*

Please, throw away the **broken** cup; you might hurt yourself.
(The participial adjective **broken** is directly describing the condition of the cup; it is not acting as a verb in the sentence.)

The cup *was broken* during the clean-up.
(The past participle *broken* is the main verb, head of the verb phrase *was broken*, in a passive construction.)

Our promotion was successful; we now have some **interested** buyers.
(The participial adjective **interested** is directly describing the buyers; it is not acting as a verb in the sentence.)

They *have interested* the audience with their sophisticated product.
(The past participle *interested* is the main verb, head of the verb phrase *have interested*, in the present perfect aspect.)

She is **disgusting**.
(The participial adjective **disgusting** is a subject complement directly describing the subject *She*; it is not acting as a verb in the sentence.)

She *is disgusting* them with her attitude.
(The present participle *disgusting* is the main verb, head of the verb phrase *is disgusting*, in the present progressive aspect.)

Quiz 2: Participial adjectives

Convert the given verbs into the most appropriate participial adjective. Give a reason for your choice of participle.

1) That restaurant has _____ waiters! (sing)
2) My grandmother always loved _____ eggs. (bake)
3) Everyone likes the store manager; she is a _____ woman. (charm)
4) The experience was difficult and _____. (exhilarate)
5) How can you mend a _____ heart? (break)

*** *In the classroom: Participial adjectives* ***

The adjectives derived from the participial forms of verbs (past participle forms such as *excited* or *written*; and present participle forms such as *thrilling* or *comforting*) present a consistent challenge. Some of the most common issues with participial adjectives are discussed here.

Choosing the correct participle form

ESL students often have trouble understanding and using the –*ed* and –*ing* forms of adjectives appropriately. It is very common to hear students say, "I am boring," or "I am confusing," when they mean, "I am bored," or "I am confused." In these cases, it is best to establish the technical differences between the two types of adjectives, coupled with a demonstration of their use, giving very easy examples, such as the following:

Situation 1: You are watching a movie.
    T: I am bored (this is how I feel; I am the receiver of the feeling) because the movie is boring (this is the description of the movie and the source of the feeling).

Situation 2: You are doing a math exercise.
    T: I am confused (this is how I feel) because the exercise is confusing (this is how I would describe it and it is the source of the confusion).

Situation 3: You like Paul very much.
    T: I am interested in Paul (this is how I feel about him) because he is an interesting guy (this is how I would describe him; he is the source of my interest

Participial adjectives vs. verbs

When a present participle is an attributive adjective, then it is fairly easy to identify it as an adjective:

> This is a very **exciting** movie.
> (**exciting** is modifying the noun *movie*)

When a present participle follows the verb *be*, then it can look like either an adjective or the main verb in a verb phrase in the continuous aspect. In these cases, present students with a situation that allows them to see the function that the participle is performing.

> This movie is **exciting**.
> (**exciting** is describing the noun *movie*; it is an adjective)

> This movie is *exciting* the children.
> (*exciting* is the action that the movie is doing to the children; it is a verb)

Another way to show the difference between the *–ing* form as a participial adjective and the *–ing* form as a verb is to elicit from the students the parts of speech in ambiguous sentences:

> Example: Paul is *entertaining*.
> T: Look at the word *entertaining* in this sentence. Can you replace it with any other adjective, for example, *nice,* as in: *Paul is nice*? If yes, then that *–ing* word is an adjective describing the subject, Paul.

> Another example: Paul is *entertaining* Grandpa with his stories.
> T: Can you replace *entertaining* with the adjective *nice*, as in: *Paul is nice Grandpa with his stories*? No. It doesn't make sense. When you can't replace the *–ing* word with another adjective, the *–ing* word could be a verb in the continuous tense.

More advanced students could also be instructed to look for the presence of an object; adjectives do not take objects, so if an object is present, then the *–ing* form is a verb.

5.2 Adjective types

Adjectives are divided into two major groups: limiting and descriptive adjectives. These two groups of adjectives have clearly different semantic functions when they modify nouns. The semantic function (the meaning that it gives) also influences adjective order in a sentence. Limiting adjectives always precede descriptive ones in sentence order. (Adjective order is discussed in more detail in section 5.4.)

Limiting adjectives include all the determiners. *(See 6 Determiners)* Descriptive adjectives can be further classified as qualifying or classifying.

Table 17: Limiting and descriptive adjectives

Limiting Adjectives	Descriptive Adjectives	
	Qualifying	*Classifying*
• Possessives • Articles • Interrogatives • Demonstratives • Quantifiers • Ordinals • Specifying adjectives	• Opinion • Size • Quality / Condition / Temperature • Age • Shape • Colour	• Age • Shape • Origin / Nationality / Style / Religion • Material • Colour • Purpose / Use / Type

Examples:

Limiting Adjective	Descriptive Adjectives		Noun
	Qualifying	*Classifying*	
several	captivating	Asian	countries
the	best	green	tea

There are two other minor subcategories of adjectives – called specifying and intensifying adjectives – within the major categories of limiting and descriptive adjectives. *(See Table 18: Types of limiting adjectives and 5.2.2.3 Intensifying adjectives)*

5.2.1 Limiting adjectives

Limiting adjectives particularize the reference of the noun. They narrow the scope and, in a way, define the noun being referred to. Most of the limiting adjectives (including all of the determining limiting adjectives) are also determiners. *(See 6 Determiners)*

In addition to determiners, limiting adjectives include a group of words called specifying adjectives. The specifying limiting adjectives add a slightly different type of limit to nouns than the determiners do. They work to make the reference to a noun more specific, without actually describing its qualities or characteristics. If used together with other limiting adjectives, the specifying limiting adjectives generally come last.

Unlike descriptive adjectives, limiting adjectives cannot postmodify a noun through a linking verb. Another important difference between limiting adjectives and descriptive adjectives is that there are different rules for combining them to modify a noun.

Here are the types of limiting adjectives, together with examples.

Table 18: Types of limiting adjectives

Type	Example
Possessive determiners my, your, his, her, its, our, your, their	**My** mother told me he was a liar.
Nouns in possessive form George's, book's, students', etc.	We are looking forward to **George's** visit.
Articles a, an, the	**A** girl came into **the** shop and bought **an** apple from **the** clerk.
Interrogative determiners whose, which, what	**Whose** book is this?
Indefinite determiners another, any, either, other, some, whatever, whichever	**Another** day passed without **any** news.
Quantifying determiners all, any, both, double, each, every, few, half, little, many, more, most, much, no, neither, several, some, such, what	**Neither** house was cheap.
Demonstratives this, that, these, those	**This** boy is sick.
Cardinal numbers one, two, three, etc.	**Four** students passed the test.
Ordinal numbers first, second, third, etc.	That's the **second** time he's done that.
General ordinals following, former, last, latter, next, penultimate, previous, subsequent, ultimate	All **subsequent** attempts failed.
Specifying limiting adjectives additional, certain, existing, main, only, other, opposite, particular, present, primary, principal, remaining, same, specific	This exit is closed; please use the **other** exit.

When not followed by a noun, most of these same words function as pronouns, or even nouns.

> Interrogative adjective: **Which** house are you planning to buy?
> Interrogative pronoun: *Which* are you planning to buy?

5.2.2 Descriptive adjectives

Descriptive adjectives name a quality or a condition of a noun. This group constitutes the majority of adjectives in English. Descriptive adjectives express the following features of nouns:

opinion, value or judgment:	a **brilliant** mathematician; an **irreplaceable** artefact; a **dubious** achievement
size:	some **gigantic** jewels; a **long** time; a **wee** tipple
condition, quality or feeling:	his **creaking** bones; some **reliable** employees; a **lovelorn** poet
age:	a **prehistoric** monster; that **old** man
shape and measurement:	an **amorphous** blob; a **10-story** building
colour:	her **violet** eyes; the **blue** ribbon
nationality, origin, style or religion:	a **Canadian** explorer; an **Elizabethan** sonnet; an **Animist** belief

material or composition: a **leather** belt; an **oil** painting
characteristics, purpose, use or type: a **caustic** chemical; a **massage** table; the **prayer** rugs; a **folding** chair

Descriptive adjectives are not mutually exclusive; many of them can modify one noun (or head) at the same time. (Considerations of adjective order are discussed in section 5.4.) There are two main types of descriptive adjectives: qualifying and classifying.

Certain adjectives may function as either qualifying or classifying. For example, **modern** may serve to describe the general condition of or opinion about something, and would therefore be a qualifying adjective.

         She's **modern**. (That's my assessment of her; she's stylish)

This adjective may also serve to describe relative age or type and would therefore be a classifying adjective.

         I prefer **modern** dance. (A style of dance pioneered in the 20th century)

5.2.2.1 Qualifying adjectives

Qualifying adjectives describe the quality of a noun. There are six sub-groups of qualifying adjectives. They modify the nouns they describe in a non-literal, less direct way than classifying adjectives do. These adjectives are more subjective in nature, with a significant element of judgment or opinion. Qualifying adjectives are also generally gradable. *(See 8.2 Gradability)* When used together with classifying adjectives, qualifying adjectives will always come first.

Here are the types of qualifying adjectives, together with examples.

Table 19: Types of qualifying adjectives

Type	*Example*
Opinion beautiful, obnoxious, intriguing, stellar, etc.	She gave a **stellar** performance last night at the theatre.
Size (judgmental assessment) big, huge, tiny, minuscule, etc.	The houses on Post Road are **huge**.
Quality / Condition / Temperature rough, silky, torn, sharp, frosty, etc.	Her hair was perfectly **silky** when she returned from the salon.
Age / Time Reference (judgmental) ancient, modern, up-to-date, etc.	They try to showcase the most **up-to-date** fashions.
Shape (judgmental assessment) voluptuous, shapeless, curvy, skinny, etc.	That suit is really **shapeless**. It wouldn't look good on him.
Colour (judgmental assessment) opalescent, greenish, etc.	The **opalescent** gems attracted everyone's attention.

5.2.2.2 Classifying adjectives

These adjectives, as their name suggests, classify the nouns they are describing. Unlike qualifying adjectives, classifying ones modify nouns directly and in a more objective, fact-based manner. These adjectives are generally non-gradable. *(See 8.2 Gradability)* When used together with qualifying adjectives, classifying adjectives will always come second.

Here are the six types of classifying adjectives, together with examples.

Table 20: Types of classifying adjectives

Type	Example
Age (literal) old, young, 10-year-old, new, etc.	My **10-year-old** cousin loves video games.
Shape / Size / Measurement (measurable) rectangular, two-meter, size nine, etc	She has a new pair of **size nine** shoes.
Nationality, Origin, Style or Religion Chinese, Shakespearean, quixotic, etc.	My professor adored **Shakespearean** sonnets.
Material wooden, plastic, silk, paper, etc.	**Paper** plates are more environmentally friendly than **plastic** ones.
Colour (literal) yellow, red, blue, pink, green, etc.	You should not advance on a **yellow** light; you must wait for the **green** one.
Purpose / Use / Type sleeping, work, racing, sports, etc.	If you plan on going camping, you need a good **sleeping** bag.

Virtually all of the purpose/use/type adjectives are either gerunds or nouns acting as adjectives.

5.2.2.3 Intensifying adjectives

Intensifying or emphasizing adjectives are used when the speaker wants to emphasize the description of an abstract or non-physical noun. If used together, intensifying adjectives come before qualifying adjectives and classifying adjectives. Some common intensifying adjectives are:

absolute	perfect	total	utter
complete	positive	true	real

The adjectives **absolute, complete, total** and **utter** are used to express strong feelings or describe extreme situations.

> **absolute** despair   a **complete** idiot
> **total** happiness   **utter** loathing

Great and **big** can also be considered intensifying adjectives. **Great** describes nouns related to qualities or feelings and **big** describes a type of person or event.

> a **big** lecturer   **great** pride
> a **big** disappointment   **great** excitement

In the majority of cases, the function of intensification is done with adverbs, not adjectives.

Quiz 3: Limiting and descriptive adjectives

Identify all of the adjectives in the passage below. Indicate whether each adjective is limiting or descriptive.

There are many Egyptian obelisks in Rome — tall, snakelike spires of red sandstone, mottled with strange writings, which remind us of the pillars of flame which led the children of Israel through the desert away from the land of the Pharaohs; but more wonderful than these to look upon is this gaunt, wedge-shaped pyramid standing here in this Italian city, unshattered amid the ruins and wrecks of time, looking older than the Eternal City itself, like terrible impassiveness turned to stone. And so in the Middle Ages men supposed this to be the sepulchre of Remus, who was slain by his own brother at the founding of the city, so ancient and mysterious it appears; but we have now, perhaps unfortunately, more accurate information about it, and know that it is the tomb of one Caius Cestius, a Roman gentleman of small note, who died about 30 B.C.

From the essay "The Tomb of Keats" by Oscar Wilde, Irish Monthly, July 1877.

Quiz 4: Descriptive adjectives: qualifying or classifying

For each of the descriptive adjectives highlighted below, indicate whether it is a qualifying or a classifying adjective.

> I had called upon my friend Sherlock Holmes upon the second morning after Christmas, with the intention of wishing him the compliments of the season. He was lounging upon the sofa in a **purple dressing**-gown, a **pipe**-rack within his reach upon the right, and a pile of **crumpled morning** papers, evidently newly **studied**, near at hand. Beside the couch was a **wooden** chair, and on the angle of the back hung a very **seedy** and **disreputable hard-felt** hat, much the **worse** for wear, and **cracked** in several places.

From "The Adventure of the Blue Carbuncle" in <u>The Adventures of Sherlock Holmes</u>, by Arthur Conan Doyle

*** *In the classroom: Adjective types* ***

The most significant student problem related to adjective type is the order of adjectives (covered in section 5.4 below). Issues related to limiting adjectives are covered in Chapter 6 Determiners. Other common student problems with adjective type are: the use of nouns as adjectives; and the correct uses of the interrogative adjectives *what* and *which*.

Possessives vs. nouns as adjectives

One common point of confusion for ESL students is the placement of nouns that serve as adjectives. When the noun is in possessive form, then it is a limiting adjective. Otherwise, it is a descriptive adjective (usually indicating type or purpose).

This differentiation is particularly troublesome in written English. Plural nouns ending in *–s* sound the same as possessive nouns ending in *–'s* and the same as plural possessive nouns ending in *–s'*. Students must be able to use knowledge of sentence structure and of grammar rules to differentiate among these in writing, as all three forms can legitimately precede and describe a noun.

a **drinks** party (plural noun acting as an adjective)
the **drink's** effect (singular possessive noun)
his **drinks'** flavours (plural possessive noun)

In most cases, it is straightforward to determine which form is correct. If the first noun is an attribute of the second, then it is a plural noun acting as an adjective. If the first noun owns, control or uses the second noun, it is possessive. A test of this case would be the ability to insert an additional adjective between the first and second noun. If it is possible to do so and still make sense, then it should be a possessive. The only question then is whether the first noun is singular or plural.

a ~~**drinks** [strange] party~~   (not a possessive)
the **drink's** [strange] effect ✓ (possessive)
his **drinks'** [strange] flavours ✓ (possessive)

Interrogative adjectives *what* and *which*

The interrogative adjectives *what* and *which* (also known as pronominal adjectives) are generally confused by learners, as the meaning of these two words are similar or the same in many languages. The concept of choice should be introduced to correct this error.

What countries would you like to visit? (no choice given)
Which countries would you like to visit: Italy, Brazil or Japan? (a choice is given)

5.3 Position of adjectives

An adjective can be put in two places in a sentence: directly beside a noun, or connected to a noun through a verb (as a complement, after a linking verb). If an adjective is placed directly next to the noun which it is modifying, it is an attributive adjective. An attributive adjective may premodify (be placed before) or postmodify (be placed right after) the noun that it is modifying. If an adjective functions as a complement, after a stative linking verb, then it is a predicative adjective.

It is **red**.
(adjective **red** is modifying the subject *it*; it is a predicative adjective following the stative verb *is*; this adjective is also the subject complement)

It is a **red** apple.
(adjective **red** is modifying the subject complement *apple* in the noun phrase *a red apple*; this is an attributive adjective)

Legal travel permits must be verified by a notary **public**.

The adjective **public** in the last example is a case of an attribute adjective that comes after a noun. It is still an attributive adjective (it is not linked to the noun through a stative verb), but it is postmodifying (it comes after the noun). *(See 5.3.1 Attributive adjectives)*

5.3.1 Attributive adjectives

Some adjectives can only be used attributively. They do not make sense if placed in the predicate after a stative linking verb.

>the **main** street ~~the street is **main**~~
>the **former** President ~~the President is **former**~~
>the **occasional** glass of wine ~~the glass of wine is **occasional**~~

Only a few attributive adjectives can appear after the nouns they modify. These have very special meanings or are usually institutional expressions.

>Professor **emeritus** (used for honorary titles, usually after retirement)
>Boston **proper** (the main, most important or central part)
>court **martial** (similar in meaning to the premodifying adjective *military*)
>Attorney **General** (describes a position with broad jurisdiction)
>notary **public** (indicates a position that serves the public)

5.3.2 Predicative adjectives

The term *predicative* comes from the term predicate. *(See 2.1.1 Subject and predicate)* Predicative adjectives are found in the predicate of a sentence and can function as subject complements of linking verbs. Linking verbs are a subcategory of stative verbs that indicate state or condition (like *feel*, *seem*, or *be*); or ones that indicate physical or emotional senses (like *look*, *smell*, or *sound*). Predicative adjectives may also function as object complements after certain verbs.

Some adjectives are restricted to predicative position and cannot be attributive. Many adjectives beginning with *a-* fall into this category.

>The cat is **asleep**. ~~It is an **asleep** cat.~~
>The girl is **afraid**. ~~She is an **afraid** girl.~~

The following adjectives are only used in predicative position:

alive	**alone**	**aware**	**glad**
sorry*	**well**	**ill***	**ready****

* sorry *and* ill *can be used attributively, but with different meanings*
** ready *can be used attributively when it is part of a compound adjective, such as* ready-made

Quiz 5: Position of adjectives
Identify if the adjectives highlighted below are predicative or attributive.

	A	P
1) The archaeologists discovered a **gigantic** cave in the Colombian forest.		
2) His sense of humor is **ingenious**.		
3) Matt feels **afraid** all the time.		
4) They took a **three-hour** tour and were **exhausted** after that.		
5) **Fewer** people showed up **this** year at the Annual Flower Festival.		
6) The presenter was quite **quick-witted**.		
7) The alpha male of the pack exhibited the **typical** behaviour for that situation.		
8) The **key** theme of the story is delusion.		
9) Wherever you want to go will be **fine**.		
10) The secretary **general** of the foundation has announced his retirement.		

Quiz 6: Categorization of adjectives
Find all the adjectives in the following excerpt from The Old Man and the Sea *and then categorize them according to the instructions in a – f below.*

> There is an old fisherman, Santiago, in Cuba who has gone eighty-four days without a catch. He is thin and gaunt with deep wrinkles in the back of his neck, ... and his hands had deep-creased scars from handling heavy fish on the cords. But none of these scars were fresh. They were as old as erosions in a fishless desert. Santiago's lack of success, though, does not destroy his spirit, and he has cheerful and undefeated eyes.
>
> (Excerpt from *The Old Man and the Sea* by Ernest Hemingway)

a) Categorize the adjectives according to type: limiting or descriptive.
b) Identify the participial adjectives.
c) Identify the adjective that is a cardinal number.
d) Identify the adjectives that derive from a noun.
e) Identify the adjective that has a prefix.
f) Identify the adjectives that have a suffix.

5.4 Order of adjectives

There are rules regarding the order of attributive adjectives in a sentence, some of them unvarying and some of them somewhat variable. One unvarying rule is in regard to the two main types of adjectives: limiting and descriptive. Limiting adjectives always precede descriptive adjectives. Specifying adjectives always follow determining adjectives and precede descriptive adjectives.

Within the class of descriptive adjectives, intensifying adjectives come first. Qualifying adjectives always precede classifying adjectives.

determining	→	specifying	→	intensifying	→	qualifying	→	classifying	
my		main		true		beautiful		old	friend

Within the broad classes of limiting and descriptive adjectives, there are many types of adjectives. Limiting adjectives have particular rules about how they may be combined with other limiting adjectives, and many of them may not be used together. *(See 6.1 Structural classification of determiners)* Descriptive adjectives have, technically, no real limit to the number and combination that could be used to describe a single noun. Within the set of descriptive adjectives, there are general, but not unvarying, rules of order. Here is an overview of adjective order:

Table 21: Limiting and descriptive adjectives, with specifying and intensifying adjectives

Limiting		Descriptive		
Determining	*Specifying*	*Intensifying*	*Qualifying*	*Classifying*
• Possessives • Articles • Interrogatives • Demonstratives • Quantifiers • Ordinals	Examples: - additional - certain - existing - main - only	Examples: - absolute - positive - total - true - utter	• Opinion • Size • Quality / Condition / Temperature • Age • Shape • Colour	• Age • Shape / Size • Origin / Nationality / Style / Religion • Material • Colour • Purpose / Use / Type

5.4.1 Order of descriptive adjectives in attributive position

In attributive position (premodifying only), more than one adjective can be used to describe a single noun. There is some disagreement among grammarians on the ordering of descriptive adjectives preceding a noun, making this topic more troublesome for ESL students.

Though not all the rules are hard and fast, there are broad rules which do not vary. No native English speaker would ever describe, for example, something from France which is also exciting as a 'French exciting' thing; it would always be an **exciting French** thing. Other ordering is less strict. Something which is **torn** and is also **old** could be correctly described as either a **torn old** thing or an **old torn** thing. The choice is dependent on emphasis, assumptions and style.

It is unusual to use more than three adjectives before a single noun. However, the following order is generally kept no matter the number or type of adjectives in the noun phrase.

Table 22: Major descriptive adjective categories for purposes of adjective ordering

Limiting Adjective	Evaluation	Physical Elements	Origin	Material	Purpose/ Type	NOUN
three	wonderful	large	Argentinean	leather	riding	jackets
another	robust	ring-shaped	southern	rubber	dog	toy

Within some of these categories, a further breakdown of descriptive adjectives is possible. There is a general convention to the ordering here, but it is somewhat less consistent. This pattern is followed roughly 80% of the time. When it is not followed, it is sometimes a stylistic choice, sometimes one more imbued with meaning.

Table 23: Full set of adjective categories for purposes of adjective ordering

Type	Deter-mining	Evaluation		Physical Elements					
		Speci-fying	Opinion / Judgment	Size	Age	Temp-erature	Shape	Condi-tion	Colour
Ex.	the	only	true	tiny	antique	cool	round	faded	red
	a		beautiful						
	her		amazing						golden

Origin		Material	Purpose / Type	NOUN	Type
Place	Religion				
German	Jesuit	ceramic	souvenir	mug	Ex.
		silk	cocktail	dress	
Swiss				watches	

the only true tiny antique cool round faded red German Jesuit ceramic souvenir mug
a beautiful silk cocktail dress
her amazing golden Swiss watches

The first example only serves the purpose of illustrating the types of adjectives in their order, since it would be highly unusual to use so many adjectives to modify one noun.

Quiz 7: Order of adjectives

a- Put the adjectives in the correct order before the noun.
b- Identify their type (opinion, size, purpose, material, etc.)

1) magenta magnificent oval plate
2) windswept vast southern beach
3) ancient precious wooden statue
4) Catholic prayer little book
5) garden plastic sun-bleached chairs
6) foggy typical British weather
7) Korean delicious sizzling BBQ
8) slender well-dressed young woman

**** In the classroom: Order of adjectives*

The order of more than two adjectives in attributive position is a topic that many ESL learners find particularly complex. They may find it difficult to understand why it is correct to say *a magnificent huge modern mansion* and it is wrong to say *a modern huge magnificent mansion*. The solution to this problem is to teach the rules of the sequence of adjectives. However, there seems to be some disagreement among grammarians on the sequence rules, which makes learners more confused. It is best to introduce this topic gradually and start from simple rules of the order of two categories of descriptive adjectives, such as *size* + *shape* + noun (a *big round* table), or *opinion* + *size* + noun (a *nice small* cup) and add more categories until the order becomes more natural. At a low level, provide learners with lots of practice and keep the categories simple. The following simplified order can be a guide to follow:

| Limiting adjective | Opinion | Size | Age | Shape | Colour | Origin | Material |

A more complex order (such as the one in Table 23) and coordinated adjectives of the same class are topics that should be introduced at a high intermediate level.

5.5 Adjective or adverb

The distinction between adjectives and adverbs is generally straightforward, and the specific vocabulary is distinct. The most obvious rule of thumb here is that adverbs very often take the form of an adjective + -*ly*, forming a completely distinct word. In some cases, however, the same word can function as either an adjective or an adverb, depending on the context. This is very confusing for students, particularly given that most of these words are very common. The most difficult distinction is in cases where the adjective follows a stative linking verb. Normally, an adverb is expected after a verb.

> The patient looks **well**.
> (adjective describing the state of the patient: in good health)
>
> We expected her to sing **well**.
> (adverb describing the quality of the action verb *sing*)

In general, the distinctions are easier to make based on sentence construction. If the word directly precedes a noun, it will be functioning as an adjective. If it directly follows an action verb or an adjective, it is an adverb. Here are the main adverbs which take the same form as adjectives.

Adjective	Adverb
an **early** riser	He rose **early** to watch the sunrise.
a **late** riser	Darren slept **late** again.
a **straight** arrow	We walked **straight** to the counter.
a **high** barrier; a **low** blow	The investigators searched **high** and **low**.
a **long** drink; a **hard** lesson	They worked **long** and **hard** to get the job done.
daily bread	They replace it **daily**.
his **wrong** answer	I must have heard that **wrong**.
some **fast** calculations	Do it **fast** or not at all.
a **short** intermission	It fell **short** of expectations.
a **direct** threat	He'll travel **direct** to San Francisco.

Some of these adverbs also have an -*ly* form: **lately**, **highly**, **hardly**, **shortly** and **directly**. These additional forms have different meanings and are not interchangeable with the adverbs given above. *(See 7.1 Adverb forms)*

There is another group of words that functions in the same way, albeit in a strictly informal manner. These words are commonly used as adverbs in their adjectival form, though they do have distinct adverbial forms. These are more common in spoken than in written English.

quick	**cheap**	**slow**	**quiet**
loud	**close**	**easy**	**clear**

Though these words have *-ly* adverbial forms, they are often used in their adjectival form, particularly when in comparative mode.

> If he looks **closer**, he'll find it. (Compare with 'more closely')
> I can breathe **easier** with you around. (Compare with 'more easily')

Quiz 8: Adjective or adverb

Identify whether the highlighted word is an adjective or an adverb and explain. (This quiz includes informal uses of adjectives as adverbs.)

1) I haven't seen any good films **lately**; and you?
2) The cheetah is one of the **fastest** animals in the world.
3) The professor won't mark any **late** assignments.
4) Melanie hates it when people speak too **loud**.
5) He was so inebriated that he couldn't even mimic a **straight** walk.
6) She was terrified of diving into the **deep** blue sea without her lifejacket.
7) The teacher lowered my mark because I handed in my assignment **late**.
8) Natalie has never tried so **hard** to achieve a goal.
9) Patients are released when they feel **well** enough to walk by themselves.
10) If you need to make an international call, please do not call **direct**.

**** In the classroom: Adjective or adverb ****

The distinction between adjective and adverb is generally a straightforward one, with fairly consistent rules. The trouble most likely to occur in the ESL classroom is the misapplication of intensifying adverbs (such as *very*) to adjectives that are already expressing an extreme state (such as *freezing*).

**** You can teach adjectives ****

The classroom activities in this unit emphasize descriptive adjectives rather than limiting adjectives. The reason for this is that descriptive adjectives allow for an enormous variety of activities which integrate all skills – including the use of limiting adjectives such as articles, demonstratives and possessives – in a natural way. (For ideas on specifically teaching limiting adjectives, see Chapter 6 Determiners.) All of these activities can be adapted to multiple levels by varying the difficulty of the adjectives used in the lesson.

Recognition activities for descriptive adjectives

These activities are ways to enrich students' ability to recognize adjectives, using a variety of tools.

Identifying parts of speech

Level: Beginner and above

Introduce adjectives in their base forms, as opposed to comparative or superlative forms. (The base form for adjectives is also known as the absolute or positive form.)

When teaching vocabulary, write new words on the board, making sure not only to demonstrate the meaning and use of the word in a sentence, but also to identify its part of speech in the context presented.

> Example: **sensitive** (adj.)
> Sue couldn't stop crying after Mark criticized her outfit; she's so **sensitive**. (It is easy to hurt Sue's feelings.)

Sorting lists into parts of speech

Level: Low intermediate and above

List words belonging to different parts of speech (nouns, adjectives, adverbs), and have students put the words on the list into the correct columns in a table.

Example list:

toothpaste	pillow	round	loudly
interesting	large	very	modern
honestly	fruit	carefully	balcony

Student output should be something like this:

Nouns	Adjectives	Adverbs
toothpaste	round	loudly
pillow	interesting	very
fruit	large	honestly
balcony	modern	carefully

Categorizing types of adjectives

Level: Beginner and above

The example activity here requires students to put adjectives into the correct category. This activity can be adapted for any level by changing the adjectives on the list.

Example adjective list:
> some; reliable; marble; rectangular; plastic; eastern; the; ancient; difficult; a; enormous; reddish; old; both; Italian; those; huge; cotton; which; lovely; small; metal; round; dirty; modern; brown; charming; well-built

Example categories and student output would be something like this:

Limiting adjective	Opinion	Size	Age	Shape	Colour	Origin	Material
some	reliable	enormous	ancient	rectangular	reddish	eastern	cotton
the	difficult	huge	old	round	brown	Italian	metal
a	lovely	small	modern	well-built			plastic
both	dirty						marble
those	charming						
which							

Categorizing positive and negative adjectives

Level: Beginner and above

In this activity, the teacher provides students with a list of adjectives and has them identify whether those adjectives express a positive or negative idea. This is good for adjectives denoting opinion or quality, or for describing personality traits.

Example list:

| outgoing | generous | shy | anxious |
| unfriendly | honest | sympathetic | sloppy |

Example student output:

Positive	Negative
outgoing	*shy*
generous	*anxious*
sympathetic	*unfriendly*
honest	*sloppy*

Morphology: Word building

Level: Adaptable to any level by choosing appropriate vocabulary and parts of speech

Word-family activities will help students remember the forms of adjectives and other parts of speech. Here are some ideas to practice word formation.

Provide students with tables like the ones shown below and have them complete the blank cells with the correct adjectives. The plain-text words in the examples below are ones which could be provided to students as a guide. The boxes with words in italics are the ones which the teacher would leave blank; the italicized words are the students' possible answers.

Noun	Verb	Adjective
danger	*endanger*	*dangerous*
attraction	attract	*attractive*
enjoyment	*enjoy*	enjoyable
creation	create	*creative*

Adjective	Opposite meaning
breakable	*unbreakable*
flexible	*inflexible*
painful	*painless*
respectful	*disrespectful*
patient	*impatient*

noun	verb	-ed/ing adjective
satisfaction	to satisfy	*satisfied / satisfying*
annoyance	to annoy	*annoyed / annoying*
embarrassment	*to embarrass*	embarrassed / embarrassing
depression	*to depress*	depressed / depressing

Morphology: Antonyms

Level: Intermediate and above

Have students re-write sentences using antonyms for the adjectives given.

> Examples:
> I think the new employee is a responsible person.
> *I think the new employee is an irresponsible person.*
>
> Sue seems efficient in what she does.
> _____
>
> He is a mature and patient person.
> _____

Brainstorming

Level: Low intermediate and above

Brainstorming, making word charts and mind-mapping are useful ways to extend students' knowledge and ability to be creative and descriptive with their use of language. In this activity, the teacher chooses any object, city, place or person and has students brainstorm as many adjectives as possible to describe them.

Example: How can you describe Paris?

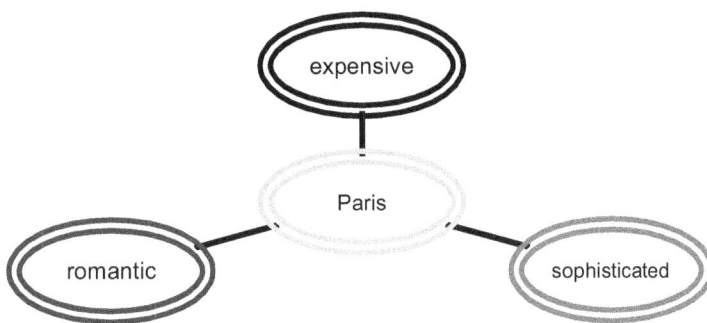

Variation: asking students to work in groups or pass their mind maps around will render better and more varied results.

Self-description

Level: Low intermediate and above

A simple and effective way to reinforce adjectives associated with personality is to get students to do a creative self-description. In the "What's in my name?" activity, students must come up with an adjective which starts with the first letter of their names: My name is **C**laire. I am a **caring** person.

Variation: Describe others in this way.
        I like **E**sther because she is **easygoing.**

Working with music and songs

Level: Intermediate and above

A simple way of using songs in the classroom is for listening comprehension gap filling activities. Find a song that has as many adjectives as possible. Two good classic examples are "Isn't She Lovely" by Stevie Wonder and "What a Wonderful World" by Louis Armstrong. Give out the lyrics of the song, but delete all the adjectives. Have students listen to the song and fill in the gaps. If the song allows for a change of adjectives, have them now substitute the adjectives in the song for other adjectives. It can be made more challenging if the students have to also take rhyme into account.

Describing feelings

Level: Beginner and above

This can be a simple miming activity. Students pick cards from a bag or box; each card has an adjective pertaining to a feeling. Students must mime the feeling for the rest of the class or group to guess. If they prefer, students can draw the feeling instead of acting it out.

Practising speaking, writing, reading and listening skills with adjectives

Most of the following activities can be adapted to practise any of the four major skills. The choice of how the activity is presented and what results students are expected to produce will determine which major skills are practised. This will also depend on the students' level.

Describing people and things

Level: High beginner and above

The teacher can ask questions using various structures for the students to practise. Here are some examples, with expected responses.

> What is Leng like? *She is tall.*
> What does Lui look like? *He has long curly hair and he is well-built.*
> Who is Mary? Which one is Mary? *She is the one with short straight hair and blue eyes.*
> What is it like? What does it look like? Can you describe it? *It is round and soft.*
> What are you looking for? *I'm looking for a heart-shaped box.*

Pictures of family members are good tools to practice descriptive adjectives connected to physical appearance and personality. Pictures of people with very distinctive features can be used to make the activity more interesting and interactive. In this activity, students practice adjectives denoting age, height, build, hair and other physical features:

> He is a middle-aged man.
> He is well-built.
> He has a long beard and a big moustache.
> His hair is also long and wavy.

Reading descriptions and correcting mistakes

Level: High beginner and above

Hand out pictures. Write descriptions of people or objects which do not exactly match the pictures. Have the students read and identify what is wrong. Students then rewrite the sentences using the correct adjectives.

This is my family. My father is a little heavy. He has long grey hair and a big moustache. My mother is very slim. She is taller than my father. Her hair is blonde and curly. My baby brother is very cute. He is wearing a purple overall. I am the girl in the picture. I have long straight hair and I am wearing a nice long dress.

Holding a fashion show

Level: High beginner and above

This activity could be done as a group project. Students design their own fashion show, where models will walk on an imaginary or real catwalk while a presenter describes the clothes. This is a fun activity for young learners.

For those groups of students who do not like dramatizing, authentic material can be used to have students practise describing clothes. Examples of authentic material could be a video clip on a famous fashion designer, or pictures from magazines.

Advertising a product

Level: High intermediate and above

This could be done as a group project. Students choose a product and use persuasive language to advertise it. For developing speaking and listening skills, the activity could be transformed into a TV or radio commercial.

Writing descriptive paragraphs

Level: Intermediate and above

This activity develops students' creative writing and vocabulary. Provide students with a descriptive paragraph from any book, magazine, or even an ESL book. First, have students identify the adjectives in the text. Then ask them to make a list of synonyms using a thesaurus. Finally, ask the students to use their creativity and rewrite the paragraph using the best synonyms they can think of. To make this activity more interactive and to integrate it with listening and speaking skills, have the students work cooperatively in small groups.

Presenting yourself

Level: Low intermediate and above

The topics of friendship or love can be very motivating. Students can write a list of adjectives describing personality, and choose the ones that best describe themselves, their ideal friends or love partners. Finally, students can write a profile for a social media page or an ad for a dating service.

6 Determiners

Determiners make up a special category of words that modify nouns (and sometimes pronouns). There are approximately 50 determiners. Although there are few determiners, they account for roughly 20% of the words used in English. Determiners include demonstratives (this, these), possessives (my, George's), interrogatives (which, whose), articles (the, a, an) and quantifiers (all, many, two). The majority of determiners may also serve other linguistic functions, such as pronoun or adverb. For example, the word **this** is a determiner in the first sentence, and is a pronoun in the second:

>He prefers **this** modified version.
>He prefers *this*.

Determiners are technically adjectives, in that they modify nouns by making them more specific in some way. But they do not describe nouns in the way that most adjectives do. Determiners put limits or a range on the noun and on any other information about the noun. These limitations are magnitude or definiteness. *(See 6.2 Functional classifications of determiners)* Determiners fall into the category of limiting adjectives. *(See 5.2.1 Limiting adjectives)* The particular functions and uses of these words are significantly different from those of most adjectives.

Unlike descriptive adjectives, determiners may sometimes carry inflection for number or gender. Another distinction of determiners is that most of them do not have a comparative form. When used together with descriptive adjectives to modify a single noun, determiners always precede any descriptive adjectives.

>**My** *new* shoes need cleaning.   ~~New my shoes need cleaning~~.

Unlike descriptive adjectives, determiners cannot postmodify a noun through a linking verb.

>I like *bright* colours.   The colours I like are *bright*.
>   (descriptive adjective)
>I like **both** colours.   ~~The colours I like are both~~.
>   (determiner)

Determiners may be subcategorized by their grammatical structure or by their linguistic function. The categories of grammatical structure for determiners are:

- Predeterminers
- Central determiners
- Postdeterminers

This categorization of determiners is only relevant if multiple determiners are used together to modify a single noun.

Determiners perform a defined set of linguistic functions as they limit nouns and noun phrases. The major functional categories of determiners are:

- Definiteness
- Magnitude

Another way to categorize determiners is based on the types of nouns that they can be paired with. Descriptive adjectives do not change based on number or countability. Determiners may change based on these factors.

> This is a *fashionable* hat.
> These are *fashionable* hats.
> This is *fashionable* clothing.

In the examples above, the descriptive adjective *fashionable* can be used whether the noun is singular (hat), plural (hats) or uncountable (clothing). This is true for virtually all descriptive adjectives. Determiners do not have this degree of flexibility. Following is a list of the determiners and the types of nouns with which they can be used. Many of these words can take other forms (pronouns, adverbs). This list applies to the words when they are functioning independently as determiners.

Table 24: Determiners and the types of nouns they can modify

Determiners	may be used with:		
	Singular Countable Nouns	Plural Countable Nouns	Un-countable Nouns
a, an, another, each, every, either, neither, one	√		
both (groups of two only), **few, fewer, fewest, many, several, two** (three, four, etc.)		√	
least, less, little, much, what (quantitative)			√
first (second, etc.), **following, next, previous, subsequent, former, latter, ultimate, penultimate**	√	√	
that, this	√		√
all, any (unstressed), **enough, more, most, other, some** (unstressed), **these, those**		√	√
any (stressed), **half** (one-quarter, etc.), **her, his, its, my, no, our, some** (stressed), **such, twice** (double, ten times, etc.), **the, their, what** (exclamatory and interrogative), **whatever, which, whichever, whose**	√	√	√

Two determiners have inflection for gender. The possessive determiners **his** and **her** show the gender of the possessor (not the possession).

6.1 Structural classifications of determiners

Structurally, determiners will always come before any descriptive adjectives. Unlike descriptive adjectives, determiners cannot be used in an endless variety of constructions. There are limits on the determiners that may be used together to modify a single noun, and there is a strict ordering among those that may be used together in those limited circumstances. This discussion of structural classifications of determiners only applies when more than one determiner is used to modify a single noun. Otherwise, a determiner is simply a determiner, with no further structural classification necessary.

In those cases when multiple determiners may be used together to modify a single noun, they must conform to the order:

predeterminer → central determiner → postdeterminer

Felicia heard about **all his many** conquests.

In the example above, **all** is a predeterminer, **his** is a central determiner, and **many** is a postdeterminer. While it is unusual to use more than one determiner at a time, it is clearly possible. The following table categorizes determiners as predeterminers, central determiners and postdeterminers. These classifications are only meaningful when more than one determiner is used to modify a single noun.

Table 25: Predeterminers, central determiners and postdeterminers

Predeterminers	Central Determiners		Postdeterminers		
all	a	neither	another	last	next
both	an	no	few	latter	other
each	any	our	fewer	least	penultimate
half (one-quarter, two-thirds, etc.)	either	some	fewest	less	previous
twice (triple, ten times, etc.)	every	that	first (second, third, etc.)	little	several
what (exclamatory)	her	the	following	many	subsequent
such	his	their	former	more	ultimate
	its	these	one (two, three, etc.)	most	
	my	this		much	
		what (quantitative and interrogative)			
		whatever			
		which			
		whichever			
		your			
		+ nouns in possessive form			

If more than one determiner is used with a single noun, no two can be from the same category, with the exceptions of possessive nouns and cardinal numbers.

~~The that dog barks at everything.~~
The neighbour's dog barks at everything.
~~Ask him if you can have another more serving.~~
Ask him if you can have **one more** serving.

Quiz 1: Order of determiners

For each sentence, choose the maximum number of determiners from the list which can be logically applied to modify the highlighted noun. Do not add any other words.

1) Sharon really enjoys visiting with _____ **old friends**.
   (all, any, following, those, twice, two)
2) I can't believe _____ huge **mess** they made.
   (a, all, George's, my, their, what)
3) _____ Benelux **countries** have high standards of living: Belgium, the Netherlands and Luxembourg.
   (a, all, least, three, twice, what)
4) This year, the kids forgot _____ **birthdays**.
   (a, both, such, their, three, parents')
5) You can take _____ **sample** you like.
   (a, any, latter, parents', their, whatever)

*** In the classroom: Determiner structure ***

Students have particular problems with handling complex possessive structures. Nouns in possessive form can function as determiners, but are also still nouns, and so the rules that apply to nouns also apply to nouns in possessive form. This is why this type of central determiner can co-occur with other central determiners. There are, essentially, two nouns (the head noun and the noun in possessive form), and each may take a determiner.

>Ann dislikes *both* **her son's** immature roommates.

In the example above, the head noun is *roommates*. It is modified by a descriptive adjective, *immature*, and three determiners: the predeterminer *both* and the two central determiners **her** and **son's**. But, in fact, the central determiner **son's** is also a noun, and it is this noun – not the head noun *roommates* – that is modified by the central determiner **her**. If the central determiner **her** were modifying the head noun *roommates*, the meaning of the sentence would be different.

Ann dislikes	both	her	son's	immature roommates.
		*modifying possessive noun **son's***	*possessive noun modifying head noun **roommates***	*(the roommates of Ann's son)*

Ann dislikes	both	her	immature roommates.
		*modifying head noun **roommates***	*(the roommates of Ann)*

The possessive central determiners, in combination with *own*, can become possessive pronouns.

>A: What a nice car! Is it *your own*?
>B: Yes, it's *mine*.

6.2 Functional classifications of determiners

There are two major functional classifications of determiners: definiteness and magnitude. Within these functional categories are more specific subcategories. The category of definiteness includes all determiners that indicate a particular selection, a known position, a definition or possession. The category of magnitude includes all indicators of quantity, size and proportion.

6.2.1 Definiteness

Determiners can indicate whether a noun is a specific instance or whether it is a general example. Determiners can indicate if the noun under discussion is exactly known or if it is unknown. In other words, they show how definite the description of the noun is. This specificity, or definiteness, is shown with articles (definite and indefinite – see section 6.4), demonstratives (which indicate some form of selection from a larger group), and other determiners that work to make a noun more definite: possessives, interrogatives and ordinals. Ordinals include both numerical ordinals (*first, second, third*) and general ordinals (*next, previous, subsequent*).

Table 26: Determiners of definiteness

Definite			Indefinite	
first (second, third, etc.)	my	their	a	what (interrogative)
following	next	these	an	whatever
former	other	this	any (stressed)	which
his	our	those	either	whichever
her	penultimate	ultimate	some (stressed; informal)	whose
its	previous	your	these (informal)	+ zero article
last	subsequent	+ nouns in possessive form	this (informal)	
latter	that			
	the			

Determiners of definiteness cannot be used together to modify the same noun. The exceptions are nouns in possessive form and ordinals.

> ~~We'll be happy with an either movie.~~
> We'll be happy with **either** movie.
> We'll be happy with **a** movie.
> We'll be happy with **your friend's** movie.

Any and **some** may also function as determiners indicating magnitude (see section 6.2.2 below). When **any** and **some** indicate an indefinite occurrence, they are sometimes called stressed (or strong). This term reflects typical pronunciation stress, not emphasis in meaning. The stressed **some**, indicating indefiniteness, is informal.

> I'll take **any** unoccupied office.
> (There is no preference or definition of which office: stressed, indicating indefiniteness.)
> Are there **any** unoccupied offices available?
> (Any quantity greater than zero: unstressed, indicating quantity.)
>
> I can see **some** guys over there.
> (There is an unknown quantity greater than one; unstressed, indicating quantity.)
> I was standing at the bus stop and **some** guy came and yelled at me.
> (The person who yelled is unknown or unidentified; stressed, indicating indefiniteness.)

*** In the classroom: Determiners of definiteness ***

The demonstrative determiners (**this**, **that**, **these** and **those**) are generally presented at a beginner level. The difficulty with these determiners at this level is that they not only carry inflection for number (the choice of determiner depends on whether the noun is a singular countable noun, a plural noun or an uncountable noun), but they also refer to close proximity (**this** and **these**) and distant proximity (**that** and **those**). This combination of concepts can be overwhelming to beginner students whose first language does not use a similar grammar.

A simple solution is to demonstrate proximity using realia (objects) and pictures to present or drill the structure until students can produce it in a more fluent and natural manner.

> **This** pen is blue. **That** pen is red.
> **These** pens are here. **Those** pens are there.

Some students have continuing difficulty remembering which demonstratives are for singular and which are for plural nouns. A mnemonic technique that is sometimes useful in these cases is to ask students to count the vowels in the words. The demonstratives with one vowel are for singular nouns; those with two are for plurals.

6.2.2 Magnitude

Determiners can indicate some element of magnitude by showing how many of something there is, or by showing how big something is. These determiners are also known as quantifiers. These determiners may indicate proportion (entirety, fraction or multiple), a specific quantity, a subjective quantity (based on personal judgment) or a comparative quantity. These determiners of magnitude are limited to single words. There are other structures, composed of multiple words, that serve a similar quantifying function (for example, *a lot of*). These structures are discussed in 6.3.

Table 27: Determiners of magnitude

Entirety	Fraction or multiple	Counters (cardinal numbers)	Subjective/ judgmental quantity	Comparative quantity
all	half (one-quarter, two-fifths, etc.)	one, two, three, etc.	enough	fewer
any (unstressed)	twice (double, ten times, etc.)		few	fewest
both			little	less
each			many	least
every			much	more
neither			several	most
no			some (unstressed)	
			such	
			what (exclamatory)	

Determiners of magnitude cannot be used together to modify the same noun, with the exception of counters (cardinal numbers).

> Elizabeth appreciates **all** classical music.
> There aren't **any** seats left.
> The Aral Sea is **one-tenth** its original size.
> The world has seen **few** leaders with the charisma of Nelson Mandela.
> Sadaharu Oh has hit the **most** home runs in professional baseball.
> There are **three fewer** entrants in the contest this year.

Any and **some** may also function as determiners indicating indefiniteness (see section 6.2.1 above). When **any** and **some** indicate quantity, they are sometimes called unstressed (or weak). When **any** is used to indicate quantity, it is usually in a negative construction, indicating an absence.

Quiz 2: Functional classifications of determiners

1) What are the major functional classifications of determiners?
2) What are the major sub-classifications of each major class?
3) What types of determiners can co-occur with determiners of definiteness?
4) What types of determiners can co-occur with determiners of magnitude?

*** In the classroom: Determiner functions ***

The functional category that tends to cause greatest confusion for students is the comparative quantity category. *(See 8.4 Comparative and superlative uses and structures)* The comparative and superlative forms of **few** (**fewer** and **fewest**), **little** (**less** and **least**), **many** (**more** and **most**) and **much** (**more** and **most**) indicate quantities which depend on other references. The implied comparison can be tough for students to ascertain.

> There are **fewer** paying customers this time.
> (The quantity of paying customers is lower than the quantity on some other occasion. The phrase *this time* indicates the reference for comparison.)

The superlative forms usually require the use of the definite article.

> Shirley scored **the fewest** points of all the competitors.

These determiners in particular lend themselves to confusion, especially when there is an accompanying descriptive adjective. The same word -- for example, **most** -- could function as a determiner or as an adverb. The context and the function of the word are the only ways to determine the part of speech.

> That is **the** *most* ridiculous thing I have seen to date.
> (Here, **most** is an adverb modifying (intensifying) the adjective *ridiculous*.)

> **Most** ridiculous things irritate me.
> (Here, **most** is a determiner modifying (quantifying) the noun *things*.)

6.3 Quantifiers

A quantifier indicates the size, frequency or quantity of a noun. In this section, the term quantifier is used in a broad sense, incorporating determiners of magnitude (see section 6.2.2 above) as well as other grammatical structures, the most common of which is partitives. These words and phrases come before any descriptive adjectives. Quantifier phrases, when they are used together with determiners to modify the same noun, precede the determiners. When used together, the order of use is:

quantifier phrase →	determiner →	descriptive adjective →	head noun
a bottle of	my	favourite	perfume

Quantifier phrases contain nouns, and the nouns in the quantifier phrase are subject to the same rules of modification as the head noun. In *a bottle of my favourite perfume*, the quantifier phrase *a bottle of* contains a noun, *bottle*, which is modified by its own determiner, *a*. *(See 6.3.1.2 Partitives)*

6.3.1 Quantifier types

Quantifiers include the full set of determiners of magnitude (see section 6.2.2 above) as well as two types of quantifying phrases. These quantifying phrases may be standard partitives using the structure *noun + of*, or they may take the form *determiner + of*.

6.3.1.1 Quantifying determiners

The determiners listed in section 6.2.2 are quantifying determiners. They indicate absolute or relative size or quantity.

6.3.1.2 Partitives

A partitive is a phrase which functions to indicate a quantity. It is most often used with uncountable nouns, but may be used with countable nouns as well. Its structure is:

noun (or noun phrase) +	**of**	+ **head noun** (or noun phrase)
(the unit of measurement)		(the thing being measured)
piles	*of*	*rubbish*
a gallon	*of*	*milk*
a glass	*of*	*wine*
two pieces	*of*	*pie*
spoonfuls	*of*	*cereal*

The noun or noun phrase in the partitive may be singular or plural. Because a partitive contains a noun, the use of determiners and adjectives can become confusing. The noun in the partitive may be modified by determiners and descriptive adjectives.

> Jimmy ate **a few big servings of** her delicious lasagna.

The head noun above is *lasagna*. It is an uncountable noun. It is modified by the determiner *her* and the descriptive adjective *delicious*. The partitive for this uncountable noun is **servings of**. The noun in the partitive is *servings*. That noun, in turn, is modified by the central determiner *a*, the postdeterminer *few* and the descriptive adjective *big*. The determiners *a* and *few* are not modifying the head noun *lasagna*. They are only modifying the noun *servings* in the partitive phrase.

The common partitive terms *percent* and *lot* are nouns, and they conform to this structure.

> Marlene has finished **twenty percent of** her requirements.
> His garden always has **a lot of** fragrant perennials.

Partitive phrases determine the number of the noun. When a partitive is applied to an uncountable noun, it has an effect on the verb form. The verb form for uncountable nouns is the same as for singular countable nouns. Plural nouns have different verb forms.

> The ice cream *was* very rich.
> (verb modifying uncountable noun *ice cream*)

> The **two scoops of** ice cream *were* very rich.
> (verb modifying plural countable noun *scoops* from partitive phrase)

6.3.2 Other quantifier phrases

There is another grammatical structure that falls somewhere between quantifying determiner and partitive. This "middle" quantifier phrase structure uses *determiner + of* to create a structure — distinct from quantifying determiners and standard partitives — that also precedes determiners. This structure only applies when the head noun or noun phrase is definite. *(See 6.4.1 Definite article)*

> I really like **most of** *my many* Irish relatives.
> Almost **half of** *all his last twenty* valiant efforts failed.

Quiz 3: Subject / verb agreement with quantifiers

Choose the correct form of the verb in brackets.
1) Many of my friends (was / were) present at the party last night.
2) All of the happiness in the world (is / are) what I wish for you.
3) Both of the girls (want / wants) to leave earlier.
4) Each of the members (are / is) delayed in their payments.
5) Two cups of flour (is / are) more than enough.

**** In the classroom: Quantifiers*

Students often have trouble with the determiners of subjective quantity: **few**, **little**, **many** and **much**.

When **few** and **little** are paired with the determiner **a**, the meaning changes. While **few** and **little** suggest insufficiency, **a few** and **a little** suggest a small amount, but not necessarily an insufficient one. **Few** and **little** always have a negative sense. **A few** and **a little** may also have a positive sense.

> A: What will you do when you finish university?
> B: I'm not sure. I have **few** options.
> (Speaker B is in a bad situation and seems to have a very small number of choices.)

> A: What will you do when you finish university?
> B: I'm not sure. I have **a few** options.
> (Speaker B seems to have some choices and is probably not in a bad situation.)

The quantifier **much** is generally used in negative statements. For positive statements, a partitive such as **a lot of** is usually preferred.

> ~~I have much money~~.
> I *don't* have **much** money.
> I have **a lot of** money.

6.4 Articles

There are three articles in English: **the**, **a** and **an**. **The** is the definite article, and **a** and **an** are the indefinite articles. The general function of **the** is to indicate known, specific or unique occurrences of something. **A** and **an** are derived from the number one. Their general function is to indicate one occurrence of something, though not necessarily a known or unique occurrence.

Articles are a subset of determiners. Structurally, they are central determiners. Functionally, they indicate definiteness and sometimes quantity. Their frequency and the nuance of their functions are such that they merit a separate discussion.

An article adds some element of reference to a noun. It does not actually describe the noun in the way that most adjectives do. It indicates something about the perspective of the speaker and the listener. It works to classify a noun as being a member of a group or as being unique in some way. It is also a central determiner. *(See 6.1 Structural classification of determiners)* Because multiple central determiners can not be used together to describe one noun, then the presence of another central determiner eliminates the need for an article.

There is another article, known as "zero article." Structurally, it is the absence of an article. It is a grammatical choice for certain indefinite nouns. Choosing when to use which form (**the**, **a/an** or **zero article**) is a challenge. There are many good techniques for making the choice. Unfortunately, even using these techniques, the rules are not always straightforward.

6.4.1 Definite article

The is the definite article. It is the most commonly used word in the English language. It is used when both the speaker and the listener (or both the reader and the writer) understand which occurrence of a noun is under discussion. It may be used with singular and plural nouns, with countable and uncountable nouns, with concrete and abstract nouns. It is generally not used with proper nouns. It is used to indicate that the noun which it is modifying has been defined in some way (it is definite). That definition may come from uniqueness, from mutual understanding or from explicit description. It is also used to indicate the general idea of a known class of something, usually in a generic statement of fact.

6.4.1.1 Uniqueness

A noun may take the definite article because it is a unique occurrence of the noun. The noun's uniqueness may stem from being the only understood case of the noun; a noun may also be understood as unique if it is described with a superlative.

the only one in existence	**the** sun
the only one in the sphere of reference	**the** receptionist
described with a superlative	**the** *longest* section

6.4.1.2 Mutual understanding

There are several conditions under which the speaker and listener (or writer and reader) may have a shared understanding of something. Even if the thing is not unique, the speaker and listener both know exactly which occurrence of the thing is being specified. When this is the case, then the definite article is needed.

The circumstances under which a mutual understanding between speaker and listener are established are: the noun has already been mentioned; the speaker and listener have a common point of reference; the reference is easy to assume; the reference is common in the culture or society.

Circumstance for mutual understanding	Examples
Noun has already been mentioned:	Eliza heard **a** voice. **The** voice was familiar. (The first mention is indefinite.)
Common point of reference:	Did you get your memo from **the** chairman? (For two employees at the same company, the reference is clear.)
Reference is easy to assume:	I made a fresh pot of coffee this morning. **The** aroma was wonderful. (Even though *aroma* has not been mentioned before, it is easy to assume that it is the aroma from the pot of coffee that is under discussion.)
Generalized mutual understanding:	Eddie hates to waste time at **the** office. (It can be assumed that this refers to a place in a building where Eddie normally works, even without knowledge of Eddie, his job, or its location.)

Some modes of communication take the definite article when referred to as a generalized concept, not a specific occurrence. Certain others do not.

> She often writes on **the** Internet. She often appears in books.
> She often writes in **the** newspaper. She often appears in magazines.

Included in this category of generalized mutual understanding are terms for eras, epochs and understood time periods. Single years do not take articles.

> They are definitely children of **the** '90s.
> That church was built in **the** middle ages.

6.4.1.3 Explicit description

In cases where a noun is defined by some clear linguistic means (not by implication or assumption or shared culture), then the definite article is required. The four most common linguistic modes of defining a noun are:

- with descriptive adjectives
- with prepositional phrases
- with relative clauses
- with infinitival phrases

When any one of these four grammatical structures sets a noun apart from other possible occurrences of that noun (making it unique in the context), then the noun requires the definite article. This applies to countable (singular and plural) and uncountable nouns.

Structure for explicit description which defines a noun	Examples
Defining descriptive adjective:	Don't eat **the** *shriveled* berries. (There are many berries and some are shriveled; it is the shriveled set that shouldn't be eaten.)
Prepositional phrase:	Did you hear **the** news *about Mr. Jones*? (The phrase beginning with the preposition *about* defines exactly which news is meant.)
Relative clause:	Introduce me to **the** man *who painted this portrait*. (The clause beginning with the relative pronoun *who* defines which man is meant.)
Infinitival phrase:	Do you have **the** motivation *to succeed*? (The infinitival phrase *to succeed* defines the type of motivation.)

6.4.1.4 Generic statements of fact

The definite article is also used to indicate a class of concrete nouns in making general statements of fact. These references do not indicate a unique occurrence of the noun, but, rather, indicate a whole group. In these cases, the definite article is only used with singular, countable concrete nouns.

> A lot has been written about **the** automobile.
> (This is a reference to the entire class of objects, automobiles.)

This sense of generic reference to an entire class of nouns can also be communicated by using the plural noun form with no article (zero article), or by using uncountable (concrete or abstract) nouns with no article.

> A lot has been written about automobiles.
> A lot has been written about happiness.

6.4.1.5 Proper place names

The use of the definite article in proper place names is subject to a separate set of rules. Some of those rules are consistent with the general rules of article use, but not all of them. They are sufficiently distinct that they merit a separate discussion.

In general, proper nouns do not take articles. City names (with the exception of The Hague) do not take articles. Streets, squares, plazas and the like generally do not take an article. When a noun is proper, it is virtually by definition a unique occurrence and the use of the definite article is redundant. But, with proper place names, there are many exceptions.

6.4.1.5.1 Proper place names that take the definite article

- Proper place names that include plurals, references to governmental structure (kingdom, union, republic, etc.) or prepositional phrases (using *of*)

Examples that take the definite article:	*Compare to:* *Similar place names (no article):*
The People's Republic of China	China
The Commonwealth of Massachusetts	Massachusetts
The Czech Republic	Slovakia
The Bay of Bengal	Botany Bay
The Cape of Good Hope	Cape Cod
The Netherlands	Holland
The Seychelles	Sri Lanka
The Statue of Liberty	Washington Monument
The Houses of Parliament	Whitehall

- Mountain ranges (not individual mountains), deserts and some bodies of water (oceans, rivers, seas – not others)

Examples that take the definite article:	*Compare to:* *Similar place names (no article):*
The Urals	Mount Fuji
The Atlantic Ocean	Lake Maricaibo
The Yangtze River	Cripple Creek
The Black Sea	Puget Sound
The Sahara Desert	Rankin Inlet

- Described regions
    The Middle East
    The Bermuda Triangle

6.4.2 Indefinite article

There are two indefinite articles in English: **a** and **an**. Indefinite articles indicate non-specific or unknown occurrences of nouns. The indefinite articles can only be used with singular, countable nouns. **Zero article** is used with plural and uncountable nouns that are indefinite. Some linguists consider zero article to be, technically, a type of indefinite article for this reason.

The uses of **a** and **an** are almost identical. Choosing between the two of them is strictly a matter of pronunciation. If the word following the indefinite article begins with a consonant sound, then use **a**. If the word following the indefinite article begins with a vowel sound, then use **an**. The choice of **a** or **an** depends strictly on the pronunciation, not the spelling, of the following word.

Generally, choosing between **a** and **an** is straightforward. There can be some difficulty when the sound of a word does not match its spelling. This is most common with words that begin with the pseudo-consonant /j/ (the "y" sound), though spelled with a vowel (such as *e* or *u*). Other areas of difficulty occur with words that are spelled with an *h*. Sometimes these words are pronounced with an initial consonant sound, sometimes with an initial vowel sound.

an egg	**a** European
an understanding	**a** uniform
an hour	**a** hospital

An indefinite article is used to indicate that the noun which it is modifying has not been defined for both the speaker and the listener (or both the writer and reader). It may be clearly defined to neither of them or to one of them, but not to both. It may be used to indicate the general idea of a class of nouns. It is used to describe people as members of a category or group. Its derivation from the word "one" is evident in its use as an occasional replacement for "one" in stating numbers.

6.4.2.1 Not defined

There are three broad situations in which a singular, countable noun might be undefined in a certain context: when the noun is first introduced; when it is given in a general sense as a point of description or background; and when it is an unknown member of a known group.

Circumstance where a noun is not defined for both speaker and listener:	Examples
First time the noun is mentioned:	Eliza heard **a** voice. The voice was familiar. (In the first sentence, the listener is hearing about the voice for the first time, so it is not yet defined (it is indefinite). After it is mentioned, the voice is understood, so in the second sentence it is definite.)
Background or hypothetical information:	Richie hopes to have **a** big house some day. He wants **an** old house with **a** beautiful garden. (Even upon the second mention, the house is still an unknown, hypothetical thing and can therefore take an indefinite article.)
Unknown or unidentified member of a known group:	She wants **a** job that is closer to her home. (Here, the membership in a group (jobs that are closer to her home) is of interest; it is not necessary to know or specify a single example.)

6.4.2.2 General idea

An indefinite article may be used to indicate a class of countable concrete nouns in making general statements. These references do not indicate a unique occurrence of the noun, but, rather, indicate a whole group.

> **An** apartment block holds many life stories.
> (This refers to apartment blocks in general, not to a single, specific but unidentified apartment block.)

This usage can also be represented by using the definite article or by using the plural noun form with no article (zero article). The difference in meaning among these choices is negligible; it is mainly a style choice.

> The apartment block holds many life stories.
> Apartment blocks hold many life stories.

6.4.2.3 Subject complements

When a singular, countable noun is acting as subject complement *(See 2.2.2 Complement)*, it may take an indefinite article. This applies to such subject complements when they identify the subject as a member of a larger group, or when they are not postmodified.

6.4.2.3.1 Known member of a larger group

When a known case of a singular, countable noun is also a member of some group, an indefinite article is used to indicate the membership in that group.

> That tree is **an** elm.
> (The specific tree is already known; the group to which it belongs is the class of trees called elms.)

An indefinite article is often used to identify people as members of any described group. It is always used with professions.

> She is studying to be **an** electrical engineer.
> (The subject *she* is known. *She* is described in relation to a larger group, the profession *electrical engineer*.)

This usage is similar in meaning to *one of the many*.

6.4.2.3.2 Unmodified subject complement

When an unknown singular, countable noun is the subject complement and is not post-modified by a prepositional phrase or a relative clause, then it will take an indefinite article.

> That is **a** difficult problem.
> (The subject complement *problem* is pre-modified with the adjective *difficult*, but is not post-modified by a prepositional phrase or relative clause.)

> That is *the* problem that we're trying to solve.
> (The subject complement *problem* is post-modified by the relative clause *that we're trying to solve*, making it definite.)

6.4.2.4 Replacement for the number "one"

In general, "one" is used for counting, while the indefinite articles are used in the situations indicated in sections 6.4.2.1 - 6.4.2.3 above.

An exception to that is in stating numbers that are literally pronounced beginning with the word *one*. Regardless of the magnitude of the number, if it begins with the word *one*, an indefinite article can be substituted. This substitution of **a/an** for *one* is far more common in spoken than in written English.

£1,000,000	one million pounds – or – **a** million pounds
1/3 off	one third off – or – **a** third off
100 miles	one hundred miles – or – **a** hundred miles
1 1/2 hours	one and one half hours – or – one and **a** half hours – or – **an** hour and **a** half

Quiz 4: A versus AN

*Complete the following phrases either with **a** or **an**:*

1) _____ game
2) _____ idol
3) _____ good apple
4) _____ dentist
5) _____ used plate
6) _____ aunt
7) _____ apricot
8) _____ hair
9) _____ horrible job
10) _____ eggplant
11) _____ heir to the throne
12) _____ iceberg
13) _____ intelligent kid
14) _____ incredible woman

*** In the classroom: Indefinite article ***

Many languages do not use articles, and there are not many straightforward rules for their use; this makes the topic of article usage a very difficult one for ESL students to grasp. The topic is also difficult for ESL teachers, particularly in trying to think of situations and contexts in which these words are used or omitted, or trying to simplify rules to make this subject memorable for students. The best way to approach articles is to present them thematically, in context. For example, omitting the indefinite article *a* before professions is a typical student mistake. ESL learners may tend to say ~~I am student~~ instead of *I am a student*. When teaching professions at a beginner level, drill as many examples of professions as possible and students will be far more likely to acquire the structure.

Another very common problem with articles is their pronunciation. Articles are unstressed words – they do not usually carry a full vowel sound. They should be pronounced with the *schwa* sound (an unstressed, short, light, *uh* sound), not the full-length syllables *ei*, *ahn* or *thee*. This is very difficult for students to internalize and should be explicitly practiced to give them the feeling for the correct rhythm of English.

6.4.3 Zero article

The absence of an article preceding a noun is not the default position; it is a grammatical choice with its own set of rules. This usage is known as **zero article**. Zero article generally indicates that the noun is indefinite (proper nouns are an exception). Zero article indicates non-specific or unknown occurrences of nouns. This usage is for plural countable nouns or uncountable nouns. The rules for using zero article are similar to those for indefinite articles **a** and **an**, but for plural and uncountable nouns.

Zero article is the appropriate choice for uncountable or plural nouns that are undefined or that represent the general idea of the head noun. Zero article may also be used to represent an undifferentiated occurrence of a countable noun such that its sense becomes the same as that of an uncountable noun.

In the examples below, the symbol ø indicates zero article.

Circumstance where a noun takes zero article:	Examples
Undefined:	Eliza heard ø voices. The voices were familiar. (On the first mention, the plural noun voices is undefined. After the first mention, the voices under discussion are understood.)
General idea:	It was a task laden with ø futility. (The nature of the futility is undefined; it is futility in general.)
Non-specific, undifferentiated:	Charles first went to ø college at the age of 15. (Not a particular college, but the concept or generalized institution of college.)

Proper nouns are viewed as definite; they are a specific occurrence of a noun. In spite of this, with the exception of some place names which take the definite article *(See 6.4.1.5.1 Proper place names that take the definite article)* and some cases where plurals are possible, proper nouns take the zero article usage.

> ø Microsoft is expanding in ø China.
> ø Edward just met ø Professor Watkins.

Quiz 5: Correct the sentences (articles)

Correct the sentences and account for your choices.

1) I studied the history at college.
2) I come from a small town in United States.
3) Telephone was invented by Alexander Bell.
4) That's good place to meet your friends.
5) The love is in the air.
6) British Isles are worth visiting in summer.
7) Gabito was famous tango dancer.
8) Last night was most amazing night I have ever had in my life.
9) Did you see Tower of London when you visited England?
10) Did you notice a girl that was standing outside the pub was crying?

Quiz 6: Fill in the blanks (articles)

*Read these paragraphs and complete the blanks with **a**, **an**, **the**, or **zero article (ø)**. There could be more than one answer.*

Paragraph A
(1) _____ deserts tend to occur in two belts that circle (2) _____ globe. Both (3) _____ Northern and Southern Hemispheres have this belt located between 15 and 35 degrees latitude, roughly centered over (4) _____ Tropic of Cancer and (5) _____ Tropic of Capricorn. This is no accident. (6) _____ sun is more directly overhead (7) _____ equatorial region so it receives (8) _____ most intense sunlight, and this solar energy heats (9) _____ air. Hot air has two important qualities: it can hold enormous quantities of moisture, and it rises up into (10) _____ atmosphere.
Source: http://www.nps.gov/archive/moja/mojadewd.htm Mojave National Preserve World Deserts

Paragraph B
It is not wrong to love (1) _____ children. But (2) _____ parents should learn how to love them. Whenever (3) _____ children go astray, wittingly or unwittingly, parents should hasten to correct their faults and bring them to (4) _____ right path. (5) _____ obligations of parents do not end with providing (6) _____ food, schooling and (7) _____ knowledge of (8) _____ worldly matters. (9) _____ children should also be provided with (10) _____ right values. They should not be made to think that (11) _____ acquisition of (12) _____ wealth is (13) _____ be-all and end-all of (14) _____ life.
Source: http://www.saibaba.ws/teachings1/saitipstoparents.htm

*** In the classroom: Articles ***

Many commonly-used phrases seem to go counter to the basic rules that students are most likely to learn about the use of articles. Countable nouns (like *school* or *plane*) can be used in their singular forms in such a way as to be essentially non-differentiable and effectively uncountable. They suggest the concept, or institution, but not any specific occurrence. Common countable nouns that take this undifferentiated, uncountable sense are institutions (school, prison), meals (breakfast, lunch, dinner) in a nonspecific context, and transportation methods, when preceded by the preposition *by*.

> She prefers to travel by ø taxi.
> (The noun *taxi* here is a concept of a travel mode; neither a specific, known taxi (definite) nor a possible single taxi (indefinite) that is a member of the population of taxis is meant here. The preposition *by* is used in these constructions for modes of transportation.)
>
> Suzette always has an apple with ø lunch.
> (The noun *lunch* here is the idea of the midday meal, not any specific, known or possible individual occurrence of it, and not in any particular place or circumstance.)

Another common point of confusion for English students is the definite or indefinite nature of the noun *time*. This noun can be countable or uncountable, definite or indefinite. The essential classroom elements for tackling this problem are providing context and giving plenty of opportunities to practise.

Shelley should have cleaned up, but she didn't have ø time.
(Indefinite, uncountable time: she didn't have time of any type.)

Shelley should have cleaned up, but she didn't have **the** time.
(Definite, uncountable time: she may have had time for other things, but not time specifically for cleaning up. There is an implied infinitival phrase when **the** is used: she didn't have the time (to clean up).)

Differentiate for students the differences between countable *time* (a good time, good times, happy times) and uncountable *time* (wasting time, standard time). Provide them with clear situational contexts for very common uses, including such standard questions as *Do you have the time?* and *What time is it?*

*** *You can teach determiners* ***

There is a great variety of material on the Internet and in ESL grammar books to practise the use of determiners. However, most of those resources are based on studying the rules in isolation and providing practice by doing rote exercises. Repetitive activities are valid and useful; however, when students want to express themselves more freely in spoken or written form, most of the time they forget the rules for using determiners.

The following suggested activities related to determiners are presented thematically, making the rules a bit more memorable for ESL students.

Articles *a* and *an* before professions

Grammar: What is his/her job? What does he/she do?
He is a dentist. She is an accountant.
(Personal pronouns are also presented: I, you, we, they)
Functional language: Asking and answering questions about occupations/professions.

At a true beginner level, present the question and the answer using pictures of different professions and occupations. Drill the questions as well as the answers to make the presentation more meaningful.

Teacher: Look at all these people in this town. They all have interesting jobs. Look at this lady. She is a doctor. (Pointing at the picture of a doctor, the teacher gets the students to repeat the sentence *She is a doctor*.)

The same procedure is done with the other jobs in the picture.

This is a good oral exercise to practise vocabulary on jobs, the indefinite articles *a* and *an* and possessive determiners:

> What is *his/her/your* job? I am *an* anthropologist.

The simple present tense of the verb *work* can also be practised, to review tense structure as well as vocabulary and the use of the articles *a* and *an*:

> What *does she do*? She *works* as *a* teacher.

Talking and asking about interesting/challenging jobs and occupations
Grammar: Articles *a* and *an* with jobs; *the* with superlatives
Vocabulary: Jobs and occupations; descriptive adjectives
Structure: I am a/an (job). It is the most (interesting/boring/challenging) job to me.
Level: Low intermediate +

Using the personalization technique, have students talk about their jobs and occupations with their classmates. Encourage students to keep on talking about their jobs and whether they like them or not. Students can also discuss the most interesting, challenging or dangerous types of jobs.

The typical line of questioning from the teacher would include: What do people do? What jobs are the most (interesting, challenging, dangerous) jobs? Why? What do people have to do in that job? What qualifications or skills do you need for that job?

Articles *a* and *an* for singular, countable objects and *zero article* for plural objects
Grammar: What is in your bag?
            I have a wallet, a USB, a pen, keys and a notebook in my bag.
Functional language: Talking about possessions; identifying objects.
Level: Beginner +

This is a good oral activity to practise singular nouns with indefinite articles and plural nouns with zero article. The teacher's bag and its contents can be used to involve the students in this activity.

> Teacher: This is my bag. It is full of things. Do you know what is in my bag? Look. (The teacher starts taking things out of the bag and names them one by one, using full sentences.)
> I have <u>keys</u>. How many keys do you see? (That question not only involves the students in the activity but also draws their attention to the rule of zero article with plural nouns.)
> I also have <u>a USB</u>. (This is a good example for showing the use of the indefinite article *a* before the sound /j/.)
> Look, I have something else. Can you guess? (The teacher has the students guess the object to involve them in the activity as well as show their previous knowledge on the topic.)

Be sure to reinforce that the article *a* is pronounced with the unstressed *schwa* sound, not with the dipthong /ei/.

Variation: Use other settings like the classroom or office. The answers to the following questions can be used to develop students' listening, speaking and writing skills. To make the activity more communicative, pair the students up.

> Teacher: Discuss with your classmates the following questions. Tell them everything that is in a room at home, or in your office. Listen carefully and take notes. Then share your notes with the class.

Variation: Add elements to the tasks that require the use of quantifiers for countable and uncountable nouns: Play a guessing game, *What is there in your bag?* to make the topic more communicative and memorable.

> T: What is there in your bag? Let's guess.
> S1: Is there a wallet?   S: Yes, there is a wallet.
> S2: Is there any tissue?   S: No, I have no tissue.
> S3: Are there any coins?   S: I have some coins.

To reinforce the structure and get the students to practise it further, the teacher can have the students say what they remember about what is in someone else's bag:

> S1: Marie has a wallet and some coins but she has no tissue.

Determiners, articles and quantifiers plus vocabulary related to food
Grammar: There are some carrots. There aren't any potatoes. There is a knife.
Functional language: Describing pictures and classifying objects/food
Level: Beginner +

Material: It will be useful to find or draw a picture of a person in the kitchen with many ingredients and utensils on a counter or table. To practise the structures orally, students describe the picture as in the examples above.

The primary purpose of the activity is oral production of descriptions. It may help to review the target structures first. Before the main speaking activity, the teacher may choose to insert a gap-filling activity in which students must fill in the blanks with the corresponding determiners. An activity of this type can help to reinforce structure and usage before students begin using the forms independently.

> Example:
> Fill in the gaps with the following words: *a, an, the, some, any,* and *lots*. Write X if no article or determiner is necessary.
>
> I went to the supermarket and I bought _____ of food. My fridge is full now. Look! There is _____ lettuce*. There are _____ of apples. I love red apples! I have _____ milk*, but I do not have _____ butter. I forgot to buy _____ butter. I also have _____ lemon, and _____ bottle of orange juice. I love _____ vegetables very much, so I bought _____ carrots*, _____ of potatoes, and _____ beans*.

(The nouns marked with * can either be preceded by zero article or the quantifier *some*.)

Zero article when referring to cities, towns, most countries, numbers, times and means of transport

Grammar: How long does it take to go from (Toronto to Vancouver by train)?
It takes (3 days, 14 hours and 42 minutes)
How far is it from (Toronto to Barrie)? It is 100 km.

Functional language: Talking and asking about time and distance using the simple present tense

Level: Beginner to low intermediate

Provide students with information on time and distances between cities or towns they are familiar with. A bus or train schedule from the Internet or any local station would work well. Have students find the information requested. This can be done as a meaningful drill to practise the structure as well as fluency, in this way:

Student 1 has the schedule with all the information and Student 2 is the customer who is planning a trip to any of the places on the list.

S1: Can I help you?
S2: Yes, please. How long does it take to go from Toronto, Ontario to Vancouver in British Columbia?
S1: It takes 3 days, 14 hours and 42 minutes by train.
S2: How far is it from Toronto to Vancouver?
S1: It is about 3360 kilometres.

Train schedule

Leaving from	Arriving at	Duration	Distance
Toronto, Ontario 22:00 on Mar 12	Vancouver, British Columbia 09:42 on Mar 16	3 d 14 h 42 m	3360 km
Vancouver, British Columbia 20:30 on Mar 12	Jasper, Alberta 16:00 on Mar 13	18 hrs 30 mins	536 km

Variation: Using the same or a similar chart, beginner students can practise asking questions using the simple present and zero article for cities or towns like this:

S1: What time does the train leave Toronto?
S2: It leaves at 10 p.m.
S1: What time does it arrive in Vancouver?
S2: It arrives at 9:42 a.m., three days later.

Zero article when referring to cities, towns, days of the week. Article *the* when referring to parts of the day, uniqueness and superlatives

Gap filling activities are useful for practising articles. They can be created from texts of various themes, by deleting the determiners, articles and quantifiers that students have already learned. Below is an example of text taken from an Internet source describing the routes, days and cities of the train called *The Canadian*.

Fill in the gaps with the articles *the*, *a*, *an*, or write *X* for zero article

___Canadian, Toronto-Vancouver

Leaving _____ Toronto, _____ Canadian crosses _____ northern Ontario, _____ vast western plains and _____ Rockies, finishing its journey in ____ Vancouver on _____ Pacific coast. You will be treated to some of _____ most beautiful landscapes in _____ Canada. _____ Canadian currently departs from _____ Toronto on _____ Tuesdays, ____ Thursdays and ____ Saturdays in _____ evening and from ___ Jasper on ___ Mondays, ____ Thursdays and ____ Saturdays. Beginning on ____ December 1, ____ Canadian will depart from ____ Toronto on ____ Tuesdays and ____ Saturdays.

Answers:
The Canadian, Toronto-Vancouver

Leaving X Toronto, *The* Canadian crosses X northern Ontario, *the* vast western plains and *the* Rockies, finishing its journey in X Vancouver on *the* Pacific coast. You will be treated to some of *the* most beautiful landscapes in X Canada. *The* Canadian currently departs from X Toronto on X Tuesdays, X Thursdays and X Saturdays in *the* evening and from X Jasper on X Mondays, X Thursdays, and X Saturdays. Beginning on X December 1, *The* Canadian will depart from X Toronto on X Tuesdays, and X Saturdays.

Shopping game

Grammar: articles *a* and *an*; nouns in the singular; simple past tense of *buy* (other tenses can be used)
Vocabulary: objects (concrete singular nouns)
Level: Beginner

Give out a list of items like the one in the example below. Students use those words to make sentences, adding one item at a time. Cue cards and pictures can be used to make the drill more challenging for beginner students.

This drill is an activity to practise the indefinite articles *a* and *an* as well as practising vocabulary, intonation and fluency.

radio – MP3 player – computer – atlas – compass
bag – map – food processor – picture

S1: Yesterday I bought a bag.
S2: Yesterday I bought a bag and a computer.
S3: Yesterday I bought a bag, a computer and an atlas.
S4: Yesterday I bought a bag, a computer, an atlas and a compass.
And so on until the list is finished.

Variation for intermediate levels and above: Review article usage in a lesson that focuses primarily on word stress and linking: articles and conjunctions are unstressed, so the rhythm of these sentences is dictated clearly and consistently by the nouns.

Talking and asking about sports and hobbies
Grammar: Zero article

Vocabulary: Leisure activities, sports and hobbies
Level: Beginner to low intermediate

Provide students with a list of activities. Make sure the nouns in the example list do not require the use of articles or any other determiner. Students must choose which activities they like doing or the hobbies they have. To make the activity more appropriate for a low intermediate level, do not guide them with any list of hobbies; instead, have them talk as freely as they can.

>Example:
>What hobbies do you have? What do you do in your spare time?
>In my spare time I play...
>.... chess
>... soccer
>... poker
>... tennis
>.... golf

To provide further practice on the theme of sports and hobbies with zero article, the teacher may ask:

>What sports or activities do people do?
>Possible answers: swimming, cycling, horseback riding, car racing, fencing, hockey, tennis, soccer, etc.

Variation:
Keep the same questions (having the students talk about their hobbies or activities in their spare time), but make sure that the nouns used in the sentences are in the plural form and the students do not add any article or determiner.

>Example:
>What hobbies do you have? What do you do in your spare time?
>I like reading ...
>... books
>... magazines
>... e-mails
>... (other)
>I like collecting
>.... stamps
>.... coins
>.... postcards
>... (other)
>
>I like....
>.... playing instruments
>.... watching movies
>.... going to concerts
>... (other)

Extension: Add countable nouns for the equipment used in sports to practise articles. The teacher may provide a list, for a matching activity – or higher-level students may generate the answers independently.

Grammar: articles *a* and *an*; zero article used with sports
Vocabulary: sports and equipment
Level: Beginner/low intermediate

Example matching activity:
What do you use to play hockey?	A bat
What do you use to play tennis?	A club
What do you use to play golf?	A stick
What do you use to play baseball?	A racquet

Talking and asking about subjects at school

Grammar: Zero article (academic subjects); article *the* with superlatives
Vocabulary: Subjects at school (history, geography, etc.)
Structure: Simple present and simple past; comparatives
Level: Low intermediate +

First, brainstorm different types of subjects people study at school and record them on the board. For example: Math, Physics, History, Philosophy, Chemistry, English, Literature, Music, Art, Information Technology, Biology.

Have the students group the subjects according to level of interest by categorizing them as *the most interesting/boring/challenging subjects at school* to help them prepare for a conversation on subjects and their preferences for those subjects.

Depending on the level, different tenses can be used. See sample questions for discussion:

> What subjects do you study/did you study at school?
> Which subject do you like/did you like the most/the least?
> Compare subjects at school. Which subject is the most challenging, difficult, easy, boring, useful, fun, etc..?

A variation with lists of superlatives: The *–th* sound is difficult for most non-native English speakers. Add a *-th* pronunciation element, both voiced and voiceless. Make a list of, say, 20 things in some sort of numbered sequential order, then do an information gap which requires questions-and-answer sequences using both *–th* sounds (the voiced sound in *the* and *-th* at the end of ordinals): What is the fourth most boring subject? The fourth most boring subject is chemistry.

Speaking skill: Interviews/surveys

Grammar: Using determiners (all, most, many, one, two, three, etc.) and quantifier phrases (half of, a lot of, fifty percent of); asking questions using various structures and tenses
Vocabulary: Varies by theme
Level: Any level

Provide students with a theme of conversation. Have students think of questions that they can ask their classmates in order to find out what their classmates think about this topic. They have to come up with at least 10 questions on the topic. Then pair them up so that the students interview their classmates and get information from them. At the end of the survey or interview, the students have to report their findings. They can report them orally or in writing, using the following structures with determiners:

    Most students in the class (think that ......)
    Three students (said they like ....)
    Only one person (does not ....)
    All of the men (have had ....)
    Half of the class (likes the idea of ....)
    None of my classmates (went to.........)

This activity can be done as a follow-up activity to many of the activities in this section, particularly after those activities which require a discussion on a certain topic.

7 Adverbs

Adverbs are words that can modify verbs, adjectives and other adverbs. An adverb may also modify a clause or an entire sentence. Occasionally, adverbs can modify or seem to modify nouns and noun phrases. They can be found in different positions in a sentence depending on what they are modifying. Some phrases and clauses can function as adverbs; they are called adverbials. Like adjectives, adverbs add meaning to a sentence, making it more precise.

In the following examples, the words in bold are adverbs, which are modifying the italicized words.

Modifying a verb:

He *behaves* **carelessly**.   He *returned* **today** from his vacation.

Modifying an adjective:

This is **extremely** *dangerous*.   Pat's house is **much** *nicer* than mine.

Modifying another adverb:

You should talk **more** *loudly*.   You **always** arrive *late*!

Modifying a clause /sentence:

He works hard **only** *when the boss is nearby*.
Fortunately, *they decided to go on with the project*.
Joan will never get back to school, **sadly**.

An adverb can sometimes modify a noun or noun phrase, as in the examples below:

The play **yesterday** was fabulous.
Only *her hairdresser* knows for sure.

Quiz 1: Adverbs modifying different parts of speech

Find the adverbs in the following sentences. Identify what they are modifying.

1) The phone was temporarily disconnected.
2) Would you like to meet early?
3) They haven't had supper yet.
4) I am extremely happy.
5) They hardly visit their friends.
6) Sometimes, I do not understand why David is so pessimistic.

7.1 Adverb forms

Although most adverbs do not have any special form, some suffixes are associated with adverbs.

-ly	-ward(s)	-wise	-long
lovingly	homeward(s)	edgewise	headlong
happily	outward(s)	likewise	overlong

Ryan sang **happily** all night.
He plunged **headlong** into the river.
The storm is believed to be heading **eastward**.

***In the classroom: Identifying adverbs ***

The most common problems ESL students have with adverbs is confusing them with adjectives. Here are some examples of the types of adverbs students may have problems with:

Adverbs and adjectives ending in –ly

The suffix –ly is most commonly connected to adverbs. But not all words ending in –ly are adverbs. For example, the word *friendly*, which is an adjective, is often confused with an adverb of manner.

The simplest way to help ESL students differentiate –ly adverbs and –ly adjectives is to look at the root of the word (without the –ly ending).

If -ly is added to an adjective, it turns the word into an adverb:

adjective + –ly = adverb:

Adjective	Adverb
careless	carelessly
true	truly
surprising	surprisingly
hopeful	hopefully

Note: Adjectives ending in –ly do not form adverbs by adding –ly: ~~friendlily~~

If –ly is added to a noun, it turns the word into an adjective:

noun + -ly = adjective:

Noun	Adjective
friend	friendly
love	lovely
cost	costly
neighbour	neighbourly

Another way to differentiate adverbs from adjectives is by focusing on the word that is being modified and its function in the sentence. If a word ending in –ly , –wise, –ward, or –long modifies a noun, it almost certainly is an adjective, since adverbs rarely modify nouns.

Same or similar form

Some adverbs have the same form as adjectives. They are sometimes called flat adverbs. The following are some of the adverbs that are included in this group:

daily   early   fast   hard   high   late   long   low   short   straight

This bread is **hard**. (adjective modifies *bread*)
I worked **hard** to get it. (adverb modifies *worked*)

To help students identify adverbs and adjectives of this type, guide them toward determining what the word is modifying.

Some adverbs have two forms, each with a different meaning:

He is **deeply** in love with Sue.	(very)
Do not go **deep** into your thoughts.	(a long way down)
They arrived **late**.	(not early)
They have been studying hard **lately**.	(recently)
She works **hard**.	(with effort)
She **hardly** works these days.	(almost never)
You can attend **free** for the first month.	(without payment)
During the first month you can attend **freely**.	(without restriction)

Introduction and practice of these adverbs in context is necessary to help students distinguish the gradations of meaning.

Quiz 2: Adverbs or adjectives

Identify whether the words in bold are adverbs or adjectives.

1. He made a **lengthwise** cut along the belly of the fish to clean it before cooking.
2. The rocket turned **earthward** soon after being launched.
3. The rocket started an **earthward** descent soon after being launched.
4. Marco is a **lovely** old man, full of energy and joy.
5. His **daily** show can now be watched online.
6. You can watch his program **daily**.
7. Have you been waiting **long**?
8. Will you cut **short** your holiday if it is necessary?

*** In the classroom: Well *or* good? ***

Learners often misuse the words **well** and **good**. Their meanings are similar, which contributes to the confusion. However, their functions in sentences are different. **Well** is an adverb, and can also be an adjective. **Good** is always an adjective.

I'm enjoying this pie. It is **good**.
(predicative adjective after the linking verb *is*, modifying the pronoun *it*)
That's a **good** movie. You should see it.
(attributive adjective modifying the noun *movie*)

He's been behaving **well**.
(adverb modifying the verb phrase *has been behaving*)
How would you like your steak? **Well** done, please.
(adverb modifying the participial adjective *done*)

Well can also be an adjective. In the sentences *I am **well*** and *You do not look **well***, it is a predicative adjective placed after the linking verbs *am* and *look*, respectively. The appropriate choice of predicative adjective – **well** or **good** – often depends on the linking verb. To describe one's general condition, several linking verbs are possible, the most common being *feel*, *look* and *be*. The meaning of **well** after these linking verbs is always *in good health*. But **good** has a different sense with different verbs:

      I feel **good**.   (generally positive condition, including physical health)
      I am **good**.   (my behaviour or talents are at a high standard)
      I look **good**.   (my appearance is attractive)

The use of **good** as a predicative adjective is increasingly used informally as a substitute for **fine** or **satisfied** after the linking verb *be* when talking about personal condition. This usage is strictly informal, as in: *How are you? I'm **good**.* or *Would you like more? No, I'm **good**.* Students may hear these informal uses among native speakers and further question their comprehension of these points as taught in the classroom. Avoid these uses in the classroom unless they come up as questions from students.

7.1.1 Spelling

An adverb is often formed by adding the suffix *–ly* to the end of an adjective. There are some basic spelling rules when adding *–ly* to adjectives to form adverbs:

Rule	Examples
1. If the adjective ends in *–y*, change the *–y* to *–i*, then add *–ly* (except one-syllable adjectives)	easy → easily happy → happily shy → shyly
2. When an adjective ends in multiple consonants + silent *e*, drop the *–e*, then add *–ly*.	possible → possibly gentle → gently
3. If the adjective ends in a single consonant + silent *e*, do not drop the *–e*, then add *–ly*.	extreme → extremely sure → surely
4. If the adjective ends in *–ll*, add only *–y*.	dull → dully full → fully
5. If the adjective ends in *–ic*, add *–ally*.	frantic → frantically automatic → automatically
6. All other cases: add *–ly*.	fiscal → fiscally spry → spryly warm → warmly

Some exceptions: true → truly, due → duly, whole → wholly, gay → gaily

7.2 Adverbials

Adverbial is the name given to the adverbial function, a function that can be realized by a single word (**home**), an adverbial phrase (**in the pool**) or an adverbial clause (**where I was born**). It is the comprehensive name for all combinations of words that can function as an adverb, including single-word adverbs. In this text, the term *adverb* refers to single-word adverbials. The word *adverbial* is used to refer to adverbial phrases and clauses.

Let's go **home**.
(**home** is a noun whose adverbial function is that of an adverb of place)

I saw him swimming **in the pool**.
(**in the pool** is a prepositional phrase functioning as an adverbial of place)

I have always lived **where I was born**.
(**where I was born** is an adverbial clause of place)

7.2.1 Adverbial phrases

Adverbial phrases (phrases acting as adverbs) can be of four types: noun phrases, prepositional phrases, infinitive phrases and compound adverbial phrases.

Noun phrases (phrases with a noun as the head) acting as adverbs always refer to time. They are also called temporal noun phrases. In the examples below, the full phrase is in bold, and the noun head of the phrase is italicized.

>I met him **this *morning***.
>We will be flying to Rome **next *week***.

Prepositional phrases (phrases with a preposition as the head) acting as adverbs refer to place, purpose, manner or time. They modify the verb of the sentence. In the examples below, the full phrase is in bold, and the prepositional head of the phrase is italicized. *(See 9.2.2.2 Adverbial prepositional phrases)*

>Suzuka went ***to* the movies**.
>She decided to see a movie ***for* distraction**.
>She traveled ***with* determination**.
>The movie started ***at* 9:15**.

Infinitive phrases (phrases with an infinitive verb form as the head) acting as adverbs refer to purpose. They are also called infinitives of purpose. Some infinitive phrases can also refer to outcome. In the examples below, the full phrase is in bold, and the infinitive form of the verb is italicized. *(See 13.6.1 Acting as adverbs)*

>Paulette listens to the radio every day **to *improve* her English listening skills**.

>I walked in **to *discover* a break-in**.

Purpose can also be expressed by the prepositional phrase *in order*, followed by a to-infinitive. (The full structure has an infinitive phrase inside a prepositional phrase.)

>**In order *to avoid* rush-hour traffic**, you should leave now.

Compound adverbial phrases are composed of two or more distinct adverbs. They refer to frequency and answer the question *how often*.

>We **almost never** go to the theatre.
>I **scarcely ever** discuss politics with strangers.

7.2.2 Adverbial clauses

An adverbial clause is part of a complex sentence. A complex sentence is made up of a main clause and one or more subordinate clauses. A subordinate adverbial clause generally modifies the verb of the main clause. (For more on clauses, consult the *You Can Teach Grammar* companion web site.) Adverbial clauses are introduced by subordinating conjunctions (also called adverbial subordinators) and they can refer to time, place, manner, reason, comparison, condition, contrast, result and purpose. *(See 10.3.3 Subordinating conjunctions and 10.3.4 Other linkers and transition signals)*

> Paul was watching TV **while I was making a delicious meal**.
> **If I see her**, I'll give her your phone number.
> **Although I was exhausted**, I waited for him.

7.2.3 Adverbs, adverbial particles and prepositions

Adverbial particles are adverbs that are considered to be dependent on the verbs that they are used with. Their modifying function as adverbs is joined to the verbs they are modifying; they do not carry full and clear meaning on their own. Many of these adverbial particles can also function as prepositions. The main difference between these adverbs and prepositions is that prepositions will have an object, while adverbs will not.

> She ran *across the road* to meet him.

Across is a preposition in this case because it is the head of the prepositional phrase that contains the object *the road.*

> Terry's voice doesn't *come* **across** well.

In this second example, **across** is not a preposition since it is not heading a prepositional phrase and it does not have an object. It is modifying the verb *come* as an adverb of manner. The word **across** on its own does not clearly convey the intended meaning. The combination of **across** with the verb is the necessary condition for the full meaning: in this case, *come across* means *project* or *leave an impression*.

Some adverbs or adverbial particles that fall into this category are:

above	aside	below	near	past
about	away	by	off	round
across	back	down	on	through
ahead	backward	forward	out	under
along	before	in	over	up
around	behind	home		

Quiz 3: Adverb or preposition
Identify whether the underlined word is functioning as an adverb or a preposition.
1) You can see the moon above the trees.
2) The toddler fell off the bed.
3) Do you think he wants to go out?
4) Please sit down.
5) We couldn't get through the gate.
6) Can I look inside?
7) They slept all through the night.
8) The book is suitable for children aged eight and above.

*** In the classroom: Adverbs and prepositions ***

Many words that are prepositions can also function as adverbs, and this can be a source of confusion for students. A way to distinguish between them is to remember that a preposition must be followed by its object. This is not the case for an adverb. In the following examples, the word *outside* is shown in its two functions: as an adverb and as a preposition.

> Let's go outside. (functioning as an adverb of place; no object required)
> Let's go outside the room. (the noun phrase *the room* is the object of the preposition *outside*).

The prepositional phrase *outside the room* functions as an adverbial of place in the second sentence. For learners, the terminology is confusing: a preposition introduces a prepositional phrase which functions as an adverbial. When covering this type of material with students, state clearly if the focus is on the words and their functions or on sentences and their parts.

Another exercise that can help students with these concepts is a kind of puzzle using sentence fragments. Students can be provided with a sentence that is cut up into words or phrases (depending on the level of the students) and they have to put the pieces in the correct order to create a sentence. This can help students to see where the prepositions and the adverbs are, and to identify any pieces that must follow them in the sentence.

7.3 Adverbs and adverbials classified by meaning

An adverb can be classified according to meaning (semantic classification). It can sometimes be classified based on the word, phrase or clause it modifies. Some adverbs can have more than one meaning or classification, which results in placing the adverbs in more than one category.

There is not complete agreement on the semantic classifications of adverbs. There are many extensive lists with exhaustive subcategories. To facilitate the easy comprehension of the different types of adverbs and how they are used, adverbs have been grouped into six major semantic categories in this chapter: manner, place, time, purpose, negation, and degree. Possible subcategories are mentioned in each section, but most are not given further attention in this text.

Position in a sentence

For clarity of meaning, an adverb or adverbial should be placed as closely as possible to the part of the sentence that it is modifying. The broad rules for placement are:
- single-word adverbs are placed before the adjectives they modify
- adverbial phrases and clauses are placed after the adjectives they modify
- adverbs and adverbials are placed directly after the verbs they modify

> That plate is **rather** *hot*. *(adverb preceding adjective)*
> That plate is *hot* **to the touch**. *(adverbial following adjective)*
> Charlie *walks* **briskly**. *(adverb following verb)*
> Charlie *walks* **with brisk strides**. *(adverbial following verb)*

If there is an object after the verb, then the adverb follows the object.

> Charlie walks *his dog* **briskly**.

There are variations to this rule for each type of adverb. The variations are given in sections 7.3.1 - 7.3.6.

7.3.1 Adverbs of manner

These adverbs provide information on the manner in which something happens. They answer the question *How?* The majority of the adverbs that end in *–ly* are adverbs of manner. Some subcategories associated with the adverbs of manner are *means*, *instrument* and *process*. No matter how they are classified, they all answer the question *How?*

Examples:
Adverbs: **well**   **badly**   **hard**   **interestingly**   **fast**   **wholly**

> You can speak English **well**.
> She plays sports **badly**.

Examples:
Adverbials: **in a crazy way**   **with a hammer**   **on tiptoes**   **like Sony does**

> She ran around **like a chicken with its head cut off**.
> You can cook artichokes **however you decide**.

Position in a sentence – adverbs of manner

Adverbs of manner are especially flexible as regards placement in a sentence. An adverb of manner may be placed before the main verb. This placement puts additional emphasis on the adverb as the most important feature.

> She **hungrily** ate the apples.
> (more emphasis on the style of the action)

If an adverbial of manner is given placement before the main verb, it is separated from the rest of the sentence with commas and modifies the whole sentence, not just the verb.

Mark and Sue, **without knowing**, bought the same car.

Adverbs may also be placed at the very beginning of a sentence. This placement sets the scene for the rest of the sentence. It modifies the entire sentence. In this placement, the adverb (or adverbial) is usually followed by a comma.

Hungrily, she ate the apples.

There are some adverbs of manner which are less flexible: **well**, **badly**, **hard** and **fast**, for example, are always placed after the verb.

He behaved **well**, so his teachers congratulated him.

Quiz 4: Placement of adverbs of manner

Put the words in the correct order, based on the intended meaning described in parentheses.

1) she the find didn't beach interestingly amusing
   (the whole situation is interesting)
2) fast Billy cleared table the
   (he did it in a speedy manner)
3) sleep went and book to the closed Nick reluctantly
   (he wished he could continue reading but he had to turn off the lights)
4) lashed in way crazy the out stranger a
   (he did it crazily)

7.3.2 Adverbs of place

These adverbs provide information about the place of action. They answer the question *Where?*

Examples:
Adverbs: **ahead   back   forward   near   outside   inside**
somewhere   there   upstairs   downstairs   underground   abroad

We lived **there** last month.
Is he **upstairs**?

Examples:
Adverbials: **at home   where people go   on the table   at school**

We live **at 67 Durham Ave**.
The books are **on the table**.
He stayed **where he was**.

Position in a sentence – adverbs of place

Adverbs and adverbials of place may be situated at the head of a sentence, separated from the rest of the sentence by commas. This usage sets the scene for the rest of the sentence.

> **At the table**, he drinks his coffee.
> (emphasis is on the fact that whatever follows happens at the table)

In rarer usage, the adverbial of place may be situated – separated by commas – between the verb and the object. This usage is poetic or literary in style. It is not recommended for everyday use.

> He drinks, **at the table**, his coffee.
> (very strong emphasis on this action taking place at the table)

If two adverbials of place occur consecutively in the same sentence, the smaller place precedes the larger.

> Let's meet **at my apartment** *in Toronto*.

These adverbials may be separated in the sentence, but only the larger place can be positioned at the front of the sentence:

> **In Toronto**, let's meet **at my apartment**.

Quiz 5: Adverbials of place

In each of the following sentences, identify the adverbials of place and their forms (adverb, prepositional phrase, etc).

1) Let's take a vacation abroad.
2) I don't know why he can't just sleep here instead of going to a hotel.
3) We were in the pool when the storm began.
4) Please deposit the cheque wherever he asked you to do so.

7.3.3 Adverbs of time

Adverbs and adverbials of time provide information on the time something happens. The broad category of adverbs of time can be subdivided. The most common usage – time-when – is given first, followed by the categories of time duration, time frequency and relative time.

7.3.3.1 Time-when

These adverbs answer the question *When?* They can be single words, noun phrases, prepositional phrases or adverbial clauses.

Examples:
Adverbs: **early**   **late**   **soon**   **now**   **tomorrow**

> I'm going to get a new TV set **soon**.
> You are **now** speaking more fluently.

Examples:
Adverbials: **last week**   **at the end of the day**   **when she arrived**

> I met him **last Tuesday**.
> Let's meet **at 7 o'clock**.

Jill went to the library **while she was waiting for her friend to come**.

Position in a sentence – adverbs of time-when

The adverbials of time-when are generally placed at the end of the sentence. However, they can be placed in other positions to give a different emphasis.

In the examples below, the facts contained in the sentences are identical. The major meaning of the sentence is changed by the placement of the adverb only. When the adverb of time is moved forward in a sentence, it places additional emphasis on the fact that the event will transpire at that particular time. Otherwise, the time element is secondary to the main verb as a point of emphasis.

I'm going to buy the tickets **tomorrow**.
(the main point is buying the tickets)

Tomorrow I'm going to buy the tickets.
(emphasis is on when the action will take place)

I am going to tell you the truth **now**.
(emphasis is on the main action)

I *am now* going to tell you the truth.
(stress is on the idea that the time is somehow unique for this event)

7.3.3.2 Time-frequency

These adverbs provide information on *how often* or *at what intervals* something happens, and can be used in the present, past and future tenses.

Examples:
Adverbs: always sometimes frequently habitually regularly repeatedly often
occasionally rarely

I **rarely** ate fish when I was a child.
He **usually** finishes work at 5.

Examples:
Adverbials: every Sunday
three times a week   every other day   almost never
every time it rains   hardly ever

During the summer, teenagers can get full time jobs.
Every Tuesday, he arrives late.
They studied English **as often as they could**.

*** In the classroom: Adverbs of frequency and their meanings ***

Choosing the correct adverb of frequency can be a challenge for learners. Giving students a meaningful method of categorization will help. The two major variables in the meanings of different frequency adverbs are implication (positive or negative) and level of frequency. The following chart helps to illustrate these concepts.

Table 28: Adverbs of frequency and their meanings

	LOW Frequency			HIGH Frequency
Positive Implication	intermittently occasionally sometimes spasmodically sporadically	commonly frequently largely normally often regularly repeatedly	chiefly generally habitually mostly predominantly primarily regularly typically usually	always constantly continuously
Negative Implication	never not ever	hardly ever infrequently not often rarely scarcely ever seldom	not generally not usually	not always

The outer corners of the grid are actual opposites:
- **sometimes**, **occasionally**, etc. are opposites of **not always**
- **never** is the opposite of **always**

When teaching these adverbs to students, it is useful to appeal to their knowledge of percentages, giving them a point of comparison. For example, **always** would be similar to 100% and **never** would be 0%. The rest of the frequency adverbs can be placed at rough intervals in between those points. Do not teach all of them at the same time; it would be overwhelming for students.

A schedule or monthly planner can be used to teach these adverbs. When an activity appears on every day of the calendar, they can say it **always** happens, when it is less frequent and irregular, it **sometimes** happens, and so on. Making sure these possibly abstract concepts become more concrete is key to preventing problems later when students have to use these adverbs independently.

Position in a sentence – adverbs of time-frequency

Adverbs and adverbials of frequency are usually placed before the main verb.

>She has **often** *come* to the meetings.
>They **sometimes** *get* together after dinner.

However, some of these adverbs can be used at the beginning or at the end of a sentence for emphasis: **usually**, **occasionally**, **sometimes**, **often**, **rarely**, **frequently** and **seldom**.

>**Sometimes** Mary develops a rash on her skin.
>They visit their aunt very **rarely**.

Never, **seldom**, **scarcely** and other similar adverbs denote a negative meaning. When these adverbs are placed at the beginning of a sentence, the word order of the sentence changes: the subject comes after the first (auxiliary) verb. This is called inversion of order. It is the word order of a question. **Seldom** and **scarcely**, however, are not used in questions.

> **Seldom** does she participate in class.
> **Never** have I told her such a lie.

When the main verb is *be*, the position of the adverbs of frequency is as follows:

Adverbs come after *be* in affirmative and negative statements.
> He *is* **usually** late but he *isn't* **always** as late as today.

Adverbs come after the subject of the sentence in interrogative sentences.
> Is *your friend* **always** so funny?

7.3.3.3 Time-duration

Adverbs of duration indicate how long something continues. They answer the question *for what length of time?* (**For** and **since** belong to this category and are discussed in *7.3.3.3.1 Relative time*.)

Examples:
Adverbs: **briefly** **temporarily** **forever** **permanently**

> He has been nagging her **forever**.
> They were **briefly** interrupted.

Examples:
Adverbials: **all day long** **day and night** **for an eternity**

> I have lived here **for three years**.
> She drank the tea **while the baby was kicking**.
> **During the whole class**, I was wishing I could be outside in the sun.

The preposition *during* can also be used to introduce a prepositional phrase that denotes time-when; the distinction is in the wording of the phrases. When *during* pinpoints a period of time that is somehow understood, then it can be the head of a prepositional phrase indicating time-when:

> Tamika always visits her grandmother **during spring break**.

In this example, the length of Tamika's visit is not indicated, only the approximate time at which it occurs.

Position in a sentence – adverbs of time-duration

Time-duration adverbs and adverbials are normally placed at the end of a sentence. When a time adverb or adverbial is placed at the beginning of the sentence, it gives additional emphasis to the duration of the action and is separated from the rest of the sentence by a comma. Certain adverbs of time-duration are placed in the middle of the sentence, immediately after the main verb and before the complement, if any: *permanently, temporarily, briefly, momentarily*.

It was **momentarily** blinding.
The flame burns **permanently** in tribute to his achievements.

7.3.3.3.1 Relative time

Relative time adverbs are a subset of duration adverbs. They are distinguished from standard duration adverbs by the requirement for *two* time references, one related to the other in the context of the sentence. They often require the verb in the main clause to be in the perfective aspect. *(See 11 Verbs and 14 Tenses)* They consist of a limited set of adverbs, and adverbials beginning with *since* and *for*.

Examples:
Adverbs: **still**   **yet**   **already**   **always**

> She hasn't arrived **yet**.
> I have **always** loved eating ice cream.

Examples:
Adverbials: **since she was born**   **since 2007**   **for a hundred days**

> We've been working on this **for ages**.
> I have lived here **since I was a little kid**.

Adverbs of relative time and their meanings

Still is used to express that an event or situation continues to happen at a particular time; it started at a previous point (known or unknown) and it continues at the point in time under discussion. It can be used in present, past and future tenses.

> I **still** work for AMC.
> (started in the past and continues now)
>
> He will **still** have time to take the plane.
> (starting now or in the future and will continue further in the future)
>
> They were **still** being searched for at 5:00 pm yesterday.
> (started in the further past and continued in the more recent past)

Already is used to express an event or situation that happened earlier than expected, or before the time under discussion.

> I am **already** exhausted.
> (expected to happen later or never; it has happened now)
>
> He has **already** seen the movie.
> (happened before now)

Yet is used to express that something has not happened up to a certain time. It gives the implication that the event is expected to happen at a later time.

> Have you filled in the form **yet**?
> (between the time when you could first do it and now)

He hadn't bought the house **yet**.
(between the further past time when it was first possible and the time in the past under discussion)

Yet is generally used in negative and interrogative sentences; however, it can also be found directly before an infinitive to denote an anticipated future start of an action.

They have **yet** to book the banquet hall for their wedding reception.
(between now and an anticipated time in the future)

Position in a sentence – adverbs of relative time

Still is placed before the main verb, but after the verb *be*.

I **still** live in Toronto.   I am **still** in Toronto.

However, for emphasis or to express surprise, for example, **still** can be used immediately after the subject in negative sentences.

He **still** hasn't finished the test! It's been two hours.

Already can be placed before the main verb and after the verb *be*. **Already** can be placed at the beginning or end of a sentence for emphasis.

The storm **already** has extremely high winds.
I've **already** seen it.
He is **already** here.
Already he is teething. He is only 4 months old!
I've seen it **already**.

Yet is placed at the end of the negative statement or question, or before an infinitive in a statement of future anticipated action.

Has he arrived **yet**?
I haven't done it **yet**.
We have **yet** to receive our invitation.

When **yet** is at the beginning of a clause, it functions as a coordinating conjunction meaning *but*. (See 10.3.1 Coordinating conjunctions)

We are in different time zones, *yet* we communicate frequently.

For is placed before a noun or noun phrase. A noun phrase beginning with **for** is most commonly placed at the end of a sentence, though it can also be found at the beginning, separated by a comma, for emphasis on the time.

We've been working on this **for** the last three hours.
For the next five minutes, he will stand as still as a statue.

Since is placed before a noun or noun phrase, or it may head an adverbial clause of relative time. The phrase or clause beginning with **since** is usually placed at the end of a sentence, though it can rarely be found at the beginning, separated by a comma, for particular emphasis on the time. Because of the common use of **since** at the beginning of a sentence to denote purpose or reason, it is best to leave a **since** adverbial at the end.

The Smithson Hat Shop has been in business **since** 1974.

Quiz 6: Adverbs of time

Identify the adverbs and adverbials of time and classify them into their four categories: when, frequency, duration and relative time.

1) Yuki has not come back since the accident happened.
2) I have to return that book to the library soon.
3) Last year, Melissa had twin baby girls.
4) Every time I call, the receptionist tells me he is busy.
5) The web site is temporarily offline for repairs.
6) Ulysses habitually visits his home town.
7) He promised he'd look for her till the end of time.

*** In the classroom: *For and* since ***

For and *since* are prepositions of time introducing an adverbial. They refer to time but in different ways. The preposition *for* denotes duration; it answers the question *How long?* The preposition *since* refers to a point in time; it answers the question *Beginning when? (See 9.3 Meanings of prepositions) Since* can also function as a conjunction introducing an adverbial clause of time. *For* and *since* are usually taught together with the present perfect tense. *(See 14.2.3 Present perfect)*

Milton has worked for IBM **since 2007**.
(adverbial prepositional phrase headed by *since* denoting the beginning of his employment with IBM)

He has been living in Canada **since his parents emigrated there**.
(adverbial clause headed by *since* denoting the beginning of his life in Canada)

Bart had not seen her **for five months**.
(adverbial prepositional phrase headed by *for* denoting the period or length of time during which he had not seen her)

7.3.4 Adverbials of purpose

Adverbials of purpose provide information on the reason something happens. They answer the questions *Why?* or *For what reason?* Adverbials of purpose are virtually always infinitive phrases, prepositional phrases or adverbial clauses of purpose. *(See 13.6.1 Acting as adverbs, 9.2.2 Functions of prepositional phrases and 7.2.2 Adverbial clauses)*

Examples:
Infinitive phrases:	**to exercise to check**	**to register to finish**
Prepositional phrases	**for fun in order to see**	**so as to understand**
Adverbial clauses:	**so I will feel better**	**so that he can find her**

Chester got a new car **to drive to work**.

I received this **for my birthday**.
He drinks **in order to forget**.
Ronald worked hard **so that he could get a promotion**.

Position in a sentence – adverbials of purpose

Adverbials of purpose are generally placed at the end of a sentence. However, they can be placed in other positions to give a different emphasis. In the examples below, the facts contained in the sentences are identical. The major meaning of the sentence is changed by the placement of the adverbial. When the adverbial of purpose is moved forward in a sentence, it places additional emphasis on the purpose of the action. Otherwise, the purpose has secondary emphasis.

Tyson has trained very hard **in order to win this important match**.
(the main point is that he is training hard)

In order to win this important match, Tyson has trained very hard.
(emphasis is on why he has trained so hard)

**** *In the classroom: Order of adverbs and adverbial phrases* ***

There are some simple rules that can help ESL learners to place adverbs and adverbials correctly in sentences. When multiple adverbs or adverbials are used in a single sentence, the usual order is:

manner + place + frequency + time + purpose

I walk **at a fast pace** *every morning* **before work**.
(manner + frequency + time)

Mechanics had to work **hard** *until morning* **to fix the problem**.
(manner + time + purpose)

However, when the verb indicates movement – as in *go, come* and *drive*, for example – this order changes as follows:

place + manner + frequency + time + purpose

I went **to the office** *by bus* **yesterday**.
(place + manner + time)

Variations on order of adverbs

The order of adverbs discussed above can be changed when the speaker wants to emphasize the information in the adverbial. In such cases, adverbs or adverbials can be placed at the beginning of the sentence. When that is done, a comma is required after the adverb or adverbial.

Every afternoon *after class*, Susan played the piano.

When using similar adverbials together, shorter adverbials will be placed before longer adverbials, and more specific adverbials precede more general ones.

Dad takes a brisk walk **before breakfast** *every day*.

Among similar adverbial phrases of the same type (manner, place, frequency), the more specific adverbial phrase comes first:

My grandmother was born **in a sod house** *on the prairie*.
She promised to meet him **for lunch** *next Tuesday*.

7.3.5 Adverbs of assertion

Positive assertion

There is only one common adverb of positive assertion, and that is **yes**. It always modifies the entire sentence or clause, and it is followed by a comma.

Yes, we can.
If you want to know, I'd say that **yes**, it is true.

Negative assertion

The most common adverbs of negative assertion are **no** and **not**. **No** is used to modify an entire sentence or a clause, and it is followed by a comma.

No, I have never seen him before.

Not modifies the main verb of a sentence by being placed after an auxiliary and before the main verb (or right after the verb *be* when it is the main verb). **Not** is often contracted to auxiliary verbs.

I might **not** make it to the due date.
She is**n't** interested.

Position in a sentence – adverbs of negative assertion

When these negative adverbs are placed at the beginning of a sentence, the structure changes: the word order is the same as that of a question. This is called inversion of order.

adverb (+ object) + *auxiliary/modal* + <u>subject</u> + *verb*

Not a penny more *will* <u>we</u> *spend*.

Other adverbs denoting negative meaning are also subject to inversion of order. *(See 7.3.3.2 Time - frequency)*

Yes and **no** may stand alone as interjections. *(See 15 Interjections)* **No** may function as a determiner. *(See 6.2 Functional classification of determiners and 6.3 Quantifiers)*

7.3.6 Adverbs of degree

Adverbs of degree are sometimes also called intensifiers. They answer the questions *How much?* or *To what extent?* They often modify adjectives or other adverbs. Some of them can modify verbs, too.

Examples:

Adverbs:	**very**	**quite**	**fairly**	**rather**	**so**
	too	**enough**	**really** (informal)	**almost**	

Mike and Sue are **very** *fond* of that puppy.
He sang that opera piece **quite** *well*.

Examples:

Adverbials: **for sure**   **to some extent**   **sort of**   **kind of**

They won't know what you're talking about, **for sure**.
Those fans love their team **as much as you could expect them to**.

The broad categories of intensification that adverbs of degree perform are emphasizing, amplifying and down-toning.

Emphasizers put additional focus on the quality of the adjective, adverb or verb being modified:

We **really** *enjoy* cold weather.
He **simply** *didn't understand* what they were saying.

Amplifiers turn the modified adjective, adverb or verb into an extreme.

It's an **absolutely** *gorgeous* ensemble.
They **heartily** *cheered* their team on.

Down-toners turn the modified adjective, adverb or verb into a lesser version.

They **kind of** *argued* about it.
Her father **mildly** *criticized* his opinions.

The emphasizing adverbs of degree **very** and **fairly** are not used with extreme adjectives (adjectives which describe an extreme quality), such as *excellent*, *horrible*, *enormous*, *huge*, *boiling*, *freezing*, *furious*, *hilarious*, *starving* and *filthy*. Extreme adjectives can be modified by **absolutely**, **completely**, **really**, **totally**, **utterly**, **simply**, **quite**, and **entirely**.

The movie was **absolutely** *hilarious*. ~~The movie was very hilarious.~~
We got **totally** *drenched*. ~~We got very drenched.~~

Position in a sentence – adverbs of degree

Adverbs (single-word) of degree are usually placed before the part of the sentence that they modify. Adverbials of degree are less consistent in their placement; they may come before or after the part of the sentence they modify, depending on length and what they are modifying. Some common adverbials of degree, such as **kind of** and **sort of**, are positioned before the parts of a sentence they modify. Many longer adverbials, which are usually modifying phrases or clauses or completing a comparison, come after.

Emily *laughed* **so hard that tears came to her eyes**.

*** In the classroom: Overuse of very ***

It is common for students (from low intermediate level and up) to overuse the adverb of degree **very**. The following example is typical of this overuse:

I went downtown with my friend the other day and we had a very good time. First we went to Bistro & Café but it was very crowded. Also, the music was very loud so we did not want to stay there for very long...

One way to solve this problem is to teach students extreme adjectives, so that they can enrich their stories or sentences with adjectives that have a stronger and more precise meaning. Another way to avoid overusing **very** is to use adverbs like **absolutely** or **extremely**.

I went downtown with my friend the other day and we had a great (very good) time. First we went to Bistro & Café but it was packed (very crowded). Also, the music was extremely (very) loud, so we did not want to stay there for very long...

7.3.6.1 Adverbs of quantity

Adverbs of quantity or measure are a subcategory of adverbs of degree. They provide detail in answering the questions *How much?* and *How many?*

Examples:

Adverbs:	completely	equally	enough	exactly	less
	little	more	much	nearly	too
	slightly	sufficiently	just	excessively	very

Elinore was **completely** shocked.
Liz **slightly** rearranged her furniture.

Examples:

Adverbials:	too much	too little	a little	as much as
	very much	twice as much	so many	a lot

The house was **too badly** damaged to be rebuilt.
Marie is **old enough** to be able to cope with this situation.

Many adverbs of quantity (**enough, little, less, least, more, most, few**) can function as determiners or quantifiers. *(See 6.2 Functional classification of determiners and 6.3 Quantifiers)*

Position in a sentence - adverbs of quantity

An adverb of quantity can be placed before the main verb, after the main verb, or after the object. It is generally placed before the adjective or clause it modifies.

I **quite** *dislike* the idea. *(before the main verb)*
They *eat* **too much**. *(after the main verb)*
I love *him* **very much**. *(after the object)*
I am feeling **less** *happy* these days. *(before an adjective)*
It is **just** *what I always wanted in life*. *(before a clause)*

Enough is an exception to this rule. It is placed after the adjective or adverb it modifies.

> *Interestingly* **enough**, the client didn't ask for a refund.
> Mariette is *old* **enough** to go to the movies with her friends.

Quiz 7: Adverb identification

Identify the adverbs or adverbials in these sentences and indicate whether they are adverbs of purpose, assertion, degree or quantity.

1) I totally agree with you.
2) I'd like to express my gratitude to all my colleagues for their support.
3) The new house was slightly larger than the old one.
4) We did it for fun.
5) Yes, I will take care of the kitten. Do not worry.

****In the classroom:* Very much *and* very ***

A typical mistake at low levels is to place the adverbial **very much** directly after the verb *like* (and before the direct object).

> ~~I like very much coffee~~.
> I like coffee **very much**.

The adverbial **very much** is modifying the whole sentence, and it should be placed at the end of the sentence, or after a direct object.

Students may use the adverb of degree **very** before the main verb, probably a literal translation from their mother tongue into English.

> ~~I very like chocolate~~.

As a solution, students can be taught to replace **very** with **really** in these structures so that they can convey their message more accurately.

*** *You can teach adverbs* ***

Some of the ideas for teaching or practising adverbs listed below are connected to other parts of speech. See the *You can teach* sections in Chapter 5 Adjectives and Chapter 11 Verbs for more ideas on teaching adverbs.

Identifying parts of speech

Level: Low intermediate
Type of activity: Identify the underlined word

Write several sentences on the board (or create a handout) with target words underlined. Students must identify whether each underlined word is an adjective or an adverb. To make this activity more challenging, have the students explain their choices and identify the word or words the adjective or adverb is modifying. Then they can make their own sentences using the underlined words. Here are some example sentences for such an activity:

1. This tablecloth is <u>lovely</u>. Where did you get it?
2. This ice cream maker is not working <u>well</u>.
3. Do you always get up <u>late</u>? Shouldn't you arrive at the office <u>earlier</u>?
4. Watch out! The burner is <u>hot</u>.
5. I did not like his performance. He spoke very <u>loudly</u>.
6. We are <u>deeply</u> sorry to give you such sad news.
7. It's one of the most <u>remarkable</u> books I've ever read.
8. He walked <u>clumsily</u> up to his car, and then fell.
9. I <u>kindly</u> suggest you fill the form out before the interview.
10. He is such a <u>lonely</u> guy.

Answer key:
1. lovely = adjective modifying the noun *tablecloth*
2. well = adverb modifying the verb phrase *is not working*
3. late = adverb modifying the phrasal verb *get up*; earlier, adverb in its comparative form, modifying the verb *arrive*
4. hot = adjective modifying the noun *burner*
5. loudly = adverb modifying the verb *spoke*
6. deeply = adverb modifying the adjective *sorry*
7. remarkable = adjective modifying the noun *books*
8. clumsily = adverb modifying the verb *walked*
9. kindly = adverb modifying the verb *suggest*
10. lonely = adjective describing the noun *guy*

Adverb formation

Level: Low intermediate
Type of activity: Complete the chart

On the board, draw a chart similar to the one in the example below, writing in either an adjective or an adverb and leaving the neighbouring box empty. Ask students to complete the blank boxes in the chart with the corresponding forms of the given words. The plain text words are provided to students as guide words; the words in italics show the expected student answers.

adjective	adverb
creative	*creatively*
happy	happily
amazing	*amazingly*
fast	fast
nice	nicely
simple	*simply*
good	*well*
terrible	*terribly*
free	*freely*
powerful	*powerfully*

Adverb or adjective?

Level: Low intermediate – Intermediate
Type of activity: Gap filling (adverbs and adjectives)

Students complete the blanks in a chosen passage. They choose their answers from a list of paired adjectives and adverbs in a box. An example is given below:

> nasty-nastily careful-carefully busy-busily heavy-heavily good-well
> slow-slowly unfortunate-unfortunately bad-badly careless-carelessly

I had a 1-_____ experience with my car last month. I was driving 2-_____ along a very 3-_____ road when it started to rain 4-_____. I did not have good wipers, as my car was quite old. The indicating light at the rear was not working 5-_____, so I definitely had to leave the road and stop the car until the rain stopped. I slowed down as every other driver did, and tried to turn 6-_____ to the right so that I could take a side road, but 7-_____, I was hit by a car whose driver did not see my maneuver. It was a minor accident, but I felt 8-_____ for having been a 9-_____driver and car owner.

To make the activity more challenging, change the order of the choices in the box.

Answer key:
1. nasty = adjective modifying the noun *experience*
2. slowly = adverb modifying the verb *driving*
3. busy = adjective modifying the noun *road*
4. heavily = adverb modifying the verb *to rain*
5. well = adverb modifying the verb *working*
6. slowly = adverb modifying the adjective *turn*
7. unfortunately = adverb modifying the clause *I was hit by a car …*
8. bad = adjective modifying the pronoun *I*
9. careless = adjective modifying the noun *driver*

Word search

Level: Intermediate and above
Type of activity: Word search

Create a word search game with the adverbs students are familiar with. This could be a review activity or a warm-up for a lesson. To make it more challenging, add adverbs which are new to the students to see if they can identify them and understand their meanings. There are many online resources for creating word search games.

Brainstorming

Level: Intermediate and above
Type of activity: Mind-mapping charts

The teacher chooses a verb and asks students to brainstorm adverbs that can describe said verb appropriately.

Example: How can people speak?

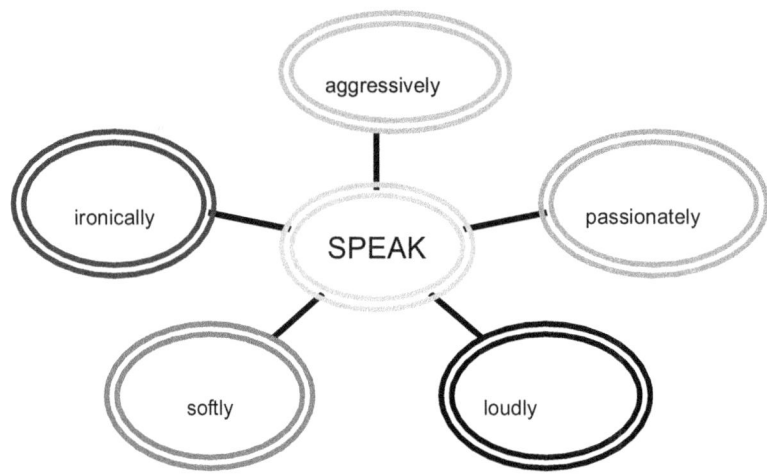

Describing actions

Level: Low intermediate and above
Type of activity: Charades, miming

Divide the class into groups or pairs. Give out a set of cards to each group. Each card contains a verb and an adverb of manner describing the verb. One student in each group must pick a card and tell their group only the verb on the card. The student must then mime the adverb, and the students in the group have to guess the adverb.

Example cards:

SPEAK	NERVOUSLY
SING	LOUDLY
WALK	SLOWLY
RUN	FAST
PLAY	QUIETLY
DRIVE	CARELESSLY
DRINK	HEAVILY

Finding the mistake

Level: Intermediate and above

Students must identify the mistakes in given sentences and explain what is wrong in each case.

1- I can type slow.
2- Maria felt happily.
3- He always is late.
4- He works every day hard in the garden.
5- Angie drives carefuly.
6- I'm going tomorrow to reserve the flight.

Answer key:
1- I can type slowly.
Explanation: *slow* is an adjective. The adverb *slowly* is required here to modify the verb *type*.
2- Maria felt happy.
Explanation: After linking verbs, use adjectives or nouns.
3- He is always late.
Explanation: adverbs of frequency are placed after the verb 'be' and before main verbs.
4- He works hard in the garden every day.
Explanation: If the sentence contains more than one adverb or adverbial in a clause, the following order is used: manner (hard), place (in the garden) and time (every day).
5- Angie drives carefully.
Explanation: this is a spelling mistake. Adverbs ending in 'l' add 'ly' without dropping the original 'l'.
6- I'm going to reserve the flight tomorrow;   or
Tomorrow I'm going to reserve the flight.
Explanation: Adverbs of time can be placed at the beginning of the sentence or at the end.

I thought it was really good!

Level: Intermediate and above

Have a discussion on movies, TV programs or music the students are fond of. Write their choices on the board. Then write some appropriate adverbs of degree on the board and ask students to express their opinions by making sentences using the adverbs in the list.

The following adverbs of degree are good choices for emphasizing opinions:

| absolutely   really   particularly   especially   extremely |
| amazingly   surprisingly   remarkably |

Expected student output would be along these lines:
His performance was remarkably good.
I think it was amazingly funny.
The scene of the murder was absolutely disgusting.

Changing meaning

Level: Upper intermediate and above

In this activity, students must create a passage which is the complete opposite of the one given to them as a sample. Choose any passage from any book – preferably a narrative piece – and give the students a copy to work with. The passage could be a complete story, or just the beginning of a story. Students have to read the passage, identify all the adverbials and then rewrite the passage changing the adverbials for some other they think will suit the context. If only the beginning of a story is given, then the students must continue it and come up with an appropriate ending. Either way, at the end of the task, the passage will look very different. Students will see how adverbs alone can change meaning completely. This activity can be done in pairs or small groups so that speaking and collaborative writing are incorporated. Encourage students to use a thesaurus to come up with better and more creative adverbs.

Note: Warn the students that there may be other parts of speech that need to be changed in the passage. Here is an example passage.

> *This is the story of a lady who was feeling very joyful. She had lived happily for many years. She had met the man of her dreams, with whom she had travelled extensively for about a year. They seldom argued, and if they did, they discussed matters in a very mature way.*
>
> *One day, not a long time ago, this lady was sitting placidly at a café waiting for her boyfriend to arrive. She was having a piece of cherry cheesecake and a coffee and enjoying it enormously. Suddenly, her cell phone rang. It was her boyfriend, who sadly said….*

Variation

In this variation, students read a passage which does not have any adverbs or adverbial phrases. They then have to add them to produce a more expressive written piece. For levels below upper intermediate, the teacher can provide guidelines such as these:

Read the passage and add the following ideas in as many places in the text as you can:
- *To add adverbials of place, think of where the action in the text took place.*
- *To add adverbials of time, think of when the action took place.*
- *To add adverbials of manner, think of how the actions were done.*
- *To add adverbials of degree, think of how strongly or weakly the actions were done.*
- *Can you think of any other adverbs or adverbial phrases? Frequency, quantity, purpose?*

8 Comparatives

Similarities and differences can be expressed through grammatical means. The size or extent of the similarities and differences is called the degree of comparison. The degree of comparison that expresses equality is called the base form of comparison. It is also called the positive or absolute form. The two degrees of comparison that express inequality are comparative and superlative.

Adjectives and adverbs have distinct forms for the comparative and superlative degrees of comparison. Nouns and verbs may be compared, but they do not change form for comparison. This chapter is focused on the special comparative forms of adjectives and adverbs.

Comparative adjectives are used to compare characteristics of two or more people, things, places or qualities. They indicate an inequality among the characteristics of a known set of nouns. Comparative adverbs are used to compare one action to another action or to the same action done by another person, or done in another time, another place or in another way.

> The grass is always **greener** on the other side of the fence.
> (comparative adjective comparing a characteristic of different *grass*)

> She can sing **more expressively** than she can act.
> (comparative adverb comparing the action *sing* to the action *act*)

Superlative adjectives compare one person or thing with others in a certain group or range. Superlative adjectives are definite; they indicate the extreme end of the comparative scale. A noun described with a superlative adjective is not exceeded by any other noun in the group for that characteristic or quality. Superlative adverbs also describe the extreme end of a range. They can compare an action to the same action done by another actor, or to the same action done in another time or place or in another way. Superlative adverbs cannot be used to compare one action to another action.

> Estelle was the **proudest** mother in the room.
> (superlative adjective comparing a characteristic of *Estelle* to that of other mothers)

> Jay worked the **hardest** of all the staff that day.
> (superlative adverb comparing the action *work* done by different people)

> ~~She can sing most expressively than she can act~~.
> (superlative adverbs cannot compare two actions)

8.1 Expressing equality and inequality

To express that people, things or actions are equal in some way, there is only one grammatical structure: *as......as*. For nouns and verbs, quantifiers (such as *much* or *many*) or adverbs are usually needed to complete the structure.

Part of speech	Equality
noun	She had *as* much **cake** *as* I did.
verb	Mary **weighs** *as* much *as* Sue does.
adjective	Laura is *as* **tall** *as* Martin.
adverb	She runs *as* **fast** *as* the wind.

Adjectives and adverbs used in this structure can have no modifications; they are kept in their base forms.

The possible modes of expressing inequality are varied. The correct grammatical structure depends on the degree of comparison (comparative or superlative) and the part of speech.

Equality	Inequality
She had as much **cake** as I did.	I want more **cake**, please.
Mary **weighs** as much as Sue does.	Tom **weighs** more than Sue.
Laura is as **tall** as Martin.	Claire is **taller** than Laura.
She runs as **fast** as the wind.	She runs **fastest** on an indoor track.

Nouns and verbs do not change form when in a structure that expresses inequality. Nouns are typically modified with determiners as a way to show comparison. Verbs are typically modified with adverbs in order to make a comparison. The actual nouns and verbs themselves do not change form. Adjectives and adverbs *do* change form when in the comparative or superlative degree of comparison. The remainder of this chapter is focused on the rules for the comparative and superlative forms for adjectives and for adverbs.

8.2 Gradability

Not all adjectives and adverbs may be compared. Those that describe some unchangeable state, place, quantity or condition (such as *dead*, *here*, *forty* or *orbital*) do not logically allow different degrees of that characteristic. Adjectives and adverbs that cannot show degree of a characteristic on a relative scale are non-gradable. Those which can show a higher or lower degree, indicating the position of the adjective or adverb on a relative scale, are gradable.

8.2.1 Gradability of adjectives

Gradable adjectives can be modified in some way to express the extent of difference or similarity among nouns. They can show that two nouns are equivalent in some way, or they can express the degree of difference between them. The list below shows degrees of comparison for the gradable adjectives **cold** and **bountiful**.

Base form	Comparative	Superlative
cold	colder/less cold	coldest/least cold
bountiful	more bountiful/ less bountiful	most bountiful/ least bountiful

A comparative adjective indicates a relative level of the characteristic of the base form of the adjective. It requires some basis of comparison for the noun it is describing:

comparison to one or more other nouns, or to the same noun in another context. It shows some inequality in the comparison, but not an extreme.

Superlative adjectives also compare one or more nouns, but they define the noun as a maximum or minimum. A noun described with an adjective in superlative form is at the extreme end of the range for that characteristic, making it a unique and identifiable occurrence of the noun. For this reason, nouns described with a superlative adjective always take the definite article. *(See 6.4.1.1 Uniqueness)*

Gradable adjectives may be modified by certain adverbs of degree – such as *somewhat, quite, very* or *extremely* – which also place the base adjective on a scale.

somewhat cold → cold → quite cold → very cold → extremely cold

Non-gradable adjectives cannot be modified by intensifying adverbs such as *somewhat, quite, very* or *extremely*, and are incompatible with comparison. With the exceptions of **few**, **little**, **many** and **much**, limiting adjectives are all non-gradable. The following are non-gradable adjectives:

| cardiopulmonary | British | former |
| possible | one-of-a-kind | two |

Some adjectives can be gradable or non-gradable depending on the meaning and position in the sentence.

a **British** idiosyncrasy (non-gradable in this context)
a very **British** mannerism (gradable in this context)

Quiz 1: Gradability of adjectives

Identify whether the adjectives below are gradable or non-gradable.

	Gradable	Non-gradable
1) impossible		
2) elated		
3) little		
4) wee		
5) homesick		
6) ninety		
7) Japanese		
8) dependent		
9) exasperating		
10) some		

8.2.2 Gradability of adverbs

A relatively small proportion of adverbs are gradable. Many adverbs do not lend themselves to degrees of comparison. Adverbs of place are definite and so are not gradable. Adverbs of degree (such as *absolutely* or *barely*) serve the purpose of describing a comparative scale and so are not themselves gradable. Some adverbs of time (such as the time-when adverbs *early* and *soon*) may be gradable. When an adverb of time is precise (such as *now* or *tomorrow*), then it is not gradable.

Adverbs of manner are generally gradable. Gradable adverbs of manner mostly modify verbs (rather than adjectives and other adverbs).

The list below shows degrees of comparison for the gradable adverbs **hard** and **beautifully**.

Base form	Comparative	Superlative
hard	harder/less hard	hardest/least hard
beautifully	more beautifully/ less beautifully	most beautifully/ least beautifully

Quiz 2: Gradability of adverbs
Identify whether the adverbs below are gradable or non-gradable.

	Gradable	Non-gradable
1) never		
2) extremely		
3) gracefully		
4) very		
5) ably		
6) always		
7) softly		
8) there		
9) more		
10) fast		

8.3 Comparative and superlative forms

Adjectival and adverbial comparatives and superlatives have three basic possible forms. The choice of form depends on the number of syllables and the nature of the comparison.

When the comparison implies a higher or increasing value, the two possible forms are:
- adding the suffix **–er** for comparatives and the suffix **–est** for superlatives
- adding the adverb **more** for comparatives and **most** for superlatives

When the comparison implies a lower or decreasing value, the only possible form is:
- the addition of the adverb **less** for comparatives and **least** for superlatives

8.3.1 One-syllable adjectives and adverbs

With one-syllable adjectives and adverbs, to indicate an increasing or greater relative value or degree, the comparative form is made by adding the suffix **–er**, and the superlative by adding the suffix **–est**. If the base form ends in the letter *e*, then the comparative and superlative are formed by adding only *–r* and *–st*.

To indicate a decreasing or lesser relative value or degree, the adverb **less** is placed before the word for the comparative form, and the adverb **least** for the superlative form.

Table 29: Comparative and superlative forms of one-syllable adjectives and adverbs

Base form	Comparative form	Superlative form
strong	strong**er** / **less** strong	strong**est** / **least** strong
fast	fast**er** / **less** fast	fast**est** / **least** fast
cheap	cheap**er** / **less** cheap	cheap**est** / **least** cheap
large	larg**er** / **less** large	larg**est** / **least** large
safe	saf**er** / **less** safe	saf**est** / **least** safe

> I am looking for **cheaper** accommodation.
> It is the **fastest** growing city in the country.
> Little kids believe others' parents are **less strong** than their own.
> That's the **least safe** measure they could have proposed.

There are few gradable adverbs which are only one syllable long. With the exception of **soon**, all one-syllable adverbs are identical to the adjectives from which they derive. This group of adverbs, which are identical in form to adjectives, are sometimes called flat adverbs. Flat adverbs take exactly the same comparative forms as their corresponding adjectives. The main gradable single-syllable flat adverbs are **deep, fast, hard, high, late, long, low, near, short** and **straight**.

Some of these adverbs also have an *-ly* form: **lately, highly, hardly, nearly** and **shortly**. These additional forms of the adverbs have different meanings than the adjective form.

There is another group of adjectives which are often used, unchanged, as adverbs although they do have a distinct *–ly* adverb form.

> **quick**   **cheap**   **slow**   **quiet**
> **loud**   **close**   **easy**   **clear**

Though these words do have *-ly* adverbial forms, they are often used in their adjectival form, especially in spoken English, and particularly when in comparative form.

> If he looks **closer**, he'll find it. (compare with **more closely**)
> I can breathe **easier** with you around. (compare with **more easily**)

For one-syllable adjectives and flat adverbs which end in a single vowel plus a consonant (except *w*), the comparative and superlative forms require a doubling of the final consonant.

Table 30: Comparative and superlative forms of one-syllable adjectives ending in vowel + consonant

Base form	Comparative form	Superlative form
hot	ho**tt**er	ho**tt**est
big	bi**gg**er	bi**gg**est
thin	thi**nn**er	thi**nn**est

There are some exceptions to this pattern. A small group of adjectives, including **fun, real, right** and **wrong**, are formed with **more / less,** or **most / least** to form comparatives and superlatives, respectively.

Table 31: Comparative and superlative forms of one-syllable adjectives: Exceptions

Base form	Comparative form	Superlative form
fun	more / less fun	most / least fun
real	more / less real	most / least real
right	more / less right	most / least right
wrong	more / less wrong	most / least wrong

To children, witches and wizards are often the **most real** characters in fairy tales; adults often consider them the **least real** ones.

Some one-syllable adjectives of abstract meaning, including **clear, safe, true, free** and **wise**, can be formed by adding the inflections **–er/-r/-est/-st** or the words **more/most**.

Base form	Comparative form	Superlative form
clear	clear**er**	clear**est**
	more clear	**most** clear
safe	safe**r**	safe**st**
	more safe	**most** safe

You can see a **clearer** picture through a microscope.
This picture in the microscope is a bit **more clear**.

It is possible to choose **more** or **most** with one-syllable adjectives to express contrast with **less** (especially in conversation), or to emphasize the comparison.

I thought summer in India was wet, but this summer here has been even **MORE wet** than the monsoon season there!
(When speaking, the word **more** would be stressed; it would be said at a higher pitch and the vowel sound would be elongated.)

Quiz 3: Correct the mistake

Indicate what is wrong in each of the following sentences, and explain why it is wrong.

1) Which is more safer, a car or a motorcycle?
2) Reading comics in class is funner than reading grammar texts.
3) I think this room is the least lightest of all the rooms in this house.
4) This bag is cuteer; you should buy it.
5) Morley runs slowwer than he used to.
6) Kitty has become fater in the last two months.

*** In the classroom: Spelling problems ***

Students are often unsure about when to double the last consonant when adding the suffixes *-er* or *–est*, as in:

big ⇨ bigger ⇨ biggest

A useful rule is that for most one-syllable words ending in a *consonant + vowel + consonant* pattern (C+V+C), the last consonant of the word doubles when adding *–er* and *–est*. This is true for the addition of all suffixes which being with a vowel, not just for *–er* and *–est*. The exceptions are cases when the final consonant is *w* or *x*.

*** *In the classroom:* Older *or* elder ***

The adjective **old** follows the rule of one-syllable adjectives to form its comparative and superlative forms: **old**⇨**older**⇨**oldest**. However, the forms **elder** and **eldest** can be used when comparing the ages of people within the same social group, especially members of a family:

Mark is my **elder** brother.

But **elder** and **eldest** are not used in the following cases:

- When comparing the ages of things, or of people who are not related

    Susan's sister is **older** than her friend's sister, Marlene.
    (*Marlene* and *Susan's sister* are not members of the same family)

    Mr. Brick's house is the **oldest** house in the neighbourhood.
    (not comparing people)

- When used after linking verbs or in predicative position

    ~~My brother Mark is *elder* than me.~~
    My brother Mark is **older** than me.

8.3.2 Adverbs greater than one syllable

With the exception of the flat adverb **early**, the comparative forms of all adverbs greater than one syllable in length are made by adding **more** or **less** and the superlative forms are made by adding **most** or **least**.

Table 32: Comparative and superlative forms of adverbs greater than one syllable

Base form	Comparative form more / less + adverb	Superlative form most / least + adverb
quickly	**more** / **less** quickly	**most** / **least** quickly
	Paul swims **more quickly** than Mark.	Mark swims the **least quickly** of anyone in the group.

8.3.3 Two-syllable adjectives

To indicate an increasing or greater relative value or degree, there is a large group of two-syllable adjectives which may be formed *either* through the addition of **–er/–est** or by a preceding **more/most**. The choice is the speaker's (or writer's). Two-syllable adjectives with stress on the first syllable can often use either form. In examples such as **quiet**, **subtle**, **shifty**, **hollow** and **saintly**, the choice is mainly for emphasis. Generally, use of **more/most** puts somewhat more emphasis on the quality of the adjective. Use of **–er/–est** puts somewhat more emphasis on the elements being compared.

Table 33: Comparative forms of two-syllable adjectives with stress on the first syllable

Base form	Comparative form adjective + -er/-r	Comparative form more + adjective
gentle	gentle**r**	**more** gentle
	Pete is **gentler** than Tom. (emphasis is Pete vs. Tom)	Peter is **more gentle** than Tom. (emphasis is gentleness)

Much of the choice comes down to the sound and flow of the language. Two-syllable adjectives with stress on the second syllable use the **more/most** form. So, adjectives such as **profound**, **discreet**, **robust** or **inane** would all take that form. Certain other two-syllable adjectives rarely, if ever, take the **–er/-est** form:

Table 34: Two-syllable adjective types that always take the more/most form for comparative and superlative

adjectives ending with: -ive	festive	~~festiver~~	more festive √
-some	fearsome	~~fearsomest~~	most fearsome √
-less	restless	~~restlessest~~	most restless √
-ous	bulbous	~~bulbouser~~	more bulbous √
-ful	bashful	~~bashfulest~~	most bashful √
-en	silken	~~silkener~~	more silken √
present participial adjectives	tiring	~~tiringer~~	more tiring √
past participial adjectives	wanted	~~wantedest~~	most wanted √

The comparative forms of two-syllable adjectives ending in *–y* (including the flat adverb **early**) is formed by changing the final *y* to *i* and adding the inflectional endings **–er** or **–est**.

To indicate a decreasing or lesser relative value or degree, the adverb **less** is placed before the adjective for the comparative form, and the adverb **least** for the superlative form.

Table 35: Comparative and superlative forms of two-syllable adjectives ending in *–y*

Base form	Comparative form	Superlative form
happy	happ**ier** / **less** happy	happ**iest** / **least** happy
silly	sill**ier** / less silly	sill**iest** / **least** silly
easy	eas**ier** / **less** easy	eas**iest** / **least** easy

I feel **happier** than ever.
This is the **easiest** task of them all.

8.3.4 Three- (or more) syllable adjectives

The comparative forms of adjectives of three or more syllables are made by adding **more** or **less**, and the superlative forms are made by adding **most** or **least**.

Table 36: Comparative and superlative forms of three- (or more) syllable adjectives

Base form	Comparative form: more / less + adjective	Superlative form: most / least + adjective
diligent	**more** / **less** diligent	**most** / **least** diligent
	Paula is **more diligent** than Marcia.	Paula is the **most diligent** receptionist I've ever known.

8.3.5 Compound adjectives

Some compound adjectives can also be used in comparative and superlative forms. Most compound adjectives will follow the same rules as three- (or more) syllable adjectives.

> **more** *coolheaded* than you'd imagine
> **the most** *mind-blowing* movie of all time

Some compound adjectives (especially hyphenated ones), which themselves contain a one- or two-syllable adjective, are changed into their comparative forms by adding –**er** or –**est** to the one- or two-syllable adjective within the compound adjective. The same rule applies to those compounds formed with irregular adjectives. (See section#)

Adjective	**Comparative**	**Superlative**
long-suffering	longer-suffering	the longest-suffering
good-natured	better-natured	the best-natured

8.3.6 Adverbial phrases

Some adverbial phrases can be used in comparative and superlative forms. These comparisons are always formed by adding **more**, **most**, **less** or **least**.

> She went inside **more** *to calm down* than *to warm up*.
> (comparing two adverbials of purpose, *to calm down* and *to warm up*)

> Of all his influences, Simon writes **most** *like Kurt Vonnegut*.
> (setting the extreme end of the range for the action *write* as the adverbial phrase of manner *like Kurt Vonnegut*)

*** *In the classroom: Over-generalizing the rules* ***

ESL learners often combine the –**er**/–**est** endings with **more** and **most**, especially on one-syllable adjectives:

> ~~This is the **most biggest** house I've ever seen.~~
> ~~Pam is **more taller** than Rex~~

Another common mistake learners make with regard to comparatives and superlatives is that they add **more** and **most** to all adjectives:

> ~~This is the **most big** house I've even seen.~~
> ~~Pam is **more tall** than Rex.~~

Consistent correction will help students get over these errors. Intervention by the teacher is often necessary with errors like these, which are so common in the classroom that they being to "sound right" to learners.

8.3.7 Irregular comparatives and superlatives

There is a set of very commonly-used adjectives and adverbs which do not follow the normal structural rules for forming comparatives and superlatives. The following table shows the most common irregular adjectives and adverbs and their comparative and superlative forms.

Table 37: Irregular comparative and superlative forms

Base form	Comparative form	Superlative form
Adjectives:		
good	better	best
bad	worse	worst
old (for members of the same social group)	elder	eldest
many	more	most
Adverbs:		
well	better	best
badly	worse	worst
Flat adverbs (words that function as both adjectives and adverbs):		
far (physical distance only)	farther	farthest
far (metaphorical distance, quantity or time)	further	furthest
little (denoting amount)	less	least
much	more	most

*** In the classroom: Irregular forms ***

After the introductory lesson on comparative and superlative forms, and some practice, it becomes simpler for students to understand that one-syllable adjectives and adverbs add **–er** or **–est** to their base forms and two- or more syllable adjectives and adverbs add the words **more** or **most** to form comparative or superlatives. However, it gets more complicated when dealing with irregular forms, which will require students to memorize the comparative and superlative, as there are no rules to follow.

At a beginner level, learning adjectives will precede learning adverbs. The adjectives *good* and *bad* are the basic irregular adjectives to teach. Students are familiar with the meaning of these two words in their base forms. However, be aware that they might apply the rule of one-syllable adjectives and think that the comparative form of *good* is ~~gooder~~. Through oral and written practice, students will get used to the irregular forms of *good* and *bad*.

good ⇨ better ⇨ best
bad ⇨ worse ⇨ worst

Other irregular adjectives and adverbs like *far* or *little* should be introduced at a low intermediate level or higher, not only because their irregular forms could be a challenge for the learners, but also for their differences in meaning:

far	⇨	farther ⇨	farthest (physical distance)
far	⇨	further ⇨	furthest (metaphorical distance, quantity, or time; also means additional, or more)
little	⇨	less ⇨	least (amount; quantity)
little	⇨	littler ⇨	littlest (size; volume)

8.4 Comparative and superlative uses and structures

Comparative and superlative forms may be used in many structures, for many purposes. The table below summarizes the major uses.

Table 38: Uses of comparative adjectives and adverbs

Comparison	Comparative Adjective	Superlative Adjective	Comparative Adverb	Superlative Adverb
one noun to one other noun	√			
one noun to many nouns	√	√		
one verb to another verb			√	
one verb to the same verb done by another actor			√	√
one verb to the same verb done in another way, time or place			√	√
one adverbial phrase to another adverbial phrase			√	

These comparisons may be further detailed by adding intensifiers or further descriptions of the comparisons through the use of adverbs. Other common uses of the comparative form include describing factual states, progressive conditions, or comparing one condition (as opposed to a thing) to another.

8.4.1 Comparing two nouns

Nouns are compared through the use of adjectives. To compare two nouns, the comparative (not superlative) form of adjectives is used. The most common sentence structure when using comparative adjectives is the following:

comparative adjective **+ than +** noun / pronoun / noun phrase / noun clause

Sue is **stronger** than *her sister.*
His proposal seems to be **less safe** than *the one from Mr. Oswald.*
The math professor is **more intelligent** than *he looks.*
This movie is **less boring** than *the other one you suggested.*

Than is used after an adjective in the comparative form when the second person or thing is mentioned in the sentence.

Two other common patterns for comparative adjectives are:

>**not as** + base form adjective **+ as** + *noun / noun equivalent*; or
>**not so** + base form adjective **+ as** + *noun / noun equivalent*
>
>He's **not as** *experienced* **as** his brother.
>
>**twice** / **three times** / **half as** + base form adjective + **as** + *noun / noun equivalent*
>
>This suitcase is **twice as** *heavy* **as** that one.

**** In the classroom: Comparing one noun to another noun ****

Comparisons of nouns can be completed with a noun, a pronoun, a noun phrase or a noun clause, following *than*. In cases where the comparison is completed with a pronoun, there can be confusion. If the noun equivalent following *than* is a noun clause with a pronoun as its subject, then the pronoun must be in subjective case.

The point of contention is when the comparison is completed with a single pronoun. Some grammar guides insist on the subjective case of a pronoun here, on the assumption that it is a case of an elided noun clause; the pronoun would be the subject of the clause, and therefore would need to be in subjective case.

>Craig is **more intellectual than** *she*.
>(Craig is **more intellectual than** *she is*.)
>
>Nobody feels **happier than** *I*.
>(Nobody feels **happier than** *I feel*.)

Use of the objective case assumes that the pronoun stands alone and is not the subject of an elided clause.

>Craig is **more intellectual than** *her*.
>Nobody feels **happier than** *me*.

Either could be correct, depending on context and emphasis. Among grammarians, there is widespread disagreement on the preferred choice. In the ESL classroom, the focus is best placed on students' ability to comprehend and communicate. If students are studying with a textbook which describes one usage over the other, focus on that usage – do not get into the fine points of subjective and objective case unless and until students understand the fundamentals of comparison. An "incorrect" choice by students in this structure is unlikely to hinder communication.

8.4.2 Comparing one noun to a group or range

To compare one noun to a larger group of nouns, both the comparative and superlative forms of adjectives are possible. The most common structures for comparative forms are given above. The superlative form does not require a *than* or *as* construction. The superlative form identifies a noun as unique and distinct from all others in a group or range, and so it is considered to be defined. As a result, any noun which is described with a superlative is defined and must take the definite article *the*.

The noun described by the superlative adjective is often followed by a defining prepositional phrase or relative clause.

the + superlative adjective

Russia is **the *largest*** country in the world.
Flying is **the *least cheap*** way to travel home from here.
Of all Van Gogh's paintings, *Starry Night* is **the *most beautiful*.**
The Godfather III is **the *least popular*** in that series of movies.

8.4.3 Comparing verbs

The comparative adverbs are used to compare one action to another action or to the same action done by another person, or in another time or place or in another way.

He speaks **more succinctly *than*** he writes.
(comparing the verb *speaks* to a different verb, *writes*)

He speaks **more succinctly *than*** his brother.
(comparing the verb *speaks* to the same action done by another person)

He speaks **more succinctly** in the morning.
(comparing the verb *speaks* to the same action done at another time)

He speaks **more succinctly** in meetings.
(comparing the verb *speaks* to the same action done in another place)

He speaks **more succinctly** with prepared notes.
(comparing the verb *speaks* to the same action done in another way)

The most common sentence structures when using comparative adverbs are the following:

comparative adverb **+ than +** noun / pronoun / noun phrase / noun clause

Sue works ***harder*** **than** *her sister* (does)
His ideas made sense ***less frequently*** **than** *the ones from Mike*.
He writes ***more eloquently*** **than** *he speaks*.
They act ***less politely*** **than** *their cousins*.

-OR-

comparative adverb **+** prepositional phrase

The doctor acted ***more professionally*** *in his office*.

Than is used after an adverb in the comparative form when the second subject doing the action is mentioned in the sentence.

Two other common patterns for comparative adverbs are:

does not + verb **+ as** + base form adverb **+ as** + noun / noun equivalent; or
does not + verb **+ so** + base form adverb **+ as** + noun / noun equivalent

> He **does not** wake up **as** *early* **as** *his brother.*

verb **+ twice / three times / half as** + base form adverb **+ as** + noun

> Mr. Smith drives **twice as** *fast* **as** *his son.*

The superlative adverbs are used in much the same way, but the comparison is by definition in the extreme and the comparison cannot be to another action.

> He speaks **the most succinctly** of the whole team.
> (comparing the verb *speaks* to the same action done by other people)
>
> He speaks **(the) most succinctly** in the mornings.
> (comparing the verb *speaks* to the same action done at different times)
>
> He speaks **(the) most succinctly** in meetings.
> (comparing the verb *speaks* to the same action done in different places)
>
> He speaks **(the) most succinctly** with prepared notes.
> (comparing the verb *speaks* to the same action done in a different way)

The definite article *the* before superlative adverbs may be dropped in informal constructions.

Quiz 4: Comparative constructions

Transform the following sentences into ones showing comparison.

1) Professor Smith is very knowledgeable. His assistant is knowledgeable as well.
2) I feel sad. I have never felt so sad.
3) *Seinfeld* is a sidesplitting comedy. I have never seen anything like that.
4) Faith's explanation was not clear to me. However, Jonathan helped me understand the concept very clearly.
5) Annabelle looked stunning at the gala party last night. Diane was also stunning. But, Meaghan was really stunning and caught everyone's attention.

*** In the classroom: Finishing the comparison ***

Comparative adjectives are followed by *than* and a noun, pronoun, noun phrase or clause. This noun phrase or noun clause is the person or thing that is being compared to the subject of the sentence. In the sentence *Mark is taller than Danny*, it is clear that Mark's height is being compared to Danny's height. This type of comparative sentence structure is very common at the beginner level. However, in the sentence *Mark is taller*, which is also grammatically correct, it is not clear to whom Mark is being compared. The idea the speaker is conveying can only be understood through context. When teaching comparative and superlative sentences, teachers also need to focus on the meaning of the comparative and superlative forms. Sometimes what is being compared is not mentioned, but it is clear to the speaker and listener, as the comparison is in context. Here is an example:

Danny has a twin brother named Mark. They look alike, but Mark is **taller**.

In the last sentence above, the explicit comparison, *than Danny*, was left unsaid. This is possible, as the context makes it clear that Mark's height is being compared to Danny's height. However, when teaching comparatives and superlatives at a beginner level, it is advisable to encourage students to finish the comparison:

> Mark is **taller**. ?? (could be ambiguous; taller than whom?)
> Mark is **taller** *than Danny*. ✓
> New York is **bigger**. ?? (could be ambiguous; bigger than what?)
> New York is **bigger** *than Ottawa*.✓

8.4.4 Adding comparative emphasis with adverbs

Some adverbs or adverbials can be placed in front of comparative adjectives and adverbs to emphasize the comparison.

Table 39: Adverbs used to emphasize comparatives

Emphasizing adverbs / adverbials	Examples emphasizing comparative adjectives	Examples emphasizing comparative adverbs
(very) much	My car is **(very) much faster** than yours.	This engine works **much more efficiently** than that one.
far	Puppies are **far more intelligent** than kittens.	Puppies act **far more intelligently** than birds.
a bit	This book is **a bit more interesting**.	He slept **a bit more soundly** with ear-plugs in.
a lot	Actually, I think it is **a lot more interesting**.	He works **a lot faster** when he is not tired.
rather	Thrillers are **rather more exciting** than dramas.	Thrillers finish **rather more excitingly** than comedies.
a little	Jim is **a little funnier** than Ben.	Jeremy jumps **a little higher** than Ben.
even	His movies are **even better** than you expect.	His speeches end **even better** than you expect.
way (very informal usage)	These shoes are **way cooler** than those boots.	He works **way harder** than anyone else.

Sometimes adverbs or adverbials can be placed in front of superlative adjectives to emphasize the comparison.

Table 40: Adverbs used to emphasize superlative adjectives

Emphasizing adverbs / adverbial phrases	Examples
by far	This is **by far the most interesting** book I've read.
easily	This is **easily the worst** movie I've had to watch.
quite	That's **quite the funniest** remark I've heard.
nearly	I'm **nearly the youngest** in the room!
without a doubt	That is **without a doubt the best** film ever produced.
unquestionably	Philip looks **unquestionably the most intriguing** of them all.

Quiz 5: Intensifying adverbs
Which sentence in each pair below is the correct one? Why?

1) a) The elderly lady walks very more energetically than her husband.
   b) The elderly lady walks much more energetically than her husband.
2) a) This is near the fastest bike I've ever ridden.
   b) This is nearly the fastest bike I've ever ridden.
3) a) He is by far the most caring nurse I've worked with.
   b) He is far the most caring nurse I've worked with.

*** In the classroom: Advanced comparative constructions ***

The structures described above are the major types of constructions ESL students should learn. However, there are other constructions that intermediate and more advanced learners could also be taught. They may be combined with the more expressive use of intensifying adverbs to help students express themselves more precisely.

comparative adjective **+ than +** same base form adjective
(used to express an extreme attribute)
   Mark is **sweeter than sweet**! (He is the perfect example of someone who is sweet.)

comparative adjective **+ and +** comparative adjective
(used to express a progressive development)
   Brad is getting **taller and taller**. (He is growing progressively, and is getting taller over time.)

the + comparative adjective **+** noun **+ , + the +** comparative adjective
(used to express a conditional relationship)
   The louder *the music,* **the more annoying** it gets. (If the music gets louder, it gets more annoying.)

comparative adjective **+ than +** different base form adjective
(used to express a difference or a replacement of a characteristic)
   She is **more studious than intelligent**. (Her achievements are due more to study than to native intelligence; the characteristic of studiousness is stronger than the characteristic of intelligence for her.)

*** You can teach comparatives ***

Many of the activities here are almost interchangeable with activities for teaching base form adjectives and adverbs. They are presented here with a focus on the comparative forms. Slight variations of these can render these activities usable for dealing with base forms, and basic variations of the activities in Chapter 5 Adjectives and Chapter 7 Adverbs can make them usable for practising comparative forms.

Finding the mistake

Level: Any level, depending on the complexity of the comparative or superlative structure.

Activities where students have to find the wrong word or structure and explain why it is wrong are excellent for reviewing or reinforcing any grammar topic. Here are some suggestions of common types of mistakes connected to comparative and superlative forms of adjectives and adverbs.

> Manuel's test is more better than Joan's test.
> It was the more boring lesson I have ever had.
> They run fastest than their peers.
> He drives carelesslier than his wife.

Describing people

Level: High beginner +

The teacher collects photos of people (or, members of the teacher's family, to personalize the activity) who show quite distinctive features: height, age, build, and hair, for example. After the teacher gives the names of the people in the photos, students are paired up and required to discuss the differences between the people, using comparative and superlative forms of descriptive adjectives. After they agree on the characteristics, they present their ideas to the class. Expected output would be something like this:

> This is Paolo, our teacher's cousin. He is taller than her bother Luigi.
> Her aunt has longer hair than her mom.

To make the activity more challenging and have the students practise comparative and superlative forms of adverbs, the teacher can present how the people in the photos are or how they do things, and then the students must create sentences or a paragraph with their conclusions, using comparative adverbs. Example output could be:

> T: My cousins Paolo and Luigi are opera singers. Paolo sings beautifully, but his brother does not sing as well.
> S: Paolo sings more beautifully than Luigi. (Or, Luigi does not sing as beautifully as Paolo does.)

Themed question and answer

Level: Low intermediate +

Choose a theme, such as animals, and give students cards or handouts with examples like the ones below, to have them discuss their ideas with their partners. (Adapted from *Excursions - Book 3* , Oxford University Press.)

> Which one is more intelligent, a dolphin or a chimpanzee?
> Which one makes longer journeys, a caribou or a whale?
>
> The largest mammal is _____
> One of the most endangered animals is _____
>
> A scorpion is more poisonous than a black mamba.   True/False
> A whale lives longer than an elephant.   True/False

Selecting the best option in a category

Level: Intermediate +

Bring flyers of different hotels, schools or tour packages. Have students read the information and then choose the best option, taking into account similarities and differences in price, quality, location, activities, etc.

Responding to questionnaires and surveys

Level: Intermediate +

This activity reinforces different grammar topics and integrates speaking, listening, reading and writing. It is very good for reviewing adjectives and their comparative or superlative forms. Choose a theme or topic such as movies, lifestyles, career, jobs, food, holiday resorts or brands. Have students think of adjectives which can be connected to those themes. Then ask the students to write a questionnaire to conduct an in-class survey based on those topics. Finally, have them present an oral or written report on their findings, including comparative and superlative forms of adjectives and adverbs. For example:

Theme: Jobs

Step 1: Students brainstorm characteristics of a job

Step 2: Write a questionnaire

> What's your job? What do you like about your job? What don't you like about your job? What do you think of your type of job? Is it more dangerous than …? Is it more highly-paid than …?

Step 3: Students do the survey and record classmates' answers.

Step 4: Presentation of the survey results; output would be similar to:

> Most of the students think their current jobs are boring.
> Peter thinks that his job is by far the most highly paid.
> All of them would love to find a more challenging job.

Comparing home towns

Level: Low intermediate +

Tell students that the theme of the lesson is their home towns. Have them first work individually. Students independently make notes on characteristics of their home towns. Encourage students to write as many details as possible. Then pair the students up and have them compare their home towns. Finally, students report their conclusions to the whole class.

Discussing movies

Level: Intermediate +

Talking about movies is a good way of practising adjectives denoting opinion: boring, fun, moving, passable, silly, dull, awful, interesting, sad, scary, good, violent, excellent, bad, etc. Students can talk or write about a movie they have seen. Then they get together and discuss their opinions by comparing ideas.

You be the judge

Level: Intermediate +

For a focus on comparative adverbs, give students a critiquing exercise. Students must make comparisons and choose a "winner." Possible themes include predicting Oscar® winners, making a sports team scouting report, doing an evaluation of different schools or classes, judging some sort of contest (singing, baking, debating), or choosing a candidate to hire from a group of qualified people. Introduce a single description of an ideal case, using targeted adverbs (the ideal candidate speaks English and French *fluently*; the ideal school enables students to adapt *easily*). Students will then compare the possible choices against those criteria.

9 Prepositions

Prepositions connect certain parts of speech to different parts of a sentence. A preposition is generally followed by a noun, a noun phrase, a pronoun or other noun equivalent (gerund or wh-clause) to form an adjective- or adverb-equivalent. (*See 9.2.2 Functions of prepositional phrases*)

Prepositions are crucial to clear English communication; three of the ten most commonly-used words in English are prepositions (**to**, **of** and **in**).

9.1 Preposition forms

Simple prepositions consist of a single word. Complex (or multiple-word) prepositions consist of more than one word.

9.1.1 Simple prepositions

Here is a list of the most common simple (one-word) prepositions. Some have more than one meaning, and some can also function as conjunctions or adverbial particles. (*See 7.2.3 Adverbs, adverbial particles and prepositions, 10.1.1 Single-word conjunctions and 11.4.2 Phrasal verbs*)

Table 41: Simple prepositions

aboard	beside	from	round
about	besides	in	since
above	between	inside	than
across	beyond	like	through
after	but	near	throughout
against	by	notwithstanding	to
along	concerning	of	toward/towards
among	considering	off	under
around	despite	on	underneath
as	down	opposite	unlike
assuming	during	out	until
at	except	outside	up
before	excepting	over	upon
behind	excluding	past	with
below	following	pending	within
beneath	for	regarding	without

The following are important, but less common, simple prepositions:

alongside	granted	plus	versus
amid	minus	save	via
anti	per		

There are not particular forms that definitively identify words as prepositions. They may sometimes be tricky to identify, because they may resemble present participles and past participles, and they may function as other parts of speech.

Some of the simple prepositions that have a form similar to participles are:

assuming	**considering**	**excluding**	**pending**
concerning	**excepting**	**granted**	**regarding**

Some of the prepositions that may function as other parts of speech are:

also conjunctions:	after	before	since	for	notwithstanding
also adverbs:	aboard	about	along	past	underneath

*** *In the classroom: Prepositions vs. conjunctions* ***

Differentiation between prepositions and conjunctions is a matter of analyzing sentence structure. To identify whether words such as **for, since, before** and **after** are prepositions or conjunctions, students should be reminded of the characteristics of these parts of speech. Conjunctions join equal elements: nouns with nouns, and clauses with clauses. Prepositions precede nouns, objective pronouns, noun phrases or noun clauses; they do not require the equivalent elements to precede them.

> I have not called Margot **since** I came back.
> (conjunction of time joining the clauses *I have not called Margot* and *I came back*)

> I have not called Margot **since** last week.
> (preposition of time followed by the noun phrase *last week*)

9.1.2 Complex prepositions

Complex prepositions are made up of two or more words. The following are the most common complex prepositions:

according to	by means of	in exchange for	in view of
ahead of	by virtue of	in favour of	next to
along with	due to	in front of	on account of
apart from	except for	in lieu of	on behalf of
aside from	for the sake of	in line with	on to / onto
at the expense of	in accordance with	in need of	out of
as a result of	in addition to	in place of	on top of
as for	in back of	in regard to	owing to
as of	in between	in relation to	prior to
as to	in case of	in return for	up to
away from	in charge of	in spite of	with regard to
because of	in comparison with	instead of	with respect to
but for	in contact with	in to / into	

Quiz 1: Simple and complex prepositions

Identify the prepositions in the sentences and state whether they are simple or complex.

1) What shall we do in regard to planning a short vacation this summer?
2) They succeeded, notwithstanding their inexperience.
3) They were all invited except me.
4) Let's make the changes along the lines he suggested.
5) They found the car along with the burned documents.

*** In the classroom: Mother tongue translation ***

There are many reasons that ESL learners find prepositions a difficult part of speech to learn and to use properly. When students have persistent preposition problems, they are very often trying to equate the functions of certain English prepositions to similar words in another language.

Different prepositions may be used in similar contexts in the learner's mother tongue. For example, the preposition of place **on** is used by a native speaker of English in the adjectival prepositional phrase **on the coast**; it may be possible that the preposition of place **in** (or its equivalent) is used in the learner's mother tongue to refer to location. Thus, the learner may wrongly say ~~My home town is in the coast~~. Another example of this case is: ~~I am interested about the job~~ (in this case the preposition **in** (not **about**) is required after the participial adjective **interested**).

The learner's mother tongue may not require a preposition in certain constructions, and therefore the learner omits a preposition that is necessary in English. For example, ~~Do you listen the radio~~? (the verb **listen** requires the preposition **to** in this context).

It could be the case that a preposition is required in the learner's mother tongue, and no preposition is used in English. Or, no preposition is used with a particular word because it is an exception to a rule. For example:

> ~~He went to home~~.
> (the preposition **to** is elided before the word **home**, but not before other nouns, as in *He went **to** his house*).
>
> ~~We held the party despite of the rain~~.
> (no other preposition is required after the preposition **despite**)
>
> ~~My house is near to the hospital~~.
> (**near** is a simple preposition; it is never followed by **to**)

One way of addressing these errors is to keep example sentences and phrases constantly visible (on the walls or on the board). Other solutions are consistent correction and continued review of the rules.

9.2 Prepositional phrases

A prepositional phrase is formed by a preposition – which is the head or nucleus of the phrase – followed by its object. The object of a preposition is also known as a prepositional complement.

9.2.1 Structures of prepositional phrases

The object of a preposition can be a noun, a noun phrase, a pronoun, a gerund or a clause – and occasionally another prepositional phrase, an adjective or an adverb. The latter is especially found in idiomatic expressions. The preposition in the phrase links the information in the object (generally a noun) to some other elements in the sentence. The preposition does not modify the noun; its only purpose is to connect, as shown below. The words in bold are prepositions – heads of prepositional phrases –

and the italicized words are the objects of the prepositions, which complete the prepositional phrases.

The most common patterns are as follows:

> **preposition + noun**
> He works **at** *night*.
> She is **in** *bed*.
>
> **preposition + noun phrase**
> I am afraid we cannot meet **in** *the afternoon*.
> They got married **on** *March 19th*.
>
> **preposition + pronoun**
> (pronouns following a preposition are always in objective form)
> Can you listen **to** *me*?
> That's **for** *him*.
>
> **preposition + gerund (or gerund phrase)**
> (a verb which follows a preposition is always in the gerund (*–ing*) form)
> Mara is interested **in** *opening a restaurant*.
> I cannot get used **to** *driving on the left*.
>
> **preposition + clause**
> (generally relative clauses with the relative pronouns *which* or *whom*)
> Della is the woman **with** *whom I'd had that huge confrontation*.
> The new committee is the group **to** *which all of the credit should go*.
>
> **wh- question word + …… + preposition** (at the end of the question)
> The wh-word in a question functions as the object of the preposition placed at the end of a question.
>
> *What* are you talking **about**? (I am talking **about** *that*.)
> *Whom** do you wish to speak **to**? (I wish to speak **to** *him*.)
> * The object form *whom* is correct; usage of the subject form *who* is more common in this stucture, even though it is the object of the verb.

Prepositional phrases can be connected with coordinating conjunctions. *(See 10.3.1 Coordinating conjunctions)* The most common conjunctions are **and** and **or**.

> The documents are either **on** *the desk* **or in** *the drawer*.
> That book can be found **in** *the mystery section* **and in** *the new releases section*.

Other, less common, prepositional phrase patterns are described on the *You Can Teach Grammar* companion web site.

Quiz 2: Prepositional phrases

Identify the prepositional phrases and indicate the type of the object of the preposition.

1) This discovery is a major step forward in gene therapy.
2) There is a way to benefit from your efforts without ruining your reputation.
3) More money should be spent on culture.
4) We will not be here in August.
5) I'd rather you didn't tell anyone about it.

9.2.2 Functions of prepositional phrases

Prepositional phrases can act as adjectives or as adverbs in a sentence.

9.2.2.1 Adjectival prepositional phrases

This type of prepositional phrase adds information about the noun or noun phrase that precedes it, just as adjectives do. A prepositional phrase follows the noun it modifies. It generally answers the question *which*?

The man **on the left** suddenly collapsed.
(**on the left** is an adjectival prepositional phrase postmodifying the noun phrase *the man*; it indicates which man: the man on the left)

Did you see *that lady* **with red hair**?
(**with red hair** is an adjectival prepositional phrase postmodifying the noun phrase *that lady*; it indicates which lady: that lady with red hair)

A noun can be modified by more than one prepositional phrase.

The house **with the wooden roof** *by the river* was sold for $200,000.

Many adjectival prepositional phrases are cases of reduced relative clauses, with the relative pronoun and verb elided.

The man (who was) **on the left** suddenly collapsed.

Adjectival prepositional phrases beginning with **of** are commonly found in partitives *(See 6.3.1.2 Partitives)* and in possessive case *(See 3.4.4.3 Case)*.

A truckload **of beets** was spilled on the highway.

A friend **of Sarah's** established a successful practice in Richmond Hill.

9.2.2.2 Adverbial prepositional phrases

This type of prepositional phrase functions as an adverb. The phrase can modify a verb, an adjective or another adverb; some adverbial prepositional phrases can modify a whole clause. *(See 7.2 Adverbials)*

We were *astounded* **at her reaction**.
(**at her reaction** is an adverbial prepositional phrase modifying the adjective *astounded*)

Is it possible to meet *early* **in the morning**?
(**in the morning** is an adverbial prepositional phrase modifying the adverb *early*)

In conclusion, the committee rejected Bob's proposal.
(**In conclusion** is an adverbial prepositional phrase modifying the whole clause *the committee rejected Bob's proposal*)

Adverbial prepositional phrases generally refer to time, place, manner and purpose. They answer the questions *when? where? how?* and *why?*

Quiz 3: Adjectival or adverbial prepositional phrase
Identify the prepositional phrases and their types (adjectival or adverbial).

1) There isn't a TV in the room.
2) The buildings in our town are pretty.
3) Try to introduce the new topic with a question.
4) I met a friend of Mark's at a party last year.
5) The girl in black should be the winner, don't you think?

***In the classroom: Order of prepositional phrases ***
ESL students whose native language is of Latin origin (Spanish and Portuguese, for example) tend to insert prepositional phrases between the subject and the verb (for example, from the quiz above: ~~Try to introduce with a question the new topic~~ or ~~There isn't in the room a TV~~). This structure is usually – but is not always – incorrect. It is technically possible to use this structure as a means of giving emphasis to the prepositional phrase. In writing, such placement would require comma separation (for example, *There isn't, in the room, a TV*; see 7.3.2 Adverbs of place). Students may latch on to such exceptions to justify their tendencies to use such constructions. Exercises which reinforce the correct structure (jumbled sentences, for example) are particularly useful for these students.

9.3 Meanings of prepositions
Prepositions define a variety of relationships among elements of a sentence. The four most common categories of meaning for prepositions are place, time, direction and transportation.

Prepositions of place are used to talk about where people or things are. They indicate a place or location. The following are the most common prepositions of place.

above	below	in	on
across	beneath	in front of	outside
among	beside	inside	over
at	between	near	past
behind	close to	next to	under

The woman is waiting **outside** the cinema.
The station is **at** the corner.
We met **near** the school.

*** *In the classroom:* In, on *and* at *as prepositions of place* ***

The use of these prepositions of place may not always be clear to ESL students. Sometimes the object of the preposition makes the choice simple: that object can only accommodate one parameter of placement. For example, the preposition **in** is probably the appropriate choice for an object that is a city name. Other prepositional objects may be able to take different prepositions, depending on the intended meaning: in particular, **on**, **at** or **in** may often be applied to the same prepositional objects, giving different meanings. Examples of these prepositions and possible objects are shown below.

in (enclosed space or defined area)	on (surface or broad space)	at (a precise location, a specific point)
Paris	a page	school
my bag	the menu	home
a car	the 3rd floor	the bottom
a row	a bus/train/plane	the back
a boat	the radio/TV	the end
the paper	the coast/beach	work
the river	an island	the bus stop
my neighbourhood	the left/right	my friend's house
the cabinet	Highway 401	the post office
the office	the door the corner	the door the office
the corner	Bay Street	the corner
Bay Street		45 Bay Street

For the objects which may take more than one preposition, the differences in meaning are illustrated as follows.

> There is a note **on** *the door.* (it is attached to the surface of the door)
> There is someone **at** *the door.* (a person is at the same location as the door)
>
> We had a fire drill **at** *the office* today. (a known location)
> I saw someone crying **in** *Mr Smith's office.* (within the walls of an enclosed office)
>
> The school is **at** *the corner* of Main and Elm. (defined intersection of streets)
> Please stack those boxes **in** *the corner.* (inside a room)
> Wait for me **on** *the corner.* (somewhere on the sidewalk near the intersection)

American English uses **on** for streets; British English uses **in**.

> Sarah grew up **on** Springfield Avenue. (American English)

Sarah grew up **in** Springfield Avenue. (British English)

For a specific address on a street, **at** is used.

Sarah grew up **at** 23 Springfield Avenue.

Prepositions of time are used to indicate general or specific times or ranges of times. The following are the most common prepositions of time:

after	**by**	**in**	**through**
at	**during**	**on**	**to**
before	**for**	**past**	**until**
between (… and)	**from (… to)**	**since**	**within**
beyond			

They have been in Boston **for** a month. (duration)
They have been in Boston **since** February 10th. (from the indicated time to now)
He worked **from** 2 p.m. **to** 5 p.m.
He rested **through** the day.
Jane will be here **within** 10 minutes.

*** In the classroom: In, on and at as prepositions of time ***

Prepositions of time **in**, **on** and **at** require lots of in-context practice. The connections between prepositions and common times or time periods are different among languages. For example, some languages will use the same preposition of time before months and days; English does not. Students need to easily recall the broad categories below:

in (months, years, periods of time)	**on** (days, dates)	**at** (precise times)
March 1997 the future the 19th century the 80s the fall / spring / winter / summer the morning / afternoon / evening	24th March 24th March, 1978 my birthday Monday Christmas Day	5 p.m. noon / night sunset Christmas / Easter present the moment
time	time	

The prepositional phrase **in time** means *before it is too late*. The prepositional phrase **on time** means *at the required time; punctual*.

We'll need your help, so please try to come **in time** to give us a hand.
She is never late for class. She always arrives **on time**.

Prepositions of direction or movement are used to talk about the direction and method by which something or someone moves. The following are the most common prepositions of direction or movement:

across	down	onto	to
around	for	out	toward
at	into	over	up
by	off		

> Move the clothes **onto** the table.
> He looked **at** me!
> Sean is leaving **for** Spain in a few days.
> I am going **to** the park now.

Prepositions of transport are used to talk about methods of transport or the position or movement of a person in relation to forms of transport.

| by | into | on | out of |
| in | off | onto | via |

The preposition **by** is mainly used to talk about how people travel or use means of transport. Most modes of transportation use the preposition **by**.

> In this city, many people go to work **by** subway.

| **by** bus | **by** bicycle | **by** car | **by** train |
| **by** coach | **by** plane | **by** streetcar | **by** taxi |

With the nouns *foot* (meaning going places by walking) and *horseback*, the preposition **on** is used.

> With this traffic, it is faster to go **on** foot than **by** car.

Following are examples of other prepositions which relate to means of transport.

> Joan was **on** the plane from NY when her dad had the accident.
> The doctor followed Jon **in** his car.
> You must get **off** the bus at the next stop.
> The thief jumped **out of** the bus and got **into** a cab.

Quiz 4: Correct the mistakes

Correct the mistakes and explain what is wrong in each case.

1) Manuel is waiting for you in the bus stop.
2) Sorry, but I thought it was at the menu.
3) When will he arrive to the office?
4) He is already in the bus.
5) You may need to change your habits and start submitting your tasks in time.
6) We do not always take vacation for summer.
7) Do you think we could meet in the corner of Oxen Road and Maxwell Drive?
8) I was born in June 5th, 1997.

Other common meanings of certain prepositions are given in the table below.

Preposition	Meaning	Examples
at	indication of direction	smile at, frown at, glare at, grin at, laugh at, shoot at, shout at, stare at, wink at
at	indication of condition	at peace, at ease, at rest, at war, at risk
at	indication of reaction	adjective + *at*: amazed at, surprised at, upset at verb + *at*: cheer at, rebel at, rejoice at
by	introduces agent (do-er) of the action in passive voice constructions	The inaugural speech was delivered by the dean.
for	indication of reason or purpose	apologize for, reward for, congratulate for, thank for, expel for, pay for, punish for
like	indication of manner or similarity	look like / be like: She is like her mother.
of	indication of possession, control or association	the edge of the table, the man of the year
to	introduces an indirect object of a verb	We gave the ticket to him.
with	indication of manner or behaviour	with care, with anger, with courage, with delight, with discretion, with pride, with thanks

***In the classroom: Focus on meanings of prepositions ***

Students often do not master correct use of prepositions until well into high intermediate or advanced levels. This is partially due to the wide variety of possible meanings and collocations. The following points should be addressed and reviewed frequently in the classroom.

More than one correct choice

Some constructions allow more than one choice of preposition, with no change in meaning:

> He pointed **at** the wall.
> He pointed **to** the wall.
> He pointed **toward** the wall.

Some prepositional choices vary between British and American English.

> It is 25 minutes **past** three. (more common in British English)
> It is 25 minutes **after** three. (more common in American English)

The teacher must avoid telling students that prepositional choices that are regional variations are wrong. Teachers should instead indicate that the choice is more appropriate for another style of English.

Choice depends on part of speech

Different parts of speech with the same root will often take different prepositions.

> He was delighted **with** the favourable outcome of the proposal.
> **To** his delight, the proposal had a favourable outcome.

The main meanings of the sentences above are the same: the recipient is affected by the emotion of delight. In the first sentence, the preposition follows the participial adjective form *delighted*; in the second, it precedes the noun form *delight*. The choice of preposition and the sentence pattern vary depending on the part of speech: *be + adjective +* **with** compared to **to** *+ one's + noun*.

Gradations of meaning

The same combination of *verb + adverbial particle (or preposition)* can have completely different meanings. Context is the only way to determine which meaning is intended. For example, the combination *put +* ***down*** can have the following meanings:

suppress	pay as a deposit	put (an animal) to death
write down	attribute	insult

Prepositions can be added as prefixes to other parts of speech to form new verbs, nouns and adjectives. Practising the morphology of these words reinforces the meanings of prepositions. Some basic examples follow:

verb	**noun**	**adjective**
download	input	in-class
update	update	ongoing
withdraw	offshoot	underpaid

9.4 Prepositional patterns

Some nouns, adjectives, and verbs are always followed by particular prepositions. Some nouns are also commonly preceded by certain prepositions. Examples of these predictable patterns are given below:

noun + preposition
- answer **to**
- agreement **with**
- complaint **about**
- solution **to**
- reply **to**
- story **about**
- advice **for**
- alternative **to**
- cure **for**
- introduction **to**
- damage **to**
- problem **with**

preposition + noun
- **out of** breath
- **under** construction
- **with** care
- **in / out of** danger
- **in / out of** debt
- **at** attention

adjective + preposition
- accustomed **to**
- bored **with**
- afraid **of**
- dependent **on**
- similar **to**
- angry **with / at** (someone) **/ about** (something)
- capable **of**
- interested **in**
- different **from**
- tired **of**

verb + preposition

argue **about / over**	care **about / for**
complain **about**	inform **about / of**
worry **about**	rely **on**
count **on**	agree **on / about** (something) **/ with** (someone)
depend **on**	hear **of**
know **about / of**	remind (someone) **of**
speak **about / of**	think **about / of**
suffer **from**	accuse (someone) **of**
concentrate **on**	introduce (someone) **to**

In the classroom: Pronunciation of prepositions

For speaking fluency, learners need good awareness of sentence stress and how stress is closely related to meaning. Prepositions are function words *(See 1.9 Content words vs. function words)*, which usually are not stressed in a sentence. However, for emphasis or contrast, the speaker may want to stress a function word, making it, in effect, a content word which carries some kind of meaning in the context of conversation. In typical use, prepositions are pronounced in their weak (unstressed) forms. When they carry particular meaning in a conversation, they are pronounced in their strong (stressed) forms.

In their weak forms, the vowels in most function words are pronounced as the *schwa* sound – a short, soft "uh" – regardless of the vowels used in spelling the word. When these words are stressed, the full vowel sound is articulated. Stressed and unstressed vowel sounds differ in their articulation, length and strength. The variation in syllable length is a particularly difficult concept for many students to master.

Preposition	Strong form pronunciation	Weak form pronunciation (ə is the schwa sound, with short length and no pronunciation stress)
at	/æt/ (as in **a**pple)	/ət/ (as in **a**bout)
for	/fɔr/ or /fɔ/ (as in h**or**se)	/fər/ (r sound is not articulated in British English)
to	/tu/ (as in sh**oe**)	/tə/ (when followed by a consonant sound) /tʊ/ (when followed by a vowel sound)
of	/ɒv/ (as in **o**dd) or /ɑv/ (as in sp**a**)	/əv/
from	/frʌm/ (as in b**u**n) or /frɒm/	/frəm/ or /frm/

In most instances, prepositions are pronounced in their weak forms.

I gave it to Dave.
(no stress on *to*; sound is similar to *tDave*)

> Here is money for the fund.
> (no stress on *for*; sound is similar to *f^ethe fund*)

When a preposition is in final position in a question, then its strong form pronunciation is used.

> What did you do it **for**?

When a contrast or other emphasis is intended, then prepositions may be stressed in mid-sentence.

> Oh, I thought this was money **from** the fund.
> (emphasis is the contrast of intention: *from* vs. *for*)

**** You can teach prepositions ****

Preposition usage is often intuitive (rather than rule-based) for teachers, and providing students with clear rules of usage can be a challenge. In addition to providing lots of speaking, listening, reading and writing practice, teachers must provide students with the technical tools: the rules. Many students will have learned prepositions by rote memorization with little connection to meaning. Where possible, teach and review prepositions in ways that are fun and memorable for students. Following are some suggestions for creating meaningful and memorable lessons on prepositions.

It's an order!

Type of preposition: Place and/or direction
Topic: Commands.
Skills: Listening and speaking
Level: Beginner (young learners)

After presenting prepositions of place (in, on, over, behind, etc.) or prepositions of direction (to, toward, through, etc.), prepare to play a game. The teacher pretends to be a commander and the kids will be soldiers. They have to follow the commander's orders in order to avoid being discovered by the enemy. The commander calls out a command for the students to perform. For example:

> Put your school bag under your desk!
> Put the chair next to the desk!
> Go behind your desk!
> Crouch under the desk!
> Move slowly toward the back of the room!

The children can take turns being the commander and giving out orders to the rest of the class.

My new living room

Type of preposition: Place
Topic: Suggesting a solution
Skills: Integrated
Level: Beginner plus

This activity integrates speaking, listening, reading and writing skills. Provide the students with a plan of a room or a house. Tell them that you have moved to a new house and that you are going to need their help to place all your furniture in the house. Divide the class into two or three groups, and give them a list of all the furniture to accommodate. Each group discusses where you should put the furniture. When each group is finished, have students share their ideas with the rest of the class. Encourage students to use the language of suggestions as well as the correct preposition of place. For example:

> You *should* put the sofa **in front of** the big window.
> *Why don't you* place the TV set **on** the shelf?

To incorporate writing practice, choose one of the student designs and have students write a paragraph describing how your furniture will look in your new living room.

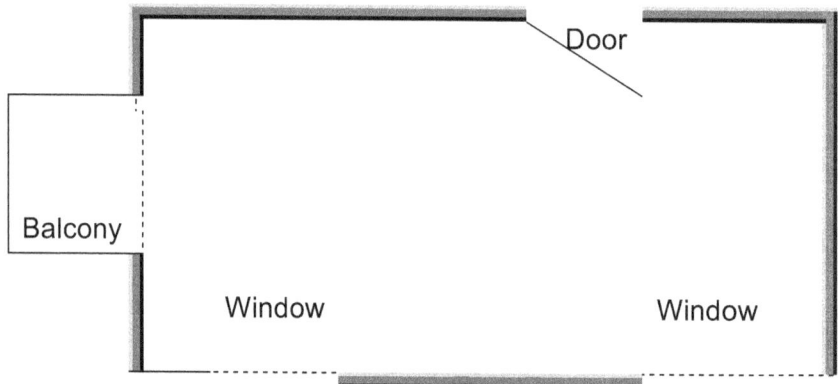

Matching cards

Type of preposition: Any
Topic: Creating prepositional phrases
Skills: Integrated
Level: Low intermediate +

This activity reviews prepositions and their possible objects. Prepare two set of cards, one with prepositions and the other one with noun phrases. Students (in pairs or groups) match the prepositions with meaningful noun phrases.

Examples:

AT	the movie theatre
ON	the kitchen table
WITH	my friend
AT	7:00 pm
ON	time

Optional: After matching prepositions with meaningful noun phrases, students may write sentences or a short paragraph. For example:

I wanted to see a movie with my friend. We agreed to meet at the movie theatre at 7:00 pm. I arrived there on time but unfortunately, I left the tickets on the kitchen table. We missed the movie.

Where were you born?

Type of preposition: Time and place
Topic: Questionnaire: classroom survey
Skills: Integrated
Level: Low intermediate +

To practise prepositions of time and place, have students create a questionnaire to find information about classmates' dates of birth, places of birth, places of residence, or other information which will elicit the desired prepositions.
Possible questions are:

When were you born? When is your birthday?
What time were you born?
Where were you born?
Where do you live?

Once the questionnaire is ready, ask students to walk around the class and find out about their classmates. They should record the answers and report them to the rest of the class. Once all students have reported their findings, have the whole class discuss any similarities (for example, people whose birthdays are on the same date, or who were born in the same country or city).

To stress or not to stress?

Type of preposition: Any
Topic: Pronunciation of weak and strong forms of prepositions
Skills: Listening and speaking
Level: All levels

Provide students with short dialogues containing examples of weak and strong prepositions. First, get them to identify all the prepositions in the dialogue. Have them work in pairs and discuss if the prepositions they have identified should be stressed or not. (Note: To do this activity, students should be familiar with the concept of stressed and unstressed words in a sentence: content and functions words.)

Check their answers. To practise sentence stress and fluency, have the students repeat each sentence in the dialogue after you. Make sure you follow the right intonation and sentence stress. Then, get them to act the dialogue out.

Optional: Students write their own dialogue, making sure they include prepositional phrases. They then act it out, showing the correct sentence stress.

Examples: (The stressed prepositions are in bold and the unstressed in italics)

> A: My name is Alex. And you?
> B: Oh, hello, Alex. I am Katrina.
> A: Hi, Katrina. Where are you **from**?
> B: I come *from* Ukraine.
>
> A: Who does this belong **to**?
> B: I don't know. It doesn't belong *to* me.

Who are they?

Type of preposition: Place (or varied types)
Topic: Identify people in a picture
Skills: Listening and speaking (reading and writing can be integrated)
Level: Beginner to Low Intermediate.

This activity requires photos or pictures showing a group of people. Hand out a copy to each student. Tell them that the people in the picture are family members (or friends, or colleagues). The students will listen to the teacher's descriptions and must then identify the people in the photo. For example:

> *My friend Mariela is in the centre. She is smiling at the camera.*
> *Her boyfriend's name is Boris. He is standing behind her. Who is*
> *the guy on the right? He is my brother, Theo. He is between Boris*
> *and my friend Pam.*

Optional: Students bring their own pictures of friends or families. They can do a similar activity as the one above, or they can ask each other questions to identify the people in the photos. For example:

> Who is the girl sitting **on** the sofa?

> She is Mariana, my sister.

Other types of prepositions can be used in this activity. For example,

> Who is the girl **with** the red bag?
> Who is the man **in** the black suit?

Are they wrong?

Type of preposition: Any
Topic: Correcting mistakes
Skills: Reading and speaking
Level: Intermediate - Advanced

Choose a text from a textbook, a magazine, or a newspaper. Make sure there are at least ten prepositions. Choose at least half of the prepositions in the text, and change them for incorrect ones. Students have to read the text and correct the prepositions that are wrong. To make the activity more challenging, have them identify the object of the preposition in each prepositional phrase.

Example:

> *Looking to somewhere to go away for a long weekend? In this time of the year, there is nowhere better than the border in England and Wales. It is full of beauty, at high hills, wooded countryside and picturesque towns and villages. Start your journey at Ludlow, which is the biggest town in the district. Cross the medieval bridge under the River Teme and enter the town on a gate in the old town walls.*

Answers:
The correct prepositions are in bold. The prepositional phrases are underlined. Prepositions that are part of a phrasal verb are in italics.

Looking **for** somewhere to *go away* for a long weekend? **At** this time of the year, there is nowhere better than the border **of** England and Wales. It is full of beauty, **with** high hills, wooded countryside and picturesque towns and villages. Start your journey **in** Ludlow, which is the biggest town in the district. Cross the medieval bridge **over** the River Teme and enter the town **through** a gate in the old town walls.
(Adapted from Opportunities – Upper intermediate - Student's book)

Collocations

Type of preposition: A combination of nouns, adjectives or verbs followed by their corresponding prepositions
Skills: Reading and speaking
Level: Intermediate - Advanced

Compile the most important prepositional patterns that students have studied during the course. Create a matching activity where students match parts of a sentence. See an example below.

Match column A to column B and complete the blanks with the correct preposition.

A

1) You can only pay
2) We need to come
3) She said she was very embarrassed
4) We should keep
5) You do not need to apologize
6) I think he is not prepared
7) You should have some respect

B

a) _____ your elders. Do not be rude!
b) _____ such a huge commitment. He needs more training.
c) _____ an agreement soon.
d) _____ credit card. Cheques are not accepted.
e) _____ anything. I was the one who was wrong. Sorry for that.
f) _____ touch. Do not forget to write to me.
g) _____ the mistake she made in her speech in front of so many people

Answers:
1-d   pay **by** credit card.
2-c   come **to** an agreement soon.
3- g   embarrassed **by** the mistake…
4- f   keep **in** touch.
5- e   apologize **for** anything.
6- b   prepared **for** such a commitment.
7- a   respect **for** your elders.

10 Conjunctions

Conjunctions are words or phrases that connect parts of a sentence to each other. Conjunctions link items of equivalent status; they can connect a noun with a noun, a verb with a verb, and so on. They do not change the meanings of the things that they connect; rather, they define the relationship between those things.

In spite of the low number of words classified as conjunctions, they appear very frequently in English. The most common conjunction is **and**, one of the five most commonly used word in the English language. The conjunctions **but** and **or** are among the 30 most frequently used words.

There are three types of conjunctions: coordinating, correlative and subordinating. Coordinating and correlative conjunctions may link words, phrases or clauses. Subordinating conjunctions link clauses (or reduced clauses) only. Other words and phrases – known as linkers or transition signals – perform functions similar to conjunctions.

*** *In the classroom: Equivalence* ***

In all cases of conjunction use, the elements that are connected by the conjunctions must be of equivalent type. This equivalence is also called parallelism.

Common errors are things like:

> ~~The country is~~ **both** ~~prosperous~~ **and** ~~it is growing~~,

where the linked elements are not the same type (an adjective and a clause, in this case). The correct versions of the previous sentence would be:

> The country is **both** *prosperous* **and** *growing*. (linking adjectives)
> The country **both** *is prosperous* **and** *is growing*. (linking phrases)

A variant of this problem is hypercorrection: students may try to add extra conjunctions, particularly if their native language uses this structure.

> ~~**Since**~~ ~~the garden is beautiful~~ **because** ~~it has nice flowers~~.

10.1 Conjunction forms

Conjunctions have three basic forms. They may be single words, stand-alone phrases, or related pairings. Correlative conjunctions are, by definition, in the form of related pairings of words or phrases within a sentence. Conjunctions that are phrases are sometimes called compound or complex conjunctions.

10.1.1 Single-word conjunctions

Single-word (or simple) conjunctions include the most commonly-used conjunctions. Following are the single-word conjunctions.

Table 42: Single-word conjunctions

after	considering	once	that	where
although	for	or	though	whereas
and	if	provided/providing	till	wherever
as	lest*	since	unless	whether
because	like	so	until	while/whilst
before	neither	supposing	when	yet
but	nor	than		

* When using **lest**, the verb in the clause following **lest** must be in the subjunctive mood.

Many of these words may also function as adverbs or prepositions. The function that the word performs in a sentence determines its part of speech in these cases.

> He completed the report **before** he went home.
> (**before** is a conjunction connecting the dependent clause *before he went home* to the independent clause *He completed the report*)

> Please complete the report *before* the end of the day.
> (*before* is a preposition, with the noun phrase *the end of the day* as its object)

> **Since** you're offering, I will have another drink.
> (**Since** is a conjunction connecting the dependent clause *Since you're offering* to the independent clause *I will have another drink*)

> We had a huge breakfast and haven't eaten *since*.
> (*since* is an adverb of time modifying the verb phrase *haven't eaten*)

10.1.2 Conjunction phrases

These phrases serve the same grammatical function in a sentence as do single-word conjunctions. In addition to these, many conjunctions are commonly introduced by the adverbs *even*, *just* or *only* to create a more specific version of the conjunctions. Examples of these include **even though**, **just as** and **only if**. Many single-word conjunctions are followed by *that* to create a conjunction phrase.

Table 43: Conjunction phrases

as if	in case	providing that
as far as	in order for	seeing that
as long as	in order that	so as + *to-infinitive*
as soon as	in order + *to-infinitive*	so that
as though	in that	such that
assuming that	in the event that	supposing that
considering that	inasmuch as	the minute
each/every time	insofar as	the moment
except that	much as	the second
given that	now that	the way
granted that	on condition that	whether or not
if only	provided that	*imperative* + and / or

The pairing of a verb in the imperative form with the single-word conjunctions **and** or **or** creates a conjunction phrase in which the two conjoined sentence parts do not seem to be equivalent. The meaning of the pairing of the imperative (with no explicit subject, only an implied one) with the conjunction (followed by a full clause, with subject) is that of a conditional, often containing a threat.

> *Stop* **or** I'll shoot!
> *Leave* **and** you'll be sorry.

10.1.3 Conjunction pairs

Conjunction pairs are sets of words that work together, though they are separated within the sentence. They work in a specific way to relate the other words, phrases and clauses to which they are connected. Conjunction pairs are always correlative conjunctions. *(See 10.3.2 Correlative conjunctions)*

Table 44: Conjunction pairs

as ... so	either ... or	neither ... nor	not (only) ... but (also)
both ... and	if ... then	no sooner ... than	whether ... or

Quiz 1: Identifying conjunctions

Indicate whether the underlined word(s) in each sentence are conjunctions or not. Give reasons for your answer.

1. Straighten up <u>or</u> you'll be sorry.
2. <u>While</u> he was traveling, Stan finished the book.
3. <u>During</u> his vacation, Stan finished the book.
4. You're just <u>as</u> cute <u>as</u> a button!
5. Ted always opens the windows <u>the minute</u> he arrives.
6. I've never seen them <u>before</u>.
7. Edith is talkative, <u>whereas</u> her sister is not.
8. Don't start <u>until</u> I tell you.
9. Can you stay <u>until</u> the end?
10. We have permission, <u>so</u> it's okay.

**** In the classroom: Same word, different part of speech ****

A great many conjunctions also function as other parts of speech (particularly prepositions). Further complicating the confusion for students is that there are similarities of meaning which may cause them to transpose words and use the incorrect part of speech. The most common occurrence of this is with subordinating conjunctions. *(See 10.3.3 Subordinating conjunctions)* For example, the subordinating conjunctions **as**, **after**, **before**, **since** and **until** may also be prepositions. Other subordinating conjunctions (such as **although**, **because** and **while**) carry meanings that are similar to prepositions (*despite*, *because of* and *during*), and are often confused with them. In addition, there is a large set of conjunctive adverbs for which the distinction between conjunction and adverb is not always obvious. (For more on conjunctive adverbs, see the *You Can Teach Grammar* companion web site.)

The most direct way of addressing this is to use a syntactic (sentence structure) approach: subordinating conjunctions must introduce clauses, and prepositions will have objects (which are not clauses).

Some pairings can be given for students to identify, or students may be asked to construct a correct pairing.

For example, with the pairs:

> during / while: math class / letter to mother
> despite / although: very hot weather / outdoor restaurant

students might construct appropriate outcomes like:

> During math class, I wrote a letter to my mother.
> (preposition with object *math class*)
> While I was in math class, I wrote a letter to my mother.
> (conjunction introducing the dependent clause *I was in math class*)

10.2 Sentence types

There are four basic sentence types. These sentence types are based on the presence and role of clauses within the sentence. The sentence types are: simple; compound; complex; and compound complex. Conjunctions may be found in all four types of sentences. They are often essential in compound, complex and compound complex sentences.

10.2.1   Simple sentences

A simple sentence contains one clause. That clause may have conjunctions within it, but it is not necessary. If a simple sentence contains conjunctions, they will be joining nouns, verbs, adjectives or adverbs (not clauses). The conjunctions that may be contained in a simple sentence are coordinating and correlative conjunctions. *(See 10.3 Conjunctions types)*

> Bob likes cheese. (one clause; no conjunctions)
> Bob *eats* **and** *drinks* heartily. (one clause; conjunction linking verbs)

10.2.2   Compound sentences

A compound sentence contains two or more independent clauses. The clauses in a compound sentence may be separated by a semicolon with a conjunctive adverb *(See 10.3.4 Other linkers and transition signals)*, by a semicolon alone, by correlative conjunctions, or by a coordinating conjunction.

> Bob likes cheese; *however*, his wife hates it. (semicolon and conjunctive adverb)
> Bob likes cheese; his wife hates it. (semicolon alone)
> **As** Bob likes cheese, **so** his wife hates it. (correlative conjunction)
> Bob likes cheese **and** his wife hates it. (coordinating conjunction)
> Bob likes cheese **but** his wife hates it. (coordinating conjunction)

10.2.3   Complex sentences

A complex sentence contains a dependent (subordinate) clause and an independent clause. These clauses may be separated by a subordinating conjunction or a relative pronoun. The correct categorization of a clause as dependent or independent is crucial to the correct usage of conjunctions and punctuation. *(See In the classroom – Subordination, at the end of section 10.3.4)*

Betty works with Annette, **though** Annette is rarely in the office.
(subordinate clause introduced by the subordinating conjunction **though**)

Betty works with Annette, who is rarely in the office.
(subordinate clause introduced by the relative pronoun *who*)

10.2.4   Compound complex sentences

A compound complex sentence contains two or more independent clauses and one or more dependent clauses. These clauses may be separated by conjunctive adverbs, semicolons, coordinating conjunctions and subordinating conjunctions.

It rained all night; *however*, we stayed dry **because** the tent was waterproof.
(independent clause introduced by a semicolon and a conjunctive adverb; dependent clause introduced by the subordinating conjunction **because**)

10.3 Conjunction types

There are three types of conjunctions: coordinating, correlative and subordinating. These three types are a guideline. There is a great deal of inconsistency in the classification of conjunctions into these categories. Sometimes classification is based on the meaning imparted by the conjunction (semantic classification), sometimes on the rules of grammatical structure for the conjunction (syntactic classification). The semantic and syntactic classifications are not always the same; there are certain conjunctions that fall into one category semantically and another syntactically.

The approach taken here is to include a range of possible conjunctions in each category and then discuss possible points of confusion or variability.

10.3.1   Coordinating conjunctions

Coordinating conjunctions connect similar things, in a roughly equivalent sense. They can connect nouns to nouns (and noun phrases), nouns to pronouns, pronouns to pronouns, verbs to verbs (and verb phrases), adjectives to adjectives (and adjective phrases), adverbs to adverbs (and adverbials), and independent clauses to independent clauses. The main coordinating conjunctions are **and**, **but**, **nor**, **or** and **yet**. The conjunctions **for** and **so** may also be classified as coordinating conjunctions, but this categorization is less clear.

Judy **and** *I* are never late. (connecting a noun and a pronoun)
Always give corrections *gently* **but** *firmly*. (adverbs)
Kevin didn't make mistakes, **but** *rather sailed through the exam*. (clauses)
The visitor didn't want to go, **nor** *did he want to stay*. (negative clauses)
The young lovers were *poor* **yet** *happy*. (adjectives)
Her advice is to *lead, follow*, **or** *get out of the way*. (verbs and verb phrase)

Semantically, coordinating conjunctions provide a logical link between ideas. They may carry a meaning of addition (called cumulative or copulative: **and**, **so**), contrast (called adversative: **but**, **yet**), choice (called alternative or disjunctive: **or, nor**) or inference (called illative: **for**, **so**). These semantic categories include **for** and **so**. When **for** is used as a conjunction, it is only used to connect clauses.

> They couldn't run fast enough, **so** they missed the bus.
> Tom will never forget that day, **for** he lost his true love to a rival.

Syntactically, coordinating conjunctions conform to some basic structural rules:
- They must connect like elements: nouns with nouns, adjectives with adjectives, and so on.
- When connecting clauses, they may not change place in a sentence; a change in position may cause the sentence to change meaning, or it will not make sense.
- They must maintain a position *between* the elements they are connecting.
- When a coordinating conjunction connects two clauses and the clauses have the same subject, it is not necessary to repeat the subject in the second clause.

Following the syntactic rules, **for** and **so** do not conform to the category of coordinating conjunctions. Using **for** and **so** (when used to mean an inference) to connect clauses, it is necessary to repeat the subject, even if it is the same in both clauses.

> ~~They couldn't run fast enough, **so** missed the bus.~~
> ~~Tom will never forget that day, **for** lost his true love to a rival.~~

The conjunctions **nor** and **so** (when used with an additive meaning) require special syntax when used to connect clauses. With these conjunctions, the subject *follows* the verb in the second clause, a process called inversion of order. In the case of **nor**, the first clause must be stated as a negative.

> Sophie is a billiards enthusiast; **so** is her friend.
> I don't drink alcohol, **nor** does my sister.

10.3.2 Correlative conjunctions

Correlative conjunctions are pairs of words that work together to show a relationship between two roughly equal elements of a sentence. The second part of the correlative pair is usually a coordinating conjunction. The main correlative conjunctions are

| as ... so | both ... and | either ... or | if ... then |
| neither ... nor | no sooner ... than | not (only) ... but (also) | whether ... or |

Correlative conjunctions are considered by many to be simply a variant form of coordinating conjunction, not a separate type of conjunction. Correlative conjunctions operate in basically the same way as do coordinating conjunctions: they link words or phrases of the same type. The main correlative conjunctions fall into the same semantic categories as do coordinating conjunctions: addition (**both...and, no sooner...than**); contrast (**as...so, not...but**); choice (**either...or, neither...nor, whether...or**) and inference (**if...then**).

> It's **neither** *fish* **nor** *fowl*. (nouns)
> I don't know **whether** *to take the train* **or** *fly*. (verb phrase/verb)

The young model was **not** *beautiful* **but** *pretty*. (adjectives)

Syntactically, the first word in the correlative conjunction pair must be placed before the first element being linked and the second word in the correlative conjunction must be placed between the elements being linked.

10.3.3 Subordinating conjunctions

Subordinating conjunctions indicate that one idea is dependent upon, or subordinate to, another. They are used to connect clauses. Subordinating conjunctions are always positioned at the beginning of a dependent (subordinate) clause. Subordinating conjunctions appear in complex sentences. Some of the main subordinating conjunctions are **after**, **because**, **before**, **if**, **since**, **unless** and **until**.

> **Unless** I get a huge raise, I'm quitting my job this year.
> The home team will surely win **if** all the players are healthy.

Semantically, subordinating conjunctions indicate that one idea is subordinate to another in the sentence. They may carry a meaning of time (**after**, **as**, **before**, **once**, **since**, **until**, **when**, **while**); result (**so**); place (**where**, **wherever**); manner (**as**); reason or purpose (**as**, **because**, **for**, **lest**, **since**); concession, comparison or contrast (**although**, **though**, **whereas**, **while**); and condition (**if**, **provided**, **providing**, **whether**).

Syntactically, subordinating conjunctions conform to some basic structural rules.
- They must connect clauses to other clauses.
- They may sometimes move around in a sentence without changing the meaning of the sentence.
- They must maintain a position *directly before* the dependent clause.
- When a subordinating conjunction connects two clauses and the clauses have the same subject, it is still necessary to repeat the subject in the second clause.

Both semantically and syntactically, subordinating conjunctions resemble adverbs, since adverbs can also refer to a whole clause. These adverbial subordinators are sometimes technically classified as conjunctions and sometimes as adverbs. Regardless of the classification, the function remains the same, and the syntactic rules are the same. *(See 10.3.4 and 10.4.3 for rules on other linkers)*

Some subordinating conjunctions appear to connect a clause to a word or phrase. In these cases, the phrases are actually reduced clauses in which the main verb is *to be*; the subject and the verb *be* are elided. The subordinating conjunctions that may work in this way are **although**, **if**, **unless**, **when**, **whenever** and **while**.

> She volunteers to help **whenever** (it is) necessary.
> Ask your teacher **if** (you are) in doubt.

In addition to the simple subordinating conjunctions listed above, some common phrases are classified as subordinators. These serve the same functions as simple subordinating conjunctions and follow the same grammatical rules. They may be called subordinators, subordinate conjunctions, subordinate clause introducers or adverbial subordinators. Following is a more complete list of these subordinators, classified by semantic category. These semantic categories have direct correlations to types of adverbs. *(See 7.3 Adverbs and adverbials classified by meaning)*

Subordinators of time
- after
- before
- since
- when
- as
- each time
- the minute/moment/second
- while/whilst
- as long as
- every time
- as soon as
- once
- until

Subordinators of result
- in order that
- so
- so that
- such that

Subordinators of purpose
- in order for
- so that
- in order that
- so as + *to-infinitive*
- in order + *to-infinitive*

Subordinators of place
- where
- wherever
- everywhere

Subordinators of manner
- as
- like (informal)
- as if
- the way
- as though
- in that

Subordinators of reason
- as
- in the event that
- lest
- because
- seeing (that)
- now (British English)
- for
- inasmuch as
- now that
- in case
- since
- so

Subordinators of concession or contrast
- although
- much as
- considering
- though
- even though
- whereas
- in that
- while/whilst

Subordinators of condition
- as long as
- if
- provided
- whether or not
- assuming (that)
- if only
- providing
- *imperative* + and
- given that
- in case
- supposing (that)
- *imperative* + or
- granted that
- on condition that
- whether

Quiz 2: Conjunction types

Identify the type (coordinating, correlative or subordinating) of the underlined conjunctions below. Identify what parts of the sentence the conjunctions are connecting.

1) <u>Seeing that</u> we're already here, let's take a look.
2) Regina looked up <u>and</u> down <u>and</u> all around.
3) The berries are easy to reach, <u>but</u> they're surrounded by thorns.
4) Let's just say that the experience left us older <u>but</u> wiser.
5) <u>Both</u> the boater <u>and</u> her dog fell asleep on the deck.

10.3.3.1 Complementizers

Subordinate clauses can take on the role of a noun in a sentence. This noun role may be that of a subject, object or subject complement. *(See 2.1 Mandatory sentence elements and 2.2 Optional sentence elements)* The word which introduces such a dependent clause is called a complementizer. The most common complementizer is *that*. The other main complementizers are *if* and *whether*. Some grammarians also include the relative pronouns *which, who* and *whom* in this category. When used before a to-infinitive, *for* also acts as a complementizer. These words are sometimes considered to be a special class of subordinating conjunction because of the role they play as the introducers of subordinate clauses.

> She said *that it was okay*.
> (complementizer *that* introducing the subordinate clause *that it was okay*, which is the direct object of the verb *said*)
>
> Please tell me *if you're coming*.
> (complementizer *if* introducing the subordinate clause *if you're coming*, which is the direct object of the verb *tell*)
>
> We never know *whether it will work*.
> (complementizer *whether* introducing the subordinate clause *whether it will work*, which is the direct object of the verb *know*)
>
> It is unusual *for John to give a recommendation*.
> (complementizer *for + to give* introducing the subordinate clause *for John to give a recommendation*, which is the subject complement)

10.3.4 Other linkers and transition signals

There is a special category of adverbs, called conjunctive adverbs, which function similarly to conjunctions; however, they are not considered conjunctions. They are also called adverbial conjunctions, transition words or linking words.

Common conjunctive adverbs are:

accordingly	consequently	however	otherwise
again	finally	indeed	therefore
also	for example	moreover	then
besides	furthermore	nevertheless	

Other common linking and transition words and phrases include:

after all	for the time being	in the long run	on the contrary
as a result	for this reason	in the meantime	on the other hand
at that time	in other words	in particular	on the whole

Semantically, many of these words and phrases are virtually identical to some conjunctions. The significant distinctions between these words and conjunctions are syntactic. These linkers take different punctuation than conjunctions do. Unlike subordinating conjunctions, they may be used in simple sentences. Subordinating conjunctions may only be used in complex sentences. *(See 10.2.3 Complex sentences)*

*** In the classroom: Subordination ***

Most of the time it is not necessary for ESL students to be aware of whether a conjunction is coordinating or subordinating. When conjunctions are operating on nouns, verbs, adjectives and adverbs, the only possible conjunctions are coordinating (or correlative). But, when connecting clauses, the nature of the clause (dependent or independent) and the nature of the conjunction (subordinating or coordinating) become important. It is not always a straightforward exercise to differentiate between them.

The most common technique for differentiating between dependent and independent clauses is the test of whether a clause can "stand alone" in a sentence. This is a good technique for introducing the topic, but it requires that the dependence of the subordinate clause is very clear. So, examples like:

Clause 1:
she is only ten years old

Clause 2:
she can't vote

make an easy-to-discern relationship: *She can't vote **because** she is only ten years old* or ***Since** she is only ten years old, she can't vote*. This type of clear distinction is needed for introducing the concept.

In reality, many clauses are not so easily differentiated. It is the very presence of the conjunction that defines dependence or independence, not the inherent meaning of the individual clauses. In the example:

Clause 1:
Fred arrived late

Clause 2:
he didn't know where to go

the causal relationship, if any, is not inherent. So, for reading and listening work, where the conjunctions are already present, the question of subordination is easily answered. But, for speaking and writing, students must be able to understand that their choices of conjunction will dictate the relationship.

The clause *Fred arrived late* may be logically treated as dependent in some situations and as independent in others. The structure of the base clause itself, then (without the conjunction), does not always define dependence. It is generally the writer's intention alone which dictates whether one clause is subordinate to another clause. It is very often *only* the presence of a conjunction which indicates this. With the clauses *Fred arrived late* and *he didn't know where to go*, it is not obvious which clause is subordinate; the specific circumstance dictates which is correct. Once subordination has been decided, then the full clause (containing the subordinating conjunction) is, by definition, a subordinate clause.

So, **because** *Fred didn't know where to go* is clearly a subordinate clause. And **because** *he arrived late* is clearly a subordinate clause. The presence of the subordinating conjunction makes it unquestionable. The correct *placement* of the subordinating conjunction, therefore, is a crucial skill.

At beginner and low intermediate levels, it is common to describe an independent clause as one that can "stand alone", using examples where the cause and effect are obvious. At higher levels, other techniques are necessary. A focus on semantics may help here. To help students practise, choose a set of subordinating conjunctions (or conjunctive adverbs) from the same semantic category (time, reason, comparison). This allows the teacher to present a set of logical questions for checking the accuracy of the relationship between the clauses.

For example, if a lesson is focused on correct use of subordinating conjunctions of reason, then independent clauses (or sentences) may be presented, and straightforward questions asked of the cause-and-effect relationship between them. If the answers to the questions are known (or assumed), then identification of the subordinate clause is clear and the application of the correct conjunction is a mechanical exercise.

Clause/sentence 1: *Sharon likes winter.*
Clause/sentence 2: *Brad became a ski instructor.*

Questions:
Do we know why Sharon likes winter? Do we know why Brad became a ski instructor? Is there a relationship between these things?

Clause/sentence 1: *They believed the rumour.*
Clause/sentence 2: *The underdog won the election.*

Questions:
Do we know why they believed the rumour? Do we know why the underdog won the election? Is there a relationship between these things?

One of the most common student errors is to use a subordinating conjunction and then to fail to include a corresponding independent clause, as in:

Although ~~the garden is beautiful and peaceful with all the flowers~~.

This is often the result of concentration on semantics rather than syntax.

10.4 Punctuation

Conjunctions often require specific punctuation. The punctuation requirements vary depending on the nature of the elements that are linked by the conjunctions.

10.4.1 Linking nouns, verbs, adjectives and adverbs

When conjunctions connect two nouns, verbs, adjectives and adverbs to one another, it is usually not necessary to include special punctuation.

The dog is old **yet** healthy.
I don't know **whether** I'm coming **or** going.

When conjunctions join more than two nouns, verbs, adjectives or adverbs, then the string of items is separated with commas. The use of a comma between the final item in the list and the conjunction is a style choice. This comma is commonly known as a serial comma or "the Oxford comma." It is strictly a case of style preference. The use (or non-use) of this comma is neither right nor wrong, but it should be consistent. If it is used once in a piece of writing, it should be used throughout that piece.

> Those things will make a man *healthy*, *wealthy*, **and** *wise*.
> (three adjectives joined by the conjunction **and** are separated by: a comma between the first and second adjectives; a serial comma between the second adjective and the conjunction)

> Those things will make a man *healthy*, *wealthy* **and** *wise*.
> (same structure without the serial comma)

In cases where the list contains separate phrases, then it may be necessary to include a serial comma for clarity of separation, so as to ensure that the conjunction is not seen as part of one of the phrases.

> Debbie's hair was *let down*, *brushed out*, **and** *pinned to the side*.

10.4.2 Linking clauses

There are several options for linking independent clauses. Independent clauses can, by definition, stand alone as separate sentences. When the ideas are closely linked, however, it may be desirable to put them together in a single sentence. If they are joined in a single sentence, they may be separated by a semicolon and nothing else.

> Fred arrived late; he didn't know where to go.

Independent clauses may not be separated by a comma alone. Linking independent clauses in this way is a very common error known as a comma splice.

> ~~Fred arrived late, he didn't know where to go.~~

When conjunctions connect independent clauses, the nature of the sentence dictates the need for additional punctuation. Many independent clauses can be joined with a conjunction and no other punctuation.

> Fred arrived late **and** he didn't know where to go.
> (two independent clauses; no additional punctuation needed)

In the above example, it is possible to separate the independent clauses with a comma. This is a style choice. Some writers prefer to use a comma between independent clauses in every case, in a style similar to that of the serial comma. *(See 10.4.1 Linking nouns, verbs, adjectives and adverbs)* When the independent clauses have a complicated structure, then the addition of a comma may be necessary for clarity, to ensure that the conjunction is not seen as part of the wrong clause.

Fred *and* Adele got distracted *and* arrived late**,** **and** they didn't know where to go.

> first independent clause: Fred **and** Adele got distracted **and** arrived late
>
> second independent clause: **and** they didn't know where to go
>
> (first clause contains two coordinating conjunctions (connecting nouns *Fred* and *Adele*, and connecting verb phrases *got distracted* and *arrived late*); without the comma, the reader might initially read the third **and** as part of the first independent clause)

When **and** connects independent clauses, there is often an additional sense of sequence and possibly of cause and effect. In the example *Fred arrived late and didn't know where to go*, it may be assumed that first Fred arrived late, then found (as a result) that he didn't know where to go. If the order changes, the meaning may change.

> Fred didn't know where to go **and** he arrived late.
> (first he didn't know, causing late arrival)

When conjunctions connect a dependent clause and an independent clause, there may be a need for additional punctuation. If the independent clause comes first, and the sentence has no further complexities, then no additional punctuation is necessary. When the dependent clause comes first, then the clauses must be separated by a comma.

> Fred didn't know where to go **because** he arrived late.
> (independent clause preceding a dependent clause)
>
> **Because** he arrived late**,** Fred didn't know where to go.
> (dependent clause preceding an independent clause)

Some subordinating conjunctions function in more than one capacity. For these, commas are needed for ease of reading. They serve as an indicator that they are introducing a certain type of clause, rather than serving another function.

The subordinating conjunction **so** has two possible meanings as a subordinator. One meaning is that the subordinate clause is the *result* of the independent clause. Another meaning is that the subordinate clause is the *reason* for the independent clause. When the former meaning (subordinate clause is the result) is intended, then a comma is needed, even if the dependent clause follows the independent clause.

> The candidate volunteered **so** he wouldn't have to wait.
> (meaning is reason; no punctuation)
>
> The candidate volunteered**,** **so** he didn't have to wait.
> (meaning is result; comma needed)

A similar situation occurs with other "multi-purpose" conjunctions. The conjunction **as** can be a subordinator conveying a sense of time, of manner, or of reason. The subordinating conjunction **since** can convey meanings of time or of reason.

When **as** and **since** convey a sense of reason, the dependent clause is usually separated from the independent clause by a comma, even when the independent clause comes first. The same is true when **as** conveys a sense of manner.

> John tiptoed into the room quietly **as** his child slept.
> (meaning is time; no punctuation)
>
> It was excellent, **as** I told you.
> (meaning is manner; comma preferred)
>
> The shoes were ice cold, **as** they had been left on the porch all night.
> (meaning is reason; comma preferred)
>
> Nobody has seen the neighbours **since** they went on vacation.
> (meaning is time; no punctuation)
>
> I refuse to help, **since** you're being such a brat.
> (meaning is reason; comma preferred)

The subordinating conjunction **while** can convey a sense of time or of contrast. When conveying contrast, the dependent clause is usually separated from the independent clause by a comma, even when the independent clause comes first.

> Stan shaved **while** the kettle boiled.
> (meaning is time; no punctuation)
>
> Betty is a brilliant artist, **while** her brother is less gifted.
> (meaning is contrast; punctuation preferred)

With subordinating conjunctions that may also be prepositions *(See 9.1.1 Simple prepositions)*, a comma ensures clarity, even when the dependent clause follows the independent clause.

> I have been waiting here *since* yesterday.
> (*since* is a preposition)
>
> I have been waiting here, **since** it's the most obvious location.
> (**since** is a subordinating conjunction – the comma makes it easier to identify it as such)

When the structure of the sentence is very complex, or if the connection between the clauses is very loose, even independent clauses should be separated with punctuation.

> Sharon wanted to see the new Italian action movie, **and** the train was running late, **and** Terry never goes out on Tuesdays, **so** I changed my mind.

Whenever a conjunction requires a punctuation mark (comma or semicolon), the punctuation comes *before* the conjunction.

It is possible to link clauses using other linkers, such as conjunctive adverbs. *(See 10.3.4 Other linkers and transition signals)* When these are used, they are followed by a comma. The conjunctive adverb may begin a sentence, or it may be offset from the other clause by a semicolon.

> Fred arrived late. *Therefore*, he didn't know where to go.
> Fred arrived late; *therefore*, he didn't know where to go.

10.4.3   Punctuation for linkers and transitions signals

Conjunctions do not always require special punctuation. When conjunctions require punctuation, the punctuation (comma or semicolon) comes *before* the conjunction (or sometimes before the independent clause; see *10.4.2 Linking clauses*). Other linking words and phrases (not conjunctions) are usually offset by punctuation, and the punctuation (comma or period) comes *after* the linking words or phrases, with other punctuation also possible before the linking word or phrase. The linking words and phrases may come at the beginning of a clause or sentence. If they begin a clause (but not a sentence), they will be preceded by a semicolon. Whether they begin a clause or a sentence, they are followed by a comma. If they end a sentence, they are preceded by a comma. If they are in the middle of a sentence, they are surrounded by commas.

> Fred arrived late **and** he didn't know where to go.
> (coordinating conjunction – no punctuation)
>
> Fred arrived late; *also,* he didn't know where to go.
> (linker/conjunctive adverb – semicolon and comma)
>
> Fred didn't know where to go **because** he arrived late.
> (subordinating conjunction with dependent clause after independent clause – no punctuation)
>
> **Because** Fred arrived late**,** he didn't know where to go.
> (subordinating conjunction with dependent clause before independent clause – comma between clauses)
>
> Fred arrived late. *As a result,* he didn't know where to go.
> (linker – start of a new sentence, followed by a comma)
>
> Fred arrived late; he didn't know where to go, *as a result.*
> (linker – end of the sentence – preceded by a comma)
>
> Fred arrived late. He didn't know, *as a result,* where to go.
> (linker in the middle of the clause – separated on both sides by commas)

It is possible to insert a dependent clause into the middle of an independent clause. In those cases, the dependent clause must be delimited by commas.

> Fred, **because** he arrived late, didn't know where to go.
> (the dependent clause **because** *he arrived late* is inserted into the independent clause *Fred didn't know where to go* and is enclosed in commas)

Conjunctions join parts of a sentence, so there must always be a "matching" element when a conjunction is used. These linking words and phrases do not have the same limitation.

> *Also,* he didn't know where to go. (acceptable sentence structure)
> ~~Because~~ ~~Fred arrived late~~. (corresponding independent clause is missing)

While the use of coordinating conjunctions to join separate sentences is discouraged, especially in formal or technical writing, it is acceptable in many contexts. These cases – usually using **and**, **but**, or **or** – are exceptions to the rule that the "matching" element must be contained in the same sentence. If not contained in the same sentence, the element which is being linked must be immediately close to the conjunction, or it must be easily understood by the reader or listener.

> I would never use the company's photocopier for personal copies. **Or** I would ask my boss if it's okay.

Quiz 3: Punctuation

The appropriate conjunctions and punctuation are missing. Insert punctuation and/or conjunctions in the blanks, as appropriate.

1. _____ that was a passing train _____ we just had an earthquake.
2. Please turn down the music _____ I complain to the management.
3. _____ you turn down the music _____ I will complain to the management.
4. I will complain to the management _____ you turn down the music.
5. Please turn down the music _____ I will complain to the management.
6. It's our anniversary _____ Tracey bought us a gift.
7. Tracey _____ it's our anniversary _____ bought us a gift.
8. Tracey bought us a gift _____ it's our anniversary.
9. _____ it's our anniversary _____ Tracey bought us a gift.
10. Traditionalists don't like that style _____ do modernists.

*** In the classroom: Punctuation ***

Conjunctions usually signal some sort of break in the logic or flow of a sentence. In spoken English, these are often marked with a change in pace or intonation. In writing, these breaks may be marked with punctuation. The greatest student problems come from using punctuation to unnecessarily mark the breaks, pauses and changes of spoken English. Errors of this type are particularly common with conjunctions, and the most common error is to follow a conjunction with a comma.

Another common error is the confusion of conjunctions with other discourse markers, which take different punctuation. *(See 10.4.3 Punctuation for linkers and transition signals)* Comma splices *(See 10.4.2 Linking clauses)* are a chronic problem. The overuse of conjunctions to join independent clauses (rather than putting them in separate sentences) results in unnecessarily long, run-on sentences. There are clear rules to address all of these problems. Frequent review of the rules, coupled with guided practice, will reduce these errors.

*** You can teach conjunctions ***

Beginners need a solid grounding in the coordinating and correlative conjunctions. The methods for teaching and reinforcing those concepts are fairly straightforward. Subordinating conjunctions require much more clarity in their introduction and practice. The use of subordinating conjunctions is an area where errors in usage are much more common, and rules and usage and punctuation may need to be reinforced from beginner through advanced levels.

Coordinating and correlative conjunctions

Some of the major considerations in teaching coordinating and correlative conjunctions are semantics and parallelism. The easiest for beginners to understand are the common coordinating conjunctions **and**, **but** and **or**. These generally have the most direct correlation to similar formations in other languages. Lists, descriptions and the consideration of options are good scenarios for introducing and practising these concepts. The less commonly used conjunctions **nor** and **yet** are a bit trickier.

Making lists

For connecting nouns using coordinating or correlative conjunctions, introduce scenarios whereby students must create and articulate lists. Role-playing a shopping activity may work well for this, or packing items for a trip.

Get students to choose from a list (from a provided list, from pictures, or from their own imaginations). They should then use complete sentences to ask about or describe their lists. Example output:

    Student A: What will you buy at the store?
    Student B: I will get eggs, milk **and** butter.

Variations: Get students to ask about or articulate choices or exceptions

    Student A: Would you prefer plastic, canvas **or** leather?
    Student B: I would like **either** canvas **or** leather, please.

Describing things

Activities where students must describe things will reinforce the conjunctions used to connect adjectives, verbs or adverbs. Provide students with pictures or with scenarios and ask them to make descriptions. Some examples of output includes:

Describing pictures:
    the man is old **but** strong (adjectives)
    they are walking **and** talking (verbs)
    it moves quickly **yet** quietly (adverbs)

Scenarios for creating descriptions could include: for adjectives, a self-description (for identifying one's self to a stranger for a meeting, say) or a guess-who (describe a known person); for verbs, a how-to (directions on making a cake or playing a game correctly); and for adverbs, a review or recounting of a performance or experience.

Considering options

The coordinating conjunctions **or**, **nor** and **yet** figure particularly in activities that include the consideration of options. A variation of this could include scenarios for making excuses. Students can be tasked with choosing items or activities in some scenario. Expressing simple preferences, selecting a gift, choosing an employment candidate, or making travel plans are some sample situations for such activities. Expected output could include:

> I don't know whether to buy the red hat **or** the green hat.
> That candidate is **neither** experienced **nor** qualified.
> The package deal to Jamaica is all-inclusive **but** expensive.

Subordinating conjunctions

Lessons that review and practise subordinating conjunctions benefit from a focus on semantics. The use of subordinators is generally easier to understand when the speaker's intent is the focus (rather than the mechanics of the structure). The structures associated with subordinating conjunctions are complex, as they require at least two subjects and two verbs in a sentence. Their close association with other discourse markers make their review still relevant even for advanced learners. Beyond the beginner and low intermediate levels, it is unusual to devote lessons strictly to conjunctions. The grammar of conjunctions will generally be combined with other concepts. Lessons that will practise the complex structures requiring conjunctions include ones that present contexts of multitasking, decision-making or deduction.

Time: multitasking

The subordinating conjunctions of time can be well-demonstrated and practised using situations that involve multi-tasking or the planning of activities. Provide students scenarios where they have multiple activities to complete in a short period of time. They must plan how to perform the tasks within the limited time. Example outputs could include:

> **As soon as** the eggs are done, I will start the dishwasher.
> I will choose my clothing **before** I go to bed.
> I can continue to make phone calls **until** the bus arrives.

Purpose / reason: decision-making

Provide students with situations related to decision-making and get them to justify their choices. Scenarios could be as simple as choosing menu items, or as deep as making life decisions like career choices or moving abroad. The expected output will have students employing conjunctions of purpose and reason.

> **Seeing as** it's on special, I'll take the lasagna.
> I would accept the lower-paying job **in order to** get experience there.
> I wouldn't choose to live in Saudi Arabia **because** it's too hot for me.

Deductions

Subordinating conjunctions that introduce conditions can be practised in activities that require the use of deduction. Any scenario that contains an unknown element (solving a mystery, making assumptions) will work to practise these forms. These could also be paired with modal verbs of deduction. Some expected outputs could include:

>**Assuming** they left on time, they'll be there by now.
>They won't be there yet **if** they didn't leave on time.
>It doesn't matter **whether or not** they left on time.

11 Verbs

Verbs are words or phrases that represent actions, processes, events or states. They are the head, or nucleus, of the predicate in a clause or sentence. Verbs may also serve the function of heading certain types of clauses which are not part of the predicate.

>Leslie **slept**.
>All the approved applicants **became** members of the club.
>The race **will start** as soon as the rain **stops**.
>A European syndicate **owns** most of the shares.

11.1 Verb forms

Most verbs do not have a distinct written form that clearly identifies them as verbs. However, there are some suffixes and prefixes that are often associated with verbs.

>**Suffixes:**
>*-ate*: alienate
>*-iate*: satiate
>*-en*: enlighten
>*-ify*: mystify
>*-ize / -ise*: recognize
>
>**Prefixes:**
>*de-*: demystify
>*un-*: unhook
>*out-*: outrun
>*over-*: oversleep
>*under-*: undercharge

Other parts of speech can sometimes act as verbs. These other parts of speech – such as nouns, adjectives or adverbs – may not change form when acting as verbs; the only way to identify their function is through context or pronunciation.

>The soldiers are equipped with powerful *arms*. (noun)
>That money **arms** the insurgents. (verb)
>
>The audience felt *calm* after the explanation. (adjective)
>They can **calm** everyone with a clear explanation. (verb)
>
>Her classmates couldn't put their drinks *down*. (adverb)
>Her classmates **down** their drinks too quickly. (verb)

11.1.1 Non-finite forms

Verbs usually appear in the dictionary in their base forms. The base form of a verb is also known as the infinitive or the bare infinitive. The base form of the verb accompanied by the particle *to* is also known as the infinitive, the to-infinitive or the full infinitive.

Verbs may appear in one of two participle forms: past participle and present participle. For regular verbs, the past participle is formed by adding *–ed* to the base form. *(See Table 47)* Present participle is formed by adding *–ing* to the base form of the verb. Gerunds are also formed by adding *–ing* to the base form. *(See Table 48)*

All these variations – the infinitive forms, the participles and gerunds – are collectively known as non-finite verb forms. Non-finite forms have no number or tense. These forms are also called verbals or non-tensed verbs, since they bear no tense markings. Non-finite verb forms have no inflection for present, past or future tense.

A verb in a non-finite form cannot form the head of a predicate on its own. It can only act as the main verb when preceded by an auxiliary verb. *(See 12.1 Auxiliary verbs)* Non-finite verb forms may be used in verb phrases and in so-called non-finite clauses. (See the *You Can Teach Grammar* companion web site.)

Table 45: Examples of non-finite verb forms

Base form / bare infinitive	Infinitive / to-infinitive	Past participle	Present participle	*Gerund*
learn	to learn	learned	learning	learning
study	to study	studied	studying	studying
go	to go	gone	going	going
be	to be	been	being	being
take	to take	taken	taking	taking
forget	to forget	forgotten	forgetting	forgetting

11.1.1.1 Base form

The base – or bare infinitive – form of a verb is the form found in the dictionary. This is the simplest and 'smallest' form of a verb. This form of verb does not stand on its own as the main verb in a sentence. It must always be accompanied by an auxiliary or modal auxiliary verb.

> Do you **study** French at school?
> He must **take** what you're giving him.
> The captain will never **forget** this day.

*** *In the classroom: Base forms* ***

Students very commonly confuse the base form of the verb with a verb in the simple present tense. The reason is simple: their forms have the same spelling and pronunciation. The way to identify whether a verb is in its base form or in the simple present tense is through context, and by looking at the sentence structure.

In *I* **study** *French at school*, the verb **study** looks the same as the base form, but it is actually a conjugated verb in the present simple form. However, in the question *Do you* **study** *French at school?*, the simple present tense is formed by the auxiliary *do* and the main verb **study** in its base form. It is not correct to say that **study** is a verb in the simple present when accompanied by an auxiliary or a modal verb. One way to reinforce the difference is to present examples where the verb must agree with a third person singular subject. In these cases, the conjugated verb and the base form do not look the same.

> I **study** French at school.   He **studies** French at school.
> Do you **study** French at school?   Does he **study** French at school?

11.1.1.2 Infinitive

The infinitive form of a verb is the base form preceded by the particle *to*. This form is generally used as a noun and it names an action or state. It cannot be the main verb in a sentence. *(See 13.4 Functions of infinitives in a sentence)*

>I like **to go** to new places as often as I can.
>**To take** a baby swimming is a great experience.
>Her new teammates hope **to learn** a lot from her.

11.1.1.3 Participle

Verbs have two kinds of participle: present and past. The present participle is formed by adding the suffix *-ing* to the base form; the past participle of regular verbs is formed by adding the suffix *-ed* to the base form. The past participles of irregular verbs are formed in different ways, depending on the verb. *(See 11.2.2.2 Irregular verbs)*

A participle is generally the head of a verb phrase in the progressive or perfective aspect, and is therefore accompanied by an auxiliary verb. *(See 12.1 Auxiliary verbs and 1.5.2 Main or auxiliary)*

>Merlin is **going** away for the summer. (present participle)
>Have you ever **studied** a second language? (past participle)
>I'd **forgotten** how big the room was. (past participle)

Despite their names, past participles and present participles do not carry tense. The tense is marked by the entire verb phrase, not the participle.

Past participles are used in passive constructions. In a passive sentence, the subject of the sentence is not the agent of the action – it receives the action of the verb. The agent of the action does not have to be named. The passive structure requires the use of the verb *be*, conjugated, plus the past participle. (For more on passive constructions, see the *You Can Teach Grammar* companion web site.)

>Active: The crowd **chased** Marshall down the street.
>Passive: Marshall *was* **chased** down the street.

Present and past participles can also be used as adjectives (called participial adjectives). *(See 5.1.3 Participial adjectives)*

11.1.1.4 Gerund

The gerund is formed in the same way as the present participle form of a verb: it is the base form with the suffix *-ing*. By definition, the gerund form is used as a noun. *(See 13.1 Functions of gerunds in a sentence)* Since gerunds and present participles look and sound identical, they can only be differentiated in context. The highlighted words below are gerunds.

>**Taking** your dog for a walk is a great way to exercise.
>John's greatest attribute is **being** calm in chaotic situations.
>The kids love **learning** about dinosaurs.

11.1.2 Finite forms

When a verb is used on its own as the main verb (the head of the predicate) in a sentence or clause, it is in a finite form. Finite forms of verbs are variations of the base form which show number (singular or plural), person (first person, second person or third person) and tense (present or past). These variations are called conjugation or inflection.

Finite verb forms are also called tensed, since they carry tense markings. Those tense markings can be visible (as in the case of the third person, singular, simple present tense) or invisible. *(See 14.1 Forms of tenses)* The table below gives examples of verbs that are inflected for person, number and tense. For each of the three example verbs, the three different persons, the two different numbers and two different tenses (in the simple aspect) are given. *(See 14 Tenses)*

Table 46: Example finite verb forms, conjugated for person, number and tense

Person	Number	Tense	Verb *to be*	Verb *to play* (regular verb)	Verb *to drive* (irregular verb)
First Person	Singular	Simple present	I **am** an accountant,	I **play** badminton on Saturdays,	I never **drive** when it snows,
		Simple past	but I **was** a teacher in the past.	but yesterday I **played** squash instead.	but I **drove** during yesterday's storm.
Second Person	Singular	Simple present	You **are** 30, right?	I heard that you **play** tennis.	He said that you **drive** a minivan.
		Simple past	For some reason I thought you **were** older.	Someone said you **played** tennis every week.	I thought you said you **drove** a sports car.
Third Person	Singular	Simple present	Marcus **is** not home right now.	Elle **plays** the violin very well.	Sandra normally **drives** to work only on Fridays,
		Simple past	He **was** home all day yesterday, though.	She also **played** the viola when she was a child.	but she **drove** today because of the rain.
First Person	Plural	Simple present	Craig and I **are** on the list now,	Maria and I **play** video games when we get together,	Alan and I **drive** the same car.
		Simple past	but we **were** not on the list yesterday.	but we **played** cards on Sunday due to the power outage.	We **drove** two different ones in the past, but it was too expensive.
Second Person	Plural	Simple present	You **are** the first people to arrive today.	You all **play** soccer too well to lose that game!	You guys **drive** all the time now!
		Simple past	Yesterday you **were** very late.	You **played** without much effort, I think.	Someone told me you **drove** only on weekends.
Third Person	Plural	Simple present	Michael and Pamela **are** upset with the results.	Tristan and Helena **play** polo when they go to Argentina.	Susan and Lenora **drive** to work every day.
		Simple past	They **were** pretty excited about the game.	They **played** for the first time in 2001.	They **drove** past us two minutes ago.

The verb *to be* is the only verb that has three different inflections for person and number in the simple present tense (*am*, *is* and *are*), and two for the simple past (*was* and *were*). For other verbs, only the third person singular shows a visible inflection or change in the simple present tense. With the exception of *to be*, the simple past tense has the same form for all persons, both singular and plural.

In the progressive and perfective aspects, the auxiliary verb will be inflected for tense and number and the main verb will be in a non-finite form. *(See 11.1.1 Non-finite forms and 14 Tenses)*

>Rose **was taking** a walk when you called.
>*was*: auxiliary verb *to be* inflected for third person singular past tense
>*taking*: main verb, present participle

>Sidney **had** already **finished** his meal when the power went out.
>*had*: auxiliary verb *to have* inflected for third person singular past tense
>*finished*: main verb, past participle

Quiz 1: Verb forms

1) *Identify the auxiliary verbs accompanying the base form verbs in the example sentences in section 11.1.1.1.*
2) *Identify the main verbs in the example sentences in section 11.1.1.2.*
3) *Identify the auxiliary verbs accompanying the participles in the example sentences in section 11.1.1.3.*
4) *Identify the part of the sentence (subject, object, etc.) that each gerund is fulfilling in the example sentences in section 11.1.1.4.*
5) *What verb has three inflections in the simple present tense?*
6) *What person/number combination has a visible conjugation in the simple present tense?*

*** *In the classroom: Verb forms* ***

Many words in English can function as multiple parts of speech. Only context and pronunciation differentiate them. Dictionaries can help students to some extent, but the classroom is likely the place where students will develop the ability to distinguish and properly apply these words in the correct context, with proper pronunciation. When words that can act as either verb or noun have two syllables or more, the pronunciation of the two forms is different. Generally, in a two-syllable word, the noun form will have the first syllable stressed (CONtract), while the verb form will have the second syllable stressed (conTRACT).

>My teenage daughter is a *REbel*. (noun)
>My teenage daughter **reBELS** against everything we say. (verb)

The participle forms of verbs are another source of confusion. Though they are non-finite forms, the names – present participle and past participle – give a strong suggestion that they carry tense. To avoid possible confusion on this point, some teachers and textbooks do not use these names. Common substitute names are *–ing form* for the present participle, and *–ed form* or *p.p.* for the past participle.

11.2 Verb classifications

In addition to the verb forms discussed above, verbs may be classified along several other dimensions. It is not always necessary for students to be explicitly aware of these classifications, but there are many times when specific distinctions can help students use different verbs more effectively, avoiding common mistakes.

The following list gives an overview of the different classifications of verbs:

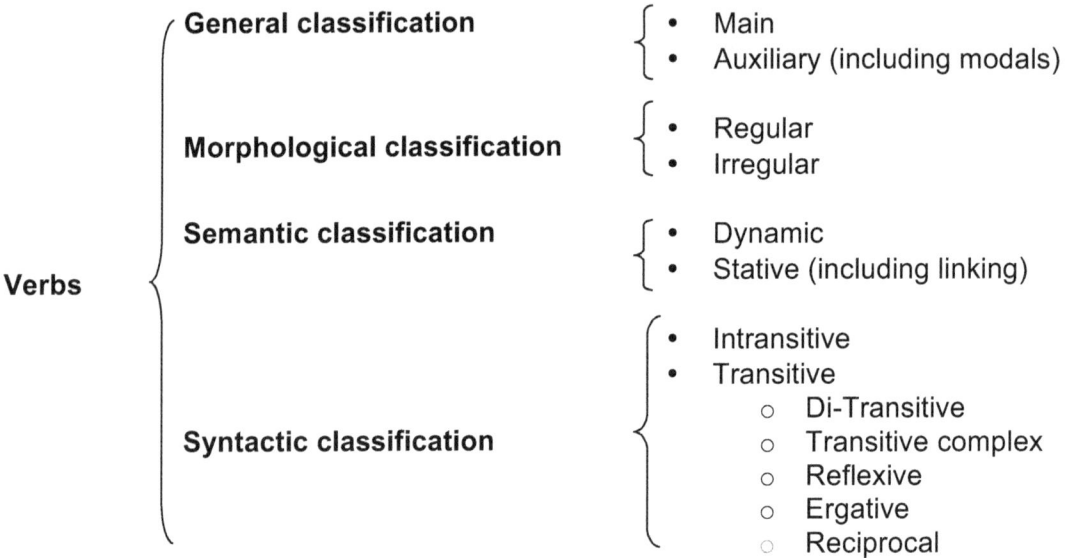

11.2.1 General classification

The general classification of verbs is into one of two categories: either main verbs or auxiliary verbs. Three verbs (**be**, **do** and **have**) have the ability to function as main verbs or auxiliary verbs; their classification depends on context.

11.2.1.1 Main verbs

Main verbs are also called lexical verbs. They are the ones that carry the meaning of the action or state in the sentence. Main verbs are the head, or nucleus, of verb phrases *(See 11.4.1 Verb phrases and 14.1 Forms of tenses)*

> Cassandra **is** an engineer.
> (**is** is the main verb, head of the predicate, inflected for the third person in the present tense, in the simple aspect)

> Carla **slept** peacefully all night.
> (**slept** is the main verb, head of the predicate, inflected for past tense, in the simple aspect)

> Mark *was* still **sleeping** at 10 a.m.
> (**sleeping** is the main verb, head of the verb phrase *was sleeping*, in the non-finite present participle form, used for the progressive aspect)

Erin *has* never **cleaned** behind the cabinet.
(**cleaned** is the main verb, head of the verb phrase *has cleaned*, in the non-finite past participle form, used for the perfective aspect)

11.2.1.2 Auxiliary verbs

Auxiliary verbs do not carry independent meaning (as main verbs do). Their function is to form grammatical structures which, together with main verbs, indicate tense and aspect. Auxiliary verbs are also called helping verbs.

There are three main auxiliary verbs: **be**, **have** and **do**. The auxiliary verb **be** is used to form verb phrases in the progressive aspect and for passive voice constructions. The auxiliary verb **have** is used to form verb phrases in the perfective aspect. These two auxiliary verbs, **have** and **be**, can be used together for verb phrases in the perfect progressive aspect. The auxiliary verb **do** is used only in the simple aspect, to express negation, interrogation, contradiction or emphasis. The auxiliaries **do** and **be** cannot be used together in the same verb phrase.

Selena **is** *waiting* for you.
(**is** is an auxiliary verb in the present tense, part of the verb phrase *is waiting*, used for the progressive aspect)

Patrick **had** never *seen* something so beautiful.
(**had** is an auxiliary verb in the past tense, part of the verb phrase *had seen*, used for the perfective aspect)

Ellen **has been** *helping* Mike with his homework for hours.
(**has** and **been** are auxiliary verbs; the first auxiliary, **has**, indicates the tense (present) of the verb phrase *has been helping*; **has** is used for perfective aspect and **been** is used for progressive aspect)

Do you *like* grammar?
(**do** is an auxiliary verb in the present tense, part of the verb phrase *do like*, used to express interrogation)

I **didn't** *know* what to say.
(**did** is an auxiliary verb in the past tense, part of the verb phrase *didn't know*; it is combined with the adverb *not* (contracted to *didn't*) to express negation in the simple aspect)

You think Bella doesn't like ice cream? Oh no, she **does** *like* it!
(**does** is an auxiliary verb in the present tense, part of the verb phrase *does like*, used to express contradiction and emphasis in the simple aspect)

Auxiliary verbs include a sub-group called modal auxiliary verbs. *(See 12.2 Modal auxiliary verbs)* These verbs, which are usually simply called modals, are different from the auxiliary verbs **do**, **be** and **have** in that they add meaning to the main verb. They are always followed by the main verb (or verb phrase) in base form.

People **must** *obey* traffic rules.
(**must** is a modal auxiliary verb expressing responsibility or obligation)

It **might** *rain* tomorrow morning.
(**might** is a modal auxiliary verb expressing possibility)

The modal auxiliary verb **will** can sometimes act like **do**, **be** and **have** in that it does not add much meaning; it simply changes time reference to future. *(See 12.3.11 Non-modal meanings)*

Mark **will** *play* tomorrow night.
(**will** is a modal auxiliary verb expressing future)

Quiz 2: Main and auxiliary verbs

There is one mistake in each of the following sentences. Identify the mistakes and explain the correct form.

1) Did you drove to school today?
2) Have you saw the movie *Reds*?
3) They were have dinner last night when the lights went off.
4) Does your sister has any kids?
5) I could skating when I was younger.

*** In the classroom: Main and auxiliary verbs ***

The most significant student problem related to auxiliary verbs and main verbs is confusion over the form of the non-finite verb which follows auxiliary verbs *be*, *do* or *have*. Students should be reminded that the possible forms of the main verbs after auxiliary verbs are non-finite forms: base form, present participle and past participle. Following are typical examples, with explanations of the errors.

He *didn't went* to school.
(the non-finite form of the main verb after the auxiliary *do (didn't)* should be the base form *go*)

You *must to stop* at the traffic lights.
(the non-finite form of the verb after a modal verb *must* should be the base form *stop*)

We *are play* chess this weekend.
(the non-finite form of the main verb after auxiliary *are* should be the present participle form *playing*)

Students sometimes have trouble differentiating main and auxiliary verbs. A simple and effective technique for reinforcing the roles of different verbs in a sentence is to conceal the parts of the verb phrase, one by one. In each case, ask the students if the sentence retains its meaning in spite of being grammatically incorrect. This shows the students quite clearly which is which in the verb phrase.

11.2.2 Morphological classification

Morphology refers to the rules via which words change form. For verbs, change in form is necessary to indicate tense and aspect. The two morphological classifications for verbs are regular and irregular. Regular verbs follow a standard set of rules for change of form. Irregular verbs do not follow these rules.

11.2.2.1 Regular verbs

The majority of verbs in English are regular verbs. This morphological classification is based on the rules via which suffixes are added to the base forms of verbs to indicate tense and aspect.

Regular verbs are so called because they conform, regularly, to a clear set of spelling rules for changing from base form to simple past and past participle forms.

Table 47: Spelling rules for regular verbs: simple past and past participle forms

Characteristics of base form verb	Rules for forming simple past and past participle
ending in consonant + *y*: **cry**	change *y* to *i* and add *–ed*: **cried**
one syllable, ending in consonant + vowel + consonant*: **brag**	double the final consonant and add *–ed*: **bragged**
two syllables, stress on second syllable: **admit**	double the final consonant and add *–ed*: **admitted**
ending in *e*: **decide**	add *d*: **decided**
ending in vowel + *l*: **travel**	American English: add *–ed*: **traveled** British English: double the final consonant and add *–ed*: **travelled**
ending in vowel + *c*: **panic**	add *-ked*: **panicked**
all other regular verbs: **walk**	add *–ed*: **walked**
* except when ending in *x* or *w*: **mix**; **vow**	add *–ed*: **mixed**; **vowed**

Present participles and gerunds also conform to a set of spelling rules. These rules apply to both regular and irregular verbs.

Table 48: Spelling rules for regular and irregular verbs: present participle and gerund forms

Characteristics of base form verb	Rules for forming present participle and gerund
ending in consonant + *e* or *-ue*: **decide**; **glue**	drop the *e* and add *–ing*: **deciding**; **gluing**
one syllable, ending in consonant + vowel + consonant*: **brag**	double the final consonant and add *–ing*: **bragging**
two syllables, stress on second syllable: **admit**	double the final consonant and add *–ing*: **admitting**
ending in vowel + *l*: **travel**	American English: add *–ing*: **traveling** British English: double the final consonant and add *–ed*: **travelling**
ending in vowel + *c*: **panic**	add *-king*: **panicking**
ending in *–ie*: **lie**	change the *–ie* to *y* and add *–ing*: **lying**
all other verbs: **walk**	add *–ing*: **walking**
* except when ending in *x* or *w*: **mix**; **vow**	add *–ing*: **mixing**; **vowing**

11.2.2.2 Irregular verbs

Irregular verbs do not conform to the spelling rules outlined in Table 47 for simple past and past participle forms. Irregular verbs might not change form at all; they might have simple past and past participle forms that look the same; or they might be different in all forms. The most commonly-used verbs are irregular verbs. Their very irregularity means that there is not a single set of rules for their morphology. For students, this means that some memorization is required. *(See Appendix I: Irregular verbs)*

Verbs	Base form	Simple past	Past participle
Regular verb: play	play	played	played
Irregular verb: cut (no changes)	cut	cut	cut
Irregular verb: find (one change)	find	found	found
Irregular verb: eat (two changes)	eat	ate	eaten

Quiz 3: Spelling

There is one spelling mistake in each of the following sentences. Identify the mistake and explain the rule of spelling for each case.

1) He carried the heavy bag up the stairs.
2) The student submited his assignment on time.
3) "How do you like the course?" "I am loveing it!"
4) "What is he doing?" "He's tieing the boat to the dock."
5) The kids are swiming in the lake.

**** In the classroom: Regular and irregular verbs ****

ESL students find it difficult to recognize if a verb is regular or irregular. The concept that most verbs are regular but that the most commonly-used verbs are irregular does not help students at beginner levels. The solution to this problem is to expose students to a variety of activities to help them visualize and memorize these verb forms. Because there are no simple rules to follow, regular exposure to the common irregular verbs – in all their forms – is necessary. The list of irregular verbs in Appendix I groups the verbs according to similar spelling, rather than alphabetically. Introducing the verbs to students in this way may aid in memorization. Wall charts displaying common irregular verbs are also useful aids.

11.2.3 Semantic classification

Semantics is the view of language concerned with the meanings of words. Verbs are classified into two semantic categories: dynamic and stative. This is sometimes called the lexical aspect of verbs.

11.2.3.1 Dynamic verbs

When a verb expresses an activity, event, or process it is called a dynamic verb. These verbs are also called action verbs. They can be used in the progressive aspect, usually without a change in meaning. They allow passive constructions when they are transitive, and they describe situations that can begin and finish. (See the *You Can Teach Grammar* companion web site for more on passive constructions.)

Some examples of common dynamic verbs include:

clean, **run** (activity)
fall, **score** (event)
grow, **create** (process)

11.2.3.2 Stative verbs

Stative verbs – also called state verbs – describe a state or condition without any action or activity taking place. The verbs in this category often describe physical, mental or emotional states; perception; possession; or communication.

Some examples of common stative verbs are:
> **be**, **love**, **seem**, **think** (physical, mental or emotional states)
> **hear**, **notice**, **remember** (perception)
> **have**, **owe**, **own** (possession)
> **agree**, **mean**, **promise** (communication)

Following is a more complete list of stative verbs.

act	get	please
agree	glow	possess
amaze	go	prefer
appear	grow	promise
appreciate	hate	prove
arrive	have	realize
astonish	hear	recognize
be	imagine	remain
become	impress	remember
believe	include	resemble
belong	involve	satisfy
come	keep	see
come out	know	seem
concern	lack	shine
consist	leave	sit
contain	lie	smell
cost	like	sound
deny	look	stay
depend	love	suppose
deserve	matter	surprise
disagree	mean	taste
dislike	measure	test
doubt	mind	think
end up	need	turn
fall	notice	turn up
feel	owe	understand
fit	own	want
forget	play	weigh
	plead	wish

Some stative verbs can also be used as dynamic verbs with a slight change in their meaning.

> Miranda **weighs** 20 pounds already.
> (**weighs** is a stative verb describing the physical state of Miranda)

> The shop assistant **weighed** the bag of apples for me.
> (**weighed** is a dynamic verb expressing the action of checking the heaviness of the apples)

For verbs that may be used as both stative and dynamic verbs, it is not always easy to recognize the semantic classification. Stative verbs cannot be used in the progressive aspect. In the cases where a normally stative verb can be used in the progressive aspect, its semantic classification is, by definition, dynamic. Dynamic verbs denote a unique reference, not a general state.

> I **love** chocolate.
> (**love** is a stative verb; it cannot be used in the progressive aspect when meaning a general emotional state of liking or preference)

> I *am* **loving** this cake.
> (**loving** is a dynamic verb, a unique reference to the action of enjoying this particular cake at the moment of speaking)

11.2.3.2.1 Linking verbs

Stative verbs contain a sub-classification called linking verbs. These verbs also describe a state or condition; however, they do so by just connecting the subject to a complement. *(See 2.2.2 Complement)* Linking verbs are always followed by a subject complement. Subject complements are always nouns (or noun phrases), pronouns or adjectives (or adjective phrases). Linking verbs are also called copulae, copulative verbs or copular verbs.

> Marianna **is** an excellent chef.
> (linking verb **is** followed by a noun phrase)

> When the sun set, the whole forest **became** dark.
> (linking verb **became** followed by an adjective)

Many verbs can function as either linking verbs or as dynamic verbs, depending on context. When a verb is a linking verb, its meaning is one of equivalence: the subject and the complement are considered to be somehow the same. If a verb is a linking verb, it should be possible to substitute the verb **be** for the verb, and still maintain the basic meaning.

> The problem **grew** bigger. ≈ The problem **is** bigger.
> (meaning is equivalence: **grew** is a linking verb)

> We **grew** some tomatoes. ≠ ~~We **are** some tomatoes~~.
> (meaning is not equivalence: **grew** is not a linking verb)

Following is a list of common linking verbs. Each is given with an example of the verb functioning as a linking verb.

act	Please act your age.	**look**	She looks great.
appear	The driver appears drunk.	**play**	The dog played dead.
arrive	The kids always arrive hungry.	**plead**	I plead ignorance.
be	Bob's happy.	**prove**	This course is proving difficult.
become	The frog became a prince.	**remain**	He remained faithful.
come	Will the criminal come clean?	**resemble**	George resembles the king.
come out	The painting came out nice.	**seem**	That doesn't seem right.
end up	The project ended up a failure.	**shine**	The sun shone golden.
fall	All the nurses fell ill.	**sit**	They're sitting pretty.
feel	I feel good.	**smell**	It smells awful.
get	Let's get married.	**sound**	Robbie sounds terrific.
glow	The whole stage glowed orange.	**stay**	The boy stayed innocent.
go	The crowd went wild.	**taste**	The coffee tastes bitter.
grow	Ed grew weary.	**test**	All the patients tested positive.
keep	How do you keep slim?	**turn**	The passengers turned green.
leave	The customer left dissatisfied.	**turn up**	My cousin turned up penniless.
lie	The baby won't lie still.		

Quiz 4: Dynamic and stative verbs

A) Identify whether the highlighted words are used correctly.

1) The flowers are **smelling** good.
2) I am **having** so much fun.
3) Are you **seeing** your doctor tomorrow?
4) He is **having** a new car.
5) The cabinet is **measuring** 3 x 4 feet.

B) What can follow a linking verb?

**** In the classroom: Dynamic and stative verbs ****

A typical student error, even at high intermediate levels, is to use stative verbs in progressive aspects. Examples of stative verbs used incorrectly in the progressive aspects are verbs expressing state, possession, necessity, perception, or communication:

~~I *am weighing* 120 pounds.~~
~~They *have been owning* a huge house by the river for a decade.~~
~~I *am wanting* to eat some chocolate cake.~~
~~Are you *hearing* that strange noise coming from downstairs?~~
~~I *was not agreeing* with you when you suggested phoning Claire.~~

The examples here are typical, and demonstrate a facility with grammatical structure: all the auxiliary verbs are properly applied. The concept to emphasize with students is the expression of state, condition or perception that is given in stative verbs. This is what makes them inappropriate for the progressive aspect.

Getting students to focus on this common error by correcting misuse is one way to raise students' awareness of the problem. If students make this type of error with any frequency, the teacher may accumulate and then distribute cases of incorrect usage and give students the task of working together to correct them.

11.2.4 Syntactic classification

Syntax refers to the rules for forming grammatically correct sentences. Syntactically, verbs fall into two major categories: transitive and intransitive. Transitive verbs may be further subcategorized. The syntactic classifications govern whether and how objects and complements may follow a verb.

11.2.4.1 Intransitive verbs

Some verbs are complete in their meaning and do not require any objects or complements; they only require a subject, a "do-er" of the action. These are intransitive verbs.

> Let sleeping dogs **lie**.
> They are **complaining**.

Lie (with the meaning *be placed somewhere*) and **complain** are two of the many intransitive verbs in English. Some verbs are always instransitive; they can't take an object. Following are some examples:

ache	**collide**	**go**
appear	**come**	**listen**
arrive	**compete**	**lie**
belong	**complain**	**matter**
chat	**depend**	**occur**

Others verbs can sometimes take an object. When these verbs take an object, they are no longer acting as intransitive verbs.

> Mike and Sophie **ate**.
> (**ate** used intransitively)

> Mike and Sophie **ate** dessert.
> (**ate** used transitively, with the object *dessert*)

There are a great many verbs like **eat**, which may function as transitive or intransitive. These are known as ambitransitive verbs.

Intransitive verbs do not take objects, but they may take adverbs.

> Mark and Sue **ate** happily.
> (**ate** used intransitively, with the adverb *happily*)

Intransitive verbs can only be used in active voice. (For more on active and passive voice, see the *You Can Teach Grammar* companion web site.)

11.2.4.2 Transitive verbs

There are verbs in English which must be followed by an object in order to fully convey their meanings. These are transitive verbs. The term transitive comes from the concept that the action of the verb travels – or transits – through the verb, from the subject to the object.

> Dora **likes** exploring.
> (**likes** is a transitive verb with the direct object *exploring*; this verb is always transitive)

Transitive verbs that require only one object are also called monotransitive verbs. Following are examples of purely monotransitive verbs:

abuse	**eat**	**like**
achieve	**follow**	**love**
bite	**gain**	**meet**
describe	**help**	**use**

Transitive verbs may be further classified based on characteristics of their subjects and objects. These classifications are ditransitive, transitive complex, reflexive, ergative and reciprocal.

11.2.4.2.1 Ditransitive verbs

Ditransitive verbs take both a direct and an indirect object. The omission of the indirect object makes the sentence either awkward or ungrammatical. Omission of the direct object makes the sentence ungrammatical.

> Lili **gave** Sue a present.
> (**gave** is a ditransitive verb with the direct object *a present* and indirect object *Sue*)

> Lili **gave** a present.
> (This sentence would be correct only if the recipient of the present (the indirect object) were clearly understood.)

> ~~Lili gave Sue.~~
> (The direct object is unknown. This sentence is grammatically incorrect.)

A sample list of ditransitive verbs is given in Appendix II: Ditransitive verbs.

11.2.4.2.2 Transitive complex verbs

Transitive complex verbs require a complement after the direct object to fully complete the meaning of the sentence. This complement can be an object complement or a locative complement (an indicator of location, usually a prepositional phrase). Transitive complex verbs are also known as factitive verbs.

Object complements are similar to subject complements *(See 2.2.2 Complement)* in that they are formed by nouns or adjectives or their equivalents. Certain complex constructions – mainly infinitive phrases and reduced clauses – may also act as object complements.

> They **deemed** *the novel* a complete success.
> (direct object: *the novel*; object complement: noun phrase *a complete success*)

> When you have a cold, you must **keep** *your feet* warm.
> (direct object: *your feet*; object complement: adjective *warm*)

> The union workers **considered** *their strike* <u>to be of utmost importance</u>.
> (direct object: *their strike*; object complement: infinitive phrase of purpose *to be of utmost importance*)

> When the assignment involved dramatic skills, the teacher **noticed** *all the students* <u>practising eagerly</u>.
> (direct object: *all the students*; object complement: participial phrase *practising eagerly* – present participle *practising* is the main verb in the reduced clause *that ... were practising eagerly*)

Some transitive complex verbs can be followed by a direct object and an infinitive without the particle *to*.

> Grandparents **let** *their grandchildren* <u>do whatever they want</u> when the parents are not watching.
> (direct object: *their grandchildren*; object complement: infinitive phrase *do whatever they want*)

Sample lists of different types of transitive complex verbs are given in Appendix III: Transitive complex verbs.

11.2.4.2.3 Reflexive verbs

Reflexive verbs are verbs that have a subject and an object with the same reference. In other words, the "do-er" of the action is the "receiver" as well. *(See 4.2.1.4 Reflexive pronouns)*

> *Lenny* **blamed** *himself* for all their hardships.
> (*Lenny* is both the subject and object of the verb **blamed**)

Sometimes verbs in English can take the prefix *self-* to convert them into reflexive verbs.

> Many authors **self-publish** their work.
> (the verb **publish** becomes reflexive with the prefix *self-*, making this sentence equivalent to *Many authors publish their work themselves*.)

Other reflexive verbs include:

convince	enjoy	kill
cut	help	pay
deny	hurt	prepare
encourage	introduce	teach

11.2.4.2.4 Ergative verbs

Ergative verbs are those that can be used transitively or intransitively. When used intransitively, the subject of an ergative verb is not the "do-er" of the action of the verb; it is the "receiver." Consider the differences between these sentences.

eat (transitive and intransitive verb; not ergative)	**break** (transitive verb; intransitive usage is ergative)
1. Mike and Sophie **ate**. (intransitive use)	4. ~~Mark broke~~. (incorrect; the receiver of the action (*the window*) should be the subject when an ergative verb is used intransitively)
2. Mike and Sophie **ate** dessert. (transitive use with *dessert* as direct object)	5. Mark **broke** the window. (transitive use with *the window* as direct object)
3. ~~Dessert ate~~. (incorrect; **eat** is not an ergative verb, so the do-er of the action should be the subject)	6. The window **broke**. (intransitive use without a clear agent or do-er; ergative use of the verb **break**)

These two sets of sentences illustrate the different features of ergative verbs. **Break** is an ergative verb; **eat** is not.

The first two examples have almost no difference in meaning except for the detail of what Mike and Sophie ate. Sentence 3 is incorrect because the subject of the sentence (*dessert*) cannot perform the action **eat** by itself; **eat** is not an ergative verb.

Sentence 4 is also incorrect because **break**, when it is a transitive verb, always requires an object that "receives" the action. The receiver of the action is not present in this sentence.

Sentences 5 and 6 are correct and seem to be similar in meaning but they have a more significant difference in meaning than 1 and 2. In sentence 5, it is clear that Mark performed the action, and Mark is the subject of the sentence. The subject is also the agent, or do-er, of the action, as it is in most active voice sentences.

However, in sentence 6, the subject of the sentence is *the window*, but it is not the agent (do-er or performer) of the action; *the window* receives the action. In this sentence, there is no clear agent. This is an example of **break** as an ergative verb. It is used intransitively because there is no object after it, but its subject is not the do-er of the action; it is the receiver.

A sample list of ergative verbs is given in Appendix IV: Ergative verbs.

11.2.4.2.5 Reciprocal verbs

Reciprocal verbs involve two agents doing the same action to or with each other. These two agents can be expressed in a sentence as two separate nouns in the subject position, a plural noun in the subject position, or a noun in the subject position and another one after a preposition. Pronouns may also fill these positions.

> Millicent and Eli **met** in South Carolina.
> (Millicent **met** Eli and Eli **met** Millicent)

> They **married** after dating for 2 years.
> (Millicent **married** Eli and Eli **married** Millicent.)

> Millicent **exchanged** vows with Eli at a Baha'i Temple.

Common reciprocal verbs in English include:

agree	**entwine**	**fight**
disagree	**exchange**	**marry**
divorce	**feud**	**meet**

Quiz 5: Transitive and intransitive verbs

Identify the highlighted verbs as intransitive, monotransitive, ditransitive, transitive complex, reflexive, ergative or reciprocal.

1) I **found** it easy to solve.
2) The new guy **watched** the movie with Yuki
3) George Foreman and Muhammad Ali **fought** in Kinshasa.
4) They **swam** in the rough river for about two hours.
5) I **considered** Mr. Rexdale's theory erroneous.
6) Sales **increased** last year.
7) When **will** they **go** to the Opera House?
8) Gloria **brought** Maryleen a gift card.
9) The movie star **sat** at the café and waited.
10) Our boss **is** always **giving** us a hard time.
11) I **watched** him leave.
12) The speaker **introduced** herself to the audience.

In the classroom: Transitive and intransitive verbs

A persistent difficulty, even for fairly advanced students, is the correct use of ergative verbs. Because the sentence subject is not the agent of the action, the sentence may appear to be one which requires a passive construction. *(See 11.1.1.3 Participle, 14.1 Forms of tenses and the You Can Teach Grammar companion web site)* A common error is to add the auxiliary *be* and use the past participle, when only the main ergative verb is required.

~~Sales were increased last year~~.
Sales **increased** last year.

The solution to this is to practise typical occurrences in context and remind students of the special status of this class of verbs.

11.3 Mood

There are four different moods in English. The mood of a verb is the speaker's (or writer's) approach to what is being said. Moods can be separated into two different kinds: factual and non-factual. Factual moods are those that describe actual actions, events or states, while non-factual moods describe actions, events or states that have not happened, are hypothetical or are just wishes.

Factual Moods
Indicative (Declarative and Interrogative)
Infinitive

Non-Factual Moods
Imperative
Subjunctive

11.3.1 Indicative mood

The indicative mood is the most commonly used mood in modern English. It includes positive and negative statements as well as questions. This mood always expresses an assertion, a negation or a question. Some grammarians divide this mood into declarative (for statements) and interrogative (for questions).

> Hilton Head is a beautiful island in South Carolina. (positive statement)
> We have never been to Hawaii. (negative statement)
> Did you see that beautiful cardinal flying by? (interrogative statement)

This is the only mood that includes all tenses and in which subject/verb agreement *(See 3.4.4.1 Number)* is utterly essential for grammatical accuracy.

11.3.2 Infinitive mood

The infinitive mood does not technically apply to verbs. It is the mood that applies to participles, gerunds and infinitives when they are not used as verbs. When verbs are in this mood they do not act like verbs, but like nouns or adjectives. *(See 11.1.1 Non-finite forms and 13 Gerunds and infinitives)*

> **To open** a can, use a can opener, not a knife.
> (infinitive as noun)
>
> The board gave us a reminder **to vote** for the new members.
> (infinitive as adjective)
>
> **Swimming** is fun, but it can be a dangerous sport if you're not careful.
> (gerund as noun)
>
> **Snapping** turtles look cute when they walk along the shore.
> (present participle as adjective)

All the non-finite verbs (verbals) highlighted above are in the infinitive mood because they are not acting as verbs and they do not have subjects.

11.3.3 Imperative mood

The imperative mood is called a non-factual mood because it describes directives (orders, requests, instructions or strong advice) that are actions, states or events that have not actually taken place yet.

The most important characteristic of sentences in this mood is that the subject can be elided – omitted – and it is understood to be the second person – you – singular or plural, depending on the context.

> Be careful!
> Listen to your friends.
> Never drink and drive.
> Don't run with scissors.

In the imperative mood, verbs are always in base form. When the directive is negative, the auxiliary **do** and the adverb *not* are used.

        Sit down!   Don't sit down!   Do not sit there!

11.3.4 Subjunctive mood

The subjunctive mood is the quintessential non-factual mood since it is used purely to describe wishes and hopes, hypothetical or imaginary situations, conditions, uncertainties or doubts. Many say the subjunctive is no longer used in English; however, it is present in many grammatical structures. The most common use of the subjunctive mood in English is in conditional sentences. (See the *You Can Teach Grammar* companion web site for more on conditionals.)

The subjunctive mood is used in subordinate clauses. It is used in hypothetical structures (especially if-clauses) and with verbs that suggest situations that have not yet happened, especially ones making suggestions or giving instructions. The following is a sample list of verbs that commonly require verbs in subordinate clauses to be in the subjunctive mood:

advise	desire	petition	resolve
ask	dictate	prefer	stipulate
beg	insist	propose	suggest
decide	intend	recommend	urge
decree	move	request	vote
demand	order	require	wish

When verbs are in present tense in the subjunctive mood, they are always in their base form. When verbs are in past tense in the subjunctive mood, they are in the same form as verbs in their simple past form in the indicative mood. The exception is the verb **be**, which has two simple past forms (*was* and *were*). The past tense subjunctive form of **be** is always **were**. For verb phrases in subjunctive mood, it is the auxiliary verb only which will be in its subjunctive form (past or present, as appropriate). When the verb in the subjunctive mood is in the negative, the adverb *not* is added.

Subjunctive following verbs of suggestion or hope:
    He wished he **were** more interested in what she was telling him.
    The court demanded that Reginald **pay** a hefty fine.
    We ask that they **not enter** until an appropriate intermission.

Subjunctive in subordinate conditional clauses:
    She agrees to press charges lest her attacker **do** it again.
    I'd believe it if it **were** true.
    If he **were** *giving* it his best effort, he would succeed

Quiz 6: Mood

Identify the mood of each of the following sentences:

1) The delegates requested that the meeting adjourn for the afternoon.
2) Isn't he a good little puppy?

3) He's such a good little puppy.
4) Get out of here!
5) Add two teaspoons of bicarbonate of soda.
6) Adding baking soda will make the batter rise.

*** In the classroom: Mood ***

The imperative and subjunctive moods tend to give students the most difficulty. Imperative sentences are constructed differently in many languages. Imperative mood allows for the elision of the subject, which is not permitted in most other English structures. Reinforcement of the circumstances under which the imperative is appropriately used (giving instructions, giving orders), together with examples, should help students to comprehend.

In many other languages, verbs in subjunctive mood have distinct conjugations. In English, verbs in subjunctive mood look exactly like other, more easily identified forms. Most textbooks treat subjunctive mood as cases where "base form" and "simple past" are used, without identifying the structure as subjunctive. This is generally an easier way to address the subject in the classroom. It is useful, however, for teachers to recognize when student errors are a result of a misunderstanding of the rules related to subjunctives. With this knowledge, appropriate rules and corrections can be given to students, with minimal confusion.

Typical subjunctive use errors include sentences like ~~I recommend you to go~~.

11.4 Verb phrases and phrasal verbs

Sentences always have a verb; however, verbs do not always look the same. Sometimes verbs are composed of more than one word. Multi-word verbs are either verb phrases or phrasal verbs. The distinction is important.

11.4.1 Verb phrases

There are two kinds of verb phrases: simple and complex. Simple verb phrases consist of only one word and that word is always the main verb. This verb always indicates tense and aspect. *(See 14 Tenses)*

Since simple verb phrases are formed by only one verb, they will always be in the simple aspect, in the affirmative, and in the active voice.

Complex verb phrases are formed by a main verb with one or more auxiliary verbs before it. All verb phrases in negative or interrogative form, in the progressive or perfective aspects, or in the passive voice are complex verb phrases. All verb phrases that include any modal auxiliaries are also complex.

The main (or lexical) verb in combination with the auxiliary determines the tense, aspect and voice.

> Please **don't stand** on the chairs.
> (Complex verb phrase in the imperative mood: auxiliary verb **don't** for negation and main verb **stand**)

We **have been working** all day.
(Complex verb phrase in the indicative mood: auxiliary verb **have** for perfective aspect, auxiliary verb **been** for progressive aspect and main verb **working**)

He **would have been arriving** at 3 pm if he hadn't missed the plane.
(Complex verb phrase in the indicative mood: modal auxiliary verb **would**, auxiliary verb **have** for the perfective aspect, auxiliary verb **been** for the progressive aspect and main verb **arriving**)

Complex verb phrases must follow a strict word order. The most important rule is that all auxiliaries must precede the main (lexical) verb. Each auxiliary will determine the form of the next constituent of the phrase, whether the next verb is the main verb or another auxiliary.

Regardless of which kinds of auxiliaries are actually used, the order of the constituents must be the following, whether some or all are present.

modal auxiliary > perfective auxiliary > progressive auxiliary > passive auxiliary > main verb

Each type of auxiliary determines the form of the next constituent

modal auxiliaries	→ followed by a base form
perfective auxiliaries	→ followed by a past participle form
progressive auxiliaries	→ followed by a present participle form
passive auxiliaries	→ followed by a past participle form

In sentences, the first constituent of a complex verb phrase will bear person and number agreement with the subject, as well as the tense. The only exception to this rule is for modal auxiliaries, which have only one form.

The politicians \<subject\>	**had** \<first auxiliary carries tense (past) and agrees with subject (third person plural); perfective auxiliary; next verb must be past participle\>			**lied** \<main verb in past participle to complete perfective construction\>	about the money.
Many teenagers \<subject\>	**would** \<first auxiliary is a modal, so does not carry tense or have agreement with subject; next verb must be in base form\>	**be** \<progressive auxiliary; next verb must be in present participle form\>		**tanning** \<main verb in present participle to complete the progressive construction\>	on a sunny day.
What \<subject\>	**has** \<first auxiliary carries tense (present) and agrees with subject (third person singular); perfective auxiliary; next verb must be in past participle form\>	**been** \<progressive auxiliary; next verb must be in present participle form\>	**being** \<passive auxiliary; next verb must be in past participle form\>	**done** \<main verb in past participle to complete passive construction\>	to fix it?

The milk	should	have	been	put	in the fridge.
<subject>	<first auxiliary is a modal, so does not carry tense or have agreement with subject; next verb must be in base form>	<perfective auxiliary; next verb must be in past participle form>	<passive auxiliary; next verb must be in past participle form>	<main verb in past participle to complete passive construction>	

11.4.2 Phrasal verbs

Phrasal verbs, which are also called multi-word verbs, are verbs formed by a main verb and a particle. A particle can be an adverb or a preposition – or both, in the case of phrasal prepositional verbs. This combination of a verb and a particle takes on a new meaning, distinct from that of the main verb on its own.

> You should never **give up** hope.
> main verb: **give** / particle: **up** / meaning of phrasal verb: abandon

> Often when two characters in a romantic comedy **make out**, something funny happens.
> main verb: **make** / particle: **out** / meaning of phrasal verb: kiss each other

Sometimes the meaning of phrasal verbs can be easily guessed from the meaning of the main verb that forms it, but much of the time the meaning of the main verb is not connected to the meaning of the actual phrasal verb in any way. These phrasal verbs that bear little or no connection to the meaning of the main verb in the phrase are called non-literal or idiomatic phrasal verbs.

Phrasal prepositional verbs are phrasal verbs that have more than one particle attached to the main verb; the second particle is always a preposition. These verbs are sometimes also called three-word phrasals.

> Bella and Mia **get along with** Jake.
> main verb: **get** / particle #1: **along** / particle #2: the preposition **with**

> She **lives up to** her mother's expectations.
> main verb: **live** / particle #1: **up** / particle #2: the preposition **to**

A list of common phrasal prepositional verbs is given in Appendix V.

11.4.2.1 Intransitive phrasal verbs

Just like regular verbs that are intransitive, intransitive phrasal verbs are not followed by a direct object.

> They searched the whole house, but the passport didn't **turn up**.

> That country is **getting ahead** due to the hard work of its citizens.

A sample list of the most common intransitive phrasal verbs is given in Appendix VI.

11.4.2.2 Transitive phrasal verbs

The majority of phrasal verbs are transitive, including phrasal prepositional verbs. There are two kinds of transitive phrasal verbs: separable and inseparable (also called non-separable).

Separable transitive phrasal verbs allow the object to be placed in between the main verb and its particle. The object may also be placed after the particle.

> When I clean the windows, please **point** every streak **out** so I can leave the windows spotless.
> (direct object appears between main verb **point** and particle **out**)
>
> Some students readily **point out** their classmates' mistakes.
> (direct object appears after the transitive phrasal verb **point out**)

There is no difference in meaning whether the object is placed after the complete phrasal verb or between the main verb and the particle. Often the length of the object will influence the placement decision, since it is generally clearer when the verb and its particle are relatively close. However, if the direct object is an objective pronoun, it *must* be placed between the main verb and its particle.

> Some students readily **point out** their classmates' mistakes. Others will rarely **point** them **out**.

A sample list of the most common separable transitive phrasal verbs is given in Appendix VII.

Inseparable transitive phrasal verbs only allow the direct object to be placed after the particle. This is true even when the direct object is a pronoun.

> Inseparable phrasal verb: **run into**
>
> Patty **ran into** Peter yesterday.
> Patty ~~ran Peter into~~ yesterday.
> Patty **ran into** him yesterday.
> Patty ~~ran him into~~ yesterday.

A sample list of the most common non-separable transitive phrasal verbs is given in Appendix VIII.

Phrasal prepositional verbs (also called 3-word phrasals) are almost always inseparable transitive verbs.

Even though most phrasal prepositional verbs are inseparable, there is a small group that allows two objects: a direct object of the main verb, placed between the verb and the first particle, and an object of the preposition, placed after the final preposition in the phrase.

Mark always **takes** his anger **out on** his little brother.
(phrasal prepositional verb: **take out on**; object of the verb: his anger; object of the preposition: his little brother)

The following is a sample list of phrasal prepositional verbs that can be used with two objects, following the pattern:

verb + object of verb + particle + preposition + object of preposition

> **fix** (someone) **up with** + (object)
> **let** (someone) **in on** + (object)
> **put** (someone) **up to** + (object)
> **put** (something) **down to** + (object)
> **take** (something) **out on** + (object)

Quiz 7: Verb phrases and phrasal verbs

Identify the full phrase in each sentence which constitutes the verb. Identify whether that phrase is a verb phrase or a phrasal verb.

1) The runner caught up with the pack after a slow start.
2) Annie could have been doing her assignment.
3) Stanley almost always throws up after a few drinks.
4) Let's call the whole thing off.
5) That little girl is singing her heart out.
6) I'll take you up on the skiing offer some day.
7) She's been intending to get that fixed for a long time.
8) The porter will be seeing to your bags.

**** In the classroom: Verb phrases and phrasal verbs ****

Phrasal verbs can be excruciatingly difficult for learners, as there is often no way to apply logic to discern the meaning of the phrase based on its component parts. For some phrasal verbs, the meaning is relatively easy to deduce (*wake up*; *break in*; *dress up*). These verbs are the best ones to start with, and may allow dissection of the form of the verb. Others, with less direct relationships to their main verbs (*get along*; *hang out*; *count on*), must be taught with a heavy reliance on context for learner comprehension. Phrasal verbs should be presented in meaningful groups and taught in the same way as one-word verbs. Often, phrasal verbs are grouped according to their main constituent or according to their particles and this only confuses students further. Since so many phrasal verbs have meanings that are dissimilar to that of their main constituents, it is safer to treat each phrasal verb as a unique occurrence.

**** You can teach verbs ****

As with all the content parts of speech, verbs should be presented in a context that is clear, allowing students to acquire the language by inferring the possible meanings of the words. As with nouns, verbs are best taught with similar counterparts that have similar meanings in small groups, or with antonyms.

Authentic material such as comic strips and some print advertisements are good ways to present verbs, as they contain visual elements which are strongly correlated to meaning. They can be a great source of graphic text that students can use to infer the meaning of different verbs and see how they are used in daily English.

Following are general ideas for presenting and practising verbs. More specific ideas for verb practice are given in Chapter 14 Tenses.

Crossword

Skills: Writing
Level: Beginner to advanced, depending on the set of verbs chosen

This is an ideal way to review form or meaning of different verbs. Crossword puzzles can help students practise different verb forms, particularly conjugations and irregular forms. They can give students extra help in spelling (with number of letters and even some letters given before they have to guess a word). Provided the instructions are clear, this could be an excellent way to review and even introduce a couple of new verbs among a majority of verbs which have already been studied.

For example, for a beginner class, the crossword clues can be verbs in the base form, and the answers in the crossword could be the past simple forms. For a low intermediate class, this can be changed to answers that include past participle forms. For intermediate and advanced classes, the clues can be the meanings of verbs (and phrasal verbs) that have been studied, and the answers are the verbs in question. Finally, for all levels, the clues can be sample sentences with blanks and the answers are the main or auxiliary verbs that would complete the sentences correctly.

Back to back crosswords

Skills: Speaking, listening
Level: Low intermediate to advanced, depending on the set of verbs chosen

Create two versions of a crossword: version A has the clues for the words missing in version B, and vice versa. Students sit back to back and rely on their aural skills as well as their knowledge of verbs to complete their version of the crossword collaboratively.

Charades

Skills: Speaking
Level: Beginner to low intermediate

This is a kinesthetic activity that appeals to all levels but is especially beneficial for beginners.

Even though dynamic verbs are the easiest to teach in terms of their meaning, the quantity and variety of verbs demand a variety of teaching activities. Playing an easy game of charades in the classroom can be an excellent and kinesthetic way of reviewing or learning the meanings of dynamic verbs.

The verbs can be written on cards and the students form groups. A student acts out the verb from a chosen card for group members to guess.

A variation of this activity could be to have the verbs described in pictures on the cards. The game evolves in the same way, but once the verb is orally guessed, the actor (or someone else from the group) has to write the verb down on the board or the back of the card. Proper spelling would count in order to get points in a competitive game setting.

Fly-swatter game

Skills: Listening, reading
Level: High beginner to intermediate

This is a kinesthetic activity that appeals to all levels. Different types of verbs (dynamic and stative, for example) can be written on cards and posted on the board or a wall in the classroom. Students line up at the other end of the classroom in two groups, and the teacher can call out a definition or just a type of verb and one student from each group will have to run to the posted verbs and use a fly-swatter to hit the card with the correct verb. The 'winner' could be the student who reaches the correct answer first.

With intermediate students who are reviewing dynamic versus stative verbs, this game can be made more challenging by adding verbs that can function as dynamic or stative depending on the context and their meaning. The clues read by the teacher then can be sentences using the verbs in a stative or dynamic form. (The verb cards should be colour-coded for stative and dynamic forms.)

Tic-tac-toe

Skills: Speaking
Level: Low intermediate to advanced

After dividing the class into two teams (or more if it is a bigger class), the teacher should draw a tic-tac-toe grid on the board, and fill each of the nine available spaces with base forms of different verbs. If the aim of the lesson is to practise the simple past forms of irregular verbs, students must provide the teacher with the correct form in order to achieve their X or O. This game can also be played with regular and irregular verbs and it can be used to practise all different forms. It can also be used as a small group game or even a pair-work game.

Another variation of this game has students provide the meanings of different verbs to get their X or O. This can be a good way to review phrasal verbs and their meaning.

For example, a mixed tic-tac-toe game for past forms could look like this:

go	show	learn
stay	be	practise
wash	cut	see

Visualization
Skills: Integrated
Level: Intermediate

Students are asked to imagine different situations with dynamic verbs. Depending on the age of the students, they could be asked to 'draw' what they see as their teacher describes it. Then students can be given sentences or situations that include only stative verbs. When they realize they cannot 'imagine' or visualize these situations as easily, they will be able to see the clear difference between these two kinds of verbs.

To-Do Lists
Skills: Reading, writing
Level: Intermediate

Students can be shown a sample to-do list and asked to identify the verbs. Then students can retell what the list says with the help of modal verbs or verb conjugation.

> *Betty must call the caterer. She might buy a new dress.*
> or
> *Betty sends the invitations. Then she cleans the carpet.*

Betty's Party Preparation List:
- *call the caterer*
- *send the invitations*
- *clean the carpet*
- *buy a new dress?*
- *organize the music*
- *repair the doorbell*

As an extension, students can make their own to-do lists and then compare them.

Simon Says
Skills: Listening, speaking
Level: High beginner – low intermediate

This children's game can be used to practise verb comprehension as well as the imperative mood. Students must follow oral instructions only when they are preceded by the phrase "Simon says..." Once a couple of rounds have been played, students can take turns giving out the oral instructions and then practise using the imperative mood themselves.

12 Auxiliary and modal auxiliary verbs

Auxiliary verbs (also called helping verbs) are words that are used with the main verbs of a sentence to form grammatical structures which indicate aspect, time, and voice. They also help to form interrogative and negative sentences. They do not carry meaning as main verbs do; their sole function is grammatical. As their name suggests, they are supplements to main verbs.

The auxiliary verbs are **be**, **do** and **have**. **Will** is sometimes considered an auxiliary verb.

Modal auxiliary verbs also work together with main verbs. Unlike the standard auxiliary verbs (**be**, **do** and **have**), modal auxiliary verbs *do* convey some meaning beyond grammatical function. Examples of modal auxiliary verbs are **would**, **should**, **can** and **might**.

12.1 Auxiliary verbs

The auxiliary verbs **be**, **do** and **have** (and sometimes **will**) perform a strictly grammatical role. The main verb in a sentence contains the primary meaning. Auxiliaries are positioned before main verbs and they make main verbs more specific by conveying aspect (progressive and perfective), time (past, present or future), passive voice, negation, interrogation, emphasis or contradiction. **Be**, **do** and **have** may also function as main verbs. The following points apply to these verbs when they are functioning as auxiliaries. More details on tense and aspect are given in Chapter 14 Tenses and Chapter 11 Verbs.

12.1.1 Auxiliary verb *be*

The auxiliary verb **be** is used to form verb phrases in the progressive aspect (past, present and future time) and for passive voice constructions. In these constructions, it is the verb **be** (not the main verb) which is conjugated to indicate past, present or future time. The present tense forms of **be** are **am**, **is** and **are**; the past tense forms are **was** and **were**. For expressing future time, **be** is accompanied by another auxiliary, **will**. For negative constructions, **not** (or its contracted form) follows the auxiliary verb.

> She **isn't** *cooking* dinner tonight.
> (**isn't** is an auxiliary verb in the negative, part of the verb phrase *isn't cooking*; present progressive tense)
>
> They **were** *told* to communicate with their lawyer as soon as possible.
> (**were** is an auxiliary verb, part of the passive voice verb phrase *were told*; simple past tense)
>
> **Will** they **be** *arriving* home by midnight?
> (**will** and **be** are auxiliary verbs, part of the verb phrase *will be arriving*; future progressive tense, in the interrogative form)

12.1.2 Auxiliary verb *have*

The auxiliary verb **have** is used to form verb phrases in the perfective aspect. In the present perfect, this auxiliary can take one of two forms: **have** or **has**. In the past perfect, **had** is the only form. For negative constructions, **not** (or its contracted form) follows the auxiliary verb.

> Penelope **has** *finished* her book.
> (**has** is an auxiliary verb in the present tense, part of the verb phrase *has finished*; present perfect tense)

> Yves **had** already *left* when Marda arrived at school.
> (**had** is an auxiliary verb in the past tense, part of the verb phrase *had left*; past perfect tense)

The auxiliary verbs **have** and **be** can be used together for verb phrases in the present perfect progressive and past perfect progressive tenses. The form of the auxiliary **be** takes its perfective form, **been**, after the auxiliaries **have**, **has** or **had**. For the future perfect progressive tense, the auxiliary **will** is combined with auxiliaries **have** and **been**.

> Francine **had been** *whipping* the cream absent-mindedly when she realized she made butter.
> (**had** and **been** are auxiliary verbs; the first auxiliary, **had**, indicates the tense (past) of the verb phrase *had been whipping*; **been** indicates the progressive aspect)

> Kali **will have been** *flying* for 10 hours by the time you get home.
> (**will** indicates the tense (future); **have** indicates the aspect is perfective; **been** indicates the progressive aspect)

12.1.3 Auxiliary verb *do*

The auxiliary verb **do** is used only in the simple aspect. It expresses negation, interrogation, contradiction or emphasis. For present time, the forms **do** or **does** (for third person singular) are used. For past time, **did** is the only form. The auxiliary **do** cannot be used together with the auxiliaries **be** or **have** in the same verb phrase. (They can be used together if one of them is a main verb, not an auxiliary.) For negative constructions, **not** (or its contracted form) follows the auxiliary verb.

> He **doesn't** *know*.
> (**doesn't** is an auxiliary verb in the negative, part of the verb phrase *doesn't know*; simple present tense)

> I **did** *intend* to go to the concert.
> (**did** is an auxiliary verb in the past tense, part of the verb phrase *did intend*, used in an affirmative sentence to give emphasis to the main verb *intend*)

> **Don't** *turn* right!
> (**don't** is an auxiliary verb in the negative, part of the verb phrase *don't turn*, used in an imperative sentence) *(See 2.5.3 Imperative sentences)*

*** In the classroom:* **Be,** *do and* **have** *as main verbs ***

The three auxiliaries (**be**, **do** and **have**) can also function as main verbs. The chart below shows different forms of these three words functioning as main verbs and as auxiliary verbs. These verbs also have participle forms.

Table 49: Examples of *be*, *do* and *have* as main and auxiliary verbs

	TIME	MAIN VERB		AUXILIARY VERB	
		SINGULAR	*PLURAL*	*SINGULAR*	*PLURAL*
BE	Present	I **am** happy.	You **are** both funny.	He **is** working.	They **are** sleeping.
BE	Past	He **was** home at 5:00.	They **were** there.	I **was** mugged.	We **were** parking.
DO	Present	She **does** my hair.	We **do** our work.	She **doesn't** drink.	**Do** you drink?
DO	Past	He **did** me a favour.	They **did** their share.	He **did** do it.	They **didn't** do it.
HAVE	Present	He **has** a sandwich.	They **have** money.	She **has** finished.	We **have** been there.
HAVE	Past	I **had** a party.	We **had** it all ready.	He **had** known.	You **hadn't** found it.

ESL learners must understand the different forms that verbs may take after these auxiliaries. The auxiliary verb **do** is always followed by a verb in its base form. The auxiliary verb **have** is followed by a verb in its past participle form. The auxiliary verb **be** is followed by a verb in present participle form for the progressive aspect. It is followed by the past participle form of a verb for passive voice constructions. *(See 11.1.1.3 Participle and 14.1 Forms of tenses)*

What **does** she *play*?
auxiliary + base form of the verb
(simple present)

He **is** *working*.
auxiliary + present participle
(present progressive)

She **has** *done* that before.
auxiliary + past participle
(present perfect)

It **is** already *done*.
auxiliary + past participle
(simple present, passive voice)

Another difficulty with these auxiliaries is when they are in the future tense. Expressing future tense requires an additional auxiliary modal verb (**will**). *(See 14.4 Future tenses)*

auxiliary **will** + <u>main verb</u> **be, do** or **have**	auxiliary **will** + <u>auxiliary</u> **be** or **have** + main verb in present or past participle
It ***will*** **be** interesting. She ***will*** **have** fun. He ***will*** **do** the dishes.	You ***will*** **be** flying. He ***will*** **have** passed. -----

239

Quiz 1: Auxiliary verbs or main verbs

*Identify whether **be**, **do** and **have** (in their different forms) are functioning as auxiliary verbs or main verbs in the following sentences.*

1) Will you be at the airport by 12:00?
2) Upon arrival, you are greeted with a bouquet of flowers and a tropical beverage.
3) By the end of the year, Pam and Greg will have achieved their goals.
4) For over two years, the team has worked hard to restructure the company.
5) You did tell Maya you were not attending the seminar. Do not change your story.

12.2 Modal auxiliary verbs

The modal auxiliary verbs (commonly referred to as modal verbs, or simply modals), are **can, could, dare, may, might, must, need, ought (to), shall, should, will**, and **would**. Other expressions often compared to modal verbs – such as **be going to, had better, have to** and **have got to** – are closely related to modals in meaning and are often interchangeable with them. They are not technically classified as modals. Due to their similarity to modal verbs, they are sometimes called semi-modals or modal phrases. *(See 12.2.2 Modal auxiliary verbs, semi-modals and modal phrases)*

Modal auxiliary verbs are a subset of auxiliary verbs. Like the primary auxiliary verbs **be**, **do** and **have**, they help the main verb to form affirmative, interrogative and negative sentences. However, they differ in that they also add meaning to the main verb. *(See Table 50)* Consider these two examples:

He **does**n't **know**.　　　　He **can**'t **know**.

The first example shows a basic usage (negation) of the auxiliary verb **does** (see preceding section) with the main verb *know*. In the second example, the auxiliary verb **can** plays a slightly different role than just negation. It carries additional meaning with it (a prohibition or a deduction).

Examples with different auxiliaries	Possible meaning
He **does**n't know.	*He doesn't know.* (No extra meaning added by the auxiliary; grammatical function of negation only)
He **can**'t know.	*deduction* that there is no way he knows OR *prohibition* that he is not permitted to know
He **might** not know.	*possibility* that he doesn't know

In the second example, the auxiliary verb **can** adds some meaning to the main verb, and thus to the sentence. This meaning is called modality. Modality describes the attitude, mood, or intention of the speaker (or writer). When the speaker feels something is necessary, advisable, preferable, permissible or possible – or when these attitudes are emphasised – modal auxiliary verbs are used. *(See 12.3 Modality)*

Unlike **be, do** and **have**, modal auxiliary verbs cannot be used as main verbs. **Need** and **dare** are exceptions.

In the classroom: Need and dare

The modals **need** and **dare** are more commonly used as main verbs, but may still be seen in modal constructions. Avoid teaching them as modals at lower levels, as their appearance as modals is relatively rare. **Dare** has fallen out of common use as an auxiliary, but can still be seen in certain texts; **need** is still sometimes used as a modal auxiliary verb.

Main verb	Auxiliary verb
I **dare** you to jump.	I **daren't** tell him. He'll be furious.
We **don't need** trouble.	He **needn't** go yet.

12.2.1 Structure of modal auxiliary verbs

A modal auxiliary verb must be followed by the main verb in its base form (bare infinitive). Some grammar books and theories consider **ought** to be an exception and describe it as a modal verb followed by a to-infinitive; however, for the sake of consistency, **ought to** will be described here as a modal verb (though it is technically a modal phrase), followed by the main verb in its base form.

He	**ought to**	*return*	those books.
<subject>	<modal auxiliary>	<main verb> (base form)	<-----object----->

It	**might**	*rain*.
<subject>	<modal auxiliary>	<main verb> (base form)

12.2.1.1 Similarities between auxiliary verbs and modal verbs

As a subset of auxiliary verbs, modal verbs naturally have many features in common with the main auxiliaries. The main similarities are the functions of negation and interrogation, and their use as pro-verbs.

12.2.1.1.1 Negation

Auxiliary verbs and modal auxiliary verbs can be followed directly by the adverb of negation **not** for the purpose of negation. Main verbs cannot be negated in this way. They require an auxiliary to carry the negation. The adverbial particle **not** can be contracted to auxiliaries and modals as **n't**.

Troy *likes* to play tennis.   Troy **does not** *like* to study.
Mildred and Tish **are** *baking* bread.   Mildred and Tish **aren't** *baking* cookies.
Carl **can** *parasail* pretty well.   Carl **can't** *bungee jump* at all.

One possible exception to main verbs requiring an auxiliary in order to negate are cases when the main verbs are **have** (meaning *possess*) and **be**.

She **isn't** here.
I **haven't** any wool.

12.2.1.1.2 Interrogation

Another similarity between auxiliary verbs and modal verbs is that they are moved in front of the subject when the structure is an interrogative one. Notice the change in word order in the interrogative form of the previous examples.

> **Does** Troy *like* to play tennis?
> **Are** Mildred and Tish *baking* bread?
> **Can** Carl *parasail* on his own?

Main verbs cannot be used in this way. They require question words, auxiliaries or modals for interrogation. The exceptions are **be** and **have** as main verbs.

> **Is** she here?
> **Have** you any wool?

12.2.1.1.3 Pro-verbs

Pro-verbs are verbs that can replace other verbs (in the same way that pronouns replace nouns) so as to avoid repetition. (*See 4 Pronouns*) Both auxiliary verbs and modal verbs can function as pro-verbs.

> A: Does he know how important it is?   B: Yes, he **does**.
> [**does** know]

> A: Why can't he come?   B: He **can**,   but he **won't**.
> [**can** come]   [**won't** come]

12.2.1.2 Differences between auxiliary verbs and modal verbs

In addition to the distinction that auxiliary verbs are purely for grammatical function and modal auxiliary verbs carry additional meaning, the main differences between auxiliaries and modals are the forms of the main verb that may follow, and the ability to change form for tense and number.

12.2.1.2.1 Form of the main verb

One of the differences between auxiliary verbs and modal verbs is the form of the main verb that follows. The auxiliary verb **do** is followed by the main verb in its base form. The auxiliaries **be** and **have** are followed by the main verb in either past or present participle form. All modal auxiliary verbs are followed by the main verb in its base form.

> We   **should**   *go*.
> <subject> <modal auxiliary>   <main verb>
>   (base form)

> He   **is**   *going*.
> <subject> <auxiliary>   <main verb>
>   (present participle)

12.2.1.2.2 Change of form for tense and number

Another difference between these two types of auxiliaries is that modal auxiliary verbs have only one form. Auxiliary verbs change form for tense (for example, **do/did**, has/had) and for number (for example, **am/is/are**, **do/does**). Modal verbs do not take any forms that show tense or number. (An exception is **could**, which may be used as a past tense form of **can**.)

I **might** swim.	I **might** swim later.
She **might** not be right.	She **might** not have been right before.
They **might** obey the rules.	They **might** obey the rules tomorrow.

Table 50: Summary of distinctions between auxiliary verbs and modal verbs

Auxiliary verbs (be, do, have)	Modal auxiliary verbs (can, must, etc.)

• help the main verb
• can be used as pro-verb
• word order:
  - after subjects in affirmative sentences
  - before *not* in negative sentences
  - before the subject in object questions*
• form negative and interrogative structures
• can be used as main verb
• show tense and number
• followed by different forms of the main verb
• do not add meaning to the verb or sentence; used only for grammatical purposes
	• help the main verb
	• can be used as pro-verb
	• word order:
	  - after subjects in affirmative sentences
	  - before *not* in negative sentences
	  - before the subject in object questions*
	• form negative and interrogative structures
	• cannot be used as main verb (except for *dare* and *need*)
	• do not show number, rarely show tense
	• always followed by the main verb in its base form
	• add meaning (modality) to the main verb and to the sentence

*See 2.5.2 Interrogative sentences

Quiz 2: Distinctions between auxiliary verbs and modal verbs

1. Which is a modal verb and why?
    a. does   b. may

2. What are the possible forms of the main verb after an auxiliary verb? After a modal auxiliary verb?

**** In the classroom: Simple present tense or base form? ****

Students generally confuse the simple present tense with the base form of the verb after a modal. It should be made clear to students that the main verb after a modal is never a verb in the present simple tense; it is always a verb in its base form. For example, in the sentence *He can speak many languages*, the modal **can** is followed by the main verb *speak* in its base form. In *He speaks many languages*, the main verb *speaks* is conjugated in the present simple tense. The source of the confusion is in cases where the base form and the simple present form look the same. In the sentences *I can speak many languages* and *I speak many languages*, the main verb *speak* looks the same, but it is not. In the first sentence, *speak* is a verb in its base form. In the second sentence, it is in the present simple tense.

12.2.2 Modal auxiliary verbs, semi-modals and modal phrases

Certain phrases function like modal auxiliaries, though they are not always classified as modal auxiliary verbs. Grammar reference books and ESL grammar texts disagree on the classification of these phrases. The most common classifications for these expressions are *semi-modal* and *modal phrase*.

Most semi-modals carry meanings similar to those of standard modal verbs.

Modal auxiliary verbs	Semi-modal counterparts
can, could	be able to
must	have to, have got to
should, ought to, must	be to, be supposed to, had better
would (past habit)	used to
may, might	be allowed to, be permitted to
should, ought to	be likely to
	would rather / would prefer / would like

Most semi-modals differ from standard modal verbs in their requirement to change form for number and tense. When the semi-modal contains **be**, **do** or **have**, it may change form.

> He **should** go.   He **is** *supposed to* go
> We **should** go.   We **are** *supposed to* go.
> We **should** have gone.   We **were** *supposed to* go.

The main verb after a semi-modal is always in its base form, regardless of the form the semi-modal takes.

*** In the classroom: Using more than one modal auxiliary verb ***

At low intermediate levels, students commonly make the mistake of combining two modal auxiliary verbs. A simple explanation will help ESL learners to realize that when a modal is used in a sentence, it behaves in an exclusive way toward all other modal auxiliary verbs.

> He ~~can must~~ go.
> They ~~will might~~ come.

The notion of modality is an essential concept for students. Students must choose one modality in these cases; they cannot express two modalities in this way. In the first sentence above, for example, if the speaker's intention is to express permission, then the correct modal verb is **can**. If the intention is expressing obligation, then **must** should be used. It is not possible to combine them in this way.

However, some modal auxiliary verbs can be used to modify some semi-modals, as in the examples below:

> He **may** *be allowed to* participate.
> They **should** *be able to* complete the test in an hour.
> His attitude **will** *have to* improve.

The subsequent discussions of modality in this chapter include modals and semi-modals; the term *modal* is used hereafter to include both categories, for brevity.

Quiz 3: Correct the errors

Identify the mistakes and explain what is wrong in each case.

1) She doesn't works on weekends.
2) Did he arrive on time? Yes, he arrived.
3) I could repaired the oven last night.
4) Do I can see the director?
5) You must to obey the rules.

12.3 Modality

Modal verbs express the attitude, mood or perspective of the speaker or writer. This expression of mood is called modality. Examples of modality are certainty, permission, assumption and suggestion. Some ESL textbooks divide these attitudes or modalities into social functions. Unfortunately, these divisions are generally not prescriptive and often overlap, leaving students at a loss over the concept of modal auxiliary verbs altogether. Many ESL textbooks and lessons draw on the communicative functions of modal auxiliary verbs and separate them according to these.

The most effective way to cover modal verbs in the classroom will depend on many factors. This textbook is addressing the subject by grouping the modal verbs according to the meaning (modality) they add to the main verb. This way of grouping modals will clarify their usage and simplify the ways they can be taught. Following are basic examples of modal verbs, labelled with their modalities.

We'll pay for it. (modality: offer)
He **can't** be a doctor. (modality: assumption)
Would you come tonight? (modality: invitation)

The following is a summary of the standard modal verbs and the different modalities that they can express. The fact that each modal has multiple modalities illustrates the complexity of this topic in the classroom.

Table 51: Summary of modal verbs and associated modalities

Modal	Modalities
can	ability, suggestion, possibility, request, offer, permission
can't	ability, assumption/deduction, prohibition
could	ability, suggestion, request, permission, possibility
couldn't	ability, assumption/deduction, request
may (not)	possibility, offer, permission
might (not)	suggestion, possibility
must	advice/recommendation, assumption/deduction, necessity/obligation
mustn't	assumption/deduction, prohibition
need (needn't)	necessity/obligation
ought to	advice/recommendation, probability, obligation/responsibility
shall	suggestion, obligation/responsibility, offer, promise
should (not)	advice/recommendation, suggestion, probability, obligation/responsibility
will (won't)	ability, certainty, obligation/necessity, request, offer, promise
would	request, offer, preference

Each modality is discussed in detail below, together with the semi-modals that express that modality.

12.3.1 Ability

can / could / will / be able to

Can is used to express present and future ability; **could** is used to express past ability; **be able to** can be used in all tenses and can change form to show a clear time frame. They all express ability; their negative counterparts – **cannot/can't**, **could not/couldn't** and **was/were not able to** – express lack of ability.

These three modals can be used to express different kinds of ability as shown in the following examples, all given in present time:

>   He **can** read German.   (knowledge)
>   She **can** type fast.   (skill)
>   I **can** climb up high mountains.   (physical ability)
>   A big dog **can** pull that sled.   (strength)
>   Roses **can't** grow in these conditions. (nature)
>   A Ferrari **can** easily reach 200 kph.   (design)

Be able to is used with similar meanings and is more flexible with time frames, as seen in the following examples, given in a mixture of tenses. The only difference between **can** and **be able to** is that the latter is used especially when referring to people or animate creatures.

>   He **is able to** read German.
>   She **was able to** type fast when she was younger.
>   I **have not been able to** climb since the accident.
>   A big dog **will be able to** pull that sled.

When **could** refers to ability, it usually has the same meaning as **was/were able to**.

> He **couldn't** see clearly before the operation.
> He **wasn't able to** see clearly before the operation.

However, **could** is not generally used when describing one action that a person was able to do on one occasion in the past; the semi-modal **be able to** is preferred.

> I **was able to** finish my homework early yesterday.
> (Instead of: ~~I could finish my homework early yesterday~~.)

The exception to this is with stative verbs. **Could** can be used for a single event in the past (and equals **was/were able to**) when used with stative verbs of perception such as *see, hear, smell, feel, taste, remember* and *understand*.

> She **could** *hear* him talking, so she knew he was home.
> She **was able to** *hear* him talking, so she knew he was home.

> They **could** *taste* all the ingredients in the complex dish.
> They **were able to** *taste* all the ingredients in the complex dish.

Some speakers intend gradations of difference between **could** and **was able to**, but these differences are individual or regional, and don't conform to generally accepted grammar rules.

In questions, the meaning remains the same; however, the word order changes slightly, as with all auxiliaries. **Can** and **could** precede subjects; **be** also precedes subjects, but **able to** follows the subject.

> **Can** you swim?
> **Could** you reach Brian via email?
> **Is** he **able to** win the game?

Will can also be used to express ability, although it is less frequently used than the rest of the modals mentioned in this section.

> This medicine **will** cure anything.
> The car **won't** go; should we call a tow truck?

Quiz 4: True or false

1) When the modal **can** is used to express ability, it refers to present and past time.
2) **Could** and **be able to** can be used to refer to a past ability that happens once.

12.3.2 Advice / recommendation

should / must / ought to / had better / have to / have got to

The modals used when giving advice are usually divided according to the strength of the advice conveyed in the sentence. They can be organized from the weakest to the strongest as in the following list:

Regular advice: should / shouldn't / ought to / ought not to
Advice with warning or threat implied: had better / had better not
Strong advice: must / have to / have got to

Should and **ought to** can be used to express advisability in almost the same way.

You **should / ought to** go home now; it's late.

The only difference between these two modals is that **ought to** is used less frequently and sometimes sounds more formal.

Had better is close to **should / ought to** in meaning, but **had better** is usually stronger. It often implies a warning or a threat of possible bad consequences. The **had** in **had better** is often contracted to the subject as **'d**.

You**'d better not** be late; passing this class depends on it.

In the interrogative form, **should** is preferred to **ought to** or **had better**.

Should I wait outside?
What time **should** I pick you up?

Must, **have to** and **have got to** are used to give strong advice. There is a difference between British and American English in this case. British English usually uses **must**, while American English usually uses **have (got) to**. However, **have (got) to** is slowly becoming more common in British English as well. These modals communicate strong advice or orders given to oneself or to others. The **have** in **have got to** is often contracted to the subject as **'ve** (or **'s** for **has** for third person singular subjects).

I **must** stop eating junk food.   He **must** stop eating junk food.
I **have to** stop eating junk food.   He **has to** stop eating junk food.
I**'ve got to** stop eating junk food. He**'s got to** stop eating junk food.

Must can also be used to express insistence or some emphasis when giving advice.

You **must** do something about your bad habits.
You really **must** accept this offer.

*** In the classroom: Should, ought to and had better ***

At intermediate level and above, students should understand that when advice is given about a past action or situation, it takes the form of criticism or regret. This may be accomplished with the modals **should** and **ought to**. The past forms of **should** and **ought to** are formed as follows:

should/ought to + *have* **+** *main verb (past participle).*

This structure is sometimes said to give hindsight advice.

I **should** *have studied* last week; I wouldn't have failed the exam.

For referring to the past, **should** is used more commonly than **ought to**.

When introduced to the semi-modal **had better**, students will naturally assume that there is an implied comparison, due to the presence of the comparative *better*. Reinforce with students that this structure has no point of comparison and means *should* or *it would be good to...*.

In spoken English, the contracted form **'d better** is very often pronounced with the **'d** elided. Students will often hear this, and may assume that *better* by itself is functioning as a modal.

>You('**d**) **better** hurry up if you want to arrive on time.

12.3.3 Suggestion
can / could / might / shall / should

Shall, should, shouldn't, can and **could** are used to give suggestions. This modality is very similar to giving advice or describing possibilities, so there are some overlapping concepts. This modality includes the use of **shall**, which is not seen in the modalities of advice and possibility.

When **shall** is used with *I* or *we* in a question, the speaker is usually making a suggestion or asking for advice. This use of **shall** can be quite formal, depending on the context. **Can, could** and **should** can be used in answers indicating possibilities or suggestions.

>**Shall** we go for a walk together?
>I'd rather not. I'm so tired, but we **can / could** watch TV together.
>
>**Shall** we dance?
>Yes, we **should**. / Let's!
>
>When **shall** I go to the bank?
>You **can / could** go there in the afternoon, but you **shouldn't** forget your chequebook this time.

Might is sometimes used to offer casual or tentative suggestions.

>That dress is too tight; you **might** ask for a bigger size.

Quiz 5: Modalities

Identify the functions of the modal verbs in the following sentences by circling the correct response.

1) Shall I make you a cup of coffee?
   (permission; necessity; request; suggestion)
2) You should obey the traffic rules.
   (offer; permission; recommendation; prohibition)
3) He ought to be more careful.
   (advice; request; possibility; necessity)
4) He'd better go home now.
   (suggestion; permission; assumption; warning)
5) You could ask her if you want.
   (request; suggestion; ability; necessity)

12.3.4 Degrees of certainty: certainty, assumption, probability and possibility

The following four modalities belong to a broader category or idea of certainty. This can aid students in their comprehension of these modals. They listed from the highest degree of certainty to the lowest.

12.3.4.1 Certainty

will

When the speaker is sure something is true in the present, no modal verb is used.

Mary **is** at home. (It is true, so the degree of certainty is 100 %.)

When the speaker is almost 100% sure something is or will be true in the future, the modal **will** is used. This modal shows certainty or confidence about the future.

I just know he **will** be late again; he always is.

12.3.4.2 Assumption

can't / couldn't / must / have to / have got to

When assumptions or deductions are made, the speaker expresses a high degree of certainty, with a slight chance of not being right.

Must (affirmative) and **can't / couldn't** (negative) express a very strong degree of certainty, but the degree of certainty is less than 100%.

She **must** be home by now; she left quite a while ago.
She **couldn't** be home yet since she lives quite far from her office.

In American English, **must not** is occasionally used to express a negative deduction or assumption in the present.

She **must not** be home yet; she works until 5 p.m. on Mondays.

These modals are also often used with the progressive structure:

modal + *be* + *present participle*.

> He **must** be working.
> She **can't** be lying about this.
> You**'ve got to** be kidding.

To express an assumption about the past, the perfect modal structure can be used: **must / can't** + *have* + *past participle*.

> She **must have been** angry after you were late again.
> She **can't have been** happy that you arrived half an hour late.

**** In the classroom: Negative forms of modals ****

ESL learners generally think that **mustn't** and **don't have to** are the exact negative counterparts of **must** and **have to**. But, often the negative form of a modal verb does not carry the opposite meaning. Pay close attention to the meaning of the modal when deciding whether to introduce negative forms in a lesson. For example, if the lesson is about expressing assumptions or deductions with modal **must** as in *She must be in a meeting*, the negative form **can't** should be presented as the opposite of **must** when expressing assumptions. However, if the lesson is about rules and obligations using **must**, as in *You must wear a uniform at school*, the negative modal that carries the opposite meaning is **mustn't**, as in *You mustn't wear jeans at school*. (See 12.3.5 Necessity / obligation / responsibility)

12.3.4.3 Probability

ought to / should / be likely to

Should, **ought to**, and **be likely to** are used to express probable guesses about the present or future with a slightly weaker degree of certainty (around 70%) than **must**, though a little higher than the modals used to describe possibilities. This group of modals show that the speaker might have some evidence in order to make a guess. When compared to **must** (used for assumptions or a higher degree of certainty) in similar examples, the following similarities and differences can be identified:

> She **must** be tired by now. (I'm almost certain that she's tired.)
> She **should** be tired by now. (I think it's highly probable, but I am not sure.)
> She **is likely to** be tired by now. (I think it's highly probable, but I am not sure.)

When **should** and **ought to** are used with the perfect modal structure, they convey hindsight advice, not probability. *(See 12.3.2 Advice / recommendation)*

12.3.4.4 Possibility

can / could / may / might

The lowest degree of certainty is possibility, and within this modality, both strong and weak possibility may be expressed. This group of modals expresses less than 50%

certainty. They generally show that the speaker's guesses are probably not based on evidence.

Can and **may** are used to describe stronger possibilities than **might** and **could**, in their affirmative and negative forms.

> I **can** make a Caesar salad; I have a recipe at home.
> She **may** know what you're talking about. I think she was eavesdropping.
>
> He **could** be a con, you know!
> She **might not** admit that she was eavesdropping.

Discussing past possibilities can be done with the perfect modal structure:

> **modal** + *have* + *past participle*
>
> She **may** *have been* in the shower when you called.
> He **might not** *have seen* you; it was quite dark at the theatre.
> They **could** *have arrived* earlier if they had found a babysitter sooner.

12.3.5 Necessity / obligation / responsibility

must / need / needn't / ought to / shall / should / will / be to / be supposed to / have to / have got to

This set of modals conveys meanings of necessity, obligation or responsibility which sometimes overlap in context; thus, they are grouped together here. They are organized from the strongest to the weakest.

Strong obligation / necessity:	must / will / be to / be supposed to / have (got) to
Regular obligation:	ought to / shall / should
Regular necessity:	need / needn't

12.3.5.1 Must, will, be to, be supposed to, have (got) to

These modals express necessity, obligation or responsibility at the highest degree. They may be differentiated based on whether the obligation or necessity comes from the speaker or some external authority. When speaking of oneself, if the speaker decides that something is important, **must** or **have got to** are used. When someone else other than the speaker makes the decision, **be to**, **be supposed to** or **have to** are generally used.

> I **must** go to the office on Saturday to finish my report.
> (speaker's sense of obligation)
>
> I'**ve got to** work harder if I want a promotion.
> (speaker's sense of necessity)
>
> I **am to** inquire at the main desk at 2:00.
> (procedure created by someone other than the speaker)

> I **am supposed to** drink eight glasses of water each day.
> (regimen designed by someone other than the speaker)
>
> I **have to** park somewhere else; otherwise, I'll get a ticket.
> (a traffic rule that was decided by law)

When talking about someone other than the speaker, the terms are interchangeable.

> You **must** provide proof of identity at the border.
> You**'ve got to** provide proof of identity at the border.
> You **are supposed to** provide proof of identity at the border.
> You **have to** provide proof of identity at the border.

The modal **will** used in the sense of necessity is more often used when speaking of another person. **Will** and **be to** have a stronger sense of direct instruction or an order.

> You **will** provide proof of identity at the border.
> You **are to** provide proof of identity at the border.

The negative form **mustn't** conveys prohibition (negative obligation). **Don't have to** is *not* the direct opposite of **have to**; it has a meaning of choice: not a prohibition, not a necessity.

> You **mustn't** cheat on the exam.   (prohibition)
> You **don't have to** come today.   (it is not necessary)

To express past time, **have to** is used instead of **must** or **have got to**. There is no other past form for **must** or **have got to** (when they mean necessity or obligation)

> I *had to return* the storybook yesterday.

12.3.5.2 Shall, should, and ought to

Should and **ought to** show obligation, and have the same meaning. They are less emphatic than **must** and **have to**. They express responsibility. However, the meaning ranges in strength from a suggestion *(See 12.3.3 Suggestion)* to responsibility or duty.

> You **should** take good care of your son.
> You **ought to** take good care of your son.

Shall is used to convey obligation in contracts and other legal documents. For this modality, it is used with third-person subjects to refer to their obligations and duties.

> The employer **shall** deduct the employee's income tax.

12.3.5.3 Need, needn't and don't need to

Need can be used as a modal verb or as the main verb in a sentence with no difference in meaning. When it is used as a main verb, it is followed by an infinitive (particle *to* + verb in base form) and takes the suffix –s in third person singular. It is used as a modal verb mainly in questions and negative sentences.

She **needs** *to buy* a new coat.	(main verb)
She **doesn't need** *to buy* a new coat.	(main verb)
She **needn't** *buy* a new coat.	(modal verb)
Need I *buy* a new coat for the winter?	(modal verb)

When **need** is used to express necessity, it is less emphatic than **must** or **have to**.

She **must** finish her project on time.
(absolute necessity)

She **needs** to finish her project on time.
(necessary, but not imperative)

Quiz 6: Modal verbs of necessity

Circle the correct statements.

1. **must** can express:
   a. recommendation b. possibility c. assumption d. obligation
2. a. **need** can only function as main verb
   b. **need** can function as a modal and as a main verb.
3. a. **should** is more emphatic than **must** when expressing obligation.
   b. **should** and **ought to** have the same meaning.

12.3.6   Requests

can / could / will / would

Requests are always in interrogative form. In these structures, the subject comes between the modal and the base form of the verb.

To ask someone to do something for someone else, **can**, **could**, **will** or **would** are used. The structure is:

> **modal +** subject **+** *main verb (base form)* ..... ?

Would you .....? and **Could you** .....? are considered more polite than **Can you** .....? and **Will you** .....? The degree of politeness, however, is often determined by the speaker's tone of voice as well.

Would you *pass* me the sugar?
Can you *buy* me some fruit?

*** In the classroom: Answers to requests ***

Some typical responses to the example requests above are: *Yes, I'd be happy to, Yes, I'd be glad to, Certainly, Of course, Yes, here you are, I'm sorry, but I can't, I'd like to, but....* and *Sure* (informal).

Could you pass me the vinegar? Yes, here you are.

Other possible answers can include the use of a different modal, such as **can**; however, **would** and **could** are not used as part of answers to polite requests.

> A: **Could** you lend me your pen?
> B: Yes, of course. / Yes, I **can**.

12.3.7 Offers

can / may / shall / will / would

Spontaneous offers can be conveyed with **will**, **shall** or **can** in affirmative statements and in the interrogative form. **Would** and **may** can convey an offer in the interrogative form only.

> I**'ll** get the phone.
> **Will** you be having the steak tonight?
> I **shall** bring the cookies.
> **Shall** I get the door for you?
> I **can** help you with that.
> **Can** I help you?
> What **would** you like to eat?
> What **may** I help you with?

12.3.8 Permission/prohibition

can / can't / could / may / may not / might / mustn't / be allowed to / be permitted to

The modals **might**, **may**, **can** and the modal phrases **be allowed to** and **be permitted to** are used to ask for permission, with different degrees of politeness.

Might I is very polite and formal; it is used less frequently than the other three.

> **Might** I borrow your dictionary?

May I is roughly as polite as **Might I**, and is considered the all-purpose permission modal.

> **May** I be excused?

Could I is more colloquial, and often more polite than **Can I**.

> **Could** I bother you for a light?

Could can sometimes be used to express past; however, when it is used to express permission it is definitely not referring to any past situations or actions.

Mustn't, can't and **may not**, as well as **be not allowed to** and **be not permitted to**, express prohibition or lack of permission.

You **mustn't** go through a red light.
They **can't** attend that seminar until they finish and pass the art class.
You **may not** speak until you are spoken to.
You **are not allowed to** leave the room.
Smoking **is not permitted** in the building.

*** In the classroom: Can I? ***

Can I is used informally, especially when the speaker is talking to someone he is quite familiar with. It is considered less polite than **May I** and **Could I**. There is a school of thought that rejects **can** for asking permission. However, the frequency with which this form is used makes it imperative for ESL teachers to acknowledge and explain this everyday usage.

Can I sit here?

Quiz 7: Defining modalities

Choose the correct meanings for the subject + modal verb combinations in the left column.

1) You mustn't…   a) You are supposed to…
2) You can't be…   b) It wasn't necessary for us to…(but we did)
3) They must be…   c) Let's…
4) They ought to…   d) He had the skill to …
5) You must…   e) They had better…
6) You should…   f) It is forbidden…
7) May I…?   g) Am I allowed to …?
8) We needn't have…   h) You are to…
9) He was able to…   i) I'm certain you aren't…
10) Shall we…?   j) I'm sure they are…

12.3.9 Preference

would prefer / would rather / would sooner

Would rather, would prefer and **would sooner** are semi-modals expressing preference. When expressing general preferences without a specific time frame, the main verb *prefer* is generally used.

I **prefer** tea **to** coffee.
(main verb *prefer* + noun + *to* + noun)

I think he **prefers** to stay at home *rather than* (to) go out tonight.
(main verb *prefer* + to-infinitive + *rather than* + to infinitive / base form)

The semi-modals **would rather**, **would prefer** and **would sooner** may also be used to express preference.

Would prefer is used to express a specific preference, choice or request. This modal generally refers to the immediate present or future. The modal **would** in this modal phrase is usually used in its contracted form **'d**.

> I**'d prefer** to watch a comedy *rather than* a thriller tonight.
> (**would prefer** + to infinitive + *rather than* + noun / to infinitive)

Would rather also conveys a specific preference or request in the immediate present or future. In addition to this, **would rather** also means the exclusion of the alternative(s) more strongly. The use of this modal phrase is also informal and generally used in the spoken form.

> I**'d rather** wait here *than* take the bus.
> (**would rather** + base form + *than* + base form)

> I**'d rather** you didn't wait here.
> (**would rather** + object + past simple form)

Notice that in spite of requiring a past form of the verb in the second example, the statement refers to the immediate present or future, not the past.

Would sooner is used in informal spoken British English to convey more than simple preferences. It can be used to express frustration or annoyance, a warning or an order. This modal phrase is also used to express immediate present or future, not past.

> I**'d sooner** make dinner myself *than* ask you.
> (**would sooner** + base form + *than* + base form)

> I**'d sooner** he didn't come to our party.
> (**would sooner** + object + past simple form)

12.3.10 Promises

will / shall

Will is used to express a promise in a simple statement, or as part of a conditional sentence.

> I **will** call you when I arrive.
> If I am elected President, I **will** work to change those laws.

Shall can also be used to express promises. It is generally used with the first person only (singular or plural).

> I **shall** never forget you.
> We **shall** be back soon.

12.3.11 Non-modal meanings

Modal verbs and modal phrases are also used with non-modal meanings to convey time frames. The use of these is explained in detail in Chapter 14 Tenses.

Will and **be going to** are used to express future time; and **would** and **used to** can be used to express past time (talking about past habits).

*** In the classroom: pronunciation of auxiliary verbs ***

Auxiliary and modal auxiliary verbs are generally unstressed words in a sentence. They are function words (words that support the structure of the sentence), not content words (words that carry substantial meaning). However, when auxiliary and modal auxiliary words are emphasized or are part of short answers, they are generally stressed. Therefore, these types of verbs have a weak and a strong form when it comes to the way they are stressed in a sentence.

The following are some examples of auxiliaries' and modal auxiliaries' weak and strong forms, depicted using the International Phonetic Alphabet (IPA). Dictionaries should show both forms, but in many cases they only give the strong form of the word. It is almost always the unstressed form of the function word which occurs in normal speech.

Modal verbs	Strong form (for emphasis or contrast)	Weak form (unstressed, normal speech)
can	/kæn/	/kən/; /kn/
could	/kʊd/	/kəd/
must	/mʌst/	/məst/; /məs/
should	/ʃʊd/	/ʃəd/

Auxiliary verbs	Strong form (for emphasis or contrast)	Weak form (unstressed, normal speech)
am	/æm/	/əm/; /m/
are	/ɑr/; /ɑ:/	/ər/; /r/
was	/wʌz/; /wɒz/	/wəz/
were	/wɜr/; /wɜə/	/wər/; /wə/
has	/hæz/	/həz/; /əz/; /z/
have	/hæv/	/həv/; /əv/; /v/
had	/hæd/	/həd/; /d/
do	/du/	/dʊ/; /də/
does	/dʌz/	/dəz/; /z/

In the following sentences, the auxiliaries and modal verbs are unstressed, as they only serve their normal grammatical function in these cases.

I should do it.
/ʃʊd/

We should have done it.
/ʃʊd/ /həv/

He has finished the job.
/həz/

They are coming soon.
/ər/

However, modal and auxiliary verbs are always stressed when they are acting as pro-verbs, in the absence of the main verb.

Are	you going abroad soon?		Yes, I	**am**.
/ɑr/				/æm/
Does	she like pizza?		Yes, she	**does**.
/dəz/				/dʌz/
Could	you speak to John?		Yes, I	**could**.
/kəd/				/kʊd/

The strong forms are also used to emphasize the modality.

She **could** be right, but I don't really think it's true.
/kʊd/ *(emphasis on the modality of possibility)*

*** *You can teach modal auxiliary verbs* ***

Following are some guidelines and reference points for developing lessons that teach or review modal auxiliary verbs in context. These ideas are listed by modality, with some suggested functions and structures. Ideas for teaching standard auxiliary verbs are described in Chapter 14 Tenses.

Some general advice for teaching modals:

1) Modal verbs should be taught in context and according to their modality or function. For example, the teacher should centre a lesson around *making requests* or *invitations*, rather than around *would*, *could* and *might*.

2) Modal verbs should be presented individually or in small groups of similar meaning. Avoid presenting them all as a list. The reason for this is that when modals are presented in groups of similar meaning (for example, *giving permission*), it will be more memorable for the students – and easier for the teacher to present.

3) Consider the level of formality and politeness. For example, *Can you close the door?* (informal request) vs. *Would you mind closing the door?* (formal request). Emphasize that intonation plays a big role in formality.

4) The level of complexity should be considered when teaching modals, taking into account whether the modals are appropriate for the students' level of English. *Can you close the door?* (Can you + verb (base form) …. ?) has a simple structure compared to *Would you mind closing the door?* (Would you mind + gerund ….?).

Modalities: Asking for and receiving advice, recommendations or suggestions

Modal verb(s)	Communicative topic	Possible use	Related language	Communicative practice
should / ought to (Low intermediate)	Going places	"Where should I go?" "You ought to visit China."	"How about…?" (Low intermediate)	Write some guidelines for a tourist.
should / must (Low intermediate)	Health	"You should drink more water." "You must lose weight."	"Why don't you…?" (Low intermediate)	Role play a check-up visit to a doctor.
should / had better (Low intermediate and above)	Manners	"You'd better be on time." "You should shake hands."	"What about…?" (Low intermediate and above)	Write or role play a 'Miss Manners' advice session.
have to / have got to (Low intermediate and above)	Career plans	"You have to finish university." "You've got to do research on the industry."	"It's better to…" (Intermediate)	Role play a career counseling session.

Modalities: Expressing obligation and responsibility

Modal verb(s)	Communicative topic	Possible exponents	Related language	Communicative practice
must / have to (Low intermediate)	Orientation on the job	"You must wear a uniform." "Do we have to sign in?"	"Are we allowed to…?" (Intermediate level)	Design an employee handbook.
should / be supposed to / be to (Intermediate and above)	School options and requirements	"We're supposed to finish this level before taking the next one." "You are to register by Tuesday."	"Is it possible…?" (Intermediate level)	Role play a university enrollment using a course schedule.
Shall (Higher levels)	Legal requirements and organizational rules	"No person shall distribute goods on this property." "Visitors shall carry identification at all times."	"It is prohibited…" (Intermediate and above)	Research laws containing this language and role play a court appearance.

Modality: Expressing necessity

Modal verb(s)	Communicative topic	Possible exponents	Related language	Communicative practice
must / have to / need (Low intermediate and above)	Traveling	"I must get to the airport on time." "You need to remove your shoes."	"It is (not) necessary to…" (Intermediate level)	Role play making arrangements for emergency travel.
need / should / have to (Low intermediate and above)	The environment	"We need to reduce greenhouse gas emissions." "We have to reduce pollution."	"It is our duty.." (Intermediate level)	Write a news article discussing the environment and what needs to be done to improve it.

Modality: Degree of certainty

Modal verb(s)	Communicative topic	Possible exponents	Related language	Communicative practice
must / have to / have got to (certain - present) (Low intermediate and above)	Detective work	"They must be out of the country by now." "It's got to be in this room somewhere."	"I'm sure…" (Low intermediate and above)	Give 'evidence' of a crime and have the students play the role of detectives, determining what is certainly true.
should / ought to (probable) (Low intermediate and above)	Waiting for a visitor	"He should be here soon." "She ought to be tired after the journey."	"…will probably/likely + verb (base form)…" (Higher level)	Role play a casual discussion about the pending arrival of an important guest.
may / could / might (possible) (Intermediate level and above)	What could it be?	"It might be for cleaning." "She could use it to keep warm."	"There is a chance that…" (Intermediate level and above)	Bring objects and have students guess what you use them for.
can't / couldn't (negative certainty) (Intermediate level and above)	Shock and surprise	"This can't be chicken!" "He couldn't be joking."	No way! Not a chance! (Intermediate level and above)	Provide written situations with an impossible element and have students produce the 'punchlines'.
will (certain future) (Low intermediate and above)	Fortune teller	"You will live a long life."	"I see…." "I predict…" (Low intermediate and above)	Give students the power to predict the future exactly. Role play a visit to a fortune teller.

Modality: Requests

Modal verb(s)	Communicative topic	Possible exponents	Related language	Communicative practice
can / will (informal) (Beginner and above)	Borrowing from friends	"Can I use your bus pass today?" "Will you give me that book later?"	"Is it okay…." "Do you mind if…" (Intermediate level and above)	Student A requests something from Student B; Student B makes excuses.
could / would (formal) (Intermediate level and above)	Style makeover	"Would you cut it a little shorter, please?" "Could I try this in another colour?"	"Would you mind + …ing?" (Intermediate level and above)	You have won a fashion and beauty makeover with a professional stylist. Role play the discussion.

Modality: Permission

Modal verb(s)	Communicative topic	Possible exponents	Related language	Communicative practice
could / may (requesting) (Low intermediate level and above)	Home stay	"Could I give it to you tomorrow?" "May I leave early?"	"Would you mind if I + verb (simple past)?" (Intermediate and above)	Have students role play a discussion of house rules.
can (not) / may (not) (giving/ denying) (Low intermediate and above)	Signs, signs	"Residents may park at the rear of the building." "You can't carry a bottle of water on the plane."	"…(not) allowed + to-infinitive." (Intermediate and above)	Discuss permissions in everyday life. Design a series of permission signs.

Modalities: Ability (knowledge, skill and capability)

Modal verb(s)	Communicative topic	Possible exponents	Related language	Communicative practice
can / be able to (Beginner and above)	Job interview	"I can speak five languages." "I'm able to adapt very quickly."	"…manage to…" (Higher level)	Role play a skills assessment or job interview
could / be able to (past ability) (Low intermediate and above)	Childhood reminiscing	"I could swim very well when I was a child."	"…used to…" (Intermediate level)	Students quiz each other about abilities they may have lost over the years.

Modality: Preference

Modal verb(s)	Communicative topic	Possible exponents	Related language	Communicative practice
would rather / would prefer (Intermediate level and above)	Everybody's favourites	"I'd rather go skating than skiing." "Would he prefer Paris or Amsterdam?"	"I'd sooner…" (Higher levels)	Write an essay about your favourite foods, restaurants and vacation spots.

Modality: Making an offer

Modal verb(s)	Communicative topic	Possible exponents	Related language	Communicative practice
will / shall (Low intermediate level)	Super polite	"I'll carry that for you." "Shall I help you with that?"	"Would you like me to…?" (Intermediate level)	Student A is a visiting VIP. Student B is trying to make a good impression by being very polite. Role play the offers to help.

Modality: Making a promise

Modal verb(s)	Communicative topic	Possible exponents	Related language	Communicative practice
will (not) (Low intermediate to intermediate levels)	Making amends	"I will come earlier tomorrow." "I won't make so much noise."	"I promise…" "I swear…"	Student A has done things to disappoint Student B and wants to make up for it. Role play the situation.

Modality: Possibility

Modal verb(s)	Communicative topic	Possible exponents	Related language	Communicative practice
can (Low intermediate level)	How do I do things here?	"You can buy your vegetables at the farmer's market." "You can get a taxi on the street."	"It is possible + to-infinitive." (Higher levels)	A new immigrant needs to know how to do everyday things. Write him an e-mail with the possibilities.

13 Gerunds and infinitives

Gerunds and infinitives are grammatical forms that have their origin in verbs, but they do not always act like verbs in sentences; they generally act like nouns. These forms are sometimes called verbals, non-tense verbs, or non-finite verbs.

Gerunds

A gerund is a non-finite, non-tense verb ending in *–ing*. It is not conjugated in any particular tense or inflected in any way (for example, by aspect, mood or person). *(See 14.1 Forms of tenses)* A gerund acts as a noun (also called a verbal noun) and it occupies the same positions in a sentence that a noun does: subject, subject complement, object of certain verbs, object of a preposition and appositive. *(See 3.2 Functions of nouns in a sentence)*

A phrase introduced by a gerund is called a gerundial phrase. Within a gerundial phrase, gerunds can be followed by complements, modifiers or objects – just as conjugated verbs do – but despite the fact that its root is a verb, a gerund cannot act as the main verb of a sentence.

> I like **running**. (simple gerund; direct object of the verb *like*)
> I enjoy **playing soccer**. (gerundial phrase; direct object of the verb *enjoy*)
> **Running** is my hobby. (simple gerund; subject of the sentence)
> **Being healthy** is my priority. (gerundial phrase; subject of the sentence.)

Infinitives

Like a gerund, an infinitive is a verb in a non-finite or non-tense form. This form may work as a noun (also called a verbal noun).

As nouns, infinitives take the same positions in a sentence as gerunds do: subject, subject complement, object of certain verbs, object of a preposition and appositive. Unlike gerunds, infinitives can also function as adverbs and sometimes as main verbs of a sentence.

An infinitive can be a two-word phrase introduced by the infinitive particle *to*, as in *I want **to go** home* and ***To eat** out in this city is very expensive*. This type of infinitive is called to-infinitive, full infinitive, or infinitive with *to*. An infinitive can also be found without the particle *to*, as in, *I heard the cat **purr***, or *She did nothing but **lie** all the time*. This one-word infinitive is called bare infinitive, base form, or infinitive without *to*.

Infinitives are not always nouns. The bare infinitive almost always has the function of the main verb in a sentence, following auxiliaries and modals, as in *He doesn't **work** on Fridays* and *You should **exercise** more*. *(See 12.2.1 Structure of modal auxiliary verbs)*

In this book, the term *infinitive* is mainly used to describe the to-infinitive, while the infinitive without *to* is called bare infinitive or base form.

A to-infinitive verb cannot act as the main verb of a sentence. As with gerunds, a to-infinitive can be followed by complements, modifiers or objects. A phrase introduced by an infinitive is called an infinitive phrase or an infinitival phrase.

I'd like **to drink a coke with lemon**.

Within the sentence, **to drink a coke with lemon** is an infinitival phrase functioning as the direct object of the verb phrase *would like*. Within the infinitival phrase, **to drink** is the head and *a coke with lemon* is the direct object of the action expressed by the to-infinitive.

Quiz 1: Gerunds and infinitives
True or false?
1) Both gerunds and infinitives always act as nouns.
2) A phrase introduced by a non-finite verb ending in *–ing* is called an infinitival phrase.
3) In the sentence *I saw him enter the house* the word *enter* is a bare infinitive.

*** In the classroom: Gerunds and infinitives ***
Understanding the form a gerund or an infinitive takes is not a real problem for ESL students. They can easily recognize that *–ing* endings might indicate the word is a gerund compared to a word preceded by the particle *to*.

>Cara *enjoys* **spending** time outdoors.
>Cara *would like* **to spend** time outdoors.

The difficulty is not the form, but the correct application. At a high beginner level, learners will be introduced to examples like the ones above. Most of the time, the words or expressions followed by gerunds or infinitives are introduced in ESL books under functional headings, such as *talking about likes/dislikes* or *preferences*. The teacher should make sure that at this stage, students have lots of examples and practice with common verbs that are followed by gerunds or infinitives, increasing the chances that they will naturally recognize the correct form to use (rather than memorizing lists).

13.1 Functions of gerunds in a sentence
The following examples show the functions of gerunds and gerundial phrases in a sentence.

Subject of the sentence

>**Smoking** is bad for your health.
>(gerund functioning as the subject of the sentence)

>**Being an actress** is what I've always wanted to do.
>(gerundial phrase functioning as the subject of the sentence; within the phrase, **Being** is a gerund followed by the subject complement *an actress*)

Subject complement

>His hobby is **watching horror movies**.
>(gerundial phrase functioning as subject complement (describing the subject, *His hobby*); within the phrase, **watching** is a gerund followed by the direct object *horror movies*)

>Another alternative could be **inviting the Robinsons**.
>(gerundial phrase functioning as subject complement (describing the subject, *Another alternative*); within the phrase, **inviting** is a gerund followed by the direct object *the Robinsons*)

Object of the main verb

Gerunds are normally direct objects. They can be the indirect objects of a few verbs.

>I enjoy **going to parties**.
>(gerundial phrase functioning as the direct object of the verb *enjoy*; within the phrase, **going** is a gerund followed by a prepositional phrase of place, *to parties*)

>He gave **partying** too much attention.
>(gerund functioning as the indirect object of the verb *gave*)

The following is an example list of common verbs that can be followed by a gerund or gerundial phrase functioning as the direct object of the verb. Only very few of these, such as *give*, *make* and *name*, allow gerunds as an indirect object. Some of the verbs in the list can also be followed by infinitives. (See section 13.4 for a sample list of verbs with infinitives and section 13.7 for verbs with both.)

verb + gerund (direct object)

admit	allow	avoid	can't help	consider
deny	discuss	dislike*	enjoy	finish
hate*	involve	like*	love*	make
mind	prefer*	propose*	recommend	regret*
resist	risk	spend (time)	suggest	tolerate

*these verbs may also be followed by infinitives; see section 13.7

>He *admits* **forging** his doctor's signature.
>The team *discussed* **hiring** an intern for the project.
>I can't *tolerate* **arriving** late for a meeting.
>He *made* **exercising** daily his priority.

Object of a preposition

A gerund or gerundial phrase following a preposition functions as the object of the preposition.

Following are sample lists of the most common combinations of (verb + preposition), (adjective + preposition) and (noun + preposition) that can be followed by gerunds, with the gerund acting as the object of the preposition.

(verb + preposition) + gerund

accuse of	admit to	apologize for	care about	concentrate on
confess to	disapprove of	feel like	forgive (s/b) for	insist on
object to	plan on	refrain from	succeed in	thank (s/b) for

He *succeeded in* **graduating** from Harvard University.
Who would *object to* **supporting** Cindy's cause?

(adjective + preposition) + gerund

angry at	accustomed to	addicted to	anxious about
bad at	committed to	devoted to	disappointed in / with
familiar with	famous for	frightened of	interested in
known for	proud of	terrified of	worried about

She was *anxious about* **speaking** publicly.
He is *frightened of* **flying**.

(noun + preposition) + gerund

addiction to	advantage of	dedication to	devotion to
excuse for	fear of	interest in	memory of
preference for	reaction to	responsibility for	talent for

Her *fear of* **failing** caused her lots of pain.
My boss has a real *talent for* **identifying** practical solutions.

In some of the patterns described above, the verbs, adjectives, and nouns are followed by *to*. In these cases, *to* is not an infinitive particle introducing an infinitive form; it is a preposition. These combinations should be followed by a gerund.

~~He admitted to have taken the money~~.
He *admitted to* **having** taken the money.

~~They are accustomed to work late on Mondays~~.
They are *accustomed to* **working** late on Mondays.

~~Her dedication to raise her children is admirable~~.
Her *dedication to* **raising** her children is admirable.

Appositive

As with any other noun, a gerund may function as an appositive. *(See 3.2 Functions of nouns in a sentence)*

Her hobby, **knitting hats**, kept her from going insane.
(gerundial phrase functioning as an appositive to the noun *hobby*)

Quiz 2: Functions of gerunds

What is the function of the gerund or gerundial phrase in the following sentences?

1) Has jogging been your pastime lately?
2) My main source of income is writing blogs.
3) What she loved most, babysitting her niece, was forbidden to her.
4) Her devotion to teaching has helped her overcome her loneliness.
5) Osvaldo regretted giving the speech.

13.2 Gerundial forms

Due to their verb base, gerunds can take different forms. These forms correspond to the aspects that verbs can take: simple, perfective and progressive. Gerunds may also take passive forms. Following are examples of the possible gerunds derived from the verb *do*.

	Simple	Passive	Perfective	Perfective progressive	Perfective passive
Gerund	doing	being done	having done	having been doing	having been done

Simple gerund is the *–ing* form of the verb.

> I am interested in **communicating** with her.

Passive gerund consists of two words: the gerund **being** and a past participle.

> They dislike **being left** behind.

Perfective gerund consists of two words: the gerund **having** and a past participle.

> They admit **having planned** the execution.

Perfective progressive gerund consists of three words: the gerund **having**, the past participle *been*, and a present participle.

> We recall their **having been drinking** through the entire weekend.

Perfective passive gerund consists of three words: the gerund **having**, the past participle *been*, and another past participle.

> Alexandra acknowledged **having been arrested** as a teenager.

Negative gerunds are formed by preceding any of the gerund forms mentioned above with the adverb *not*.

> She regrets **not having been informed** about the accident sooner.

Quiz 3: Gerundial forms

Which sentence contains a perfective passive gerund?
a. She remembers having had an argument with Rob before she fainted.
b. I am sure they enjoyed having been guided through the whole process.

Which sentence contains a perfective negative gerund?
a. They recall not having learned that topic.
b. They do not recall having learned that topic.

13.3 Other uses of gerunds

In addition to their main roles as noun equivalents in sentences, gerunds are used in the following ways:

13.3.1 After certain words or expressions

Certain standard expressions use the gerund form.

> No **parking**. (found in signs)
> There is no **smoking** in the building

13.3.2 After possessives

A gerund can be used after possessive adjectives (determiners) or possessive nouns which indicate the do-er of the action indicated by the gerund. This structure is often used in formal English.

> I was shocked at *his* **coming** to the ceremony.
> I was shocked at *John's* **coming** to the ceremony.
> *His* **being** a teacher made his father feel very proud.

An objective pronoun can sometimes precede a gerund. This structure is less formal than the previous one because its surface structure is ungrammatical. It is incorrect to place a noun (the gerund in this case) after an objective pronoun. However, this form is seen more often than its grammatically correct equivalent.

> I was shocked at him **coming** to the ceremony.

13.3.3 As nouns related to leisure, hobbies or jobs

In their role of naming actions, gerunds are commonly used to describe leisure and professional activities.

canoeing	**fishing**	**gliding**	**golfing**
manufacturing	**skiing**	**surfing**	**writing**

A gerund is always used after the verbs *go* or *come* when referring to sports or leisure activities.

> They went **rafting** this weekend.
> They agreed to come **skiing**.

This category is particularly confusing to students because it does not conform to the rule of nouns being replaceable by *it*.

*** *In the classroom: Gerund and present participle* ***

Both gerunds and present participles are words formed from a verb by adding *–ing* to the base form. The difference is that a gerund functions as a noun and a present participle mainly functions as the main verb of a tense in the progressive aspect. *(See 11.1.1.4 Gerund, 14.2.2 Present progressive and 14.3.2 Past progressive)*

> He recommended **visiting** the Royal museum. (gerund)
> We *are* **visiting** the Royal museum tomorrow. (present participle, main verb, part of the verb phrase *are visiting*, present progressive tense)

One of the typical mistakes at a beginner level is that students add the auxiliary verb *be* before a gerund, thinking that the *–ing* word is part of a progressive tense.

Students might say:

> ~~I like be walking~~.   instead of   I like **walking**.

Or, they might omit the auxiliary verb *be* in a progressive tense:

> ~~I walking~~.   instead of   I *am walking*.

To solve this problem, the teacher should provide students with lots of practice using a functional context such as *talking about likes and dislikes* (like + gerund), or *talking about actions happening now* (be + present participle).

One way to recognize if a word or phrase is a gerund is by replacing it with the pronouns *it*, *this*, or *that*. If the sentence still makes sense, then the word or phrase is a gerund, not a verb.

Gerund
I like *running*. (I like it.)
I like *playing soccer*. (I like that.)

Continuous/progressive aspect
I am *running*. (~~I am it~~)
I am *playing soccer*. (~~I am that~~)

At an intermediate level and above, another way of recognizing whether the *–ing* word is a gerund or a present participle is to look at the position of the *–ing* word in a sentence: Is it the subject, a subject complement, the object of a verb or the object of a preposition? If so, then it is a gerund. Is it the main action verb of a sentence? If so, then it is a participle.

> His hobby is **playing** *squash*.
> (**playing squash** is a gerundial phrase, subject complement of *His hobby* after the main linking verb *is*)

> He *is* **playing** squash.
> (**playing** is a present participle verb, main verb in the sentence, part of the verb phrase *is playing*, forming the present progressive tense)

Quiz 4: Gerund or present participle?

Identify whether the –ing word in each of the following sentences is a gerund (or gerundial phrase) or a present participle.

1) They finished <u>painting</u> the house.
2) What is he <u>doing</u> right now?
3) He told me to stop <u>talking</u> nonsense.
4) Will you be <u>driving</u> all the way down on your own?
5) <u>Listening</u> to Mozart relaxes me so much.

*** In the classroom: –ing *form after verbs of perception* ***

Verbs of perception (such as *see, feel, hear, observe* and *notice*) are usually followed by an infinitive. They can also be followed by the *–ing* form of a verb, as in *I saw the accused entering the building*. This *–ing* form is *not*, as is often mistakenly thought, a gerund. It is the present participle form of an action verb. In *I saw the accused entering the building*, the *–ing* form *entering* is a participle because it comes from a reduced noun clause, as in *I saw <u>that the accused was entering</u> the building*.

13.4 Functions of infinitives in a sentence

The following examples show the functions of infinitives and infinitival phrases in a sentence

<u>Subject of the sentence</u>

Gerunds serve as sentence subjects more commonly than infinitives do. When an infinitive is the subject of a sentence, it is always in the to-infinitive form (never the bare infinitive).

To learn a new language is comparatively easy.
(infinitival phrase functioning as the subject of the sentence; within the phrase, **To learn** is an infinitive, followed by the direct object *a new language*)

To offer kids a healthy environment is very important.
(infinitival phrase functioning as the subject of the sentence; within the phrase, **To offer** is an infinitive, followed by the indirect object *kids* and the direct object *a healthy environment*)

<u>Subject complement</u>

Although infinitives can act as subjects of sentences, it is more common to place the infinitive after a linking verb, making it a subject complement.

My wish is **to travel all around the world**.
(infinitival phrase functioning as complement to the subject *My wish*; within the phrase, **to travel** is an infinitive followed by the adverbial phrase of place *all around the world*)

He seems **to know everything**.
(infinitival phrase functioning as the complement to the subject *He*; within the phrase, **to know** is an infinitive followed by the direct object *everything*)

Object of the main verb

The following is an example list of common verbs that can be followed by an infinitive or infinitival phrase functioning as the direct object of the verb. Some of the verbs in the list can also be followed by gerunds. (See section 13.1 for verbs with gerunds and section 13.7 for verbs with both.)

verb + infinitive (direct object)

afford*	agree	choose	decide	deserve*
dislike*	dread*	expect	hate*	hesitate
hope	intend*	manage*	offer	pretend
promise	refuse	threaten*	want	wish

* these verbs may also be followed by gerunds; see section 13.7

> I *expect* **to arrive** on time.
> The patient *refused* **to eat**.
> He *hopes* **not to continue** with the task.

If two infinitives are joined with the conjunctions *or* or *and*, the second infinitive is most commonly in its base form (without the particle *to*).

> He promised **to come** and **help** us.

A noun or pronoun may sometimes appear between a verb and an infinitive. In these cases, the function of the infinitive varies depending on the main verb. Sometimes the infinitive is a direct object of the verb, sometimes it is an object complement, and sometimes the noun and infinitive work together as a single unit to form a direct object. The following categories describe these cases in more detail.

The following is a list of verbs that can be followed by a pronoun or noun and an infinitive. In these cases, the infinitive still functions as the direct object of the main verb. The noun or pronoun (which falls between the main verb and the infinitive) is the indirect object.

verb + pronoun/noun (indirect object) **+ infinitive** (direct object)

advise*	ask	beg	challenge
command	direct	encourage*	forbid*
instruct	order	persuade	remind
request	teach	tell	urge

* *advise*, *encourage* and *forbid* can also be followed by a gerund if there is no indirect object

> I *begged* him **to come** and **apologize** to her.
> She *asked* the girls **to eat** some vegetables.

Object complement

The following is an example list of verbs that can be followed by a pronoun or noun and an infinitive. In these cases, the infinitive functions as the object complement.

verb + noun / pronoun (direct object) **+ infinitive** (object complement)

allow	assume	believe	consider
elect	expect	feel	help*
hire	invite	judge	let*
make*	permit	warn	

* *help*, *let* and *make* can be followed by bare infinitives after the noun / pronoun

> The committee *hired* <u>Mark</u> **to be** their chairman.
> Penelope *warned* <u>him</u> **to stay** away from her.

<u>Object of a preposition</u>

There are a few prepositions that take an infinitive after them. These prepositions are:

> but   except   like

> What else can you do *but* **tell** the truth?
> We had no choice *except* **to refuse** their invitation.
> He wants to do something *like* **watch** TV or **go** to a movie.

If a verb precedes these prepositions, then they will take the bare infinitive. If a noun precedes these prepositions, they will be followed by a to-infinitive.

<u>Appositive</u>

Infinitives and infinitival phrases may function as appositives. *(See 3.2 Functions of nouns in a sentence)*

> Their idea, **to go camping in the mountains,** was a good one after all.
> (infinitival phrase functioning as appositive to the subject *Their idea*)

Quiz 5: *Functions of infinitives*

What is the function of the underlined infinitives and infinitive phrases in each of the following sentences?

1) I was told <u>to arrive</u> one hour before.
2) My decision, <u>to rent the apartment</u>, was not accepted by my parents.
3) He can't do anything but <u>wait</u>.
4) My favourite indulgence is <u>to curl up by the fire with a glass of wine</u>.
5) <u>To wear casual clothes</u> in the office is not allowed.

13.5 Infinitival forms

Due to their verb base, infinitives can take different forms. These forms correspond to the aspects that verbs can take: simple, perfective and progressive. Infinitives may also take passive forms. Following are examples of the possible infinitives derived from the verb *do*.

	Simple	Passive	Perfective	Perfective progressive	Perfective passive
Infinitive	to do	to be done	to have done	to have been doing	to have been done

Simple infinitive may take the to-infinitive form or the bare infinitive form (without the particle *to*).

Many verbs can only take the to-infinitive. (*See sample list in section 13.4*)

>Paige *would love* **to see** the movie.

Certain verbs can only take the bare infinitive. Following is a sample list:

Verb types that only take bare infinitive

Causative verbs:
- *have, make, let*

He *let* the children **go** home earlier.
I'll *have* my students **edit** their work.
They *made* her **cry**.*

*In the passive form, the verb *make* takes the to-infinitive: She *was made* **to cry**.

Perception verbs:
- *see, watch, feel, hear, observe, notice, smell*

I *saw* the accused **enter** the building.
We *watched* the girls **take** the bus.
I *felt* a presence **stand** behind me.

Certain verbs or clauses can be followed by either to-infinitive or bare infinitive.

>I *helped* my cousin **carry** the suitcase.
>I *helped* my cousin **to carry** the suitcase.
>The first thing I'd *do* is **take** a hot shower.
>The first thing I'd *do* is **to take** a hot shower.

Passive infinitive is formed by **to be** and a past participle.

>Frank hates **to be overlooked.**

Perfective infinitive is formed by **to have** and a past participle.

>The snow seemed **to have stopped**.

Perfective progressive infinitive is formed by **to have**, the past participle **been**, and a present participle.

>He is thought **to have been smuggling** alcoholic drinks for months.

Perfective passive infinitive is formed by **to have**, the past participle **been**, and another past participle.

>The organization is lucky **to have been given** a tax break.

Negative infinitives are formed by preceding any of the infinitive forms mentioned above with the adverb *not*. The adverb *never* can also be used to negate an infinitive.

>He promised **not to share** this information with anyone in the group.

It is better to have loved and lost than **never to have loved** at all.

Quiz 6: To-infinitive or bare infinitive?

Which of the verbs below must be followed by bare infinitive? Which ones can be followed by either bare or to-infinitive?

1) help
2) see
3) would love
4) feel

13.6 Other uses of infinitives

In addition to their main roles as noun equivalents in sentences, infinitives are used in the following ways:

13.6.1 Acting as adverbs

Infinitives can act as adverbs which modify the adjectives they follow. They may also act as adverbs of purpose when they follow verbs.

Acting as adverbs after certain adjectives

Generally, the adjectives that take an infinitive are adjectives which describe people's character or emotions, or adjectives which express willingness or unwillingness.

The following is an example list of common adjectives that can be followed by a to-infinitive acting as an adverb:

adjective + infinitive (adverb)

amazed	anxious	astonished	determined	eligible
fortunate	glad	happy	hesitant	liable
likely	pleased	ready	relieved	reluctant

I was *glad* **to hear** from you.
She's *reluctant* **to go** there.

Often the infinitive or infinitival phrase will modify an adjective – or an adverb – preceded by the adverbs *too* or *enough*. When this is the case, the infinitive sometimes conveys an idea of result or consequence. The possible structures are:

too + adjective/adverb + **infinitive**   OR   adjective/adverb + **enough** + **infinitive**

I am *too* <u>tired</u> **to go** for a walk.
She typed *too* <u>slowly</u> **to be** hired as a secretary.

You're <u>good</u> *enough* **to be** a teacher.
They worked <u>hard</u> *enough* **to earn** their pay.

The infinitive can also be preceded by a prepositional phrase headed by the preposition *for* and followed by a noun or pronoun. The possible structures are:

too + adjective/adverb **+ for +** noun/pronoun **+ infinitive**   OR
adjective/adverb **+ enough + for +** noun/pronoun **+ infinitive**

>No way! It is *too* late *for* you **to go** out.
>He works *too* little *for* his boss **to promote** him.
>The car is cheap *enough for* me **to afford**.
>Patrick plays well *enough for* his coach **to put** him on the team.

Acting as adverbs of purpose
An infinitive or infinitival phrase can introduce an infinitival adverbial phrase of purpose. *(See 7.3.4 Adverbials of purpose)* This phrase can also be seen as a shortened and equivalent form of the prepositional phrase headed by *in order to*.

>She came to Toronto **to study** English. (*in order to study English*.)

13.6.2   Acting as adjectives
An infinitive can act as an adjective following certain nouns. These nouns are usually derived from verbs that can take an infinitive as an object. Following is an example list of nouns that may be followed by infinitives acting as adjectives.

noun + infinitive (adjective)

advice	attempt	chance	decision	goal
hankering	motivation	need	order	permission
plan	proposal	recommendation	refusal	reminder
request	requirement	suggestion	tendency	wish
way	yearning			

>I have a *hankering* **to go** dancing.
>A *yearning* **to see** her again overwhelmed him.
>The *requirement* **to inspect** all machinery is part of the maintenance code.

13.6.3   After wh- words in noun clauses
An infinitive can be found in noun clauses after question words like *where, who, whom, how,* and *what*. It is a common structure used in indirect questions or reported speech.

>I have not decided *where* **to go** for my vacation.
>Do you know *whom* **to call** in case of an emergency?
>Can you tell me *what* **to do**?

After *why*, however, a bare infinitive is used in direct questions:

>*Why* not **go** now?   *Why* **stay** here?

Quiz 7: Functions of gerunds and infinitives
Identify the function of the underlined non-finite form in the sentences.

1) He mentioned <u>taking</u> the subway to his office instead of <u>walking</u>.
2) The teacher reminded the students <u>to submit</u> their homework by noon.
3) I was advised <u>to buy</u> the latest gadget.
4) My boss seems <u>to be</u> in a good mood today, don't you think?
5) <u>Admitting</u> the truth was his biggest challenge.
6) His passion is <u>to collect</u> all sorts of gemstones.
7) There is nothing <u>to regret</u>.
8) I called Farah <u>to remind</u> her of her appointment with the dentist.
9) The prize, <u>to travel solo in a hot-air balloon</u>, was not sanctioned by the organizers of the contest.

*** In the classroom: Ellipsis of the infinitive phrase ***

In common usage, to-infinitives may be reduced to the particle *to*, without mention of the verb itself. This generally happens when the verb (the entire infinitive phrase) is understood by both the speaker and the listener. The omission of commonly-understood words is known as ellipsis.

A: Would you like to invite the Carltons for dinner?   B: I don't want **to**.
[**to invite** the Carltons]

I am sorry I didn't phone you. I meant **to**.
[**to phone** you]

13.7 Verbs followed by gerunds *or* infinitives

Many verbs can be followed by either of these non-finite verbs, the gerund or the infinitive. For some verbs, there is virtually no change in meaning between gerund and infinitive; for others, the difference is substantial.

13.7.1   No change in meaning

The following is an example list of verbs that can be followed by either a gerund (or gerundial phrase) or an infinitive (or infinitival phrase), with no significant change in meaning.

advise	**afford**	**arrange**	**dread**	**forbid**
intend	**learn**	**neglect**	**propose**	**threaten**

Gertrude *learned* **to sing.**
Gertrude *learned* **singing**.

I can't *afford* **to take** private dancing lessons.
I can't *afford* **taking** private dancing lessons.

Though the meaning is not changed by the choice of gerund or infinitive, some of these verbs (for example, *advise* and *forbid*) require a change in structure. With these verbs, use of the infinitive requires an indirect object directly after the verb.

verb + gerund:	I *advise* **getting** up at 6 a.m. The director *has forbidden* **wearing** jeans.
verb + indirect object + infinitive:	I *advised* <u>the guests</u> **to get** up at 6 a.m. The director *has forbidden* <u>us</u> **to wear** jeans.

13.7.2 Little difference in meaning

Some verbs can take either a gerund or an infinitive as direct object or complement, with slight differences in meaning between the two. The differences in meaning are related to: the source of the action; whether the action is habitual; and a sense of progress or completion.

13.7.2.1 Considering the do-er of the actions

Since gerunds and infinitives are derived from verbs and can function as nouns, they can have combined characteristics of these two parts of speech (noun and verb). Their use sometimes depends on whether they are acting more like a verb or more like a noun. When a verb form is acting as a noun that states an action, that action must have a do-er or performer.

When an infinitive acts as a complement or object of another verb, it can be seen to exhibit verb-like qualities in that it indicates who the performer of the action (described by the infinitive) is.

>Henry *doesn't like* **to smoke**.
>(Henry, the subject or performer of the action *doesn't like*, is also the one who performs (or does not perform) another action: **to smoke**)

>They *love* **to sing**.
>(the subject of the verb *love* is also the performer of the action **to sing**; perhaps this is one of their hobbies)

When gerunds are used following a verb, they exhibit more noun-like properties. Even though they also derive from verbs, gerunds can be classified as single events or moments, more than as general actions. When gerunds are used, the do-er or performer is sometimes not the same as the subject of the main verb; or, the do-er of the action might be unclear or indefinite. Furthermore, gerunds can also be modified by a possessive adjective showing the "do-er" or "performer".

>Henry *doesn't like* **smoking**.
>(the subject of *doesn't like*, Henry, is not necessarily the one who would be doing the action **smoking**; it is possible that Henry doesn't like when other people smoke)

>They *love* **singing**.
>(the do-er or performer of the verb *love* is not necessarily the same as the performer of **singing**; they might love to be the audience for any singing)

Following is an example list of verbs which can take both gerund and infinitive, with a difference in meaning which is related to the do-er of the action. These are verbs which describe a person's feelings or attitudes.

(cannot) bear	bother	deserve	hate	like
loathe	love	prefer	(cannot) stand	(not) tolerate

After the phrases *would like*, *would love*, *would hate* and *would prefer*, an infinitive form always follows.

> I *would like* **to invite** you to my 50th birthday party.
> I am sure he *would prefer* **to stay** home.

13.7.2.2 Particular habits vs. general enjoyment

Following is an example list of verbs which can take both gerund and infinitive, with a difference in meaning which is related to whether the action is habitual. These verbs may also have differences of meaning as described in section 13.7.2.1 above. In the cases described here, the do-er of the action named by the gerund or infinitive is understood to be the subject of the main verb.

dislike	**hate**	**like**	**love**	**prefer**

Some grammarians agree that when these verbs are followed by an infinitive, it suggests a regular or habitual action performed by the subject of the sentence. On the other hand, when these verbs are followed by a gerund, they denote the idea of general (not necessarily habitual) enjoyment.

> I *like* **to get up** early in the morning and **meditate** for half an hour.
> (the subject of the sentence enjoys these activities and does them as a habit)

> I *love* **listening** to music.
> (the subject of the sentence enjoys this activity; however, the sentence doesn't necessarily show that it is a habitual action.)

This slight difference in meaning is greatly influenced by the context these verbs are used in.

13.7.2.3 Progress versus completion

Following is an example list of verbs which can take both gerund and infinitive, with a difference in meaning which is related to time or progress. This set of verbs describes the beginning, continuing or ending of situations.

begin	**cease**	**commence**	**continue**	**manage**	**start**

With these verbs, the gerund is often favoured as complement; however, when either the gerund or the infinitive is possible, the slight change in meaning implies a difference in time, completion or progress. When the gerund is used, the focus is on the continuation of the action or its progress. When the infinitive is used, the focus is a point in time, not the duration or the completion of the action.

He *starts* **crying** when he thinks about her.
(he cries for the duration of the time that he thinks about her, from when he starts thinking till he stops thinking about her; it can also be said that the focus is on the process of crying)

He *starts* **to cry** when he thinks about her.
(as soon as his thoughts are about her – from that point in time – he cries; the focus is on the starting point, and the duration of the crying is unclear)

Henry *managed* **studying** for his French exam.
(focus is on the fact that Henry was, at some time, engaged in the process of studying; whether he finished or not does not seem to be important in this case)

Henry *managed* **to study** for his French exam.
(focus is on the fact that the study was completed)

If the main verb is in a continuous tense, an infinitive (not a gerund) is usually used.

I *was starting* **to work**.
~~I was starting working~~.

When these verbs are followed by verbs expressing cognition, such as *understand, know* and *believe*, an infinitive is used.

I *began* **to understand**.
~~I began understanding~~.

13.7.3 Change in meaning

Following are verbs which can take both gerund and infinitive, with a significant difference in meaning.

remember   forget   stop   regret   mean

The differences in meaning for gerund and infinitive following **try**, **need** and **deserve** are discussed on the *You Can Teach Grammar* companion web site.

13.7.3.1 Time of the action: remember, forget, stop and regret

With the main verbs **remember**, **forget**, **stop** and **regret**, there seems to be a string of two actions and the order of these actions is determined by the form (gerund or infinitive) used after the main verb. The choice of gerund or infinitive denotes a change in time reference.

When the main verb is followed by an infinitive, the action expressed by this infinitive seems to happen (or not) *after* the action expressed by the main verb. With the verb *forget* (in the affirmative), this means that the action of the infinitive does not happen; first it is forgotten, so it therefore does not take place.

Alison *remembered* **to study** biology.
(Alison first remembered, then studied)

> Kent *forgot* **to call** Sue on her birthday.
> (Kent first forgot, and thus then did not call Sue)

> Mortimer *stopped* **to look** at his reflection in the mirror.
> (Mortimer stopped whatever he was doing first, and then looked at himself in the mirror.)

> I *regret* **to tell** you that you've been drafted.
> (I regret it, and then tell you)

When *stop* is followed by the infinitive, it is used as an infinitive of purpose. *(See 13.6.1 Acting as adverbs)*

When the main verb is followed by a gerund, the action expressed by the gerund happened (or must happen) *before* the action expressed by the main verb.

> Alison *remembered* **studying** biology and not understanding any of it.
> (Alison first studied some time in her past, and then remembered it as a bad experience)

> Kent *forgot* **calling** Sue on her birthday, and sent her a happy belated birthday message the next day.
> (Kent first called Sue to wish her a happy birthday, and then forgot that he had done it; that's why he tried to apologize by sending her a belated birthday message)

> Mortimer *stopped* **looking** at his reflection on the mirror
> (Mortimer was looking at himself in the mirror first, and then stopped)

> I *regret* **saying** that you've been drafted; it was a bad joke.
> (I first said it, and then regretted it when I saw your reaction)

Regret is used with the infinitive almost exclusively for giving bad news; it is more widely used with the gerund to imply that the subject is sorry about the action in the gerund.

13.7.3.2 Intention or involvement: *mean*

Mean followed by the infinitive implies an intention to do something. This structure is most often used to say that the intention was there, but the action described by the infinitive did not happen.

> I *meant* **to call** him but I got distracted and I forgot.

When followed by a gerund, *mean* takes on a completely different meaning; it is the same as *involve*.

> Being a teacher *means* **working** extra hours to mark homework.

Quiz 8: Choose the correct form

Fill in the blanks with the correct non-finite form (infinitive (to-infinitive or bare infinitive) or gerund) of the verb in parenthesis. Account for your choice.

1) I watched her (1)_____(cross) the road from the moment she left the corner shop till she got to the other end of the road but I did not think her (2) _____(be) drunk at all.

2) I still remember (3) _____(visit) my friend's grandma in those sunny summer days at the village. She was delighted (4) _____(see) us, and (5) _____(show) us her appreciation for those afternoon visits, she would let us (6) _____(dress up) with her most exquisite costumes from the days when she was an actress. We would never forget (7) _____(put) her clothes back in the attic, or else she would not allow us (8) _____(wear) them ever again.

3) She regrets not (9) _____(listen) to her brother's advice. He was right. Now, she has to apologize to her boss for not (10) _____(call) the insurance company on time.

*** In the classroom: Gerund or infinitive after certain verbs ***

There are no rules for which verbs will be followed by gerunds and which will be followed by infinitives, and this is a huge frustration for students. Making the correct choices ultimately comes down to a combination of memorization and repeated exposure. One solution is drilling the structures when first presented as a way to repeat patterns and get used to them. But most important is to do communicative practice and have the students understand how to use these verbs in context.

As for the structures discussed in sections 13.7.2 and 13.7.3, it will not be until an intermediate stage that students will learn how to master the usage of gerunds and infinitives with different meanings.

That said, the main problem in most levels is that not all *–ing* words are gerunds and not all phrases introduced by *to* are infinitives.

*** You can teach gerunds and infinitives ***

The following are ideas to help ESL students learn and practise when to use gerunds and infinitives. All the activities suggested in this section are designed to develop speaking, listening, reading or writing skills. These activities are communicative complements to the gap-filling, choose-the-best-answer, or complete-the-blank types of activities that can be found in most ESL textbooks.

The activities below are presented according to difficulties, or students' levels, and include the communicative function and the suggested gerund or infinitive patterns for the corresponding topics.

Function: Asking and talking about likes/dislikes
Structure: like/love/dislike/hate + gerund or to-infinitive
Skill: Speaking
Level: High beginner
Type of activity: Survey

The teacher hands out a list of leisure activities and has students choose their three favourite ones.

- listen to music
- play soccer
- watch videos
- play chess
- go camping
- study English
- ride horses

After choosing their favourite activities, the students must go around the class and ask their classmates what their favourite activities are. It could be by asking yes/no questions (as in, *Do you like listening to music?* or *Do you like to listen to music?*), or wh-questions (such as *Which of the activities do you like to do?*, or *What do you like doing?*). When they get all their classmates' answers, they must present to the class how many people in the class like doing certain things.

Function: Talking about preferences and giving opinions
Structure: prefer/would prefer/would like + to-infinitive
Skill: Speaking
Level: Low intermediate – Intermediate +
Type of activity: Discussion using pictures of places and people

Students in pairs or groups talk about the places or people in supplied pictures. Students may be given questions to start the discussion, such as:

- *Which of these places would you like to go to on vacation and why?*
- *Which of the people in the photographs would prefer to go to the places in the pictures, do you think?*

Function: Recognizing structure: Various patterns of gerunds and infinitives
Skill: Reading comprehension
Level: Intermediate +
Type of activity: Discovering grammar: Recognition of gerunds and infinitives

Choose a paragraph from a textbook, magazine, or newspaper article that is appropriate for the students' level and that contains various examples of gerunds and infinitives. Get the students to identify gerunds and infinitives in the article.

Following is an excerpt from an article used as an example of what can be done in this type of activity.

The Psychology of Passive Income
<u>Relying</u> on passive income is comfortable when the economy is running smoothly. But when things get bumpy, what can you do <u>to keep</u> your attitude calm and your outlook positive? Downturns are part of every cycle and we need <u>to learn</u> <u>to cope</u> with them. Here are some ideas for <u>doing</u> that...."
Source: 2009 Mary Lloyd - http://www.copypastearticles.com/article/47195/the-psychology-of-passive-income/

To make it more challenging, ask students to explain how many different cases they could find and what the rules are. Example:

<u>Relying</u>: a gerund as subject of the sentence; <u>to keep</u>: a to-infinitive expressing purpose; <u>to learn</u>: a to-infinitive as direct object of the verb need*; <u>to cope</u>: a to-infinitive as direct object of the verb* to learn*; <u>doing</u>: a gerund as object of the preposition* for.

Or, the teacher can make comprehension questions on the text that encourage students to answer using a gerund or infinitive. Example:

According to the writer, what is comfortable when the economy is running smoothly? (Relying on passive income)
What do we need to learn? (To cope with downturns)

Function: Giving advice and recommendations using different structures
Possible structures, depending on the level:
    advise + pronoun + to-infinitive: *I advise you to reserve the tickets in advance.*
    advise + gerund: *I advise reserving the tickets in advance.*
    recommend + gerund: *I recommend reserving the tickets in advance.*
Skill: Speaking and/or writing
Level: Low intermediate - Intermediate +

This activity could be done as a speaking or writing activity. The teacher asks for advice from the students on visiting the students' hometowns or countries (recommendations on where to go or what to do). Have the students brainstorm all the places the teacher can visit or activities to do when visiting these places. Encourage them to give advice or recommendations (written, spoken or both) using some of the structures they have learned and to give further details about the places to visit.

Function: Talking about permission
Structure: let + pronoun + bare infinitive vs. allow + pronoun + to-infinitive
Skill: Speaking and/or writing
Level: Intermediate +
Type of activity: Situation sentences

Have students speak or write about their upbringing and what they were or weren't permitted to do at school or home. Example:

    When I was in grade two, my teacher *did not allow* us **to write** with pens. However, she *let* us **use** coloured pencils and markers for drawing.

Function: Talking about perceptions

Structure: appear/seem/look + to-infinitive (to be)
Skill: Speaking
Level: Intermediate +

Show pictures of different people's faces and expressions and have the students describe what they perceive the people in the pictures are feeling, using the structure above. For example:

>(Picture of someone sad)   S: He seems to be sad / disappointed.

Function: Talking or writing about past memories

Structure: remember + gerund; (modals *used to* and *would* (+ bare infinitive) can be used in this context as well)
Skill: Speaking and/or writing
Level: Intermediate +
Type of activity: Situation sentences

Tell students to choose a nice past memory from when they were younger and share it with the class. It can be done orally or in writing. In their retelling of what they remember, they can use the structures described in the heading above and any other gerund or infinitive structure that the situation calls for, such as *forget, try*, etc. See the example below:

> When I was a kid, I *remember* **going** to my grandma's home on Sundays. I *used to* **help** in the kitchen. We *would* **cook** chocolate biscuits or orange cake for tea. I always *forgot* **to sift** the flour *before* **adding** the eggs and I got very upset about that, but my grandma *tried* **to remind** me of that step, always with a smile.

Function: Adapting

Structure: be used/accustomed to + gerund
Skill: Speaking
Level: Intermediate +

Have students talk about how they liked or didn't like doing certain things and how that has changed in the present. For example:

> When I came to this country I didn't understand people speaking fast, but now I am *used to* **understanding** English when someone talks to me fast.

Function: Requesting politely

Structure: would you mind + gerund?
Skill: Speaking
Level: Low Intermediate +

Provide students with cards on various situations. Place the card face down and have students pick up one card. The student who picks up the card will make a polite request of another student, using the verb and object on the card.

Cards:
- speak louder
- turn the TV off
- switch on the light
- clean the cup
- close the door
- make some coffee
- pass the sugar

Student A: *Would you mind* **speaking** louder?
Student B: No, not at all.

Function: Talking about obligations and responsibilities
Structure: remember/forget + to-infinitive; (modals *should/shouldn't/must/mustn't/have to* + base form can also be used in this context)
Skill: Speaking and/or writing
Level: Intermediate +

Present the following situation to students and get them to write down as many ideas as possible, expressing what someone mustn't forget, or must remember to avoid the following problems:

T: Jonathan is very absentminded and forgets his obligations and responsibilities. Also, his room is very messy and he needs some reminders. Can you help? This is the list:
- ✓ He doesn't take the garbage out every day.
- ✓ He doesn't keep the milk in the fridge.
- ✓ He doesn't do his homework every day.
- ✓ He doesn't put his dirty clothes in the hamper.
- ✓ He wakes up too late every day.
- ✓ He pays his bills too late.

Expected performance:
Jonathan must remember to take the garbage out every day.
He shouldn't forget to put the milk in the fridge

Function: Talking about jobs and qualifications
Structure: various uses of gerund and infinitives (for example: need + to-infinitive; have to + base form; wh-words + to-infinitive, etc.)
Skill: Speaking and/or writing
Level: Low Intermediate +

Students in pairs or groups first decide on an interesting or out-of-the-ordinary job or profession and then discuss what qualifications or skills the candidate needs to have. For example:

An astronaut
Qualities: The candidate *has to* **be** very intelligent; he or she *needs* **to be** healthy; they *should* **be** *willing* **to sacrifice** their personal life, etc...

14 Tenses

The concept of verb tense almost always brings to mind the concept of time: past, present and future. While this is an essential element of verb tense, it is not the whole picture. Correct application of tense requires a knowledge of both time and aspect.

Technically, the term *tense* applies only to the time component of a verb's conjugation (past, present, future). Other features (such as relation to other events; whether the action is at a single point in time; whether the action is completed; and whether the action is ongoing) are known as the *aspect*.

For example, a verb that is related in time to another event is expressed in the perfective aspect. The perfective aspect may have a past, present or future time. In the example *Conrad* **has served** *all the guests; now they are happy*, the verb phrase **has served** is in the present time (it describes a present situation, action or condition) and the perfective aspect (this aspect describes actions in relation to now, or in relation to other events).

In classroom situations, the distinction between time and aspect is not analyzed to this depth; the combination of time and aspect is generally known simply as the tense, and is taught as a stand-alone concept. In the example above, the verb form **has served** would be taught as a verb in the present perfect tense; it is generally not useful to explicitly teach the two separate technical elements. That said, students must have some grasp of the implications of both portions of each tense (time and aspect) in order to apply the correct tense in a given situation. The job of the teacher is to instill in students an understanding of any tense's particular use in its context (in this case, present perfect tense to describe recent past actions).

Tense (time)

The tense of a verb is an indicator of the time when the event or situation takes place. Grammatically, there are three possible "times" an event or situation can take place in: the past, the present and the future. Verb tense dictates the form that a verb takes in a given context. When a verb changes form (conjugates) to show tense, it is said to be marked, or inflected, for tense.

In English, the present and past are clearly marked tenses: the verb forms for present and past give an indication of time. Verbs marked for present tense take place at or near the time of speaking or writing. Verbs marked for past tense take place before the time of speaking or writing.

> Everything **looks** great.
> (verb *look* marked (inflected) for present tense; it is happening now)
>
> The passengers **saw** the robbery.
> (verb *see* marked (inflected) for past tense; it happened before now)

Future time events take place after the time of speaking or writing. The future time in English is different from present and past because verbs in the future tense are not marked. Future tense verbs stay in base form and are coupled with **will** or **be going to**.

All trends **will come** back eventually.
(verb *come* in base form, preceded by *will*)

We**'re going to travel** to Europe next week.
(verb *travel* in base form, preceded by *are going to*)

Because the head verb is not inflected (it stays in its base form), some grammar books do not consider this a tense in the same sense as verbs in past and present times. For this reason, future tenses are categorized differently in many texts. The functions and structures remain the same, regardless of the classification.

Quiz 1: Tense (time)

Indicate the tense (time) of each of the sentences.

	Present	Past	Future
1. Lisa is going to make lots of money.			
2. Marion is working on a special project.			
3. Florence cut her finger chopping onions.			
4. Yves hasn't studied much.			
5. Fidel will become a legend.			
6. It had been a while since they'd talked.			

*** In the classroom: Presenting time ***

Understanding time references is crucial to correctly applying tenses. It is therefore essential that teachers be able to express the intended time references clearly. There are several options for achieving this.

Teachers can use body language and signaling with the thumb (like when hitch-hiking) pointing backwards, to indicate the past. A walking motion can indicate movement towards the future. This visual and kinesthetic representation of time can sometimes be a help to lower level students.

However, this is not necessarily easy or comprehensible for all students. In certain cultures, the past is considered something you can see because you have lived through it already, so it cannot be "behind" you; the future is unknown and cannot be seen, so it would be behind you. This atypical interpretation serves to illustrate that not all body language is understood in the same way, so teachers should use many different methods to deliver the same message, ensuring a better chance of comprehension by all students.

When represented pictorially, tenses are often plotted on timelines similar to the ones used to represent history.

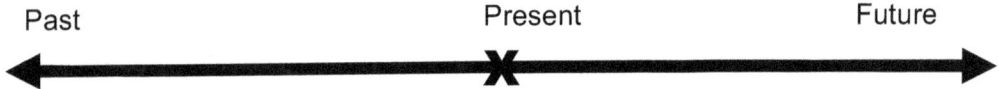

Typically, the present is marked with an **X**, the past is placed to its left and the future to its right. This representation makes sense and helps some students, but other students find it too abstract or too linear to comprehend.

When time is thought of as a period of time rather than a particular point in time, a "boxed" representation of the timeline can sometimes aid comprehension.

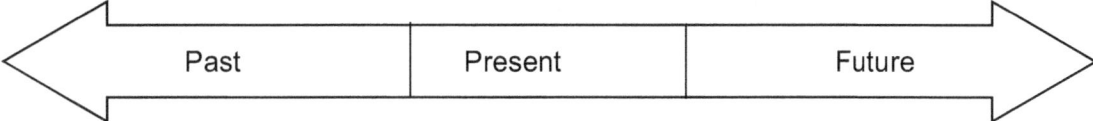

Present time: Today **is** Monday.
Short shorts **are** trendy nowadays.
Past time: Laura **went** to the zoo yesterday.
Baggy jeans **were** trendy in the past.

Aspect

The grammatical aspect of a verb is the speaker's experience of the event or situation. The way the speaker lives, views or understands the event or situation is revealed in the grammatical aspect the speaker chooses for the verb. The speaker may view or experience the event as being completed (perfective), as being ongoing (progressive) or as taking place at a point in time (simple). Grammatical aspect is not inherent in the verb; it is added by the speaker or writer when conjugating the verb.

There are four different possible grammatical aspects in English: simple, progressive, perfective and perfect progressive (a combination of perfective and progressive).

Table 52: Grammatical aspects of verbs

Aspect	Meaning	Examples
Simple	- Used to express habitual actions; also for an event or state that happens at one moment (a point in time), that is permanent, or that is complete - Affirmative form of the verb does not require an auxiliary - Interrogative and negative forms require an auxiliary (for the future simple, the verb always requires an auxiliary)	Elena sleeps soundly during the weekend. *(affirmative)* Elena doesn't sleep soundly every day. *(negative)* Does Elena sleep soundly at home? *(interrogative)* Doesn't Elena sleep soundly at home? *(negative interrogative)*
Progressive	- Used to express ongoing, incomplete, or extended but temporary actions - Focus on the duration of an event or state; or, the speaker is experiencing the event or state at the very moment of speaking - Requires the auxiliary verb *be* and changes the form of the main verb to the present participle (*-ing*)	Erin is typing. *(affirmative)* Erin is not typing. *(negative)* Is Erin typing? *(interrogative)* Isn't Erin typing? *(negative interrogative)*
Perfective	- Connects two different times demonstrating the relevance of a past event or state with another time - Requires the completion of the action in the main verb - Expresses the consequences of a past event or state - Requires the auxiliary *have* and changes the form of the main verb to the past participle	I have seen that film twice. *(affirmative)* I haven't seen that film. / I have never seen that film. *(negative)* Have you seen that film? *(interrogative)* Haven't you seen that film? *(negative interrogative)*
Perfect Progressive	- Used to express the consequence or relevance of an ongoing or incomplete action to another particular time; emphases are the ideas of non-completion, interruption or duration - Describes how a past ongoing or incomplete action affects another time - Requires the auxiliary verb *have*, the auxiliary verb *be* in past participle form (*been*) and changes the form of the main verb to the present participle (*-ing*)	Janet has been taking classes all summer. *(affirmative)* Janet has not been taking classes all summer. *(negative)* Has Janet been taking classes all summer? *(interrogative)* Hasn't Janet been taking classes? *(negative interrogative)*

*** In the classroom: Aspect ***

Aspect is easily identified because of the corresponding markings (*be* + *-ing* for progressive aspect; *have* + past participle for perfective aspect) for each possible aspect, but it is a concept that most ESL students struggle with. Timeline representation can fail to accurately represent the aspect of a verb, and this can further confuse students. The safest and clearest approach is to teach different aspects separately and make sure that students do not confuse one with another.

The aspects in English do not always have a direct correspondence to similar aspects in other languages. Students will naturally try to equate them, and teachers have to be aware of when this is happening so they can correct and direct appropriately.

14.1 Forms of tenses

The system of forming tenses in English is straightforward and almost mechanical in nature. The rules of formation apply consistently to all the tenses and allow easy identification of the form. The system is depicted in the following tables, using the verb **show** as an example.

Forms of the verb *show*:
- Base form: show
- Simple present, third person singular: shows
- Past participle (*show* is irregular) shown
- Infinitive: to show
- Simple past: showed
- Present participle: showing

Table 53: Forms of tenses in affirmative statements

Aspect / Time	Simple	Progressive	Perfective	Perfect progressive
Present	I/you/we/they **show**	I *am* **showing**	I/you/we/they *have* **shown**	I/you/we/they *have been* **showing**
		you/we/they *are* **showing**		
	he/she/it **shows**	he/she/it *is* **showing**	he/she/it *has* **shown**	he/she/it *has been* **showing**
Past	I/you/he/she/it/we/they **showed**	I/he/she/it *was* **showing**	I/you/he/she/it/we/they *had* **shown**	I/you/he/she/it/we/they *had been* **showing**
		you/we/they *were* **showing**		
Future	I/you/he/she/it/we/they *will* **show**	I/you/he/she/it/we/they *will be* **showing**	I/you/he/she/it/we/they *will have* **shown**	I/you/he/she/it/we/they *will have been* **showing**

Table 54: Forms of tenses in negative statements

Aspect / Time	Simple	Progressive	Perfective	Perfect progressive
Present	I/you/we/they *do not* **show**	I *am not* **showing**	I/you/we/they *have not* **shown**	I/you/we/they *have not been* **showing**
		you/we/they *are not* **showing**		
	he/she/it *does not* **show**	he/she/it *is not* **showing**	he/she/it *has not* **shown**	he/she/it *has not been* **showing**
Past	I/you/he/she/it/we/they *did not* **show**	I/he/she/it *was not* **showing**	I/you/he/she/it/we/they *had not* **shown**	I/you/he/she/it/we/they *had not been* **showing**
		you/we/they *were not* **showing**		
Future	I/you/he/she/it/we/they *will not* **show**	I/you/he/she/it/we/they *will not be* **showing**	I/you/he/she/it/we/they *will not have* **shown**	I/you/he/she/it/we/they *will not have been* **showing**

Table 55: Forms of tenses in affirmative or negative interrogatives

Aspect / Time	Simple	Progressive	Perfective	Perfect progressive
Present	***do*** I/you/we/they ***(not)*** show	***am*** I ***(not)*** showing ***are*** you/we/they ***(not)*** showing	***have*** I/you/we/they ***(not)*** shown	***have*** I/you/we/they ***(not) been*** showing
	does he/she/it ***(not)*** show	***is*** he/she/it ***(not)*** showing	***has*** he/she/it ***(not)*** shown	***has*** he/she/it ***(not) been*** showing
Past	***did*** I/you/he/she/it/we/they ***(not)*** show	***was*** I/he/she/it ***(not)*** showing ***were*** you/we/they ***(not)*** **showing**	***had*** I/you/he/she/it/we/they ***(not)*** shown	***had*** I/you/he/she/it/we/they ***(not) been*** showing
Future	***will*** I/you/he/she/it/we/they ***(not)*** show	***will*** I/you/he/she/it/we/they ***(not) be*** showing	***will*** I/you/he/she/it/we/they ***(not) have*** shown	***will*** I/you/he/she/it/we/they ***(not) have been*** showing

Quiz 2: Forms

Analyze the tables above and then answer the following questions.

1) What do all present and past simple tenses have in common? (two main characteristics)
2) What do all progressive tenses have in common? (two main characteristics)
3) What do all perfective tenses have in common? (two main characteristics)
4) What is the word order for all the auxiliaries in the perfect progressive tense?
5) What do all tenses have in common? (two main characteristics)

Passive forms

The tense forms given in Tables 53 - 55 are all in the active voice form, in which the subject is the do-er or performer of the action in the main verb. Passive voice is the structure used when the subject *receives* the action in the main verb. Each tense has a corresponding passive voice form, as shown in the table below. (For more on active and passive voice, consult the *You Can Teach Grammar* companion web site)

Table 56: Examples of tenses in active and passive voice

Tense	Active voice form	Passive voice form
Present simple	They show it.	It is shown.
Past simple	They showed it.	It was shown.
Future simple	They will show it.	It will be shown.
Present progressive	They are showing it.	It is being shown.
Past progressive	They were showing it.	It was being shown.
Future progressive	They will be showing it.	It will be being shown.
Present perfect	They have shown it.	It has been shown.
Past perfect	They had shown it.	It had been shown.
Future perfect	They will have shown it.	It will have been shown.
Present perfect progressive	They have been showing it.	It has been being shown.
Past perfect progressive	They had been showing it.	It had been being shown.
Future perfect progressive	They will have been showing it.	It will have been being shown.

14.2 Present tenses

The following sections describe each of the present tenses (present simple, present progressive, present perfect, present perfect progressive). The forms and uses are described, along with some basic visual depictions and concept questions which may be used to present and discuss the tenses in the classroom, as well as descriptions of the uses of the tense.

14.2.1 Present simple

The following table depicts the different possible forms of the present simple tense.

Table 57: Forms of the present simple tense

		Examples:
Affirmative statement	I / you / we / they + *finite verb* (simple present: looks the same as non-finite base form)	You **work** hard.
	he / she / it + *finite verb* + **s** (simple present: looks the same as non-finite base form + **s**)	She **sleeps** well.
Negative statement	I / you / we / they + **do not** + *verb* (base form) // or **don't** + *verb* (base form)	We **do not see** each other often. // We **don't see** each other often.
	he / she / it + **does not** + *verb* (base form) // or **doesn't** + *verb* (base form)	He **does not work out** at the gym. He **doesn't work out** at the gym.
Affirmative interrogative	**do** + I / you / we / they + *verb* (base form)	Where **do** you **stay** when you go visit her?
	does + he / she / it + *verb* (base form)	**Does** she **cry** when the lights go out?
Negative interrogative	**do** + I / you / we / they + **not** + *verb* (base form) // or **don't** + *subject* + *verb* (base form)	**Do** you **not know** the answer? // **Don't** you **know** the answer?
	does + he / she / it + **not** + *verb* (base form) // or **doesn't** + *subject* + *verb* (base form)	Why **does** he **not call**? // Why **doesn't** he **call**?

For negative interrogatives, when the adverb *not* is contracted with the auxiliary (as in *don't* and *doesn't*), the full contracted form is placed before the subject.

Exception to the present simple structure: the verb *be*

The verb *be* is an exception to the negative and interrogative structures in the present simple tense. When *be* is the main verb in a sentence, it does not require the auxiliary verb *do* in order to form negative or interrogative sentences. Thus, the adverb *not* can attach to the main verb *be*, and can modify it directly for negative sentences. For interrogatives, *be* precedes the subject. Furthermore, the verb *be* has different forms for each person so it does not follow the rule of adding *–s* for third person singular.

Table 58: Simple present (finite) forms of the verb *be*

		Examples:
Affirmative statement	I + **am** // or I +**'m**	I **am** thirsty. I**'m** hungry, too.
	you / we / they + **are** // or you / we / they + **'re**	You **are** a great friend. They**'re** wonderful students.
	he / she / it + **is** // or he / she / it + **'s**	It **is** a grey day. She**'s** very happy about it.
Negative statement	I + **am not** // or **'m not**	I **am not** sure. I**'m not** sure.
	you / we / they + **are not** // or **aren't** // or **'re not**	They **are not** right. They **aren't** right. They**'re not** right.
	he / she / it + **is not** // or **isn't** // or **'s not**	It **is not** true. It **isn't** true. It**'s not** true.
Affirmative interrogative	**am** + I	**Am** I included in the mailing list?
	are + you / we / they	**Are** we in that picture?
	is + he / she / it	Where **is** John? // **Is** he here?
Negative Interrogative	**am** + I + **not**	Why **am** I **not** there?
	are + you / we / they + **not** // or **aren't** + you / we / they	**Are** you **not** aware of the situation? **Aren't** you aware of the situation?
	is + he / she / it + **not** // or **isn't** + he / she / it	What **is** she **not** supposed to do? What **isn't** she supposed to do?

For negative interrogatives, when the adverb *not* is contracted with the auxiliary (as in *aren't* and *isn't*), the full contracted form is placed before the subject.

The contraction **ain't**, though used very frequently, is generally not recognized as correct English. It is a present simple negative form of *be* (and sometimes *have*), and may be used with all persons and numbers. It is a very informal, colloquial – and common – structure. The following lines from pop songs illustrate some uses.

I ain't moving; I've been here long before. *(ain't = am not)*
Ain't that a shame? *(ain't = isn't)*
Everything means nothing if I ain't got you. *(ain't = haven't)*

Uses of the present simple tense

The following uses are organized from the most frequently used for this tense, to the least used or most rare. When choosing examples and teaching this tense to ESL students, the most common uses should be taught first, since students will encounter them (and use them) more frequently.

Uses	Examples
1. to give personal information	My name **is** Clara. I **am** from Spain. This **is** my friend Jean. He **comes** from France.
2. to describe emotions, preferences, likes and dislikes	Priscilla **loves** iced coffee. Melman **doesn't enjoy** loud music.
3. to describe habits and routines	Sue Ellen **brushes** her teeth twice a day. Preston **doesn't study** every day.
4. to describe general facts or truths, or generalizations	The sun **doesn't go** around the earth; it **is** the other way around! People in Asia **consume** more rice than people in North America.

Uses	Examples
5. to talk about timetables and schedules	Trains **leave** here every 15 minutes. The break **doesn't start** until 10:30 a.m.
6. to give instructions and directions	You **walk** 100 meters north and then you **turn** right. (instructions can also be expressed with the imperative mood. See 11.3.3 Imperative mood)
7. to describe reactions, feelings or states that are ongoing, with *stative verbs*	Most people **believe** politicians lie. The soup **smells** delicious!
8. to narrate plot events when discussing literature, movies or plays (in reviews, reports, summaries, etc.)	Andy **lies** on the sidewalk bleeding and **thinks** about his decision to join the Royals. (Re: *On the Sidewalk Bleeding* by Evan Hunter) Romeo **believes** Juliet is dead and **decides** to take his own life, too. (Re: *Romeo and Juliet* by Shakespeare)
9. to tell jokes and /or anecdotes	Why **does** little Billy **throw** the butter out the window? To see a butterfly! Suddenly, Mary **walks** into the room and everyone **stops** talking.
10. to describe commitments or requirements when they happen	I **promise** I will work hard at it. The president **demands** to know what the worst-case scenario is.
11. to describe timeframes in time clauses in future sentences	When I **see** him, I will tell him about it. He won't attend school when his parents **come** to visit from Mexico.
12. to state the condition in the if-clause of conditional sentences	If he **studies**, he will pass the test. You will understand if I **explain** it again.
13. to summarize, write abstracts, or give the result of research reports in academic writing	The article **includes** information about three different types of coniferous trees. After careful study of all factors, it **is** clear that social media marketing **prevails** for this product.
14. to mean simple past tense in newspaper headlines	Boy, 17, **fires** gun at school

Representations of the concept of the present simple tense

Following are examples of different possible ways of representing and describing this tense. These examples are illustrative, not exhaustive.

In the drawing on the left, the protagonist is represented by the stick-man figure. The event is represented by the **X**. The protagonist and the event are in the present and there is no connection with or reference to past or future times.

In the drawing on the right, the concept of *present* is depicted as a grouped series of **X**s which are clustered around a generalized idea of *now*.

The example sentence demonstrates the use of present simple to talk about habitual actions.

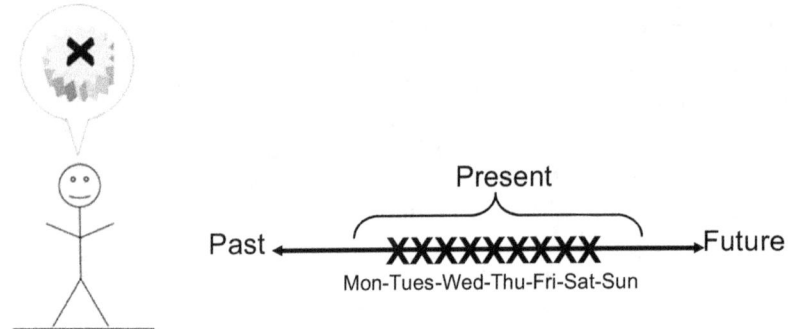

Jack **walks** his dog every evening.

Following are basic concept questions which can help in recognizing when it is appropriate to use the present simple tense to describe habitual actions or constant states.

Is the action finished? → NO
→ Is it a habitual, regular or constant action? → YES *(This is a continuous state, a condition, a fact, or something that happens regularly)*
→ Present simple

*** In the classroom: Present simple ***

The present simple is usually the tense that students learn first and it is one of the most common tenses in English. As a tense that includes the simple aspect it denotes a complete event or state and its occurrence is most closely related to the present time. Students do not seem to encounter too many problems when learning this tense, except for the use of the third person singular form (adding the –s). This is a mechanical mistake and it does not reflect the students' comprehension of the tense itself. Mechanical drills can be used for practice, but they often do not work. A funny statement with alliteration may be more memorable and thus more effective for some students.

For younger students, try: *Sammy snake slitherSSS and hisseSSS.*
For more mature students, try: *Sinatra, the sassy singer, singSSS soulfully.*

Spelling can sometimes be a problem when adding –s to the verb in third person singular. The most common variations are the following:

Rule	Examples	
verbs ending in consonant + y: change the *–y* to *–i* and add *–es*	hurry → deny → employ → buy →	hurries denies employs buys
verbs ending in *–ch, –o, –ss, –sh, –x*: add *–es*	watch → go → express → wash → mix →	watches goes expresses washes mixes

14.2.2 Present progressive

The present progressive is also called present continuous. It is often taught to students at the beginner levels. It is the tense used to describe ongoing, incomplete or extended but temporary present-time actions.

The following table depicts the different possible forms of the present progressive tense.

Table 59: Forms of the present progressive tense

		Examples
Affirmative statement	I + **am** + *present participle* // or **'m**	I **am writing** right now. I**'m writing** right now
	you / we / they + **are** + *present participle* // or **'re**	You **are working** hard. You**'re working** hard.
	he / she / it + **is** + *present participle* // or **'s**	She **is sleeping** well. She**'s sleeping** well.
Negative statement	I + **am not** + *present participle* // or **'m not**	I **am not resting** enough. I**'m not resting** enough.
	you / we / they + **are not** + *present participle* // or **aren't** // or **'re not**	We **are not getting** together today. We **aren't getting** together today. We**'re not getting** together today.
	he / she / it + **is not** + *present participle* // or **isn't** // or **'s not**	He **is not working** out right now. He **isn't working** out right now. He**'s not working** out right now.
Affirmative interrogative	**am** + I + *present participle*	Where **am** I **sleeping** tonight?
	are + you / we / they + *present participle*	**Are** you **staying** there for two nights?
	is + he / she / it + *present participle*	Why **is** she **crying**? **Is** John **hoping** for good weather?
Negative interrogative	**am** + I + **not** + *present participle*	Which course **am** I **not passing**?
	are + you / we / they + **not** + *present participle* // or **aren't** + *subject* + *present participle*	**Are** you **not studying** for the test? **Aren't** you **studying** for the test?
	is + he / she / it + **not** + *present participle* // or **isn't** + *subject* + *present participle*	**Is** she **not visiting** her aunt this month? // **Isn't** she **visiting** her aunt this month?

For negative interrogatives, when the adverb *not* is contracted with the auxiliary (as in *aren't* and *isn't*), the full contracted form is placed before the subject.

The spelling rules for transforming a verb into its present participle form are given in section 11.2.2.1.

Uses of the present progressive tense

The following uses are organized from the most frequently used for this tense, to the least used or most rare. When choosing examples and teaching this tense to ESL students, the most common uses should be taught first, since students will encounter them (and use them) more frequently.

Uses	Examples
1. to describe ongoing actions at the moment of speaking / writing	A lot of people **are ordering** coffee right now; I'll wait. Look! Benny **is wearing** his new uniform.
2. to describe current ongoing actions	He**'s working** on a new marketing strategy this week. The Maple Leafs **are playing** better this season.
3. to describe progress	Thank goodness traffic **is thinning** out. Tom is on a diet and he**'s losing** lots of weight.
4. to describe future plans	We**'re leaving** on the 16th, so everything has to be finished by then. The students **are not presenting** their monologues until next month.
5. to describe unplanned, often undesired events; often described with adverbs such as *always, continually, constantly* or *forever*.	He**'s** constantly **forgetting** to take out the trash. They**'re** forever **complaining** about having too much homework. My sister**'s** always **borrowing** my clothes without asking first.
6. to be indirect or more polite	I**'m hoping** the doctor won't take long. **Is** he **running** behind? We**'re wondering** if it is okay to sit over here while we wait.

Exception to present progressive uses: Stative verbs

Verbs that express states or verbs that have a stative meaning do not describe actions. *(See 1.5.3 Dynamic or stative and 11.2.3.2 Stative verbs)* These verbs describe conditions that are understood to exist (on a continuing basis). As such, they are not used in the progressive aspect.

For example, the verb *seem* is stative, while the verb *jump* is not. Therefore,

> Paul **is jumping** down the stairs. → is correct
> ~~Paul is seeming happy.~~ → is not correct

Nevertheless, some of these verbs can be used in the progressive aspect with a slight change in meaning.

This sample drink **tastes** too sweet.	→	the stative verb *taste* used in present simple form describing the ongoing state of the drink; as is often the case with stative verbs, it is followed by an adjective phrase
That customer **is tasting** every sample available.	→	the commonly stative verb *taste* used in a non-stative way to describe the action (dynamic verb sense) of drinking or eating something for the first time; it is, thus, used correctly in the progressive aspect and is followed by a noun phrase functioning as direct object

Representations of the concept of the present progressive tense

Following are examples of different possible ways of representing and describing this tense. These examples are illustrative, not exhaustive.

In the drawing on the left, the protagonist is represented by the stick-man figure. The event is represented by the **X**. He is standing astride the **X**, indicating an exact confluence of the actor, the action and the present time. There is no connection to past or future times.

In the drawing on the right, the concept of *present* is depicted as a single **X**, which indicates a precise idea of *now* on a time continuum.

The example sentence demonstrates the use of present progressive to talk about an action at the moment of speaking.

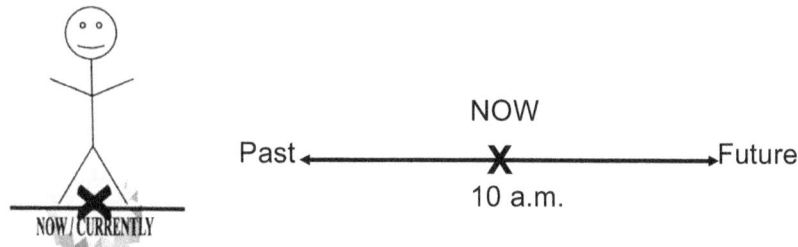

Jack **is walking** his dog now. (It's 10 a.m. now.)

Following is a basic set of concept questions which can help in recognizing when it is appropriate to use the present progressive tense to talk about an action at the moment of speaking.

Is the action finished? → NO *(It is not finished, but it has started – it is continuing)*
   → Is it a habitual, regular or constant action? → NO *(It is a specific or unique, event; it is not a continuous state or something that happens regularly)*
      → Is it related to another time? → NO *(This action has no relationship to any other event or known point in the past or future)*
         → Present progressive

*** In the classroom: Present progressive ***

When students are first introduced to the present progressive tense, the easiest concept is its general use to describe actions that are happening now. Other uses of this tense are frequent and the slight change in meaning (between exactly right now and a generally current now, for example) can lead to some misunderstandings.

Another typical mistake is that students forget the auxiliary verb and use only the main verb in present participle form. When this tense is taught to beginner levels, clear and frequent explanations of the need for the auxiliary are essential. Written and oral drills are a good way to prevent or fix this problem.

14.2.3 Present perfect

The present perfect is the first of the perfective tenses that students encounter. It is taught to students who have already learned the simple and progressive (past and present) tenses. It can be confusing and misleading for students because its name suggests present time, but its uses are mainly connected to the past time. In general, the present perfect tense is used to describe actions that occurred some time in the past but are somehow connected to the present (they are important in the present context or they are still happening). It is sometimes helpful to identify this tense as the "present-past" mix.

The following table depicts the different possible forms of the present perfect tense.

Table 60: Forms of the present perfect tense

		Examples
Affirmative statement	I / you / we / they + **have** + *past participle* // or **'ve**	I **have seen** better movies. I**'ve seen** better movies.
	he / she / it + **has** + *past participle* // or **'s**	She **has taken** lessons all her life. She**'s taken** lessons all her life.
Negative statement	I / you / we / they + **have not** + *past participle* // or **haven't** // or **'ve not**	I **haven't noticed** how beautiful it looks until now! I **have not seen** such lovely grounds. I**'ve not paid** attention before.
	he / she / it + **has not** + *past participle* // or **hasn't** // or **'s not**	It **has not stopped** raining in three days. It **hasn't warmed** up, either. It**'s not been** very pleasant.
Affirmative interrogative	**have** + I / you / we / they + *past participle*	**Have** they **watched** any new episodes online?
	has + he / she / it + *present participle*	Why **has** it **taken** so long for you to respond?
Negative interrogative	**have** + I / you / we / they + **not** + *past participle* // or **haven't** + subject + *past participle*	**Have** I **not sent** the payment yet? I'm so sorry! // **Haven't** I **sent** the payment yet?
	has + he / she / it + **not** + *past participle* // or **hasn't** + subject + *past participle*	What **has** he **not done** this time? // What **hasn't** he **done** this time?

The present perfect is formed with the past participle form of the main verb. *(See 11.1.1 Non-finite forms)*

Uses of the present perfect tense

The following uses are organized from the most frequently used for this tense, to the least used or most rare. When choosing examples and teaching this tense to ESL students, the most common uses should be taught first, since students will encounter them (and use them) more frequently.

Uses	Examples
1. to describe a past experience with an unknown time frame but relevant to the present time	Renata **has travelled** all around Europe; she can recommend the best places for you to visit. I don't want to watch that movie; I'**ve** already **seen** it.
2. to describe a past event or action that is still going on in the present	They **have worked** for the same company for the last 20 years. He **hasn't golfed** since last summer.
3. to describe a past event or action that has a result in the present	The photocopier **has broken down**, so we can't prepare the handout for the class. His proposal **has been accepted** and the renovations start next week.
4. to summarize as part of a conclusion, or to cite in academic writing	This essay **has proven** that the underlying factors that cause poverty are systemic. Shakespeare's female characters **have** always **been portrayed** as strong women in spite of Hamlet having stated "Frailty, thy name is woman" (Act 1, scene 2.)

Representations of the concept of the present perfect tense

Following are examples of different possible ways of representing and describing this tense. These examples are illustrative, not exhaustive.

In the drawing on the left, the protagonist is represented by the stick-man figure. The event is represented by the **X**. He is thinking about event (the **X**), which is to the reader's left, above the stick-man figure, indicating that the event took place in the past. The arrow indicates that this past event is somehow relevant in the present.

In the drawing on the right, the event is depicted as a single **X** to the left of the present time, beside a **?**, indicating a time in the past that is unknown or simply unmentioned.

The example sentence demonstrates the use of present perfect to talk about an action that has taken place at an unknown point in the past. The completion of the action (but not the specific time of the action) is of interest.

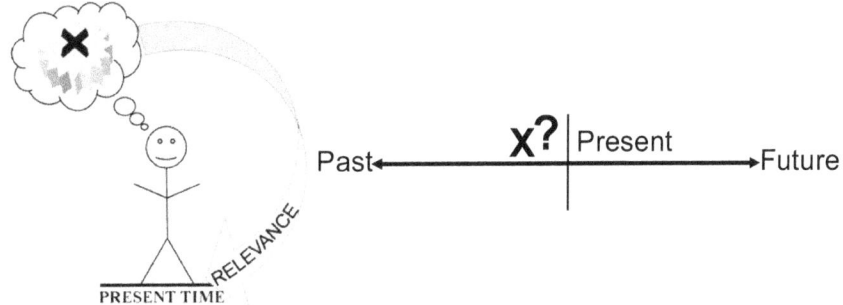

Jack **has** already **walked** his dog.

Following is a basic set of concept questions which can help in recognizing when it is appropriate to use the present perfect tense to talk about a completed event at an unknown time in the past.

Is the action finished? → YES
> → Do we know when it happened? → NO *(Just a general knowledge that it is some unknown time in the past; precise time is not known)*
>> → Is it important or relevant to now? → YES *(The fact that the action happened is of interest in the current context)*
>>> → Present perfect

**** In the classroom: Present perfect ****

There are three very common difficulties for students in mastering the present perfect. First of all, students must learn to use a completely new structure with the verb *have* as auxiliary (instead of *do* or *be*, which they would have learned before). Making sure students know the difference between auxiliary and main verbs can prevent this difficulty from becoming a problem.

Also, students have to learn a new form of the verb: the past participle. To help with this transition, the present perfect should be introduced with regular verbs since their past participle form is the same as the past simple form.

Finally, the main problem students encounter when learning this tense is how to use it properly and the difference between this tense and past simple. Clarify that if there is a connection to the present time, they should be inclined to use the present perfect. If the action is clearly only in the past or the exact time that it happened is understood, then past simple is the best choice. Exercises and drills that combine the uses of both tenses are highly recommended to prevent or solve this problem.

14.2.4   Present perfect progressive

The present perfect progressive is also called present perfect continuous. It is mainly used to describe ongoing actions that began in the past and are not yet complete or finished. The following table depicts the different possible forms of the present perfect progressive tense.

Table 61: Forms of the present perfect progressive tense

		Examples
Affirmative statement	I / you / we / they + **have been** + *present participle* // or **'ve been**	Marc and I **have been training** for a marathon. We**'ve been planning** our regimen carefully.
	he / she / it + **has been** + *present participle* // or **'s been**	He **has been running** for an hour! Martin**'s been waiting** for him.
Negative statement	I / you / we / they + **have not been** + *present participle* // or **haven't been** // or **'ve not been**	You **have not been attending** regularly; is something wrong? You **haven't been** sick, have you? I heard you**'ve not been** well.
	he / she / it + **has not been** + *present participle* // or **hasn't been** // or **'s not been**	She **hasn't been working** very hard this semester. She**'s not been studying**, either. She **has not been trying** at all.
Affirmative interrogative	**have** + I / you / we / they + **been** + *present participle*	Where **have** you **been staying**? You could've come to our place!
	has + he / she / it + **been** + *present participle*	**Has** it **been raining** all day long?
Negative interrogative	**have** + I / you / we / they + **not been** + *present participle* // or **haven't** + subject + *present participle*	**Have** you **not been following** the news? **Haven't** you **been following** the news?
	has + he / she / it + **not been** + *present participle* // or **hasn't** + subject + *present participle*	Why **has** he **not been doing** all his assignment? Why **hasn't** he **been doing** all his assignments?

Uses of the present perfect progressive tense

The following uses are organized from the most frequently used for this tense to the least used.

Uses	Examples
1. to describe a past event or action that is definitely still going on in the present; sometimes the emphasis is on the length of the action.	He**'s been working** for the same company since he graduated. It's been 25 years already. He **has been writing** his memoirs ever since I can remember; I wonder when he'll be done.
2. to describe a past event or action that is unfinished or incomplete; the emphasis is on the event being temporary	I**'ve been reading** about Slavic languages lately. *(this is a temporary interest)* They **have been looking** for her for 48 hours already. It's been so long and they still haven't found her. It's so sad!
3. to describe a past event that has an effect or consequence in the present with emphasis on the length or duration	She's exhausted; she**'s been playing** in the pool for four hours straight. They **have been waiting** for their server for 40 minutes; I think they've decided to leave.
4. to describe a past repeated action that continues into the present	I**'ve been trying** to reach them all evening and I still haven't gotten through.

Exception to the present perfect progressive uses: Stative verbs

Verbs that express states cannot be used in any of the progressive aspects. *(See 11.2.3.2 Stative verbs)*

Representations of the concept of the present perfect progressive tense

Following are examples of different possible ways of representing and describing this tense. These examples are illustrative, not exhaustive.

In the drawing on the left, the protagonist is represented by the stick-man figure. The event is represented by a series of **X**s. The representation of the stick-man performing the original action is to the reader's left, indicating that the event began in the past. The series of **X**s leading from the initiation of the event to now indicate that the action has continued from its start until the present time.

In the drawing on the right, the time of the event is depicted as a range to the left of (and including) the present time, indicating a duration for the event.

The example sentence demonstrates the use of present perfect progressive to talk about an action that began in the past and continues in the present.

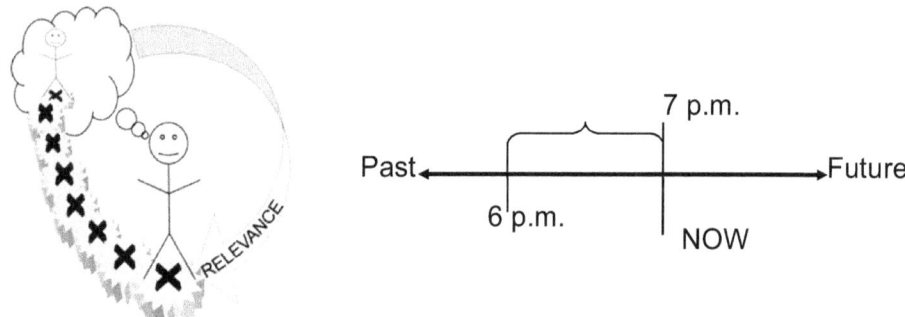

Jack **has been walking** his dog for one hour.

Following is a basic set of concept questions which can help in recognizing when it is appropriate to use the present perfect tense to emphasize the duration of an ongoing action.

Is the action finished? → NO *(The action is not definitively finished; it may possibly finish exactly at the time of speaking or writing, but it did not finish before that; the emphasis here is not on completion, but on duration)*
→ Is it a regular, constant or habitual action? → NO *(It is not a state or condition or fact or habit; it is a distinct or unique action)*
→ Is it related to another time (past or future) or event? → YES *(For present perfect progressive, it began in the past, though it is not finished)*
→ Is it related to another event or known time in the past? → YES *(It began in the past)*
→ Present perfect progressive

*** In the classroom: Present perfect progressive ***

The present perfect progressive is very closely related to the present perfect tense. In fact, these two tenses are sometimes interchangeable when it comes to describing an event that started in the past and continues in the present (the main use of the present perfect progressive). This tense should be taught after students have a strong grasp of the present perfect.

When teaching the present perfect progressive, clarify the differences between this tense and the present perfect. Even though sometimes they are interchangeable, this is not always the case and this can confuse students. As a rule of thumb, students should be reminded that if the event is incomplete or transitory, the progressive tense is preferred. Also, if the duration or length of the event is emphasized, it is better to choose the present perfect progressive.

Students often find the word order for this tense to be complicated. A useful tip here is that the name of the tense dictates the order of the two auxiliaries that are included in the tense: first perfect (*have + been*), then progressive (*present participle*).

When talking about past repeated actions that continue in the present, clarify that when the rate of recurrence of the repeated action is mentioned, then present perfect is used, not present perfect progressive.

> Clotilde **has dropped** her bag *ten times* already.
> ~~Clotilde **has been dropping** her bag ten times already.~~

Quiz 3: Present tenses

Read the sentences below and indicate whether they are using the correct present tense form. Explain your answers.

1) I am brushing my teeth every day.
2) Mildred is reading that trendy, recently-released novel.
3) Elmer has been reading that book four times already. He knows it by heart.
4) The train is leaving every fifteen minutes. The next one is at 4:15.
5) Florence has been living in Toronto since she was a teenager; she knows the city like the back of her hand.

14.3 Past tenses

The following sections describe each of the past tenses (past simple, past progressive, past perfect and past perfect progressive). The forms and uses are described, together with some basic visual depictions and concept questions which may be used to present and discuss the tenses in the classroom, together with descriptions of the uses of the tense.

14.3.1   Past simple

The past simple is used to describe completed events and actions. The following table depicts the different possible forms of the past simple tense.

Table 62: Forms of the past simple tense

		Examples
Affirmative statement	I / you / he / she / it / we / they + *finite simple past verb* (finite simple past construction: looks like non-finite base form + **ed**) (or irregular past verb formation: see 11.2.2.2)	Ellen **started** her show in the late nineties. The sleek new rocket **soared** into the sky. We **complained** to the management. Marco **saw** the ghost and **screamed**.
Negative statement	I / you / he / she / it / we / they + **did** + **not** + *verb* (base form) // or subject + **didn't** + *verb* (base form)	I **did not know** that it was true. We **didn't expect** bad weather, but it rained all week.
Affirmative interrogative	**did** + I / you / he / she / it / we / they + *verb* (base form)	Why **did** she **cry**? **Did** they **agree** to sell the house?
Negative interrogative	**did** + I / you / he / she / it / we / they + **not** + *verb* (base form) // or **didn't** + subject + *verb* (base form)	**Didn't** she **know** this would happen? What **did** he **not understand**?

For negative interrogatives, if the adverb *not* is contracted with the auxiliary, the entire contracted form is placed before the subject.

Exception to the past simple structure: the verb *be*

The verb *be* is an exception to the standard negative and interrogative structures in the past simple tense. When this verb is the main verb of the sentence, it does not require the aid of the auxiliary verb *do* in order to form negative or interrogative sentences. *(See 14.1 Forms of tenses)*

Table 63: Simple past (finite) forms of the verb *be*

		Examples
Affirmative statement	I / he / she / it + **was**	I **was** in high school in the 1990s.
	you / we / they + **were**	Elliot and Shirley **were** very happy together.
Negative statement	I / he / she / it + **was** + **not** // or **wasn't**	She **wasn't** sure she wanted to jump in the pool. I **was not** sure, either.
	you / we / they + **were** + **not** // or **weren't**	We **were not** part of the committee, so they **weren't** interested in us.
Affirmative interrogative	**was** + I / he / she / it	**Was** Melanie at her house when you called?
	were + you / we / they	**Were** we on the list or did you have to tip the bouncer?
Negative interrogative	**was** + I / he / she / it + **not** // or **wasn't** + I / he / she / it	Why **was** our food **not** ready? Why **wasn't** our food ready?
	were + you / we / they + **not** // or **weren't** + you / we / they	**Were** they **not** away on vacation? **Weren't** they away on vacation?

For negative interrogatives, if the adverb *not* is contracted with the auxiliary, the entire contracted form is placed before the subject.

Uses of the past simple tense

The following uses are organized from the most frequently used for this tense, to the least frequently used.

Uses	Examples
1. to describe finished past events	She **stayed** up so late that she **was** overtired and **didn't sleep** well.
2. to describe events in the past with a definite and known past time reference	The Second World War **ended** in 1945. Marlon **met** his son yesterday for lunch.
3. to describe past events with unknown but implied or understood past time reference	Shakespeare **wrote** more than ten comedies. (General knowledge allows people to know the time reference.) Do you remember when that teacher **ran** out of the classroom crying? (Time reference is understood between the participants.)
4. to describe past states	He **looked** so sad! Do you know what happened to him?
5. to describe past habits (to describe past habits that have been changed, the semi-modal *used to* is used)	Every morning she **went** to the gym, **showered** and **went** to work. Lilian **used to smoke** but she **didn't use to drink** when she was in high school. **Did** you **use to smoke** too? (See 12.2.2 for more information on *used to*)
6. to narrate – in order – events that happened in the past. (the order used in the sentence is the same order in which events happened, unless indicated otherwise by conjunctions or transition signals)	The hawk **perched** on the branch, **looked** around and **dove** towards its prey. (Order of events is the same as stated in this sentence.) Ulises **called** out her name when he **saw** her. (In this case, *saw* happened before *called*; that is clarified by the use of *when*)
7. to report things somebody said in the past (reported speech)	The journalist **explained** that the vote **went** well. She **asked** if you **wanted** extra ketchup with these fries.

Representations of the concept of the past simple tense

Following are examples of different possible ways of representing and describing this tense. These examples are illustrative, not exhaustive.

In the drawing on the left, the protagonist is represented by the stick-man figure. The event is represented by an **X**. The action is in the protagonist's mind, to the reader's left, indicating that the event happened in the past. The event is not connected to the present or future in any explicit way.

In the drawing on the right, the event is indicated by an **X** on a time continuum, indicating that it happened (and finished) at a known time (yesterday) before the present.

The example sentence demonstrates the use of past simple to talk about a discrete action that was completed at a known time in the past.

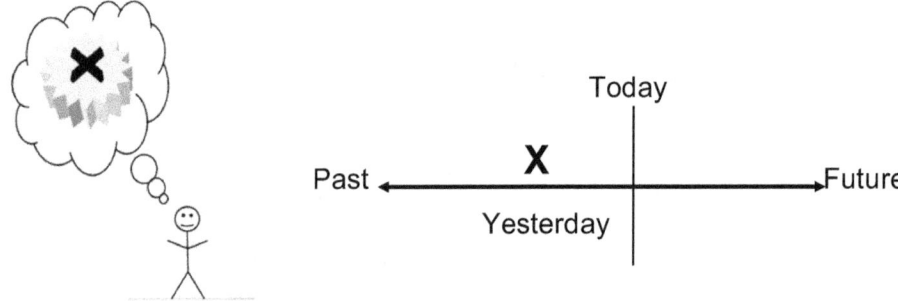

Jack **walked** his dog yesterday.

Following is a basic set of concept questions which can help in recognizing when it is appropriate to use the past simple tense to talk about a unique action completed at a known time in the past.

Is the action finished? → YES
   → Do we know when it happened? → YES *(The speaker and the listener have some common understanding of the timeframe of the event in the past)*
      → Is it important when it happened? → YES *(The understanding of the timeframe is somehow relevant or useful for understanding)*
         → Was it happening before another action we are talking about? → NO
            → Was it at the same time as another action? → NO
               → Past simple

*** In the classroom: Past simple ***

Students do not have too many difficulties when learning the past simple tense. Mistakes happen when they do not remember to use the auxiliary verb *did* properly. This can be prevented and solved with some drills.

When learning about the formation of regular verbs, students need to be taught about how to properly add *–ed* to the verbs. *(See Table 47)*

Furthermore, students need to be taught how to pronounce the verb once the suffix *–ed* is added. The three possible pronunciations (/d/, /t/ and /ɪd/) need to be explained and practised so students can fully and fluently use this tense in written and spoken form.

14.3.2   Past progressive

The past progressive is also called past continuous. It is often taught to students once they have already learned present simple, present progressive and past simple. It is used for actions that were under way at the same time as other actions in the past.

The following table depicts the different possible forms of the past progressive tense.

Table 64: Forms of the past progressive tense

		Example
Affirmative statement	I / he / she / it + **was** + *present participle*	When you arrived, I **was getting** ready.
	you / we / they + **were** + *present participle*	Lois and Clark **were discussing** their future when I dropped by.
Negative statement	I / he / she / it + **was** + **not** + *present participle* // or **wasn't** + *present participle*	It **was not raining** at 5 am. Mary **wasn't using** any special equipment to do that.
	you / we / they + **were** + **not** + *present participle* // or **weren't** + *present participle*	Judy and I **were not paying** attention when it happened. You **weren't studying**, were you?
Affirmative interrogative	**was** + I / he / she / it + *present participle*	**Was** he **acting** strangely when you saw him?
	were + you / we / they + *present participle*	Where **were** we **sitting**? I can't remember.
Negative interrogative	**was** + I / he / she / it + **not** + *present participle* // or **wasn't** + subject + *present participle*	Why **was** she **not talking** to him? Why **wasn't** she **talking** to him?
	were + you / we / they + **not** + *present participle* // or **weren't** + subject + *present participle*	**Were** they **not playing** well together? **Weren't** they **playing** well together?

For negative interrogatives, if the adverb *not* is contracted with the auxiliary, the entire contracted form is placed before the subject.

Uses of the past progressive tense

The following uses are organized from the most frequently used for this tense, to the least frequently used.

Uses	Examples
1. to describe ongoing actions at a particular time in the past	At 9 pm last night, Mia and her cousins **were** still **running** around and **playing**.
2. to describe a past action that was interrupted by another past action	Casey **was working** on her final assignment paper when her computer reset itself and she lost everything.
3. to describe two simultaneous past actions	The kids **were playing** while the adults **were getting** lunch ready; it was a perfect summer day.
4. to describe the background of a story and / or another action	The guests **were walking** around and **admiring** the art pieces when the stranger appeared. The sun **was shining** and birds **were singing** on that lovely morning.
5. to describe events that are repeated	Back then she **was** always **reading** romantic novels and **daydreaming**.
6. to make a polite request with the verb *wonder*	We **were wondering** if we could share this table.

Exception to the past progressive uses: Stative verbs

Verbs that express states cannot be used in any of the progressive aspects. (See *11.2.3.2 Stative verbs*)

Representations of the concept of the past progressive tense

Following are examples of different possible ways of representing and describing this tense. These examples are illustrative, not exhaustive.

In the drawing on the left, the protagonist is represented by the stick-man figure. The event is represented by an **X**. The representation of the stick-man performing the original action is to the reader's left, indicating that the event took place in the past. The presence of the protagonist and the event on the same spot indicates that the protagonist was performing the action at the point in time in the past that he is thinking about. The drawing does not explicitly depict any other past time reference (such as a *when*-clause or a specific time or date), though these are common in past continuous constructions. In the classroom, these elements might need to be added. There is no connection to present or future times.

In the drawing on the right, the time of the event is depicted as a range to the left of the present time, indicating an ongoing action. The action coincides with another past action on the timeline.

The example sentences demonstrate the use of past progressive to talk about the background to another event, and to talk about a past action that was interrupted.

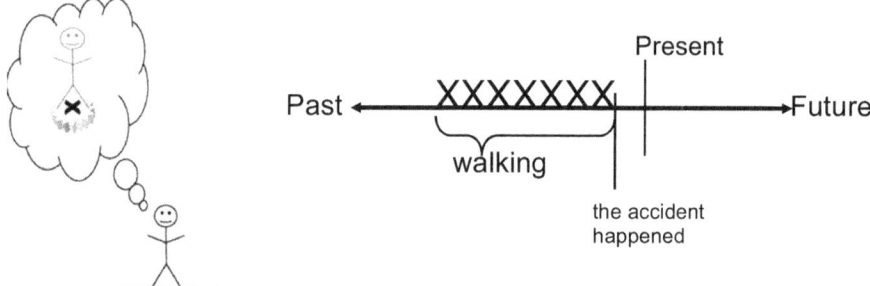

Jack **was walking** his dog when the accident happened.

The following concept questions can help to determine when it is appropriate to use past progressive to talk about an action or event in the past that was interrupted by another event.

Is the action finished? → YES
- → Do we know when it happened? → YES *(The speaker and the listener have some common understanding of the timeframe of the event in the past)*
  - → Is it important when it happened? → YES *(The understanding of the timeframe is somehow relevant or useful for understanding)*
    - → Was it happening before another action we are talking about? → YES
      - → Was it finished or completed before the other action? → NO *(It may have finished at the same time as the other action, but it was not fully completed before the other action)*
        - → Was it interrupted by the other action? → YES
          - → Past progressive *(describing an interrupted action)*

**** In the classroom: Past progressive ****

The difficulties of learning past progressive are similar to the difficulties in the present progressive when it comes to internalizing form and structure. Clarify the use of the auxiliary verb *be* in this tense, and that there is no need for any other auxiliary. Students sometimes over-generalize and transfer knowledge and rules of other tenses onto the new ones they are learning, creating sentences with mistakes like the one below:

~~Did she was playing when you called?~~

Students can sometimes confuse the ongoing nature of the past progressive and consider this a way to make a reference or connection between a past event and the present.

~~Meryl **was living** in Toronto since 2001.~~
Meryl **has lived / has been living** in Toronto since 2001.

Since the present perfect and the present perfect progressive are usually taught after students learn the past progressive, this mistake is difficult to prevent. However, it should be addressed and it might be a good chance to then introduce the present perfect to students.

14.3.3 Past perfect

The past perfect is taught to students who have already learned the present and past simple and progressive tenses, as well as the present perfect tense. In contrast to the present perfect, this tense offers less difficulty because students already know of the use of the verb *have* as an auxiliary and they have a better general knowledge of the language by the time past perfect is introduced. The following table depicts the different possible forms of the past perfect tense.

Table 65: Forms of the past perfect tense

		Examples
Affirmative statement	I / you / he / she / it / we / they + **had** + *past participle* // or **'d** + *past participle*	When Juliet woke up, Romeo **had** already **taken** the poison.
Negative statement	I / you / he / she / it / we / they + **had** + **not** + *past participle* // or **hadn't** + *past participle* // or **'d not** + *past participle*	I **had not understood** the instructions. They **hadn't finished** dinner yet when I arrived. We**'d not recognized** you at first.
Affirmative interrogative	**had** + I / you / he / she / it / we / they + *past participle* // or **'d** + *past participle*	Where **had** the waiter **left** the purse you thought you**'d lost**?
Negative interrogative	**had** + I / you / he / she / it / we / they + **not** + *past participle* // or **hadn't** + subject + *past participle*	**Had** you **not heard** the news? **Hadn't** he **said** you could go with them too?

For negative interrogatives, if the adverb *not* is contracted with the auxiliary, the entire contracted form is placed before the subject.

Uses of the past perfect tense

The following uses are organized from the most frequently used for this tense to the least frequently used.

Uses	Examples
1. to describe a past event or state that happened before another past event or a certain time in the past	We got married in 2003 after we **had dated** for four years. I knew the movie wasn't going to be very good when the protagonist **had** already **solved** the main conflict by minute 15.
2. to describe a past event that had a consequence at another later past time	There was no chance of getting a refund because the company **had gone** bankrupt.
3. to report past events (reported speech)	The report said that the authorities **had declared** the elections void because of fraud.

Representations of the concept of the past perfect tense

Following are examples of different possible ways of representing and describing this tense. These examples are illustrative, not exhaustive.

In the drawing on the left, the protagonist is represented by the stick-man figure. The event is represented by an **X**. The representation of the original action is to the reader's left, indicating that the event took place in the past. The protagonist is also contemplating another past time. The completion of the main event is somehow relevant to that other known time in the past. There is no connection to present or future times.

In the drawing on the right, the times of two events are depicted to the left of the present time, indicating completion in the past. The two events are labeled on the timeline, with one event to the left of the other, indicating that it occurred first. An arrow is also used to indicate that by the time one event occurred, the other event had already taken place; it is the first event on the time continuum.

The example sentence demonstrates the use of past perfect to talk about the completion of one event in relation to another event in the past.

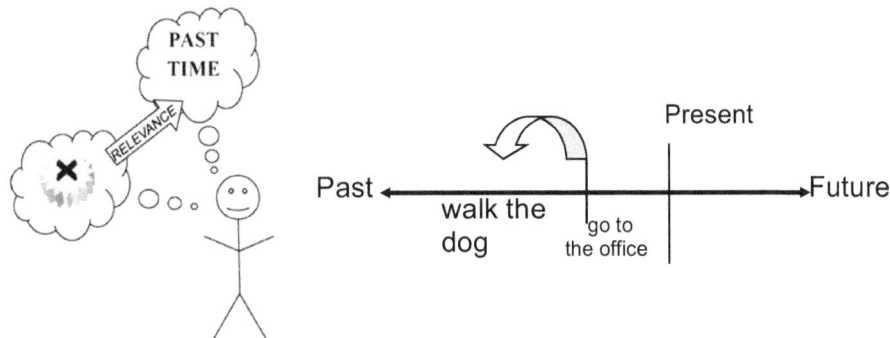

Jack **had walked** his dog before he went to the office.

The protagonist experienced the event in the past and it is relevant or connected to another past time. There are no other connections to any other time but the past.

Following is a basic set of concept questions which can help in recognizing when it is appropriate to use the past perfect tense to talk about one event in the past in relation to another event in the past.

Is the action finished? → YES
    → Do we know when it happened? → YES *(The speaker and the listener have some common understanding of the timeframe of the event in the past)*
        → Is it important when it happened? → YES *(The understanding of the timeframe is somehow relevant or useful for understanding)*
            → Was it happening before another action we are talking about? → YES
                → Was it finished or completed before the other action? → YES
                    → Past perfect

*** In the classroom: Past perfect ***

The difficulties students faced and hopefully overcame when learning the present perfect will have prevented some potential problems with the past perfect. This tense is often taught as and referred to as the "past of the past." Because its uses are quite straightforward, students have significantly fewer issues with it than with other tenses.

The main problem for students with this tense is a tendency to overuse it. Students have learned that the past perfect is used when an action happened before another action in the past, so they may use it when talking about a sequence of events (which would usually require past simple). To avoid this problem, the uses of past perfect and past simple should be compared and reviewed together after students learn both of them.

14.3.4 Past perfect progressive

Past perfect progressive is also called past perfect continuous. It is used to describe past events that were in progress during some known time or known event in the past. The past perfect progressive is very closely related to the past perfect tense. Differences in meaning between the two can be minute. This tense should only be taught after students have a strong understanding of the past perfect.

The following table depicts the different possible forms of the past perfect progressive tense.

Table 66: Forms of the past perfect progressive tense

		Examples
Affirmative statement	I / you / we / he / she / it / they + **had been** + *present participle*	Thomas **had been cooking** for five hours and he still had to prepare dessert.
Negative statement	I / you / he / she / it / we / they + **had** + **not** + **been** + *present participle* // or **hadn't been** + *present participle* // or **'d not been** + *present participle*	They **had not been going** regularly. We **hadn't been driving** long when we ran out of gas. She**'d not been checking** the indicators; that's why it happened.
Affirmative interrogative	**had** + I / you / we / he / she / it / they + **been** + *present participle*	**Had** you **been working** there for a long time before they fired you?
Negative interrogative	**had** + I / you / we / he / she / it / they + **not** + **been** + *present participle* // or **hadn't** + subject + **been** + *present participle*	Why **had** he **not been watching** for the signal? Why **hadn't** she **been handing** in her assignments?

Uses of the past perfect progressive tense

The following uses are organized from the most frequently used for this tense to the least frequently used.

Uses	Examples
1. to describe a past event or action that was in progress before another event or time in the past	Hector **had been working** for the same company for twenty years when they appointed him CEO.
2. to describe the duration of a past event or action before another past event or time reference; the emphasis is on the length or duration of the action	The students **had been writing** their final essays for forty-five minutes when the fire alarm rang and chaos ensued. Eleonora **had been working** on her PhD for years before she realized she didn't actually like philosophy.
3. to describe a past repeated action that happened before another past event or time	The machine **had been making** strange noises for a couple of weeks before it failed completely.

Exception to the past perfect progressive uses: Stative verbs

Verbs that express states cannot be used in any of the progressive aspects. *(See 11.2.3.2 Stative verbs)*

Representations of the concept of the past perfect progressive tense

Following are examples of different possible ways of representing and describing this tense. These examples are illustrative, not exhaustive.

In the drawing on the left, the protagonist is represented by the stick-man figure. The event is represented by a series of **X**s, which indicates that the event continues over time. The representation of the action is to the reader's left, indicating that the event took place in the past. The protagonist is also contemplating another past time, and the action series continues from its origin into that known past time. A clear relationship of relevance between the main event and the other past time or event is not always needed, particularly when using this tense to provide background. There is no connection to present or future times.

In the drawing on the right, the times of two events are depicted to the left of the present time, indicating completion in the past. The two events are labeled on the timeline, with one event to the left of the other, indicating that it occurred first. The first event is depicted as a series of **X**s, indicating that it took place over some period of time. An arrow is also used to indicate that by the time one event occurred, the other event had already begun.

The example sentence demonstrates the use of past perfect progressive to talk about the duration of an event prior to another event in the past.

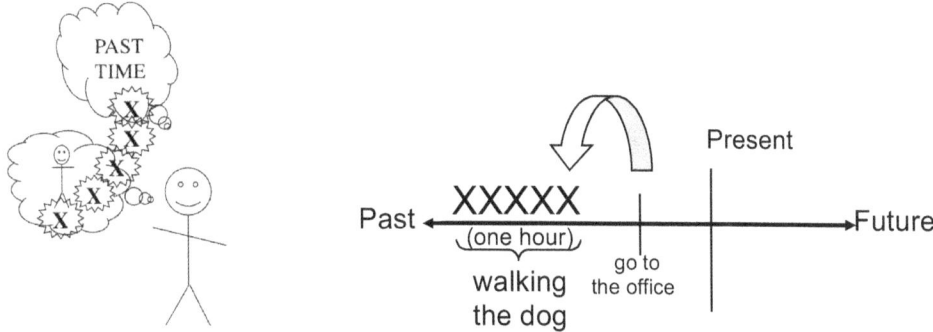

Jack **had been walking** his dog for an hour before he went to the office.

Following is a basic set of concept questions which can help in recognizing when it is appropriate to use the past perfect progressive tense to talk about the duration of a past action in relation to another past action.

Is the action finished? → YES
→ Do we know when it happened? → YES *(The speaker and the listener have some common understanding of the timeframe of the event in the past)*
→ Is it important when it happened? → YES *(The understanding of the timeframe is somehow relevant or useful for understanding)*
→ Was it happening before another action we are talking about? → YES
→ Was it finished or completed before the other action? → NO
→ Was it interrupted by the other action? → NO *(Not completed and not interrupted – therefore, it was continuing)*
→ Past perfect progressive

*** In the classroom: Past perfect progressive ***

As with the present perfect tenses, when teaching the past perfect progressive it is necessary to clarify the differences between this tense and its non-progressive counterpart.

Students might forget one of the auxiliaries or mix their order when using this tense in written or spoken form. This can be solved with meaningful drills.

Quiz 4: Past tenses

Choose the best past tense form to complete the sentences. Explain your choices.

1. Ian (pass) his final exam and graduated.
   a. was passing   b. had passed   c. passed

2. They phoned me while I (do) my presentation. It was embarrassing.
   a. was doing   b. had been doing   c. did

3. They (already leave) when she arrived.
   a. already left   b. had already left   c. had already been leaving

4. Apollo 11 (land) on the moon on July 20, 1969.
   a. was landing   b. landed   c. had been landing

5. They gave her the medal because she (finish) the race in third place.
   a. was finished   b. had finished   c. had been finishing

6. Doris (try) to reach her secretary all day and she finally received a message saying he'd quit.
   a. tried   b. had tried   c. had been trying

14.4 Future tenses

The following sections describe each of the future tenses (future simple, future progressive, future perfect and future perfect progressive). The future tenses differ from the present and past tenses in that the main verbs are not marked (inflected) for the future tenses. The modal auxiliary *will* is used to form the future tenses. The phrase *be going to* is also used to form future constructions.

14.4.1 Future simple

The future simple tense is used to describe events that are expected or predicted to happen in the future. It is formed with the modal auxiliary verb *will* and the main verb in its base form.

Table 67: Forms of the future simple tense

		Examples
Affirmative statement	I / you / we / he / she / it / they + **will** + *verb* (base form) // or **'ll** + *verb* (base form)	I think she **will stay** there all day and work. Hurry or we**'ll get** there late.
Negative statement	I / you / we / he / she / it / they + **will not** + *verb* (base form) // or **won't** + *verb* (base form) // or **'ll not** + *verb* (base form)	I **will not pay** any more money. You **won't understand** my handwriting; let me read it to you. He's a liar; he**'ll not receive** my vote.
Affirmative interrogative	**will** + I / you / we / he / she / it / they + *verb* (base form)	**Will** the Prime Minister **be** available to answer some questions later?
Negative interrogative	**will** + I / you / we / he / she / it / they + **not** + *verb* (base form) // or **won't** + subject + *verb* (base form)	Why **will** they **not listen** to reason? Why **won't** you **stay** just a little bit longer with us?

For negatives, the adverb *not* is contracted to *will* as *won't*. For negative interrogatives, if the adverb *not* is contracted to *will*, the entire contracted form *won't* is placed before the subject.

Uses of the future simple tense

The following uses are organized from the most frequently used for this tense to the least frequently used. The modal auxiliary *will* is used for a variety of purposes, all of which are expressions of possible future action. The uses listed here are ones that are most closely tied to the idea of future time; other moods (ability, certainty, obligation, necessity, request, offer, hope, promise, threat, warning) are described in more detail in *Chapter 12 Auxiliary and modal auxiliary verbs*.

Uses	Examples
1. to predict events based on opinions or subjective evidence	You **will marry** a tall, handsome man. The baby **will** probably **look** like you.
2. to make formal predictions (compare with use of *be going to* for informal predictions, below)	The rain **will make** the morning commute slower than usual, so motorists are advised to take this into consideration tomorrow.
3. to make decisions about the future at the moment of speaking*	A: That's the doorbell, can someone please check? B: I**'ll get** it. (Looking at the menu) Mmm ... I**'ll have** the steak, please.
4. to talk about informal arrangements* (compare with use of *be going to* for formal plans and arrangements, below)	After they finish shopping, they**'ll share** a taxi. On trips to New York, we **won't stay** anywhere north of 23rd Street.
5. to express determination	Looking at the bike catalogue Sarah said, "I **will save** my money and I **will buy** my own bike in a month!"

* These uses are almost always in the contracted (**'ll** or **won't**) forms.

Will and *be going to*

A structure known as the going-to future is frequently taught to ESL learners at lower levels. Its uses are similar to those of the future simple, and its structure is also similar, substituting the phrase *be going to* for *will*. When using this form, it is necessary to conjugate *be* (in the phrase *be going to*) appropriately.

Despite their sometimes seemingly interchangeable nature, these two forms are used to express different concepts. Therefore, students need to be taught what those uses are so that they can use them properly and fully understand the implications and the underlying meanings of sentences using these tenses.

Uses of *going-to* future	Examples
1. to describe future plans that have been arranged already	Maiko and I talked earlier and we **are going to meet** after lunch tomorrow.
2. to make predictions based on evidence	That bookcase is not straight and all the heavy books are on one side; it**'s going to fall** sideways.
3. to make informal predictions	The rain**'s going to make** the morning commute a real pain!

Representations of the concept of the future simple tense

Following are examples of different possible ways of representing and describing this tense. These examples are illustrative, not exhaustive.

In the drawing on the left, the protagonist is represented by the stick-man figure. The event is represented by an **X**. The event is to the reader's right, indicating that the event takes place in the future. There is no connection to present or past times.

In the drawing on the right, the time of the event is depicted to the right of the present time, indicating completion in the future.

The example sentence demonstrates the use of future simple to talk about an informal arrangement in the future.

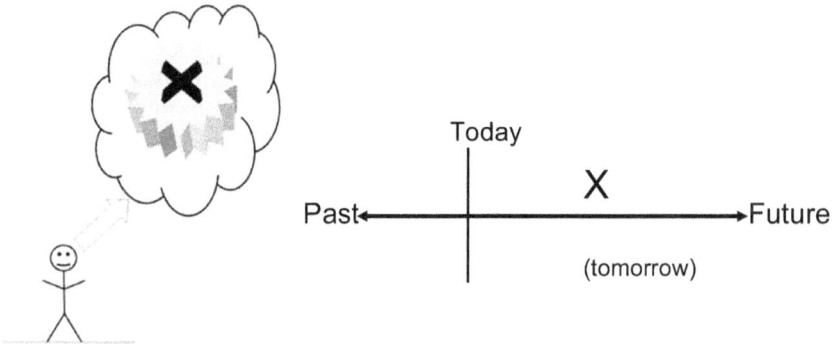

Jack**'ll walk** his dog tomorrow.

Following is a basic set of concept questions which can help in recognizing when it is appropriate to use the future simple tense for an informally arranged action at a known future time.

Is the action finished? → NO
→ Is it a regular, constant or habitual action? → NO
→ Is it related to another time (past or future) or event? → YES
→ Is it related to an event or known time in the past? → NO
→ Is it related to another event or known time in the future? → YES
(Related to a known time in the future: tomorrow, 2:00, in 100 years)
→ Will it finish before or at the same time as another action in the future? → NO *(Related to a time, not to another action)*
→ Will it be in progress in the future? → NO *(Not an ongoing action; it is an informal arrangement)*
→ Future simple

*** In the classroom: Future simple ***

The future simple is usually taught after students learn at least the present and the past simple. The fact that main verbs are in base form in the future simple tense means that students have fewer chances to make mistakes with form.

If students learn the present progressive tense before the going-to future, they will likely confuse them or make mistakes with one or more of the components of the verb phrase. One possible way to prevent or solve this is to leave some time between them (do not teach them one after the other) and to have visual aids around the classroom that will remind them of the structure of each tense.

14.4.2 Future progressive

The future progressive is also called future continuous. It is used to describe future events that will still be in progress at the time under discussion. Because it is not used nearly as often as other tenses, it is usually introduced at the intermediate or advanced levels.

Table 68: Forms of the future progressive tense

		Examples
Affirmative statement	I / you / we / he / she / it / they + **will be** + *present participle* // or **'ll be** + *present participle*	Debbie and Nick **will be getting** their pictures taken after the ceremony. He'll **be regretting** that forever.
Negative statement	I / you / we / he / she / it / they + **will not be** + *present participle* // or **won't be** + *present participle* // or **'ll not be** + *present participle*	You **will not be wasting** any more time online. They **won't be giving** us any more credit. I'll **not be taking** any trips with them again.
Affirmative interrogative	**will** + I / you / we / he / she / it / they + **be** + *present participle* or **'ll** + subject + **be** + *present participle*	What **will** you **be doing** this time next year? What'll you **be doing** this time next year?
Negative interrogative	**will** + I / you / we / he / she / it / they + **not be** + *present participle* // or **won't** + subject + **be** + *present participle*	**Will** you **not be staying** longer? Why **won't** you **be coming** in April?

Uses of the future progressive tense

The following uses are organized from the most frequently used for this tense to the least frequently used.

Uses	Examples
1. to describe an action or event that will be in progress at some point in time in the future	Next year in April, my brother **will be getting** married. Tomorrow at noon, Boris **will be meeting** with his lawyer.
2. to describe events that are supposed to happen and which may make other events possible or have certain consequences	Kitty **will be dropping** by tomorrow after work. Do you want to come by so you can meet her? I'll **be finishing** this in a minute and then you can use the computer.
3. to describe an event or inquire about the future politely	**Will** you **be taking** your vacation days all at once? Where **will** Mr. Morris **be taking** his dinner today?

Exception to the future progressive uses: Stative verbs

Verbs that express states cannot be used in any of the progressive aspects. *(See 11.2.3.2 Stative verbs)*

Representations of the concept of the future progressive tense

Following are examples of different possible ways of representing and describing this tense. These examples are illustrative, not exhaustive.

In the drawing on the left, the protagonist is represented by the stick-man figure. The event is represented by an **X**. The protagonist pictures himself astride the event, indicating that he is picturing himself in the middle of doing the action. This depiction of the protagonist and the action in the thought bubble is to the reader's right, indicating that the event will be taking place in the future. There is no connection to present or past times.

In the drawing on the right, the times of two events are depicted to the right of the present time, indicating activity in the future. One event is depicted as a series of **X**s, showing it is an ongoing action. The second event is depicted inside the continuing event, indicating that they are occurring simultaneously.

The example sentence demonstrates the use of future continuous to talk about an action that will be in progress at a known future time.

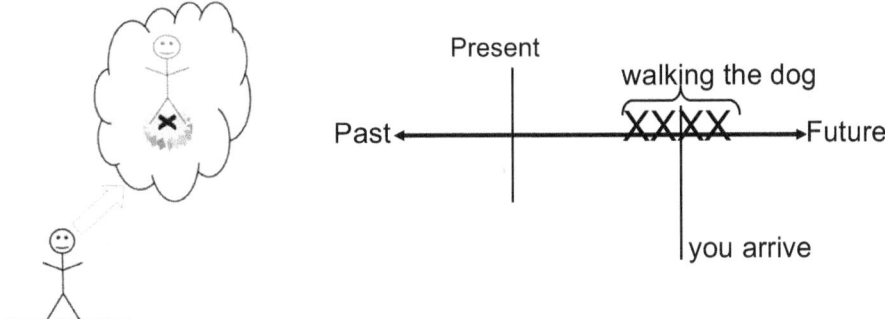

Jack **will be walking** his dog when you arrive.

Following is a basic set of concept questions which can help in recognizing when it is appropriate to use the future progressive tense to talk about actions that will be under way at a described time in the future.

Is the action finished? → NO
    → Is it a regular, constant or habitual action? → NO
        → Is it related to another time (past or future) or event? → YES
            → Is it related to an event or known time in the past? → NO
                → Is it related to another event or known time in the future? → YES
(Related to a known time in the future: a definite time, like tomorrow or 2:00, or linked to an event such as "when I am older")
                    → Will it finish before or at the same time as another action in the future? → NO *(It won't be finished, it will be continuing)*
                    → Will it be in progress in the future? → YES *(An ongoing action)*
                    → Future progressive

**** In the classroom: Future progressive ****

When students are first introduced to the future progressive tense they generally do not find it too challenging, since they will probably have learned all the other progressive tenses and probably some perfect progressive tenses. Students should already know how to form present participles and how to use more than one auxiliary verb in a verb phrase.

The challenge for students learning this tense lies in the difference between this tense and the future simple. The focus must be on whether the action will be in process or ongoing at a particular time in the future.

14.4.3 Future perfect

The future perfect is used to describe events that will be finished before some other reference point in the future. It is taught to students at the high intermediate and advanced levels. The low frequency of its usage means that students can communicate well in English without having learned this tense. It is quite possible that students who develop a feel for the language will be able to understand and use this tense even if they have never learned it formally in class.

Table 69: Forms of the future perfect tense

		Examples
Affirmative statement	I / you / we / he / she / it / they + **will have** + *past participle* // or **'ll have** + *past participle*	Timothy **will have completed** his studies by June next year. I**'ll have forgotten** all this by the time I take the exam.
Negative statement	I / you / we / he / she / it / they + **will not have** + *past participle* // or **won't have** + *past participle* // or **'ll not have** + *past participle*	We **will not have finished** by 5:00. She **won't have worked** there for three months if they fire her tomorrow. She**'ll not have heard**; she's on vacation for the next three weeks.
Affirmative interrogative	**will** + I / you / we / he / she / it / they + **have** + *past participle*	**Will** you **have received** more stock of this new game before tomorrow?
Negative interrogative	**will** + I / you / we / he / she / it / they + **not have** + *past participle* // or **won't** + subject + **have** + *past participle*	**Will** they **not have encountered** these problems by then? You go to the movies almost every day! Which movie **won't** you **have seen** by next Friday?

Uses of the future perfect tense

The future perfect is used in one major way:

Use	Examples
1. to describe an event or action that will have been completed before a certain time in the future	At the end of this month, I **will have worked** as a teacher for twenty years. The principal has left for the day. If you come tomorrow at 9:00, she **will have arrived** and she'll be ready to meet with you.

Representations of the concept of the future perfect tense

Following are examples of different possible ways of representing and describing this tense. These examples are illustrative, not exhaustive.

In the drawing on the left, the protagonist is represented by the stick-man figure. The event is represented by an **X**. The time of the completion of the action is uncertain in this case. The protagonist is also contemplating another time, definitely in the future. The important element is the completion of the action in relation to some time or event in the future; the action will finish before the other future time or event under discussion.

In the drawing on the right, the times of two events are depicted to the right of the present time, indicating completion in the future. The two events are labeled on the timeline, with one event to the left of the other, indicating that it occurs first.

The example sentence demonstrates the use of future perfect to talk about the completion of one event in relation to another event in the future.

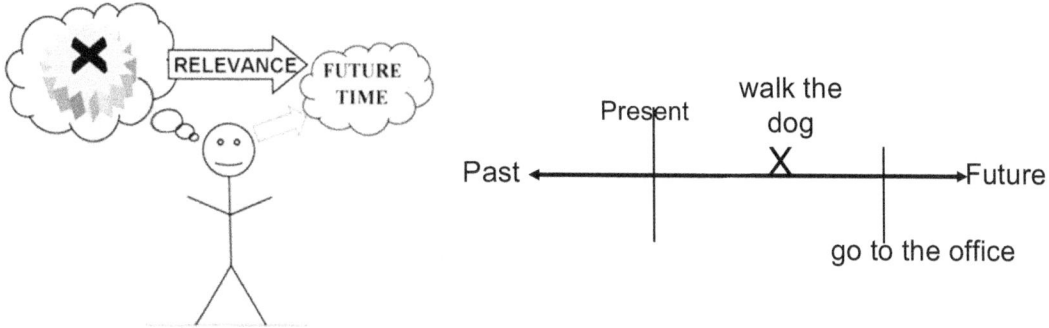

Jack **will have walked** his dog before he goes to the office.

Following is a basic set of concept questions which can help in recognizing when it is appropriate to use the future perfect tense.

Is the action finished? → NO
   → Is it a regular, constant or habitual action? → NO
      → Is it related to another time (past or future) or event? → YES
         → Is it related to an event or known time in the past? → NO
            → Is it related to another event or known time in the future? → YES *(Related to a known time in the future: a definite time, like next year, or linked to an event such as "by the time I get home")*
               → Will it finish either before or at the same time as another action in the future? → YES *(It will finish before another event or known time)*
                 → Will it still be happening at the same time as another event or known time in the future? → NO *(It will be finished)*
                   → Future perfect

**** In the classroom: Future perfect ****

This tense only has one use and it is so specific that it is only taught to high intermediate and advanced learners. If students have learned other tenses correctly before this one and they are able to use other tenses effectively, this tense will not pose many difficulties.

14.4.4 Future perfect progressive

The future perfect progressive is also called future perfect continuous. It is closely related to the future perfect and the future progressive tenses. The main focus is the idea that the event or action is incomplete or temporary. Though the tense is progressive, the sense is that the action has continued for some time, but is essentially finished by the time under discussion.

Table 70: Forms of the future perfect progressive tense

		Examples
Affirmative statement	I / you / we / he / she / it / they + **will have been** + *present participle* // or **'ll have been** + *present participle*	Tammy **will have been teaching** at our school for two years by the end of next month. She**'ll have been teaching** for two years.
Negative statement	I / you / we / he / she / it / they + **will not have been** + *present participle* // or **won't have been** + *present participle* // or **'ll not have been** + *present participle*	Next year, you **will not have been working** long enough to qualify for a pension. You need another year. You **won't have been** working long enough. You**'ll not have been working** long enough.
Affirmative interrogative	**will** + I / you / we / he / she / it / they + **have been** + *present participle*	How long **will** Zoe **have been studying** medicine by the time she graduates?
Negative interrogative	**will** + I / you / we / he / she / it / they + **not have been** + *present participle* // or **won't** + subject + **have been** + *present participle*	**Will** they **not have been selling** those beyond their expiration date? **Won't** you **have been standing** too long by now? Please take a seat!

Uses of the future perfect progressive tense

The future perfect progressive is used to describe one main concept:

Use	Examples
1. to describe an event or action that will be ongoing at a certain time in the future; it also highlights the duration of the action	At the end of this month, I **will have been working** as a teacher for twenty years without ever stopping or changing jobs! At this time tomorrow, the manager **will have been reviewing** resumes all morning and she'll be ready to interview appropriate candidates.

Exception to the future perfect progressive uses: Stative verbs

Verbs that express states cannot be used in any of the progressive aspects. *(See 11.2.3.2 Stative verbs)*

Representations of the concept of the future perfect progressive tense

Following are examples of different possible ways of representing and describing this tense. These examples are illustrative, not exhaustive.

In the drawing on the left, the protagonist is represented by the stick-man figure. The event is represented by a series of **X**s, indicating a continuing activity. The protagonist is also contemplating another action or known time that is definitely in the future. The starting point of the main action may be in the past, present or future. The key point is that the action will continue up to the known point in the future.

In the drawing on the right, the times of two events are depicted to the right of the present time, indicating activity in the future. One event is depicted as a series of **X**s, showing it is an ongoing action. The second event is depicted at the edge of the continuing event, indicating that they are coinciding.

The example sentence demonstrates the use of future perfect progressive to talk about an action that in progress (and probably finishing) at a known future time.

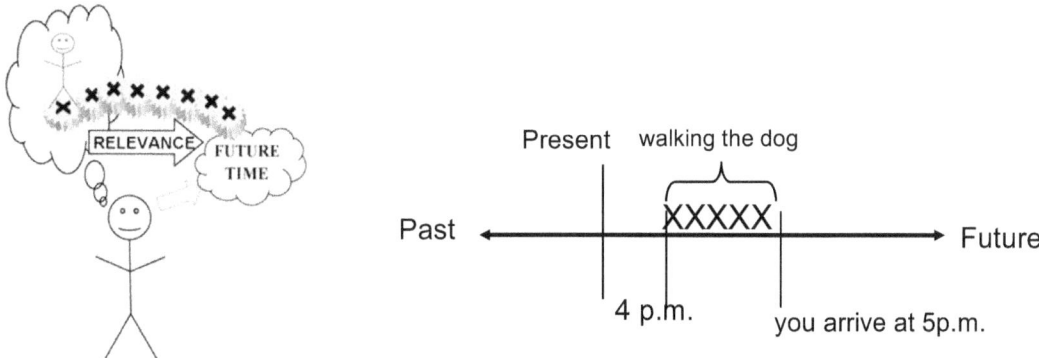

Jack **will have been walking** his dog for an hour by the time you arrive.

Following is a basic set of concept questions which can help in recognizing when it is appropriate to use the future perfect progressive tense.

Is the action finished? → NO
   → Is it a regular, constant or habitual action? → NO
      → Is it related to another time (past or future) or event? → YES
         → Is it related to an event or known time in the past? → NO
            → Is it related to another event or known time in the future? → YES
            (Related to a known time in the future: a definite time, like next year, or linked to an event such as "by the time I get home")
               → Will it finish either before or at the same time as another action in the future? → YES *(It will finish at the same time as another event or known time; or our interest in it will be finished)*
                  → Will it still be happening at the same time as another event or known time in the future? → YES *(It will coincide with the future event)*
                     → Future perfect progressive

*** In the classroom: Future perfect progressive ***

When teaching students to recognize the future perfect progressive, they will have virtually no difficulties; the form is regular and obvious. On the other hand, when teaching students to use the future perfect progressive, the context will have to be very clear and specific since there is only one concept for which this tense is necessary. If students are provided with the proper context for practice and they are at a high intermediate or advanced level, they will be able to learn and use this tense well.

Quiz 5: Future tenses

Fill in the blanks with the correct form of the future tenses and explain your choices.

1) At 10 am next week, we (drive) _____ to Hilton Head island.
2) The music is too loud; the baby (wake up) _____; I just know it!
3) If you don't pass your class, you (not be able) _____ to apply for a bursary.
4) In a few years all the buses (accept) _____ electronic payment only.
5) This dress is perfect for the party and it fits well! I (take) _____ it!
6) He is so exhausted that tomorrow he (sleep) _____ in.
7) No later than next year, my parents (buy) _____ a new condo on the beach and we'll be able to go.
8) Before next week is over she (stay) _____ with us for 2 months.

14.5 Tenses tree

The following set of yes/no questions can be used to determine which tense to use in a given situation. These questions can provide the basis for concept questions in the classroom for checking student comprehension.

Is the action finished?							Result
Y — Do we know when it happened?	**Y** — Is it important when it happened?	**Y** — Was it happening before another past action that we are talking about?	**Y** — Was it finished or complete before the other action?				Yes → Past Perfect – *We had eaten by the time Phyllis arrived.*
			N — Was it interrupted by the other action?				Yes → Past Progressive – *I was working on this when you called.*
							No → Past Perfect Progressive – *Shawn had been saving for years when the market crashed.*
		N — Was it at the same time as another action in the past?					Yes → Past Progressive – *The patient was watching TV when he took his medicine.*
							No → Simple Past – *The patient took his medicine at 2 o'clock.*
	N						No → Present Perfect – *The maintenance workers have repaired the pipes.*
	N — Is it important or relevant to now?						Yes → Present Perfect – *I'm pretty sure she has taken all the training courses.*
							No → Simple Past – *She won a singing contest.*
N — Is it a regular, constant or habitual action?							Yes → Present Simple – *She wakes up around 4:00 every morning and can't get back to sleep.*
N — Is it related to another time (past or future) or event?	**Y** — Is it related to an event or a known time in the past?						Yes → Present Perfect Progressive – *We have been waiting for the bell to ring since noon.*
	N — Is it related to another event or known time in the future?	**Y** — Will it be finished before or during another future action?	**Y** — Will it still be happening at the same time as another event or known time in the future?				Yes → Future Perfect Progressive – *Bob will have been working for 45 years when he retires next December.*
							No → Future Perfect – *Sam will have moved by the time you graduate.*
			N — Will it be in progress in the future?				Yes → Future Progressive – *Tom will be traveling when you come for a visit.*
							No → Future Simple – *I will begin the new course next week.*
		N — Future simple (several possible variations)					Based on objective, clear evidence: → "Going to" modal phrase – *With these statistics, the market is going to improve.*
							Prediction: → Future Simple – *The athlete's strength will improve.*
							Decision at the time of speaking: → Future Simple – *Mmm, I will have the spaghetti, please.*
							Expression of determination: → Future Simple – *I will finish this.*
N							No → Present Progressive – *We are waiting for the bell to ring.*

*** You can teach tenses ***

General ideas and pointers

Tenses are best taught in a meaningful context. If the context is clear and creates the need for students to use that particular tense, then students will practise it authentically and learn the most important part of these lessons first: when to use each tense. The form and structure of each tense is something that students can practise through drills and regular exercises.

If students do not know how to use tenses correctly then they will not understand what others really say or write or the context in which things are said – nor will they be able to communicate their ideas effectively.

The knowledge of how to use tenses goes hand in hand with learning verbs and the general structure of sentences in English and should, therefore, not be taught in isolation.

Specific ideas for different tenses

TENSE:	Present simple	SKILLS:	Reading / speaking / listening
TOPIC:	Schedules	LEVEL:	Beginner
Description:	Use bus, train and flight schedules. An information gap activity in which one student has part of the information and the other has what's missing can work very well to get students practising this use of the present simple - What time does the train from Toronto to Ottawa leave? / It leaves at 6 pm. - How long is the trip? / What time does it arrive in Ottawa? / It arrives at 8 pm.		

TENSE:	Present simple	SKILLS:	Reading / writing
TOPIC:	Science	LEVEL:	Beginner / low intermediate
Description:	Simple science experiments and facts can also bring interesting content and an ideal context for practising this tense. Have students do simple experiments and write out conclusions using the present simple tense.		

TENSE:	Present simple	SKILLS:	Writing / reading
TOPIC:	Personal information	LEVEL:	Beginner
Description:	This is one of the first tenses to be taught to students, and this type of exercise provides a great opportunity to get to know students (and for them to get to know each other). Students are asked to create an information sheet about themselves. In it, students can describe their daily routines, their likes and dislikes and even give directions on how to get to their favourite places, all using the present simple tense only.		

TENSE:	Present simple	SKILLS:	Reading / speaking
TOPIC:	Recipes	LEVEL:	Beginner / low Intermediate
Description:	Another good information gap activity can be done with simple recipes. These can have the instructions all written in present simple and two or more students can work collaboratively to put the instructions in order or complete them using the different information each of them has. - Do we have to melt the butter first or mix the eggs? - My instructions say we mix the eggs first.		

TENSE:	Present progressive	SKILL:	Speaking
TOPIC:	Describing pictures	LEVEL:	Beginner / low intermediate
Description:	Photographs and pictures from magazines are excellent resources for practising and teaching the present progressive. Using this tense, students can describe what is happening in the images. This typical practice exercise can be turned into a game once students are more comfortable with the tense. Three students come to the front of the class and receive a file folder each. Two of the file folders have a picture inside, and the third is empty. Taking turns, the students must describe what they see in the pictures, including the student who has no picture (who must imagine a picture). The rest of the class has to guess which student had no picture. With practice, students get very good at this game and it's hard to tell who doesn't have a picture.		

TENSE:	Present progressive	SKILL:	Speaking
TOPIC:	Charades	LEVEL:	Beginner
Description:	Playing charades is a popular way to practise present progressive. A student comes to the front and performs an action and the rest of the class must shout out what the student is doing.		

TENSE:	Present progressive	SKILLS:	Reading / writing
TOPIC:	Planning	LEVEL:	Beginner / low intermediate
Description:	Students can create a daily planner and fill it with activities they would like to do in their future and then write about it. This type of exercise can also easily include future simple tenses (using *will* and *going to*).		

TENSE:	Present progressive	SKILLS:	Reading / speaking
TOPIC:	News / current affairs	LEVEL:	Low intermediate
Description:	For adult students, a brief look at headlines in newspapers can provide some current affairs topics to discuss in class using the present progressive. (Choose ongoing situations rather than news items that report one-time events, since these would be discussed using the simple past instead.)		

TENSE:	Present perfect	SKILLS:	Writing / speaking / listening
TOPIC:	Your experience	LEVEL:	Intermediate
Description:	Students' past experiences and their life stories are ideal topics to use with the present perfect. Students can develop "have you ever …?" questionnaires and ask around the class. For further written practice, students can write a paragraph comparing their results, which they can plot in a graph. (For example, 50% of students have traveled abroad.) There are many songs (for example, "I Still Haven't Found What I'm Looking For," by U2) that can be used to accompany this lesson.		

TENSE:	Present perfect	SKILLS:	Reading / speaking
TOPIC:	Receipts	LEVEL:	Intermediate
Description:	Receipts from groceries stores or others kinds of stores can be brought in and students can guess why each person has bought each thing. Try to make sure the dates on the receipts are not visible and tell students they are doing 'detective' work. (For example, "This person has bought three cartons of milk because she has five cats." Or "This person has chosen whole wheat bread because they are health conscious.")		

TENSE:	Present perfect	SKILL:	Speaking
TOPIC:	Guessing	LEVEL:	Intermediate
Description:	Scenes from movies can be shown with or without sound and students can guess what has just happened before that scene.		

TENSE:	Present perfect progressive	SKILLS:	Reading / writing
TOPIC:	Celebrities	LEVEL:	Intermediate
Description:	A famous person's biography or list of biographical facts can be used to describe actions which the person started in the past and which they still continue to do. Choose celebrities that the students know or are interested in; otherwise, the interest in the activity will be too low. Also, it is imperative that the celebrities are still alive, or students will not be using the tense authentically.		

TENSE:	Present perfect progressive	SKILL:	Speaking
TOPIC:	Through my window	LEVEL:	Intermediate
Description:	With magazine pictures that depict people performing different kinds of actions, students can create short written dialogues or skits in which they talk about the person in the picture. They can imagine that the picture is what they see through their window and they are not very happy with their neighbours. For example, if the picture shows a person painting on an easel they could say: "My neighbour has been listening to his loud music all morning. He says it inspires him to paint, but it annoys me."		

TENSE:	Past simple	SKILLS:	Reading / speaking or writing
TOPIC:	History	LEVEL:	Low intermediate
Description:	Ask students to do research and present information on historic events from their countries.		

TENSE:	Past simple	SKILL:	Speaking
TOPIC:	What we did on the weekend	LEVEL:	Beginner
Description:	Students can tell the class what they did on the weekend as a narrative. To make this into a game, ask students to include one or more events or details that are not true and the rest of the class must discover which ones are not true.		

TENSE:	Past simple	SKILLS:	Listening / speaking / writing
TOPIC:	Summarizing a movie	LEVEL:	Low intermediate
Description:	Divide the class into groups. Show each group a different portion of a movie scene. Ask students to create a brief summary of what they saw and be ready to re-tell it to the class. Each group re-tells its part of the movie scene. When they all finish, the class as a whole must agree on the order in which these parts happened. Show the whole scene for the class to check if their prediction was correct.		

TENSE:	Past progressive	SKILLS:	Speaking / listening
TOPIC:	Detectives	LEVEL:	Intermediate
Description:	Do a detective role play in which students need to ask each other, "What were you doing when the necklace was stolen?" Depending on the number of students in class, this can be done as a whole class activity or in smaller groups. You can even assign students different roles.		

TENSE:	Past progressive	SKILL:	Speaking
TOPIC:	What were you doing?	LEVEL:	Low intermediate
Description:	Give each student a card with a verb written on it. The verbs must all be action verbs that students can perform in class in one minute. Tell students not to show the cards to their classmates. Tell them that you will leave the room for one minute at a time. Each student must simply perform the action on the card as soon as the teacher leaves, and stop as soon as the teacher comes back. As a final instruction, tell them they must also look around while they perform their action. Leave the room and come back one minute later and ask the students about their classmate: "What was Paula doing when I was outside?"		

TENSE:	Past perfect	SKILLS:	Reading / speaking
TOPIC:	Re-telling stories	LEVEL:	Intermediate / high intermediate
Description:	Give students stories that have many steps in a sequence, with a clear time frame for each. Ask them to retell the story in half the number of sentences and summarize using the past perfect tense.		

TENSE:	Past perfect progressive	SKILLS:	Reading / speaking / writing
TOPIC:	Sentence puzzles	LEVEL:	Intermediate
Description:	Create sentences / situations with two actions; one action must be clearly before the other, and must be long. The situations must be written without proper grammar. Split each situation in two and give out the pieces to different students in the class. Students must find their partners and then together re-write the sentences so that they are correctly expressed. One sentence will have to contain past perfect progressive. This can even be made into a race and the winners can receive some kind of prize.		

TENSE:	Future simple	SKILL:	Speaking
TOPIC:	Lists	LEVEL:	Low intermediate
Description:	Create shopping lists or to-do lists for fictional characters and ask students to predict what they think these characters will do. Since these will be predictions highly influenced by their opinions, this exercise is a good example where *will* is preferred to *going to*.		

TENSE:	Future simple	SKILLS:	Listening / speaking
TOPIC:	Sci-Fi	LEVEL:	Low intermediate
Description:	Watch snippets of science fiction films as an introduction. Then ask students to make their own predictions about what life will be like on Earth (or other planets) in the distant or near future.		

TENSE:	Future simple	SKILLS:	Speaking / reading
TOPIC:	Ordering	LEVEL:	Low intermediate
Description:	Bring menus from different restaurants (or have students create them so that they can practise food and restaurant vocabulary as well) and ask students to role-play ordering at a restaurant, making sure to use *will* when they decide what they will eat and drink.		

TENSE:	Future simple	SKILLS:	Speaking / listening
TOPIC:	Threats and warnings	LEVEL:	Intermediate
Description:	Play a chain game with threats / warnings in which each student must use the previous main clause as an if-clause in their sentence. Challenge students to see how long two different groups can go, or how long the whole class can go. For example, student A says, "If you don't do your homework, you will not pass." Student B then replies, "If you don't pass, your parents will be upset." Student C might then say "If your parents are upset, they won't let you come to the party." And so on, until the whole chain can be summarized by repeating the first if-clause of the chain and the very last main clause: "If you don't do your homework, your parents won't let you go to the party."		

Structure:	Going-to future	SKILL:	Speaking
TOPIC:	Weather forecasts	LEVEL:	Beginner
Description:	Use weather charts for students to predict weather conditions for later in the week, with some evidence in front of them.		

Structure:	Going-to future	SKILLS:	Reading / speaking / listening
TOPIC:	Arranging a meeting (1)	LEVEL:	Low intermediate
Description:	Pair students up and give them two different daily planners with a variety of appointments and tasks already planned. Their goal is to find a time when they can meet. Each of them must ask the other to meet at a certain time and the answer is bound to be "I can't; I'm going to see my dentist at that time. How about (insert another date and time)?" and so on, until they find a suitable time for both. Make sure the planners are accurately created to just leave one possibility.		

TENSE:	Future progressive	SKILLS:	Reading / speaking / listening
TOPIC:	Arranging a meeting (2)	LEVEL:	Low intermediate / intermediate
Description:	The daily planner activity described above using the going-to future can be slightly changed so that it asks the students to use future progressive instead. The planners should have shaded areas that show the duration of the events / activities and then students will be using the tense more accurately. - Let's meet on Tuesday at 4 pm. - I can't. I will be spending the afternoon at a conference.		

TENSE:	Future progressive	SKILLS:	Speaking / listening
TOPIC:	Making excuses	LEVEL:	Intermediate
Description:	Students can create short role-play situations in which one person wants to meet with or invite another to do something together, while the other really does not want to go. Instruct the students who supposedly do not want to go to make up funny excuses of things they will be doing at the time, using future progressive. The funnier the excuses, the more memorable the learning experience will be for the whole class.		

TENSE:	Future progressive	SKILLS:	Writing / speaking
TOPIC:	Being super polite	LEVEL:	Intermediate +
Description:	Once students learn past progressive, modal verbs used for politeness, and the future progressive tense, they can be asked to create dialogues (and possibly act them out) in which one of the characters is extremely polite and uses all these tenses and special forms when speaking. Others in the skit are not as polite and sometimes misinterpret the polite language and take it rather literally. (This activity will work best with high intermediate and advanced students, as it also helps students discuss and learn register as well as culture.)		

TENSE:	Future perfect / future perfect progressive	SKILLS:	Speaking / writing / reading
TOPIC:	Goals	LEVEL:	High intermediate / advanced
Description:	Have students discuss their own future goals and visions of where they will be, what they will have done and what they will have been doing with the use of these two tenses. You can ask them to create a little poster with a picture and a set of 10 sentences using these tenses. Make sure they do not put any obviously revealing information about themselves (name, home town) on the posters. When everyone is finished, the teacher can display all the posters around the classroom and students must guess which of their classmates created which poster.		

15 Interjections

Interjections are exclamatory words or phrases which express emotions: anger, surprise, joy, doubt, irony, agreement, disappointment, wonder, hesitancy, recognition, greeting and many others. They stand alone and do not have a grammatical connection to other words, phrases or clauses. Even when interjections are completely set apart – with a capital letter and a terminating punctuation mark – they do not form a complete grammatical sentence; they are considered sentence fragments.

The following are examples of interjections.

ugh	**wow**	**yikes**	**oops**	**ouch**	**yes**
well	**oh**	**hmm**	**duh**	**hey**	**aha**

The emotions expressed by interjections are also marked by intonation and variation of the voice pitch (in spoken English), or by punctuation (in writing). The most common punctuation mark used with interjections is the exclamation mark (!), which expresses strong feelings. Commas (,), dashes (-) or interrogative marks (?) can also be used with interjections. A comma or dash can indicate a pause in speech (perhaps the time the speaker needs to think of what to say next), or can simply offset the interjection from the rest of the sentence. An interrogative mark can indicate doubt, confusion or surprise.

> **Lord!** I can't believe what he has just said.
> **Huh?** I don't know what you are suggesting.
> **Well,** I think it'd be a good idea to invite Jeannette to the party.

Interjections are not generally used in formal writing, except when the writer is quoting some other person directly. They are very common in informal writing (such as text messages, blogs and emails to friends), in cartoons (comic strips, graphic novels) and in dialogs (in plays or novels).

15.1 Interjection forms

Interjections can be one word or a phrase. Many interjections also function as other parts of speech. When they are interjections, they express independent ideas.

> **Absolutely!** I agree with you.
> (**Absolutely!** is an interjection expressing approval, encouragement or agreement; it usually functions as an adverb)
>
> **Great!** Your idea is going to be implemented.
> (**Great!** is an interjection expressing enthusiasm; it usually functions as an adjective)
>
> **Big deal!**
> (an interjection phrase expressing indifference, nonchalance or disdain; it could also function as a noun phrase)

Interjections are sometimes composed of independent consonant- or vowel-like sounds. Many of these interjections are classed as paralanguage: utterances which have meanings and spellings unique to the language, but which are often not considered to be true words.

> **Oh!** That is so funny! (to add emphasis)
> **Shhh!** Do not disturb him. (to ask someone to be quiet)
> **Pst! Pst!** Can you come closer? (to call someone's attention)

Interjections can be onomatopoeic; they imitate the sounds of people, animals and nature.

> **Oink! Oink!** (sound made by a pig)
> **Ahem!** (sound of clearing the throat)
> **Achoo!** (sound of sneezing)
> **Whoosh!** (sound of a brisk wind)

15.2 Interjection placement

An interjection is usually placed before any associated sentences or ideas. In speaking, an interjection can use varied intonation patterns. In writing, an interjection is followed by a comma when it is still contained within the sentence structure, but precedes the sentence.

However, interjections can be found in different parts of a sentence: at the very end, or anywhere in the middle. Generally, interjections in the middle of a sentence are used to make a pause in the conversation, to show that the speaker is thinking of what to say next, or to show that the speaker is doubtful. In writing, interjections in the middle of a sentence are offset by commas.

If they are completely separate from sentences, or if they end a sentence, interjections are followed by a terminating mark (exclamation mark, question mark or period).

> **Hello.** How can I help you?
> **Ugh!** This is disgusting.
> **Well,** I am not sure, **hmm,** if I would like to tell the kids about the move.

Sometimes two interjections can be combined, separated by a comma.

> A: It's a very aggressive schedule you have.
> B: **Yes, exactly!** I will be very happy to finish this work soon.
> (**Yes** is an interjection expressing assertion; **exactly** indicates agreement or recognition)

> The answer is right in front of you! **Um, hello?**
> (**Um** is an interjection to indicate hesitancy; **hello** is used here to indicate that the listener should pay attention, an indicator that they missed something obvious.)

*** In the classroom: Interjections ***

Overdoing interjections
Because interjections add strong emotion to one's speech or writing, they should be used with moderation. The expressiveness of interjections can be a temptation for many: a way to avoid using more complicated structures to express an idea. Or, they may just feel like a fun way to express oneself. The problem with overuse is that it tends to make the speaker or writer sound cartoon-ish and unsophisticated.

> **Yikes!** How the time is flying. **Alas,** I have been falling behind. **Egad!** The deadline is looming. **Gadzooks,** will I get the job done!?

Translation for meaning
Interjections are not exclusive to the English language. Many languages have this type of speech, with distinct meanings and phonological characteristics. For high level students, a discussion of how interjections are said in their mother tongue is a great way to introduce the concept of English interjections.

This type of discussion is a good introduction to teaching interjections based on semantics, integrating meaning, intonation, pronunciation and usage. In some cases, interjections can have different meanings which can only be realized through intonation and context. One example is Aah!

> Aah, what a wonderful view! (expressing surprise or amazement)
> Aah, I'm sorry to hear that. (expressing sympathy)
> Aah! I get it now. (expressing understanding)

Quiz: Defining interjections
Indicate which of the following statements are true of interjections.

a) They modify others parts of a sentence or clause.
b) They can be one word or a phrase.
c) They are always placed before a sentence or clause.
d) They are always marked with an exclamation mark.
e) Meaning is affected by intonation.

*** You can teach interjections ***

Following are some ideas to help students identify the meaning of interjections, and use them in speech or writing.

Matching
Give the students a list of sentences and the same number of bubbles with interjections in them. They have to complete the comments with the corresponding sentence. See some examples below for low levels:

1. I am not sure if I am going to tell her that.
2. Is this cherry cheesecake?
3. That hurts.
4. Our team won.

Answer key: 1. Well; 2. Yummy!; 3. Ouch! 4:Hurray!

To make the activity more challenging, get the students to create short dialogues which include the sentences with the interjections, or the interjections on their own. For higher levels, use more sophisticated interjections and no situation or sentence for them to match. They have to complete the comments with a suitable sentence.

What would you say?

Create a context in which interjections can be used. Write the situations on different cards and distribute them to half of the students in a group. Student A reads the situation and student β expresses his feelings using the appropriate interjections.

Student A: If you catch your fingers on the door, what would you say?
Student B: Ouch!

Other possible situations:
      You figured something out (aha!)
      You do not agree with something or someone (absolutely not!)
      Something smells bad (pew!)
      Something feels great (aaah!)
      I made a small mistake (oops!)

How many can you find?

Pair student up and supply them with a list of emotions. Each pair has to brainstorm as many interjections as they know related to that emotion. Students then must create situations or mini-dialogues to illustrate the meanings of the interjections.

Examples of emotions and possible interjections on those categories:
      surprise: wow; oh, no; eh?; huh?
      disgust: yeech; ugh; eew; ick
      agreement: absolutely; agreed; okay; yes
      joy and excitement: yippee; eureka; yeah; woo-hoo

Fun with comics

Choose an appropriate selection of comic strips, taking into consideration students' ages and interests, and the type and variety of interjections the strips contain. Begin with a reading exercise which requires students to identify and describe the sound and function of the interjections that appear in the strip. Follow up by assigning students a drawing and writing task of creating their own strip which uses the targeted interjections. As a variation, delete the interjections from the original strips and ask students to add appropriate ones.

Appendices

Appendix I: Irregular verbs

Example list of irregular verbs, grouped by similiarity of conjugation

Base Form	Simple Past	Past Participle	Base Form	Simple Past	Past Participle
beat	beat	beaten	**begin**	**began**	**begun**
beget	begot	begotten	**drink**	**drank**	**drunk**
bite	bit	bitten	**ring**	**rang**	**rung**
break	broke	broken	**sing**	**sang**	**sung**
choose	chose	chosen	**sink**	**sank**	**sunk**
drive	drove	driven	**spring**	**sprang**	**sprung**
ride	rode	ridden	**stink**	**stank/stunk**	**stunk**
eat	ate	eaten	**swim**	**swam**	**swum**
fall	fell	fallen			
forbid	forbade	forbidden	build	built	built
forget	forgot	forgotten	bend	bent	bent
forgive	forgave	forgiven	burn	burnt*	burnt*
get	got	gotten/got	cleave	cleft	cleft
give	gave	given	creep	crept	crept
freeze	froze	frozen	deal	dealt	dealt
hide	hid	hidden	dream	dreamt*	dreamt*
prove	proved	proven	feel	felt	felt
rise	rose	risen	keep	kept	kept
shake	shook	shaken	kneel	knelt	knelt
shave	shaved	shaven	learn	learnt*	learnt*
shrink	shrank	shrunken	leave	left	left
speak	spoke	spoken	lend	lent	lent
steal	stole	stolen	light	lit	lit
swell	swelled	swollen	lose	lost	lost
take	took	taken	mean	meant	meant
tread	trod	trodden	meet	met	met
wake	woke	woken	send	sent	sent
weave	wove	woven	shoot	shot	shot
write	wrote	written	sleep	slept	slept
			smell	smelt*	smelt*
become	**became**	**become**	spell	spelt	spelt
come	**came**	**come**	spend	spent	spent
			spill	spilt*	spilt*
be	was / were	been	spoil	spoilt*	spoilt*
can	could	been able to	sweep	swept	swept
do	did	done	weep	wept	wept
go	went	gone			
lie	lay	lain	**bring**	**brought**	**brought**
run	ran	run	**buy**	**bought**	**bought**
see	saw	seen	**fight**	**fought**	**fought**
show	showed	shown*	**think**	**thought**	**thought**
wear	wore	worn	**catch**	**caught**	**caught**
			teach	**taught**	**taught**
			seek	**sought**	**sought**

* Regular *(-ed)* form is also commonly used.

Base Form	Simple Past	Past Participle	Base Form	Simple Past	Past Participle
bet	bet	bet	bleed	bled	bled
bid	bid	bid	breed	bred	bred
burst	burst	burst	feed	fed	fed
cast	cast	cast	lead	led	led
cost	cost	cost	plead	pled*	pled*
cut	cut	cut	speed	sped	sped
fit	fit	fit			
hit	hit	hit	bind	bound	bound
hurt	hurt	hurt	find	found	found
knit	knit	knit	grind	ground	ground
let	let	let	wind	wound	wound
put	put	put			
quit	quit	quit	dive	dove*	dove*
read	read†	read†	hear	heard	heard
rid	rid	rid	hold	held	held
set	set	set	have	had	had
shed	shed	shed	lay	laid	laid
shut	shut	shut	make	made	made
slit	slit	slit	pay	paid	paid
spit	spit	spit	say	said	said
split	split	split	sell	sold	sold
spread	spread	spread	tell	told	told
sweat	sweat	sweat	shine	shone	shone
thrust	thrust	thrust	shoe	shod*	shod*
wed	wed	wed	sit	sat	sat
wet	wet	wet	slide	slid	slid
			win	won	won
hew	hewed	hewn			
mow	mowed	mown	cling	clung	clung
sew	sewed	sewn	dig	dug	dug
shear	sheared	shorn*	fling	flung	flung
sow	sowed	sown	hang	hung	hung
			sling	slung	slung
bear	bore	born	slink	slunk	slunk
swear	swore	sworn	spin	spun	spun
tear	tore	torn	stick	stuck	stuck
			sting	stung	stung
blow	blew	blown	strike	struck	struck
draw	drew	drawn	string	strung	strung
fly	flew	flown	swing	swung	swung
grow	grew	grown	wring	wrung	wrung
know	knew	known			
throw	threw	thrown	stand	stood	stood
slay	slew*	slain*	understand	understood	understood

* Regular *(-ed)* form also commonly used.
† Pronounced /red/

Appendix II: Ditransitive verbs

Example list of verbs that may take both a direct object and an indirect object

advance	fold	prepare
allow	forbid	promise
ask	forge	read
assign	forgive	recite
award	forward	refuse
bake	fry	reimburse
begrudge	get	remit
bet	give	rent
boil	grant	reserve
brew	grill	roll
bring	grind	save
build	guarantee	scramble
buy	hand	sculpt
call	hum	secure
carve	knit	sell
catch	lease	send
clean	leave	sew
cook	lend	show
crochet	light	sing
deal	lose	spare
deny	mail	spin
design	make	steal
develop	mix	stitch
do	mold	take
draw	offer	teach
earn	order	tell
embroider	owe	throw
ensure	paint	toss
envy	pass	weave
excuse	pay	whistle
fetch	play	win
fix	pluck	wish
flash	pour	write

Either of the objects (the direct or the indirect) of a ditransitive verb can be used as the subject of the sentence in a passive voice.

Appendix III: Transitive complex verbs

Example list of transitive verbs whose objects may take an object complement

appoint	get	prefer
baptize	have	presume
believe	hold	proclaim
call	imagine	pronounce
catch	keep	rate
christen	lead	report
consider	leave	see
crown	like	send
declare	make	smell
deem	name	spot
discover	need	think
drive	notice	turn
elect	observe	vote
find	overhear	want

Some transitive complex verbs can be followed by a direct object and an infinitival clause without *to*.

Example list of transitive complex verbs that can be followed by an infinitival clause without *to*

feel	help	overhear
have	let	see
hear	make	sense
	notice	watch

Some transitive complex verbs can take a locative complement. Locative complements are adverbials (often prepositional phrases) written directly after the direct object of a transitive complex verb, defining the time or place of the object in relation to the verb. (For example, in *Take me to the store*, the prepositional phrase *to the store* is a locative complement.)

Example list of transitive complex verbs that may take a locative complement

bring	lead	set
drive	place	show
get	put	stand
lay	send	take

Appendix IV: Ergative verbs

Example list of common ergative verbs

accelerate	deploy	hang	rattle
acculturate	derail	harden	reboot
activate	detonate	harmonize	recycle
align	dilate	hasten	redden
attach	dim	heal	regrow
awaken	distill	honk	rejuvenate
back up	dock	hurt	reload
bake	download	hush	relocate
bend	drag	ignite	rest
blacken	drain	improve	reverse
bleed	drill	increase	revive
blow up	drive	inflame	rewind
boast	drop	inflate	ripen
boil	drown	jam	roast
bounce	dry	land	rock
break	duplicate	launch	roll
brighten	empty	lean	rotate
bruise	end	lengthen	run
burn	entwine	lighten	rupture
burst	erode	line up	rush
calm down	escalate	lock	sail
change	expand	loosen	scatter
cheer up	factor	lower	scramble
choke	fail	madden	scroll
close	fast forward	march	separate
collapse	fasten	melt	shake
combine	fatten	mend	shatter
compile	fill up	merge	shift
connect	fire	mix	shine
cook	flash	moisten	shorten
count	flatten	move	shrink
crack	flip	open	shut
crash	float	overcook	simplify
crumble	flood	overwork	sink
crumple	flush	park	skip
dampen	fly	pass	slam
darken	fold	play	slide
deactivate	fracture	please	slow
deaden	freeze	plunge	smash
decelerate	fry	pop	soak
decrease	gather	pull over	soften
deepen	graduate	quicken	spill
deflate	grieve	quieten	spin
deform	grow	radiate	splash
dent	halt	raise	splatter

splinter	stretch	threaten	unfasten
split	suspend	tighten	unfurl
start	sway	tire	unlock
starve	sweep	toast	unravel
steer	sweeten	toughen	unwind
stick	swing	train	upload
stiffen	tame	transfer	wave
stop	tangle	transform	weaken
straighten	tear	tuck	widen
strangle	thaw	turn	wind
strengthen	thicken	twist	worsen

Appendix V: Phrasal prepositional verbs

Example list of common phrasal prepositional verbs

add up to	come down with	live up to
break out of	come up with	look down on
brush up on	cut down on	look forward to
carry on about	do away with	look up to
carry on with	fall back on	make up for
catch up on	fall behind in/on	put up with
catch up with	feel up to	run out of
check up on	hold on to	stand up for
close in on	keep up with	take out on
		watch out for

Phrasal prepositional verbs are always transitive and inseparable. See also Appendix VIII: Inseparable transitive phrasal verbs

Appendix VI: Intransitive phrasal verbs

Example list of common intransitive phrasal verbs

back down	drop out	look out
blow up	eat out	make up
branch out	end up	move in
break down	fall behind	move out
break in	find out	nod off
break up	get along	pass on / away
calm down	get away	pass out
carry on	get back	show off
catch up	get up	show up
check in	give in	shut up
check out	give up	stand out
cheer up	go back	stand up
come about	go on	take off
come by	grow up	throw up
come to	hang up	turn around
dress up	hold on	wake up
drop in	lie down	work out

Appendix VII: Separable transitive phrasal verbs

Example list of common separable transitive phrasal verbs

back up	hand in	stand up
break up	hand out	take back
bring about	hand over	take in
call off	keep up	take off
check out	lay off	take over
chop up	let down	talk over
clean out	look up	tell off
count in / out	make up	think through
do over	mix up	tire out
eat up	pay back	try on
figure out	point out	turn on
find out	put away	use up
fix up	rule out	wake up
give back	set up	wind up
give out	show off	write down

Appendix VIII: Inseparable transitive phrasal verbs

Example list of common non-separable transitive phrasal verbs

bear with	get on	look into
break into	get through	pay for
call for	go for	pick on
care for	go into	run into
check on	go through	see to
come across	hang out	stick to
come by	jump to	take after
count on	look after	tell on
count out	look for	touch on

Answer key

Chapter 1 – Parts of Speech

Quiz 1: Nouns
baby is a countable (singular), concrete, common noun
pigs is a countable (plural), concrete, common noun
dirt is an uncountable, concrete, common noun
Sue is a countable (singular), concrete, proper noun
brother's is a countable (singular), concrete, common, possessive noun
proposal is a countable (singular), abstract, common noun.

Quiz 2: Pronouns
We is a subjective personal pronoun, which refers to the writer and others in the writer's group
this is a demonstrative pronoun referring to a known thing that is close in time or importance to the writer and reader
himself is a reflexive pronoun referring to Stuart
me is an objective personal pronoun replacing the writer
somebody is an indefinite pronoun referring to an unknown person
him is an objective personal pronoun replacing Mike
I is a subjective personal pronoun referring to the writer
everyone is an indefinite pronoun referring to all members of a group
one another is a reciprocal pronoun referring to everyone, acting upon everyone
What is an interrogative pronoun referring to the unknown name of the man
who is a relative pronoun referring to the man in the main clause
I is a subjective personal pronoun referring to the writer
mine is a possessive personal pronoun referring to a possession of the writer
you is a subjective personal pronoun referring to the reader
me is an objective personal pronoun referring to the writer
yours is a possessive personal pronoun referring to a possession of the reader

Quiz 3: Adjectives
a is a limiting adjective modifying the noun *man*
handsome is an attributive descriptive adjective modifying the noun *man*
middle-aged is an attributive compound participial descriptive adjective modifying the noun *man*
the is a limiting adjective modifying the noun *shore*
the is a limiting adjective modifying the noun *morning*
his is a limiting adjective modifying the noun *house*
the is a limiting adjective modifying the noun *city*
his is a limiting adjective modifying the noun *wife*
their is a limiting adjective modifying the noun *children*
three is a limiting adjective modifying the noun *children*
shocked is a predicative participial descriptive adjective modifying the pronoun *they*
a is a limiting adjective modifying the noun *frown*
a is a limiting adjective modifying the noun *tone*
no-nonsense is an attributive compound descriptive adjective modifying the noun *tone*
oldest is an attributive superlative descriptive adjective modifying the noun *child*
bad is an attributive postmodifying descriptive adjective modifying the pronoun *something*
terrible is a predicative descriptive adjective modifying the pronoun *you*

Quiz 4: Adverbs
carelessly is an adverb of manner modifying the verb *drives*
Unfortunately is an adverb of manner modifying the entire sentence *we do not accept credit cards*
always is an adverb of time (frequency) modifying the verb phrase *get up early*
early is an adverb of time (when) modifying the phrasal verb *get up*
very is an adverb of degree modifying the adjective *nice*
there is an adverb of place modifying the verb *going*
today is an adverb of time (when) modifying the verb *going*
to be a doctor is an adverbial phrase of purpose modifying the verb *studying*
Frankly is an adverb of manner modifying the clause *I think it's ridiculous*

Quiz 5: Verbs
stretches is a main dynamic intransitive verb (simple present form)
stretches is a main dynamic transitive verb (simple present form)
ran into is a main dynamic transitive irregular phrasal verb (simple past form)
will be flying is a main dynamic intransitive verb (future continuous form, with **will** and **be** as auxiliary verbs)
Are is a main stative intransitive irregular verb (simple present form, interrogative mood)

Quiz 6: Conjunctions
and is a coordinating conjunction connecting the verb *stumbled* to the phrasal verb *fell down*
because is a subordinating conjunction connecting the independent clause *He stumbled and fell down* to the dependent clause *he was drunk*
whether ... or is a correlative conjunction pair connecting the verb phrase *to stay in this city* and the verb phrase *move to Denver*

Quiz 7: Prepositions
in is a preposition of place; it is the head of the adverbial prepositional phrase of place *in Paris*, modifying the verb *born*
on is a preposition of time; it is the head of the adverbial prepositional phrase of time *on October 26th*, modifying the verb *born*
over is a preposition of direction/movement; it is the head of the adverbial prepositional phrase of direction *over the rough surface*, modifying the verb *ran*
with is a preposition of possession; it is the head of the adjectival prepositional phrase **with** *a green roof*, modifying the noun phrase *that building*
at is a preposition of place; it is the head of the adverbial prepositional phrase of place *at the next intersection*, modifying the verb *turn*
of is a preposition of possession; it is the head of the

adjectival prepositional phrase *of England*, modifying the noun phrase *the Queen*
for is a preposition of purpose; it is the head of the adverbial prepositional phrase of purpose *for a haircut*, modifying the verb *go*
in is a preposition of manner; it is the head of the adverbial prepositional phrase of manner *in a loud voice*, modifying the verb *gave*

Chapter 2 – Parts of a Sentence
Quiz 1: Mandatory sentence elements
The subjects are highlighted in bold. The categorization of the underlined section is given in parentheses.

1) **He** told me <u>he would come.</u> (clause)
2) <u>Arriving home</u>, **he** found out he had lost his keys. (phrase)
3) **He** told me he would come <u>by 7 p.m.</u> (phrase)
4) **My closest friend** will get married soon after graduation. (phrase)
5) <u>Although he was exhausted,</u> **he** managed to finish the assignment. (clause)
6) **Eating in restaurants** is very expensive these days. (phrase)
7) **He** came home directly <u>after school.</u> (phrase)
8) **He** came home directly <u>after he finished school.</u> (clause)
9) **He** wants <u>to come to the party.</u> (phrase)
10) **I** have been studying for the test <u>since last week.</u> (phrase)
11) **I** have been studying for the test <u>since I left my job.</u> (clause)
12) Do **you** know her <u>pretty well</u>? (phrase)
13) **I** do not know <u>how I will get there.</u> (clause)
14) <u>Injured in the war</u>, **he** could never work again. (phrase)

Quiz 2: Optional sentence elements
1) My sweater is <u>different from yours.</u> (subject complement)
2) I <u>found my jacket.</u> (predicate)
3) They looked <u>tired.</u> (subject complement)
4) His peers <u>acknowledge his efforts.</u> (predicate)
5) <u>The man at the corner</u> sells popcorn. (subject)
6) What does <u>she</u> like to eat? (subject)
7) We saw <u>the building we are going to move into.</u> (direct object)
8) Would you mind meeting him <u>before noon</u>? (adverbial)
9) He drove <u>carefully.</u> (adverbial)
10) We painted the room <u>purple.</u> (object complement)
11) He told <u>me</u> to mind my own business. (indirect object)
12) They will go <u>to the port.</u> (adverbial)
13) They gave <u>the judge</u> all the documents. (indirect object)

Quiz 3: Simple sentence structure
A)
1- I have given this exercise to hundreds of people.
a. I: subject
b. have given this exercise to hundreds of people: predicate
c. have given: main verb (dynamic; transitive; verb phrase; head of the predicate)
can be further broken down as: *have*: auxiliary verb; *given*: main verb in past participle form
d. this exercise: direct object (noun phrase)
e. to hundreds of people: indirect object (introduced by preposition *to*)

2- He ate the pizza in a hurry.
a. He: subject
b. ate the pizza in a hurry: predicate
c. ate: main verb (dynamic; transitive; head of the predicate)
d. the pizza: direct object (noun phrase)
e. in a hurry: adverbial of manner

B)

1.) The children seem awfully quiet tonight.			
Subject	Verb	Subject Complement	Adverbial
The children	seem	awfully quiet	tonight
2.) Could you lend me that magazine when you're done?				
Subject	Verb	Direct Object	Indirect Object	Adverbial
you	could lend	that magazine	me	when you're done
3.) I find the hamburgers at this restaurant overcooked most of the time.				
Sub.	V.	Direct Object	Object Complement	Adverbial
I	find	the hamburgers at this restaurant	overcooked	most of the time
4.) Jim's tools don't work on 220-volt power sources.			
Subject	Verb	Adverbial	
Jim's tools	don't work	on 220-volt power sources	

Quiz 4: Variations on subject and object
A-
1) Cleaning the house is time-consuming. <u>It is time-consuming cleaning (or to clean) the house.</u>
2) Andy should have won the race. <u>It is Andy who should have won the race.</u> or <u>The one (or person) who (or that) should have won the race is Andy.</u>
3) To sleep for a full eight hours seems impossible. <u>It seems impossible to sleep for a full eight hours.</u>
4) What I wanted to show you was the new shopping centre. <u>It was the new shopping centre that I wanted to show you.</u> or <u>The new shopping centre was what I wanted to show you.</u>

B-
1) We always find being here so peaceful. <u>We always find it so peaceful being (or to be) here.</u>
2) The summers here make staying outdoors imperative. <u>The summers here make it imperative to stay outdoors.</u>

C-
1) I think <u>there</u> is a thunderstorm coming. (introducing a subject)
2) <u>It</u> 's late. (talking about time)
3) <u>There</u> are two certainties in life: death and taxes. (emphasizing existence)
4) <u>It</u> seems a little dark. (describing surroundings)

Quiz 5: Sentence types
1) What a wonderful sight! *Exclamatory*
2) They haven't arrived yet. *Declarative negative*
3) Did you ever tell him about the situation? *Interrogative – yes/no question*

4) How long did you say it was? *Interrogative – wh-question*
5) I am a fool, aren't I? *Interrogative – tag question*
6) Add two eggs and mix well. *Imperative*
7) Are you coming with us or taking the bus? *Interrogative – alternative question*
8) You will get that promotion. *Declarative affirmative*
9) Don't you like it? *Interrogative negative*
10) That's it. *Declarative affirmative*

Chapter 3 - Nouns
Quiz 1: Functions of a noun in a sentence
1) We named the baby <u>Alec</u> after his grandfather.
Alec is functioning as the object complement of the direct object *the baby*
2) When you buy something from a shop, you are making a <u>contract.</u>
contract is part of the noun phrase *a contract*, which is functioning as the direct object of the verb phrase *are making*
3) Janice and Boris are antique <u>dealers</u>.
dealers is the head of the noun phrase *antique dealers*, which is the subject complement
4) The <u>tower</u> was built in 1989.
tower is the head of the noun phase *the tower*, which is functioning as the subject
5) Lucerne, a magnificent <u>city</u>, is located on Lake Lucerne.
city is the head of the noun phrase *a magnificent city*, which is functioning as an appositive

Quiz 2: Commonality and concreteness
1) Hello! This is <u>Philip</u>, the estate <u>agent</u>.
Philip: proper and concrete; **agent**: common and concrete
2) The <u>hairdryer</u> I bought yesterday was faulty.
hairdryer: common and concrete
3) The <u>law</u> is on his side.
law: common and abstract
4) They are agents from the <u>National Revenue Service</u>.
National Revenue Service: proper and abstract
5) <u>Ainsley</u> had a <u>smile</u> on her face.
Ainsley: proper and concrete; **smile**: common and concrete

Quiz 3: Countability
1) His **understanding** of the **topic** is quite remarkable for his **age**.
understanding: uncountable; **topic**: countable, singular; **age**: countable, singular
2) What about **accommodation**? Do you know where to stay for the two **weeks**?
accommodation: uncountable; **weeks**: countable, plural
3) Are you willing to give him any **advice** on this **matter**?
advice: uncountable; **matter**: countable, singular
4) That's too much **mayonnaise** for my **taste**.
mayonnaise: uncountable; **taste**: uncountable

Quiz 4: Inflection and collective nouns
Come on and hear! Come on and hear! **Alexander's** *(genitive)* ragtime **band**! *(collective)*
Come on and hear! Come on and hear! It's the best **band** in the land!
They can play a bugle call like you never heard before
So natural that you want to go to war
I'm a Yankee doodle dandy,
Yankee doodle do or die.
A real live **nephew** *(masculine gender)* of my **Uncle** *(masculine gender)* Sam,
Born on the 4th of July.
I've got a Yankee doodle sweetheart,
She's my Yankee doodle joy.
Yankee doodle came to London,
Just to ride the **ponies** *(number)*.
I am a Yankee doodle **boy**. *(masculine gender)*

Chapter 4 – Pronouns
Quiz 1: Subjective and objective pronouns
The correct personal pronouns are in bold. The type of pronoun and the antecedent are in parentheses.
1) Did you talk to the Joneses? Would you like to invite **them** *(objective pronoun; the Joneses)* to the meeting?
2) The cartons of milk are on the counter, ready for you to put **them** *(objective pronoun; the cartons of milk)* away in the fridge.
3) Maria said **she** *(subjective pronoun; Maria)* would never be able to accept that Paul did not love **her** *(objective pronoun; Maria)*.
4) Caroline is here with the little puppy. Please tell **her** *(objective pronoun; Caroline)* to wash **it** *(objective pronoun; the little puppy)* with this shampoo for pets.
5) Harry has been away for 5 months. I am so looking forward to seeing **him** *(objective pronoun; Harry)* after such a long time.
6) "Farah, I've chosen to watch this movie. Would **you** *(subjective pronoun; Farah)* like to watch **it** *(objective pronoun; the movie)* with **me** *(objective pronoun; the speaker)*?"
7) **I** *(subjective pronoun; the speaker/writer who is named after the pronoun – cataphoric reference)*, (your name here), agree to the terms on this contract.

Quiz 2: Personal pronouns and their forms

Subjective	Objective	Possessive
I	me	mine
you	you	yours
he	him	his
she	her	hers
it	it	its
we	us	ours
you	you	yours
they	them	theirs

Quiz 3: Pronoun identification
1) <u>Something</u> is burning. Can <u>you</u> go check in the kitchen?
Something: indefinite pronoun in subjective case, functioning as subject of the sentence;
you: personal pronoun in subjective case functioning as subject of the sentence
2) Show <u>me</u> <u>those</u> over there, please.
me: personal pronoun in objective case functioning as indirect object of the main verb;
those: demonstrative pronoun in objective case functioning as direct object of the main verb
3) <u>They</u> wrote the letter, <u>which</u> described their situation.
they: personal pronoun in subjective case functioning as subject of the sentence;
which: relative pronoun in subjective case functioning as subject of the relative clause
4) <u>This</u> is the girl <u>that</u> I saw at the beach.
this: demonstrative pronoun in subjective case

functioning as subject of the sentence;
that: relative pronoun in objective case functioning as the direct object of the main verb in the relative clause
5) Praising oneself is not always recommended during a job interview.
oneself: reflexive pronoun in objective case functioning as direct object of the non-finite verb *praising*
6) Manuel and Parisa talk to each other every day.
each other: reciprocal pronoun in objective case functioning as object of the preposition *to*
7) What do you want to do during your holiday?
what: interrogative pronoun in objective case functioning as direct object of the main verb *do*
8) A friend of his lent us a tent for the camping trip.
his: personal pronoun in possessive case functioning as object of the preposition *of*

Quiz 4: Correct the errors
1) Every morning Nicholas shaved him before he went to work.
Mistake: *him* / Explanation: The sentence is not clear: *him* probably refers to Nicholas, and should then be changed into the reflexive pronoun *himself*. However, if *him* refers to another man, there should be a clear reference, an antecedent, which is not present in this sentence.
2) He doesn't know nothing.
Mistake: *nothing* / Explanation: English does not allow double negatives like other languages do. The correct pronoun is *anything*; or the verb should be in its positive form, *knows*
3) A friend of me is coming later.
Mistake: *me* / Explanation: The structure *noun + of ...* requires the possessive pronoun, in this case, *mine*
4) That boy which you can see over there is Marietta's son.
Mistake: *which* / Explanation: The relative pronouns *who* or *that* are used to refer to a person; *which* is used to refer to an object or thing
5) The two apple cakes we cooked were not good. None had enough apples.
Mistake: *none* / Explanation: The indefinite negative pronoun *none* is used to refer to groups of more than two people or things; *neither* is used for groups of two people or things

Chapter 5 – Adjectives
Quiz 1: Adjective forms
A. The possible adjective forms are given in italics.

	Adjective form
1) satisfaction	*(un)satisfactory* *(un/dis)satisfied/-ing*
2) humour	*humourous* *humourless*
3) degrade	*(non-)degradable* *(un)degraded/-ing*
4) religion	*(non-/ir)religious*
5) radiate	*radiant* *radiated/-ing*
6) envy	*envious* *(un)enviable*
7) waste	*wasteful* *wasted/-ing*
8) spirit	*spiritual* *(dis)spirited/-ing*
9) shine	*shiny* *shined/-ing*
10) hate	*hateful* *hated/-ing*

B. The parts of speech of the highlighted words are described after each sentence.

1) Susan plans to study **Italian** next year.
noun (object of the verb study*)*
2) That method is **wasteful**.
adjective (modifying the noun method *after the stative verb* is*)*
3) Dad just taught me a **magic** trick.
adjective (modifying the noun trick*)*
4) The **cowardly** lion makes me laugh.
adjective (modifying the noun lion*)*
5) That style should appeal to the **creative** among us.
noun (object of the verb appeal*; additional clue is the presence of* the *with no other noun)*

Quiz 2: Participial adjectives
The correct participial adjectives are given in bold.

1) That restaurant has **singing** waiters!
present participle form to indicate the do-er of the verb (the waiters); the waiters are the source of the singing
2) My grandmother always loved **baked** eggs.
past participle form to describe the condition of the eggs – the eggs are recipients of the verb bake*; grammatically, it is possible to say* My grandmother always loved baking eggs, *but in that case,* baking *is not acting as an adjective; it is acting as the object of the verb* loved.
3) Everyone likes the store manager; she is a **charming** woman.
present participle form to indicate the do-er of the verb; the store manager creates the feeling, she is the source – everyone likes her, they are **charmed**
4) The experience was difficult and **exhilarating**.
present participle form to describe the source of the feeling of exhilaration (The experience)
5) How can you mend a **broken** heart?
past participle form to indicate the condition of the noun (heart)

Quiz 3 – Limiting and descriptive adjectives
The adjectives are highlighted in bold. The limiting adjectives are also italicized.

There are ***many*** Egyptian obelisks in Rome – **tall**, **snakelike** spires of **red** sandstone, **mottled** with **strange** writings, which remind us of ***the*** pillars of flame which led ***the*** children of Israel through ***the*** desert away from ***the*** land of ***the*** Pharaohs; but more **wonderful** than these to look upon is ***this*** **gaunt**, **wedge-shaped** pyramid standing here in ***this*** Italian city, **unshattered** amid ***the*** ruins and wrecks of time, looking **older** than ***the*** Eternal City itself, like **terrible** impassiveness turned to stone. And so in ***the*** Middle Ages men supposed this to be ***the*** sepulchre of Remus, who was slain by ***his*** **own** brother at ***the*** founding of ***the*** city, so **ancient** and **mysterious** it appears; but we have now, perhaps unfortunately, more **accurate** information about it, and know that it is ***the*** tomb of ***one*** Caius Cestius, ***a*** Roman gentleman of **small** note, who died about 30 B.C.

Quiz 4: Descriptive adjectives: qualifying or classifying
The adjective type is given in italics after each highlighted adjective.

I had called upon my friend Sherlock Holmes upon the second morning after Christmas, with the intention of wishing him the compliments of the season. He was lounging upon the sofa in a **purple** *(classifying: colour)* **dressing** *(classifying: purpose)*-gown, a **pipe** *(classifying: purpose)*-rack within his reach upon the right, and a pile of **crumpled** *(qualifying: condition)* **morning** *(classifying: type)* papers, evidently newly **studied** *(qualifying: condition)*, near at hand. Beside the couch was a **wooden** *(classifying: material)* chair, and on the angle of the back hung a very **seedy** *(qualifying: opinion)* and **disreputable** *(qualifying: opinion)* **hard-felt** *(classifying: material)* hat, much the **worse** *(qualifying: condition/opinion)* for wear, and **cracked** *(qualifying: condition)* in several places. A lens and a forceps lying upon the seat of the chair suggested that the hat had been **suspended** *(qualifying: condition)* in this manner for the purpose of examination.

Quiz 5: Position of adjectives

	Attributive	Predicative
1) The archaeologists discovered a **gigantic** cave in the Colombian forest.	√	
2) His sense of humor is **ingenious**.		√
3) Matt feels **afraid** all the time.		√
4) They took a **three-hour** tour and were **exhausted** after that.	three-hour	exhausted
5) **Fewer** people showed up **this** year at the Annual Flower Festival.	fewer, this	
6) The presenter was quite **quick-witted**.		√
7) The alpha male of the pack exhibited the **typical** behaviour for that situation.	√	
8) The **key** theme of the story is delusion.	√	
9) Wherever you want to go will be **fine**.		√
10) The secretary **general** of the foundation has announced his retirement.	√	

Quiz 6: Categorization of adjectives
The adjectives are highlighted in bold. The limiting adjectives are also italicized.

There is *an* **old** fisherman, Santiago, in Cuba who has gone *eighty-four* days without *a* catch. He is **thin** and **gaunt** with **deep** wrinkles in *the* back of *his* neck,...and *his* hands had **deep-creased** scars from handling **heavy** fish on *the* cords. But none of these scars were **fresh**. They were as **old** as erosions in *a* **fishless** desert. **Santiago's** lack of success, though, does not destroy *his* spirit, and he has **cheerful** and **undefeated** eyes.

Participial adjectives: **deep-creased**; **undefeated**
Cardinal number: **eighty-four**
Adjectives that derive from a noun: **fishless**; **Santiago's**; **cheerful**
Adjective that has a prefix: **undefeated**
Adjectives that have a suffix: **fishless**; **cheerful**

Quiz 7: Order of adjectives
1) magnificent oval magenta plate (opinion + shape + colour)
2) vast windswept southern beach (size + condition + origin)
3) precious ancient wooden statue (opinion + age + material)
4) little Catholic prayer book (size + religion + purpose)
5) sun-bleached plastic garden chairs (condition + material + purpose/type)
6) typical foggy British weather (opinion + condition + origin)
7) delicious sizzling Korean BBQ (opinion + condition (or temperature) + origin)
8) well-dressed slender young woman (opinion + size + age)

Slender can also function as an opinion adjective. If considered an opinion adjective, the order of *well-dressed* and *slender* would be the writer's choice.

Quiz 8 – Adjective or adverb
1) I haven't seen any good films **lately**; and you? *(adverb modifying the entire clause* I haven't seen any good films*)*
2) The cheetah is one of the **fastest** animals in the world. *(adjective modifying the noun* animals*)*
3) The professor won't mark any **late** assignments. *(adjective modifying the noun* assignments*)*
4) Melanie hates it when people speak too **loud**. *(adverb (informal; formal use would be* loudly*) modifying the verb* speak*)*
5) He was so inebriated that he couldn't even mimic a **straight** walk. *(adjective modifying the noun* walk *– presence of article* a *is a clue)*
6) She was terrified of diving into the **deep** blue sea without her lifejacket. *(adjective modifying the noun* sea*; deep as an adverb modifying a colour adjective is possible, but in the common phrase* deep blue sea, *it is the sea that is deep, not the colour blue)*
7) The teacher lowered my mark because I handed in my assignment **late**. *(adverb modifying the phrasal verb* handed in*)*
8) Natalie has never tried so **hard** to achieve a goal. *(adverb modifying the verb* tried*)*
9) Patients are released when they feel **well** enough to walk by themselves. *(adjective completing the pronoun* they *through the stative verb* feel*)*
10) If you need to make an international call, please do not call **direct**. *(adverb modifying the verb* call*)*

Chapter 6 – Determiners
Quiz 1: Order of determiners
1) Sharon really enjoys visiting with *those two* –or- *all those* old friends.
2) I can't believe *what a* huge mess they made.
3) *All three* Benelux countries have high standards of living: Belgium, the Netherlands and Luxembourg.
4) This year, the kids forgot *both their parents'* birthdays. (makes the assumption of two parents)
5) You can take *whatever* –or- *any* sample you like.

355

Quiz 2: Functional classifications of determiners
1) What are the major functional classifications of determiners? *Magnitude and definiteness*
2) What are the major sub-classifications of each major class?
Magnitude: entirety; fraction or multiple; counters; subjective quantity; comparative quantity
Definiteness: definite; indefinite
3) What types of determiners can co-occur with determiners of definiteness?
nouns in possessive form; and ordinals
4) What types of determiners can co-occur with determiners of magnitude?
1) *cardinal numbers*
2)

Quiz 3 – Subject / verb agreement with quantifiers
1) *Many* of my friends **were** present at the party last night.
2) *All* of the happiness in the world **is** what I wish for you.
3) *Both* of the girls **want** to leave earlier.
4) *Each* of the members **is** delayed in their payments.
5) *Two* cups of flour **are** more than enough.

Quiz 4 –A versus AN
Complete the following phrases either with **a** *or* **an***:*
1) *a* game   8) *a* hair
2) *an* idol   9) *a* horrible job
3) *a* good apple   10) *an* eggplant
4) *a* dentist   11) *an* heir to the throne
5) *a* used plate   12) *an* iceberg
6) *an* aunt   13) *an* intelligent kid
7) *an* apricot   14) *an* incredible woman

Quiz 5: Correct the sentences (articles)
1) I studied ø history at college. (general idea; academic subject)
2) I come from a small town in **the** United States. (proper place name including a plural)
3) **The** telephone was invented by Alexander Bell. (general idea of telephones)
4) That's **a** good place to meet your friends. (a known member of a larger group)
5) ø Love is in the air. (uncountable; general concept)
6) **The** British Isles are worth visiting in summer. (proper place name including a plural)
7) Gabito was **a** famous tango dancer. (unmodified subject complement; used with professions or jobs)
8) Last night was **the** most amazing night I have ever had in my life. (superlative)
9) Did you see **the** Tower of London when you visited England? (place name with "of")
10) Did you notice **the** girl that was standing outside the pub was crying? (defined by a relative clause)

Quiz 6: Fill in the blanks (articles)
Paragraph A
1) ø (general idea of the plural noun *deserts*; **The** is also possible here; general idea)
2) **the** (only one exists; unique; the *globe* in this reference is the earth)
3) **the** (named regions; the single article applies to both *Northern* and *Southern*)
4) **the** (proper place name containing the preposition *of*)
5) **the** (proper place name containing the preposition *of*)
6) **The** (only one exists; unique)
7) **the** (singular, countable noun *region* is defined by the descriptive adjective *equatorial*)
8) **the** (*sunlight* defined by the phrase *most intense*, containing the superlative *most*)
9) **the** (easy to assume which air is meant: the air in deserts)
10) **the** (unique to the environment: the atmosphere of the earth)

Paragraph B
1) ø (general concept of children, not any specific group of children)
2) ø (or **the**) (general concept of parents, not a specific group of parents (although it is possible to assume that these are the parents of the children just referred to; this is the writer's choice, and would generally only work well if the reader could easily understand which group of parents is under discussion))
3) ø (or **the**) (same as 2) above)
4) **the** (or **a**) (extreme descriptive adjective *right* suggests that the noun *path* is unique – there can only be one path that is right (if the sense is that there is more than one possible right path, then the indefinite article is possible))
5) **The** (*obligations* defined by the prepositional phrase *of parents*)
6) ø (general idea of the uncountable *food*, not any specific food)
7) ø (or **the**) (general idea of knowledge of worldly matters, not specific knowledge (or, the sense that the prepositional phrase *of worldly matters* is sufficiently descriptive to make the knowledge specific))
8) ø (plural noun *matters* not sufficiently defined by the descriptive adjective *worldly* to make it a unique set of matters)
9) ø (or **the**) (same as 2) above)
10) **the** (or ø) (same as 4) above, except that the noun is plural, so the indefinite choice requires zero article rather than the indefinite article)
11) **the** (*acquisition* defined by the prepositional phrase *of wealth*)
12) ø (uncountable noun *wealth* as a general concept, not any particular wealth)
13) **the** (applies to both *be-all* and *end-all*, idiomatic noun phrases which are defined by the prepositional phrase *of life*)
14) ø (*life* as a general, uncountable concept, not any particular life)

Chapter 7 – Adverbs
Quiz 1: Adverbs modifying different parts of speech
The adverbs are highlighted in bold. The words, phrases or clauses that they are modifying are underlined. The part of speech or part of a sentence that is modified is given in italics after the sentence.

1) The phone was **temporarily** disconnected. *(adjective)*
2) Would you like to meet **early**? *(verb in infinitive form, which is acting as the object of the verb* like*)*
3) They haven't had supper **yet**. *(main clause)*
4) I am **extremely** happy. *(adjective)*
5) They **hardly** visit their friends. *(verb)*
6) **Sometimes**, I do **not** understand why David is **so** pessimistic. *(sometimes is modifying the entire*

sentence (both clauses); not *is modifying* understand *(verb);* so *is modifying* pessimistic *(adjective))*

Quiz 2: Adverbs or adjectives
1) *adjective modifying the noun* cut
2) *adverb modifying the verb* turned
3) *adjective modifying the noun* descent
4) *adjective modifying the noun* man
5) *adjective modifying the noun* show
6) *adverb modifying the verb phrase* can watch
7) *adverb modifying the verb phrase* have been waiting
8) *adverb modifying the verb phrase* will cut

Quiz 3 - Adverb or preposition
1) You can see the moon <u>above</u> the trees. *(preposition)*
2) The toddler fell <u>off</u> the bed. *(preposition)*
3) Do you think he wants to go <u>out</u>? *(adverb)*
4) Please sit <u>down</u>. *(adverb)*
5) We couldn't get <u>through</u> the gate. *(preposition)*
6) Can I look <u>inside</u>? *(adverb)*
7) They slept all <u>through</u> the night. *(preposition)*
8) The book is suitable for children aged eight and <u>above</u>. *(adverb)*

Quiz 4: Placement of adverbs of manner
1) Interestingly, she didn't find the beach amusing.
2) Billy cleared the table fast.
3) Nick reluctantly closed the book and went to sleep.
or: Nick closed the book reluctantly and went to sleep.
4) The stranger lashed out in a crazy way.

Quiz 5: Adverbials of place
The adverbials are highlighted in bold. The form of the adverbial is given in parentheses.
1) Let's take a vacation **abroad**. *(adverb)*
2) I don't know why he can't just sleep **here** *(adverb)* instead of going **to a hotel**. *(adverbial prepositional phrase)*
3) We were **in the pool** *(adverbial prepositional phrase)* when the storm began.
4) Please deposit the cheque **wherever he asked you to do so**. *(adverbial clause)*

Quiz 6: Adverbs of time
The adverbs and adverbials are highlighted in bold; the types of adverbials are given in parentheses.

1) Yuki has not come back **since the accident happened**. *(prepositional phrase as adverbial of relative time)*
2) I have to return that book to the library **soon**. *(adverb of time-when)*
3) **Last year**, Melissa had twin baby girls. *(noun phrase as adverbial of time-when)*
4) **Every time I call**, the receptionist tells me he is busy. *(adverbial phrase as adverbial of frequency)*
5) The web site is **temporarily** offline for repairs. *(adverb of time-duration)*
6) Ulysses **habitually** visits his home town. *(adverb of frequency)*
7) He promised he'd look for her **till the end of time**. *(prepositional phrase as adverbial of relative time)*

Quiz 7: Adverb identification
The adverbs and adverbials are highlighted in bold. Their types are given in parentheses.

1) I **totally** agree with you. *(degree)*
2) I'd like to express my gratitude to all my colleagues **for their support**. *(purpose)*
3) The new house was **slightly** larger than the old one. *(quantity)*
4) We did it **for fun**. *(purpose)*
5) **Yes**, I will take care of the kitten. Do not worry. *(assertion)*

Chapter 8 – Comparatives
Quiz 1: Gradability of adjectives

	Gradable	Non-gradable
1) impossible		√
2) elated	√	
3) little	√	
4) wee		√
5) homesick	√	
6) ninety		√
7) Japanese	generally not gradable, but possible	√
8) dependent	√	
9) exasperating	√	
10) some		√

Quiz 2: Gradability of adverbs

	Gradable	Non-gradable
1) never		√
2) extremely		√
3) gracefully	√	
4) very		√
5) ably	√	
6) always		√
7) softly	√	
8) there		√
9) more		√
10) fast	√	

Quiz 3: Correct the mistake
1) Which is ~~more~~ safer, a car or a motorcycle?
*the comparative form of **safe** is simply **safer**; combining **more** or **most** with an –er/–est form is unnecessary and incorrect*
2) Reading comics in class is ~~funner~~ **more fun** than reading grammar texts.
*the comparative form of **fun** is **more fun***
3) I think this room is the least light~~est~~ of all the rooms in this house.
*for comparative and superlative adjectives indicating lower degrees of comparison, **less** and **least** are the only possibilities; –er and –est are only for higher degrees of comparison*
4) This bag is ~~cuter~~ **cuter**; you should buy it.
adjective ending in –e adds only –r (not –er) for comparative form
5) Morley runs ~~slowwer~~ **slower** than he used to.
when the final consonant is –w, it should not be doubled when adding –er
6) Kitty has become ~~fater~~ **fatter** in the last two months.
adjective ending in consonant-vowel-consonant doubles the final consonant when adding –er

Quiz 4 – Comparative constructions

1) Professor Smith's assistant is **as knowledgeable as** Professor Smith.
2) This is **the saddest** I've ever felt. OR
I feel **sadder** than I have ever felt. OR
I have never felt **sadder**.
3) Seinfeld is **the most sidesplitting** comedy I've ever seen.
4) Jonathan's explanation was **clearer** than Faith's explanation. OR
Faith's explanation was **less clear** than Jonathan's explanation.
5) Meaghan was **the most stunning** woman at the gala. OR
Meaghan was **more stunning** than Annabelle and Diane.

Quiz 5: Intensifying adverbs
The correct sentences are listed. The reasons are given in italics.

1)   b) The elderly lady walks much more energetically than her husband.
much *emphasizes the comparative adverb* more energetically, *which compares the way the lady walks to the way her husband walks;* very *is not used on it own as an intensifier for comparative or superlative forms*
2)   b) This is nearly the fastest bike I've ever ridden.
nearly *is an adverb which emphasizes the superlative adjective* the fastest; near *is not an intensifying adverb*
3)   a) He is by far the most caring nurse I've worked with.
the adverbial phrase by far *is used to emphasize superlative adjectives; the adverb* far *emphasizes comparative adjectives*

Chapter 9 - Prepositions
Quiz 1: Simple and complex prepositions
The prepositions are highlighted in bold; the type is given in italics.

1) What shall we do **in regard to** *(complex)* planning a short vacation this summer?
2) They succeeded, **notwithstanding** *(simple)* their inexperience.
3) They were all invited **except** *(simple)* me.
4) Let's make the changes **along** *(simple)* the lines he suggested.
5) They found the car **along with** *(complex)* the burned documents.

Quiz 2: Prepositional phrases
The prepositional phrases are highlighted in bold. Each preposition's object's type is given in italics.

1) This discovery is a major step forward **in gene therapy**. *(noun phrase)*
2) There is a way to benefit **from your efforts** *(noun phrase)* **without ruining your reputation**. *(gerund (verb) phrase)*
3) More money should be spent **on culture**. *(noun)*
4) We will not be here **in August**. *(noun)*
5) I'd rather you didn't tell anyone **about it**. *(pronoun)*

Quiz 3: Adjectival or adverbial prepositional phrase
The prepositional phrases are highlighted in bold. Their types are given in italics.

1) There isn't a TV **in the room**. *(adverbial of place)*
2) The buildings **in our town** are pretty. *(adjectival – modifying* the buildings*)*
3) Try to introduce the new topic **with a question**. *(adverbial of manner)*
4) I met a friend **of Mark's** *(adjectival – modifying* friend*)* **at a party** *(adverbial of place)* **last year**. *(adverbial of time)*
5) The girl **in black** *(adjectival – modifying* the girl*)* should be the winner, don't you think?

Quiz 4: Correct the mistakes
The correct prepositions are given in bold; the explanations are in italics.

1) Manuel is waiting for you ~~in~~ **at** the bus stop. *(specific location)*
2) Sorry, but I thought it was ~~at~~ **on** the menu. *(surface)*
3) When will he arrive ~~to~~ **at** the office? *(specific, known location;* arrive *is generally followed by* at *when referring to small places;* in *is used with big places, generally cities or countries, as in:* arrive **in** England*)*
4) He is already ~~in~~ **on** the bus. *(bus, train and plane use* on*)*
5) You may need to change your habits and start submitting your tasks ~~in~~ **on** time. *(punctually)*
6) We do not always take vacation ~~for~~ **in** summer. *(period of time)*
7) Do you think we could meet ~~in~~ **at** the corner of Oxen Road and Maxwell Drive? *(specific location;* **on** *is also possible)*
8) I was born ~~in~~ **on** June 5th, 1997. *(date)*

Chapter 10 - Conjunctions
Quiz 1: Identifying conjunctions
The part of speech and the explanation are given in italics.

1) Straighten up <u>or</u> you'll be sorry. *conjunction (specifically, a coordinating conjunction of choice) – connecting the (elided, imperative mood) clause* Straighten up *to the clause* you'll be sorry
2) <u>While</u> he was traveling, Stan finished the book. *conjunction (specifically, a subordinating conjunction of time) – introducing the subordinate clause* while he was traveling *and defining its relationship to the main clause* Stan finished the book
3) <u>During</u> his vacation, Stan finished the book. *not a conjunction – preposition followed by the noun phrase (object of the preposition)* his vacation
4) You're just <u>as</u> cute <u>as</u> a button! *not conjunctions (technically adverbs) – connecting an adjective (*cute*) and a noun phrase (*a button*)*
5) Ted always opens the windows <u>the minute</u> he arrives. *conjunction (specifically, a subordinating conjunction of time) – introducing the subordinate clause* the minute he arrives *and defining its relationship to the main clause* Ted always opens the window
6) I've never seen them <u>before</u>. *not a conjunction – adverb of time modifying the verb* seen
7) Edith is talkative, <u>whereas</u> her sister is not. *conjunction (specifically, a subordinating conjunction of contrast) – introducing the subordinate clause* whereas her sister is not *and defining its relationship to the main clause* Edith is talkative

8) Don't start until I tell you. *conjunction (specifically, a subordinating conjunction of time) – introducing the subordinate clause* until I tell you *and defining its relationship to the main (elided, imperative mood) clause* Don't start
9) Can you stay until the end? *not a conjunction – preposition of time followed by the noun phrase (object of the preposition)* the end
10) We have permission, so it's okay. *conjunction (specifically, a subordinating conjunction of reason) – introducing the subordinate clause* so it's okay *and defining its relationship to the main clause* We have permission

Quiz 2: Conjunction types
The conjunction types and the sentence parts they connect are given in parentheses.

1) Seeing that we're already here, let's take a look. (subordinating; connecting the subordinate/dependent clause *seeing that we're already here* to the independent clause *let's take a look*)
2) Regina looked up and down and all around. (coordinating; connecting the adverbials *up*, *down* and *all around*)
3) The berries are easy to reach, but they're surrounded by thorns. (coordinating; connecting the independent clauses *The berries are easy to reach* and *they're surrounded by thorns*)
4) Let's just say that the experience left us older but wiser. (coordinating; connecting the adjectives *older* and *wiser*)
5) Both the boater and her dog fell asleep on the deck. (correlative; connecting the noun phrases *the boater* and *her dog*, which comprise the subject of the sentence)

Quiz 3: Punctuation
The possible conjunctions and appropriate punctuation are given in bold.

1) **Either** that was a passing train **or** we just had an earthquake.
2) Please turn down the music **before** I complain to the management. OR
Please turn down the music **lest** I complain to the management.
3) **Unless** you turn down the music, I will complain to the management.
4) I will complain to the management **unless** you turn down the music.
5) Please turn down the music **or** I will complain to the management. OR
Please turn down the music**;** I will complain to the management. OR
Please turn down the music**.** I will complain to the management.
6) It's our anniversary **and** Tracey bought us a gift. OR
It's our anniversary**, so** Tracey bought us a gift. OR
It's our anniversary**;** Tracey bought us a gift. OR
It's our anniversary**.** Tracey bought us a gift.
7) Tracey**, since** it's our anniversary**,** bought us a gift. OR
Tracey**, because** it's our anniversary**,** bought us a gift. OR
Tracey**, as** it's our anniversary**,** bought us a gift.
8) Tracey bought us a gift **because** it's our anniversary. OR
Tracey bought us a gift **since** it's our anniversary. OR
Tracey bought us a gift**, as** it's our anniversary.
9) **Since** it's our anniversary, Tracey bought us a gift. OR
Because it's our anniversary, Tracey bought us a gift. OR
As it's our anniversary, Tracey bought us a gift.
10) Traditionalists don't like that style**, nor** do modernists. OR
Traditionalist don't like that style **nor** do modernists.

Chapter 11 - Verbs

Quiz 1: Verb forms
1) *Auxiliary verbs are underlined.*
<u>Do</u> you **study** French at school?
He <u>must</u> **take** what you're giving him.
The captain <u>will</u> never **forget** this day.
2) *Main verbs are underlined.*
I like <u>to go</u> to new places as often as I can.
<u>To take</u> a baby swimming is a great experience.
Her new teammates hope <u>to learn</u> a lot from her.
3) *Auxiliary verbs are underlined.*
Merlin <u>is</u> **going** away for the summer.
<u>Have</u> you ever **studied** a second language?
I'<u>d</u> **forgotten** how big the room was. *(contracted form of* had*)*
4) *Part of the sentence is given in parentheses.*
Taking your dog for a walk is a great way to exercise. *(subject)*
John's greatest attribute is **being** calm in chaotic situations. *Subject complement)*
The kids love **learning** about dinosaurs. *(direct object)*
5) *What verb has three inflections in the simple present tense?* **to be**
6) *What person/number combination has a visible conjugation in the simple present tense?* **third person singular**

Quiz 2: Main and auxiliary verbs
The corrections to the main verbs are given in bold. Associated auxiliary verbs are in italics. Explanations are in parentheses.

1) *Did* you ~~drove~~ **drive** to school today? *(the main verb used with* do *in an interrogative structure must be in base form; the auxiliary verb is the only one that is inflected for tense and number)*
2) *Have* you ~~saw~~ **seen** the movie 'Reds'? *(the main verb used with* have *in a perfective structure must be in past participle form)*
3) They *were* ~~have~~ **having** dinner last night when the lights went off. *(the main verb used with the auxiliary* be *in a progressive structure must be in present participle form, not base form)*
4) *Does* your sister ~~has~~ **have** any kids? *(the main verb used with* do *in an interrogative structure must be in base form)*
5) I *could* ~~skating~~ **skate** when I was younger. *(the main verb following an auxiliary modal verb must be in base form)*

Quiz 3 – Regular and irregular verbs
The correct spelling is in bold. The spelling rule is in parentheses.

1) He ~~carryed~~ **carried** the heavy bag up the stairs. *(verbs ending in –y change the –y to –i, then add –ed)*

2) The student ~~submited~~ **submitted** his assignment on time. *(verbs ending in consonant + vowel + consonant double the final consonant, then add –ed)*
3) "How do you like the course?" "I am ~~loveing~~ **loving** it!" *(verbs ending in –e drop the –e, then add –ing)*
4) "What is he doing?" "He's ~~tieing~~ **tying** the boat to the dock." *(verbs ending in –ie change the –ie to –y, then add –ing)*
5) The kids are ~~swiming~~ **swimming** in the lake. *(verbs ending in consonant + vowel + consonant double the final consonant, then add –ing)*

Quiz 4: Dynamic and stative verbs
A) Correct forms are indicated. Reasons are in parentheses.

1) ~~The flowers are smelling good~~. The flowers **smell** good. *(general condition, not a specific, one-time incident)*
2) I am **having** so much fun. *(correct usage; reference is to the experience at the time of speaking)*
3) Are you **seeing** your doctor tomorrow? *(correct usage; use of see is a reference to the action of having a meeting, not the perceptive meaning)*
4) ~~He is having~~ a new car. He **has** a new car. *(meaning is possession, not action)*
5) ~~The cabinet is measuring~~ 3 x 4 feet. The cabinet **measures** 3 x 4 feet. *(general state, not a specific, one-time incident)*

B) What can follow a linking verb? **A noun, noun phrase, pronoun, adjective, or adjective phrase.**

Quiz 5: Transitive and intransitive verbs
Verb types are given in parentheses.

1) I **found** it easy to solve. *(transitive complex: object it and object complement easy to solve)*
2) The new guy **watched** the movie with Yuki. *(monotransitive: direct object the movie followed by adverbial with Yuki)*
3) George Foreman and Muhammad Ali **fought** in Kinshasa. *(reciprocal: George Foreman fought Muhammad Ali and Muhammad Ali fought George Foreman)*
4) They **swam** in the rough river for about two hours. *(intransitive: no object, only adverbials of place and time)*
5) I **considered** Mr. Rexdale's theory erroneous. *(transitive complex: object Mr. Rexdale's theory and object complement erroneous)*
6) Sales **increased** last year. *(ergative: sales were increased by an unnamed agent)*
7) When **will** they **go** to the Opera House? *(intransitive: no object, only an adverbial)*
8) Gloria **brought** Maryleen a gift card. *(ditransitive: direct object a gift card and indirect object Maryleen)*
9) The movie star **sat** at the café and waited. *(intransitive: no object)*
10) Our boss **is** always **giving** us a hard time. *(ditransitive: direct object a hard time and indirect object us)*
11) I **watched** him leave. *(transitive complex: direct object him and object complement infinitive leave)*
12) The speaker **introduced** herself to the audience. *(reflexive: subject the speaker and object herself are the same)*

Quiz 6: Mood
Mood is given in parentheses.

1) The delegates requested that the meeting adjourn for the afternoon. *(subjunctive)*
2) Isn't he a good little puppy? *(indicative – interrogative)*
3) He's such a good little puppy. *(indicative – declarative)*
4) Get out of here! *(imperative)*
5) Add two teaspoons of bicarbonate of soda. *(imperative)*
6) Adding baking soda will make the batter rise. *(infinitive)*

Quiz 7: Verb phrases and phrasal verbs
The full verb is in bold. The type is in parentheses.

1) The runner **caught up with** the pack after a slow start. *(phrasal verb)*
2) Annie **could have been doing** her assignment. *(verb phrase)*
3) Stanley almost always **throws up** after a few drinks. *(phrasal verb)*
4) Let's **call** the whole thing **off**. *(separable phrasal verb)*
5) That little girl **is singing** her heart out. *(verb phrase)*
6) I'll **take** you **up on** the skiing offer some day. *(separable phrasal verb)*
7) She's **been intending** to get that fixed for a long time. *(verb phrase)*
8) The porter **will be seeing to** your bags. *(verb phrase will be seeing to containing the phrasal verb seeing to)*

Chapter 12 - Auxiliary and modal auxiliary verbs

Quiz 1: Auxiliary verbs or main verbs
Be, do and have are highlighted; their functions are given in italics.

1) Will you **be** at the airport by 12:00? *main verb; auxiliary will is used to show future tense and is placed to make the sentence interrogative*
2) Upon arrival, you **are** greeted with a bouquet of flowers and a tropical beverage. *auxiliary verb; used with the main verb greeted (past participle) to form the passive voice*
3) By the end of the year, Pam and Greg will **have** achieved their goals. *auxiliary verb; used with the auxiliary will and the main verb achieved (past participle) to form the future perfect*
4) For over two years, the team **has** worked hard to restructure the company. *auxiliary verb; used with the main verb worked (past participle) to form the present perfect*
5) You **did** tell Maya *auxiliary verb; used with main verb tell (base form) to show emphasis*
you **were** not attending the seminar. *auxiliary verb; used with particle not to create negative and main verb attending (present participle) to form past progressive*
Do not change your story. *auxiliary verb; used with particle not to create negative of the main verb change (base form) in an imperative sentence*

Quiz 2: Distinctions between auxiliary verbs and modal verbs
1) b. **may** is a modal verb. It adds meaning (modality) to the main verb (**may** can express possibility, permission or an offering).
2) After the auxiliary verb **do** (including the forms **does** and **did**), the main verb is in base form. After the auxiliary verb **be** (including the forms **am**, **is**, **are**, **was**, **were** and **been**) the main verb is in the present participle (-*ing*) form for progressive tenses, or in the past participle (-*ed*) form for passive voice sentences. After the auxiliary verb **have** (including the forms **has** and **had**), the main verb is in past participle form. After modal verbs, the main verb is in base form.

Quiz 3: Correct the errors
1) She doesn't works on weekends.
Correct answer: She doesn't work on weekends.
The base form of the verb should be used after the auxiliary verb **does**.
2) Did he arrive on time? Yes, he arrived.
Correct answer: Yes, he did. (*Yes, he arrived* is grammatically correct)
The auxiliary **did** should be used as a pro-verb to avoid repetition of the main verb in the short answer.
3) I could repaired the oven last night.
Correct answer: I could repair the oven last night.
The base form of the verb should be used after the modal **could**.
4) Do I can see the director?
Correct answer: Can I see the director?
The modal **can** doesn't take another auxiliary to form the interrogative.
5) You must to obey the rules.
Correct answer: You must obey the rules.
After the modal **must**, the base form of the verb should be used.

Quiz 4: True or false
1) False. **Can** is used to refer to present or future times. To refer to past time, **could** or **was/were able to** should be used instead.
2) False. **Could** is used for general abilities in the past. **Be able to** is used when the action denoting ability occurred once. (Exception for stative verbs of perception.)
   1.

Quiz 5: Modalities
1) Shall I make you a cup of coffee? (suggestion)
2) You should obey the traffic rules. (recommendation)
3) He ought to be more careful. (advice)
4) He'd better go home now. (warning)
5) You could ask her if you want. (suggestion)

Quiz 6: Modal verbs of necessity
1) **must** can express
   a. recommendation   c. assumption   d. obligation
2) b. **need** can function as a modal and as a main verb.
3) b. **should** and **ought to** have the same meaning.

Quiz 7: Defining modalities
   1. f
   2. i
   3. j
   4. e
   5. h
   6. a
   7. g

8. b
9. d
10. c

Chapter 13 - Gerunds and infinitives

Quiz 1: Gerunds and infinitives
Answers are given in italics.
1) Both gerunds and infinitives always act as nouns. *False. Gerunds generally act like nouns but infinitives can act as nouns, verbs and adverbs.*
2) A phrase introduced by a non-finite verb ending in –*ing* is called an infinitival phrase. *False. It is called a gerundial phrase.*
3) In the sentence *I saw him enter the house* the word *enter* is a bare infinitive. *True. It is the base form of the verb without the infinitive particle.*

Quiz 2: Functions of gerunds
The gerunds and gerundial phrases are highlighted. The functions are given in italics.

1) Has **jogging** been your pastime lately? *(subject of an interrogative sentence)*
2) My main source of income is **writing blogs**. *(gerundial phrase functioning as subject complement)*
3) What she loved most, **babysitting her niece**, was forbidden to her. *(gerundial phrase functioning as an appositive to the noun phrase* what she loved most*)*
4) Her devotion to **teaching** has helped her overcome her loneliness. *(gerund functioning as object of the preposition* to*)*
5) Osvaldo regretted **giving the speech**. *(gerundial phrase functioning as direct object of the verb* regretted*)*

Quiz 3: Gerundial forms
Which sentence contains a perfective passive gerund?
   b. I am sure they enjoyed having been guided through the whole process.

Which sentence contains a perfective negative gerund?
   a. They recall not having learned that topic.

Quiz 4: Gerund or present participle?
1) They finished painting the house. *gerund*
2) What is he doing right now? *present participle*
3) He told me to stop talking nonsense. *gerundial phrase (talking nonsense)*
4) Will you be driving all the way down on your own? *present participle*
5) Listening to Mozart relaxes me so much. *gerundial phrase (Listening to Mozart)*

Quiz 5: Functions of infinitives
1) I was told to arrive one hour before. *direct object of the verb* told
2) My decision, to rent the apartment, was not accepted by my parents. *appositive*
3) He can't do anything but wait. *object of the preposition* but
4) My favourite indulgence is to curl up by the fire with a glass of wine. *subject complement*
5) To wear casual clothes in the office is not allowed. *subject of the sentence*

361

Quiz 6: To-infinitive or bare infinitive?
1) help *(can be followed by either)*
2) see *(followed by bare infinitive)*
3) would love *(followed by to-infinitive)*
4) feel *(followed by bare infinitive)*

Quiz 7: Functions of gerunds and infinitives
Functions are given in italics.

1) He mentioned <u>taking</u> *(gerund functioning as direct object of main verb* mentioned*)* the subway to his office instead of <u>walking</u>. *(gerund functioning as the object of the preposition* of*)*
2) The teacher reminded the students <u>to submit</u> *(infinitive functioning as the direct object of the main verb* reminded*)* their homework by noon.
3) I was advised <u>to buy</u> *(infinitive functioning as the direct object of the main verb* was advised*)* the latest gadget.
4) My boss seems <u>to be</u> *(to-infinitive as the head of the phrase* to be in a good mood, *which is functioning as a subject complement after the linking verb* seem*)* in a good mood today, don't you think?
5) <u>Admitting</u> *(gerund functioning as the subject of the sentence)* the truth was his biggest challenge.
6) His passion is <u>to collect</u> *(infinitive as the head of the phrase* to collect all sorts of gemstones, *which is functioning as subject complement after the verb* is*)* all sorts of gemstones.
7) There is nothing <u>to regret</u>. *(infinitive functioning as adjective describing the indefinite pronoun* nothing*)*
8) I called Farah <u>to remind</u> *(infinitive as the head of the phrase* to remind her of her appointment, *which is functioning as an adverbial of purpose)* her of her appointment with the dentist.
9) The prize, <u>to travel solo in a hot-air balloon</u>, *(infinitive as the head of the phrase* to travel solo in an air balloon, *which is functioning as an appositive to the noun phrase* the prize*)* was not sanctioned by the organizers of the contest.

Quiz 8: Choose the correct form
Answers are given in italics.

1) I watched her (1) *cross (bare infinitive after verb of perception* watch; *-ing form in this structure would be a reduced form of a verb in the progressive aspect, which would mean that the action was still happening – in this case, the action was completed)* the road from the moment she left the corner shop till she got to the other end of the road but I did not think her (2) *to be (infinitive after the objective pronoun* her *(object of the main verb* think*); object complement)* drunk at all.

2) I still remember (3) *visiting (gerund after* remember *when the action of visiting was completed in the past)* my friend's grandma in those sunny summer days at the village. She was delighted (4) *to see (to-infinitive after the adjective* delighted*)* us, and (5) *to show (infinitive of purpose, introducing the adverbial clause* to show us her appreciation..., *modifying the clause* she would let us...*)* us her appreciation for those afternoon visits, she would let us (6) *dress up (bare infinitive after verb* let*)* with her most exquisite costumes from the days when she was an actress. We would never forget (7) *to put (infinitive after the verb* forget, *to show that the action of putting happened after the action of not forgetting)* her clothes back in the attic, or else she would not allow us (8) *to wear (infinitive after the verb* allow*)* them ever again.

3) She regrets not (9) *listening (gerund after the verb* regret *to show that the action of not listening was completed in the past)* to her brother's advice. He was right. Now, she has to apologize to her boss for not (10) *calling (gerund after the preposition* for*)* the insurance company on time.

Chapter 14 - Tenses

Quiz 1: Tenses (time)

Sentences	Present	Past	Future
Lisa is going to make lots of money.			√
Marion is working on a special project.	√		
Florence cut her finger chopping onions.		√	
Yves hasn't studied much.	√		
Fidel will become a legend.			√
It had been a while since they'd talked.		√	

Quiz 2: Forms
Answers are given in italics.

1) What do all present and past simple tenses have in common?
they only need one verb (no auxiliary) for affirmative statements; they need the auxiliary do *(in present or past form) to form negatives and interrogatives*
2) What do all progressive tenses have in common?
they require the verb be *(conjugated into the appropriate form) as an auxiliary; they require the present participle form of the main verb*
3) What do all perfective tenses have in common?
they require the verb have *as an auxiliary; they require the past participle form of the main verb*
4) What is the word order for all the auxiliaries in the perfect progressive tense?
it is the same order as the name of the aspect: first, perfect (have + past participle), then progressive (be + present participle)
5) What do ALL tenses have in common?
any needed auxiliaries are placed before the main verb; the subject is placed immediately after the first auxiliary in interrogative forms

Quiz 3: Present tenses

1) I ~~am brushing~~ brush my teeth every day. *(describing a habitual action (every day), so present simple tense is correct)*
2) Mildred *is reading* that trendy, recently-released novel. *(present progressive tense correctly describes a current event that is incomplete)*
3) Elmer ~~has been reading~~ has read that book four times already. He knows it by heart. *(present perfect progressive cannot be used with the amount of times (or the frequency) that an event happens; present perfect is better since it is an event in the past that has finished and has connection to the present.)*

4) The train ~~is leaving~~ *leaves* every fifteen minutes. The next one is at 4:15. *(present simple should be used to describe schedules like the one in this example)*

5) Florence *has been living* in Toronto since she was a teenager; she knows the city like the back of her hand. *(present perfect progressive correctly describes an event that started in the past and continues in the present; however, the present perfect could also be used correctly in this sentence, changing the focus from the length of time she's been living in Toronto, to the fact that she really knows her way around the city)*

Quiz 4: Past tenses

1) Ian *passed* his final exam and graduated.
c. passed. This is the best choice because it shows a completed event in the past with an understood time reference.

2) They phoned me while I *was doing* my presentation. It was embarrassing.
a. was doing. This is the best choice because the past event (doing the presentation) was in progress at the time the person received the phone call and it was probably interrupted for at least a couple of seconds.

3) They *had already left* when she arrived.
b. had already left. This is the best choice because it shows that this event clearly happened before the second even mentioned (she arrived.)

4) Apollo 11 *landed* on the moon on July 20, 1969.
b. landed. This is a finished past event with a definite time.

5) The gave her the medal because she *had finished* the race in third place.
b. had finished. This is the best choice because it describes an action that happened before another action. (simple past is also acceptable here, to describe a completed action)

6) Doris *had been trying* to reach her secretary all day and suddenly she received a message saying he'd quit.
c. had been trying. This is the best choice because it describes a long past event relevant to another past action that happened later. It is also a repeated past event or action before another event.

Quiz 5: Future tenses
Answers are given in italics.

1) At 10 am next week, *we will be driving (ongoing future action at a particular time)* to Hilton Head island.

2) The music is too loud; the baby *is going to wake up (prediction with objective evidence)*; I just know it! *(If "I just know it" means that the conclusion is based on evidence, then the going-to future is preferred; the will future is equally plausible)*

3) If you don't pass your class, you *will not be able to (threat)* to apply for a bursary.

4) In a few years, all the buses *will accept (prediction based on an opinion)* electronic payment only.

5) This dress is perfect for the party and it fits well! I*'ll take (decision at the moment of speaking)* it!

6) He is so exhausted that tomorrow he *is going to sleep (plan)* in.

7) No later than next year my parents *will have bought (future event to be completed before another future time reference)* a new condo on the beach and we'll be able to go.

8) Before next week is over she *will have been staying (future event that will be in process before another time in the future)* with us for 2 months.

Bibliography

"150 Words which are both Verbs and Nouns." *English Banana*. N.p. 15/05/2010. Web. 15 Mar 2012. <http://www.englishbanana.com/top-free-printable-worksheets/150-words-which-are-both-verbs-and-nouns.html>.

Abbott, Barbara. "Definite and Indefinite." *Encyclopedia of Language and Linguistics*. 2nd ed. Elsevier, 2008. Web.

"Adjectives: Coordinate or Cumulative." UMass Amherst Writing Program, n.d. Web. 15 Apr 2008. <umass.edu/writingprogram/>.

Almaas, Roy. "Time Chart Explanations." *Anglaide*. N.p., 16/10/2010. Web. 17 Mar 2012. <http://www.anglaide.com/Grammar/Anglaide_Overview.pdf>.

Ansell, Mary. "English Grammar: Explanations and Exercises." *Scribd.*. 2000. Web. 15 Jul 2010. <scribd.com>.

Azar, Betty Schrampfer. *Basic English Grammar*. Englewood Cliffs, NJ: Prentice Hall Regents, 1984. Print.

Badalamenti, Victoria and Carolyn Henner-Stanchina. *Grammar Dimensions, Book One, Form, Meaning, and Use*. Boston: Heinle and Heinle, 1993. Print.

Baskerville, William Malone, and James Witt Sewell. *An English Grammar*. 1895. eBook. <http://www.gutenberg.org/>.

Bieri, Adolfo. "Verbs list." *The Irregular Verbs*. N.p., 30/05/2010. Web. 15 Mar 2012. <http://www.theirregularverbs.com/verbList.php?page=1>.

Bond, Karen. "The Subjunctive." *Karen's Linguistics Issues, Free resources for Teachers and Students of English* . N.p., 08/07/2010. Web. 15 Mar 2012. <http://www3.telus.net/linguisticsissues/subjunctive.html>.

Brizee, Allen. "Intransitive Phrasal Verbs." *Purdue Online Writing Lab*. Purdue University, 12/07/2010. Web. 15 Mar 2012. <http://owl.english.purdue.edu/owl/resource/630/04/>.

Brown, Goold. *A Grammar of Grammars*. 1851. eBook. <http://www.gutenberg.org/>.

Canary, Robert. "Verbs with Indirect Objects." University Of Wisconsin, Parkside, 03/07/2010. Web. 15 Mar 2012. <http://homepages.uwp.edu/canary/grammar_text/37-vb-ditr.html>.

Carter, Ronald, and Michael McCarthy. *Cambridge Grammar of English: A Comprehensive Guide*. Cambridge University Press, 2006. Print.

Celce-Murcia, Marianne, and Diane Larsen-Freeman. *The Grammar Book - An ESL/EFL Teacher's Course*. 2nd ed. Heinle & Heinle, 1999. Print.

Collins Cobuild English Usage. HarperCollins, 1992. Print.

"Conjunctions." Bow Valley College Learning Resource Services, n.d. Web. 15 Jul 2010.

"Conjunctions." *Humber School of Liberal Arts and Science*. Humber College Department of English, n.d. Web. 1 July 2010. <http://www.humber.ca/liberalarts/las-writing-centre/handouts>.

Darling, Charles. "Count and Non-Count Nouns." *Guide to Grammar and Writing*. Capital Community College Foundation, 19/08/2007. Web. 15 Mar 2012. <http://grammar.ccc.commnet.edu/grammar/noncount.htm>.

Dixon, R.M.W. *A Semantic Approach to English Grammar*. Second Edition. Oxford University Press, 2005. Print.

Dow, John. "English Grammar in English." *Scribd.*. 15 Oct 2008. Web. 14 Apr 2010. <http://www.scribd.com>.

Downing, Angela, and Philip Locke. *English Grammar: A University Course*. Second Edition. Routledge, 2006. eBook.

"English words whose meaning is changed by a difference in stress accent." *Second Language LCC, Vernon / Manchester CT USA Language School*. N.p., 15/05/2010. Web. 15 Mar 2012. <http://yoursecondlanguage.com/resources/english.nouns.verbs.accented.shtml>.

Fernald, James C. *English Grammar Simplified*. 1916. eBook. <books.google.com>.

Finney, C.E.A. "The subjunctive mood in English - a guide to usage." *God Save the Subjunctive*. N.p., 08/07/2010. Web. 15 Mar 2012. <http://www.ceafinney.com/subjunctive/guide.html>.

Francis, Gill, Susan Hunston, and Elizabeth Manning, eds. "Grammar Patterns 1: Verbs." *The Bank of English*. Collins Cobuild, 26/06/2010. Web. 15 Mar 2012. <https://arts-ccr-002.bham.ac.uk/ccr/patgram/>.

Fuchs, Marjorie, Miriam Westheimer, and Margaret Bonner. *Focus On Grammar, Volume A, An Intermediate Course for Reference and Practice*. White Plains, NY: Addison-Wesley, 1994. Print.

"Guide to Grammar and Writing." Capital Community College Foundation, n.d. Web. 20 Mar 2007. <grammar.ccc.commnet.edu/grammar/>.

Haines, Simon, Mark Nettle, and Martin Hewings. *Advanced Grammar in Use*. Cambridge University Press, 2007. Print.

Hartmann, Pamela, Annette A. Zarian, and Patricia A. Esparza. *Tense Situations: Tenses in Contrast and Context*. Westlake Village, CA: IPS Publishing, 1984. Print.

Heycock, Caroline, and Anthony Kroch. "Pseudocleft connectivity: Implications for the LF interface level." University of Edinburgh and University of Pennsylvania, 1996. Web. 23 Aug 2008.

Johnson, Samuel. *A Grammar of the English Tongue*. 1812. eBook. <http://www.gutenberg.org>.

Jones, Leo. *Use of English: Grammar Practice Activities (Student's Book)*. Cambridge University Press, 1995. Print.

Kastovsky, Dieter, ed. *Studies in Early Modern English*. Berlin: Walter de Gruyter, 1994. Web. <books.google.com>.

Kosur, Heather Marie. "Verb Aspect: Simple, Perfect, Progressive, Perfect-Progressive." *Language Study @ suite 101*. N.p., 09/08/2010. Web. 15 Mar 2012. <http://heather-marie-kosur.suite101.com/verb-aspect-simple-perfect-progressive-perfect-progressive-a228686>.

Leech, Geoffrey, and Jan Svartvik. *A Communicative Grammar of English*. Longman, 1975. Print.

Lester, Mark. *Grammar and Usage in the Classroom*. 2nd ed. Allyn and Bacon, 2001. Print.

Lester, Mark. *Grammar in the Classroom*. Macmillan, 1990. Print.

Lester, Mark. *Practice Makes Perfect Advanced English Grammar for ESL Learners*. McGraw-Hill, 2010. Print.

Maddox, Maeve. "Careful with Words Used as Noun and Verb." *Daily Writing Tips*. N.p., 25 06 2007. Web. 15 Mar. 2012. <http://www.dailywritingtips.com/careful-with-words-used-as-noun-and-verb/>.

Malouf, Robert. "The order of prenominal adjectives in natural language generation." Rijksuniversiteit Groningen, 2000. Web. 12 Mar 2008.

Master, Peter. "Pedagogical Frameworks for Learning the English Article System." . San Jose State University, n.d. Web. 16 Apr 2007.

McArthur, Tom. "Determiner." *Concise Oxford Companion to the English Language*. Oxford University Press, 1998. Web. 15 Aug 2009. <http://www.encyclopedia.com>.

McCarthy, Michael, and Felicity O'Dell. *English Phrasal Verbs in Use: Advanced*. Cambridge University Press, 2007. Print.

McFadyen, Heather. "What Is An Adjective?." *The Writing Centre - HyperGrammar*. University of Ottawa, n.d. Web. 20 Mar 2007. <arts.uottawa.ca/writcent>.

Molczanow, Aleksy. "Set Reference Relationships and the Phrasal Syntax of Quantifiers in English." Studia Anglica Posnaniensia XXIX. (1994). Web. 15 Jun. 2009.

Murphy, Raymond. *Essential Grammar in Use*. 3rd ed. Cambridge University Press, 2007. Print.

Oliver, Dennis. "The Present Perfect Tense #3." *Dave's ESL Cafe*. N.p., 22/07/2011. Web. 17 Mar 2012. <http://www.eslcafe.com/grammar/present_perfect_tense03.html>.

Olsen, Judy Winn-Bell. *Communication Starters and Other Activities for the ESL Classroom*. Englewood Cliffs, NJ: Alemany Press, Prentice Hall Regents, 1977. Print.

Onions, C.T. *Modern English Syntax*. 7th ed. Routledge, 1974. Print.

Parrott, Martin. *Grammar for English Language Teachers*. Cambridge University Press, 2000. Print.

Partee, Barbara H. "Topic, Focus and Quantification." University of Massachusetts, n.d. Web. 15 Jun 2009.

"Phrasal Verb Dictionary." *English Page*. Language Dynamics, 13/07/2010. Web. 15 Mar 2012. <http://www.englishpage.com/prepositions/phrasaldictionary.html>.

"Phrasal Verbs." *English Club*. N.p., 12/07/2010. Web. 15 Mar 2012. <http://www.englishclub.com/grammar/verbs-phrasal-verbs_2.htm>.

Poehland, Joerg. "Tenses Table." *Englisch-Hilfen*. N.p., 16/10/2010. Web. 17 Mar 2012. <http://www.englisch-hilfen.de/en/grammar/tenses_table.pdf>.

Quirk, R, S Greenbaum, G Leech, and J Svartvik. *A Comprehensive Grammar of the English Language*. Longman, 1985. Print.

Quirk, Randolph, and Sidney Greenbaum. *A University Grammar of English*. Longman, 1973. Print.

Richards, Jack, and Theodore Rodgers. *Approaches and Methods in Language Teaching*. 2nd ed. Cambridge University Press, 2001. Print.

Riggenbach, Heidi and Virginia Samuda. *Grammar Dimensions, Book 2A, Form, Meaning, and Use*. Boston: Heinle and Heinle Publishers, 1993. Print.

Rinvolucri, Mario. *Grammar Games: Cognitive, Affective and Drama Activities for EFL Students*. New York: Cambridge University Press, 1984. Print.

Rinvolucri, Mario and Paul Davis. *Dictation*. New York: Cambridge University Press, 1988. Print.

Rinvolucri, Mario and Paul Davis. *More Grammar Games*. New York: Cambridge University Press, 1995. Print.

Roach, Peter. *English Phonetics and Phonology*. Cambridge University Press, 2000. Print.

"Regular Verbs." *English Club*. N.p., 30/05/2010. Web. 15 Mar 2012. <http://www.englishclub.com/vocabulary/regular-verbs-list.htm>.

Romero, Maribel. "On Concealed Questions and Specificational Subjects." University of Pennsylvania, 22 May, 2003. Web. 23 Aug 2008.

Sevastopoulos, Julie. "Past Perfect." *Grammar Quizzes, Practice on Points of English Grammar*. N.p., 22/07/2011. Web. 17 Mar 2012. <http://www.grammar-quizzes.com/past3b.html>.

Simmons, Robin L. "The Concrete Noun." *Grammar Bytes*. N.p. 17/08/2007. Web. 15 Mar 2012. <http://www.chompchomp.com/terms/concretenoun.htm>.

"Simple Present Use." *English Grammar Online 4U*. N.p., 16/10/2010. Web. 15 Mar 2012. <http://www.ego4u.com/en/cram-up/grammar/simple-present/use>.

Swan, Michael. *Grammar*. Oxford University Press, 2005. Print.

Swan, Michael. *Practical English Usage*. Oxford University Press, 1995. Print.

"The Basic Elements of English." English Department at the University of Calgary, 1998. Web. 1 July 2010. <ucalgary.ca/UofC/eduweb/grammar>.

Tom, Abigal and Heather McKay. *The Card Book*. Englewood Cliffs, NJ: Alemany Press, Prentice Hall Regents, 1991. Print.

"Understanding Verbs: Gerunds, Participles, and Infinitives." University of Houston Victoria Academic Center, 2005. Web. 23 Jun 2009. <uhv.edu/ac/>.

Ur, Penny. *Grammar Practice Activities: A Practical Guide for Teachers*. New York: Cambridge University Press, 1988. Print.

Ur, Penny. *Grammar Practice Activities Paperback with CD-ROM: A Practical Guide for Teachers*. 2nd ed. Cambridge University Press, 2009. Print.

"Use of tenses." *Language and Learning Online*. Monash University, 16/10/2010. Web. 15 Mar 2012. <http://www.monash.edu.au/lls/llonline/writing/general/lit-reviews/3.2.xml>.

"Verb Tense Tutorial." *English Page*. N.p., 16/10/2010. Web. 17 Mar 2012. <http://www.englishpage.com/verbpage/verbtenseintro.html>.

Willis, Dave. *Collins Cobuild Intermediate English Grammar*. HarperCollins, 2000. Print.

Willis, Dave. *Collins Cobuild Student's Grammar*. Self-Study Edition. HarperCollins, 1991. Print.

Zamparelli, Roberto. *Layers in the Determiner Phrase*. University of Rochester, 2000. Web.

Index

a bit
    as emphasizing adverbial, 165
a few
    comparison with *few*, 107
    number, 58
a little
    as emphasizing adverbial, 165
    comparison with *little*, 107
    number, 58
a lot
    as emphasizing adverbial, 165
a lot of
    partitive for positive statements, 107
a/an. *See* indefinite articles
    central determiner, 101
    choice based on pronunciation, 111
    determiner of indefiniteness, 103
    limiting adjective indicating number, 73
ability
    modality, 246
aboard
    preposition and adverb, 172
    simple preposition, 171
about
    adverbial particle, 130
    preposition and adverb, 172
    simple preposition, 171
above
    adverbial particle, 130
    preposition of place, 9, 176
    simple preposition, 171
absolute
    intensifying adjective, 84
absolutely
    interjection, 337
abstract nouns, 1, 34
abuse
    monotransitive verb, 223
accordingly
    conjunctive adverb, 197
accusative case. *See* objective case
accusative pronouns. *See* objective pronouns
accuse of
    followed by gerund, 268
accustomed to
    followed by gerund, 268
ache
    intransitive verb, 222
achieve
    monotransitive verb, 223

achoo
    interjection, 338
across
    adverbial particle, 130
    preposition of direction/movement, 9
    preposition of movement, 179
    preposition of place, 176
    simple preposition, 171
act
    linking verb, 221
    stative verb, 219
action verbs. *See* dynamic verbs
active voice, 222
addicted to
    followed by gerund, 268
addiction to
    followed by gerund, 268
additional
    specifying adjective, 82
adjectival prepositional phrases, 10, 175
    reduced relative clauses, 175
adjective forms, 73
    comparative adjectives, 151, 152
    compound adjectives, 74
    descriptive adjectives, 73
    limiting adjectives, 73
    participial adjectives, 77
    prefixes, 74, 76
    suffixes, 74, 76
    superlative adjectives, 151, 153
adjective phrases, 14
adjective types, 80
    attributive adjectives, 86, 87
    classifying adjectives, 81, 83
    descriptive adjectives, 81, 82
    intensifying adjectives, 84
    limiting adjectives, 81
    predicative adjectives, 86, 87
    qualifying adjectives, 81, 83
    Table 17 Limiting and descriptive adjectives, 81
adjectives, 4, 73
    adjectival prepositional phrases, 10
    attributive adjectives, 4, 87
    classifying adjectives, 83
    comparative adjectives, 151, 152
    compound adjectives, 5
    descriptive adjectives, 4, 81, 82
    determiners, 4, 99
    distinction from adverbs, 91
    gradability, 152
    gradable adjectives, 4

intensifying adjectives, 84
limiting adjectives, 4, 81
non-gradable adjectives, 5
order of adjectives, 88
participial adjectives, 5, 77
predicative adjectives, 4, 87
qualifying adjectives, 83
semantic functions, 80
superlative adjectives, 151, 153
admit
   verb followed by gerund, 267
admit to
   followed by gerund, 268
advantage of
   followed by gerund, 268
adverb forms, 5
   adverbials, 128
   comparative adverbs, 151
   suffixes, 126
   superlative adverbs, 151
adverb types, 5
   adverbials of purpose, 140
   adverbs of assertion, 142
   adverbs of degree, 6, 142
   adverbs of manner, 6, 132
   adverbs of place, 6, 133
   adverbs of purpose, 6
   adverbs of quantity, 144
   adverbs of time, 6, 134
   Table 3 Adverb types, 6
adverbial clauses, 130
   adverbials of comparison, 130
   adverbials of condition, 130
   adverbials of contrast, 130
   adverbials of manner, 130
   adverbials of place, 130
   adverbials of purpose, 130
   adverbials of reason, 130
   adverbials of result, 130
   adverbials of time, 130
   position in a sentence, 132
adverbial conjunctions. *See* conjunctive adverbs
adverbial infinitive phrases, 129
adverbial particles, 130
   distinction from prepositions, 130
adverbial phrases, 14, 129
   adverbials of frequency, 129
   adverbials of manner, 129
   adverbials of place, 129
   adverbials of purpose, 129
   adverbials of time, 129
   compound adverbial phrases, 129
   infinitive phrases, 129
   noun phrases, 129
   position in a sentence, 132
   prepositional phrases, 129
adverbial prepositional phrases, 10, 129, 176
adverbial subordinators, 195, *See* subordinating conjunctions
adverbials, 17, 19, 125, 128
   adverbial phrases, 129
   placement in a sentence, 19, 21
adverbials of comparison, 130
adverbials of condition, 130
adverbials of contrast, 130
adverbials of degree, 143
adverbials of frequency, 129
adverbials of manner, 129, 130, 132
   placement in a sentence, 21
adverbials of place, 129, 130, 133
   placement in a sentence, 21
adverbials of purpose, 129, 130, 140
   position in a sentence, 141
adverbials of quantity, 144
adverbials of reason, 130
adverbials of relative time, 138
adverbials of result, 130
adverbials of time, 129, 130
   placement in a sentence, 21
adverbials of time-duration, 137
adverbials of time-frequency, 135
adverbials of time-when, 134
adverbs, 5, 125
   adding comparative emphasis, 165
   adverbial particles, 130
   adverbial prepositional phrases, 10
   adverbials, 17, 19
   adverbs of assertion, 142
   adverbs of degree, 142
   adverbs of quantity, 144
   adverbs of time, 134
   comparative adverbs, 151
   distinction from adjectives, 92, 127
   distinction from conjunctions, 190
   distinction from prepositions, 130, 131
   flat adverbs, 126
   gradability, 153
   order of adverbs, 141
   position in a sentence, 132
   superlative adverbs, 151
   Table 39 Adverbs to emphasize comparatives, 165
   Table 40 Adverbs to emphasize superlatives, 165
adverbs of manner, 6
adverbs of assertion, 5, 142
   position in a sentence, 142
adverbs of degree, 6, 142

adverbs of quantity, 144
   modifying gradable adjectives, 153
   non-gradable, 153
   position in a sentence, 143
adverbs of manner, 132
   gradability, 154
   position in a sentence, 132
adverbs of measure. *See* adverbs of quantity
adverbs of place, 6, 133
   non-gradable, 153
   position in a sentence, 133
adverbs of purpose, 6
   infinitives, 277
adverbs of quantity, 144
   position in a sentence, 144
adverbs of relative time
   position in a sentence, 139
adverbs of time, 6, 134
   duration, 137
   frequency, 135
   gradability, 153
   when, 134
adverbs of time-duration
   position in a sentence, 137
   relative time, 138
adverbs of time-frequency
   position in a sentence, 136
   Table 28 Adverbs of frequency, 136
adverbs of time-when
   position in a sentence, 135
adversative conjunctions. *See* coordinating conjunctions - semantics
advice
   followed by infinitive, 277
advice/recommendation
   about past events, 248
   modality, 247
advise
   followed by gerund *or* infinitive, 278
   followed by indirect object and infinitive, 273
   subordinate clause subjunctive, 228
affirmative declarative sentences, 25
afford
   followed by gerund *or* infinitive, 278
   verb followed by infinitive, 273
afraid
   predicative adjective, 87
after
   conjunction, 190
   conjunction and preposition, 172, 191
   preposition and conjunction, 172
   preposition of time, 9, 178
   simple preposition, 171
   subordinating conjunction, 8, 195
   subordinator of time, 196
after all
   linker, 197
again
   conjunctive adverb, 197
against
   simple preposition, 171
agree
   reciprocal verb, 226
   stative verb, 219
   verb followed by infinitive, 273
aha
   interjection, 337
ahead
   adverb of place, 133
   adverbial particle, 130
ahem
   interjection, 338
ain't, 296
alive
   predicative adjective, 87
all
   determiner of magnitude, 104
   general indefinite pronoun, 56
   indefinite pronoun, 56
   number, 58
   predeterminer, 101
   quantifier indefinite pronoun, 57
allow
   infinitive as object complement, 274
   verb followed by gerund, 267
almost
   adverb of degree, 143
alone
   predicative adjective, 87
along
   adverbial particle, 130
   preposition and adverb, 172
   simple preposition, 171
alongside
   simple preposition, 171
already
   adverb of relative time, 138
   position in a sentence, 139
also
   conjunctive adverb, 197
alternative conjunctions. *See* coordinating conjunctions - semantics
alternative questions, 26
although
   conjunction, 190
   elision of subject and *be*, 195
   similar to *despite*, 191
   subordinating conjunction, 195
   subordinator of contrast, 196
always

adverb of relative time, 138
adverb of time-frequency, 135, 136
am
   form of *be*, 296
   in present progressive, 299
am not
   in negative questions, 27
amaze
   stative verb, 219
amazed
   followed by infinitive, 276
   participial adjective, 78
amazing
   participial adjective, 78
ambitransitive verbs, 222
amid
   simple preposition, 171
among
   preposition of place, 176
   simple preposition, 171
amused
   participial adjective, 78
amusing
   participial adjective, 78
anaphoric reference, 47, 56, 64
and
   conjunction, 190
   connecting infinitives, 273
   coordinating conjunction, 8, 192, 193
   in comparative structures, 166
   linking independent clauses, 201
   to begin a sentence, 204
angry at
   followed by gerund, 268
another
   indefinite pronoun, 56
   limiting adjective indicating number, 73
   number, 58
   postdeterminer, 101
   quantifier indefinite pronoun, 57
antecedent, 47, 51, 55, 64
anti
   simple preposition, 171
anticipatory *it*. See preparatory *it*
anxious
   followed by infinitive, 276
anxious about
   followed by gerund, 268
any
   central determiner, 101
   determiner of indefiniteness, 103
   determiner of magnitude, 104
   indefinite pronoun, 56
   number, 58
   quantifier indefinite pronoun, 57
anybody
   affirmative sentences, 59
   general indefinite pronoun, 56
   indefinite pronoun, 56
   interrogative sentences, 58
   negative sentences, 58
   number, 57
anyone
   affirmative sentences, 59
   indefinite pronoun, 56
   interrogative sentences, 58
   negative sentences, 58
   number, 57
anything
   affirmative sentences, 59
   general indefinite pronoun, 56
   indefinite pronoun, 56
   interrogative sentences, 58
   negative sentences, 58
   number, 57
apologize for
   followed by gerund, 268
apostrophe
   placement with multiple possessors, 42
   use in possessive case, 42
appear
   intransitive verb, 222
   linking verb, 221
   stative verb, 219
appoint
   verb taking object complement, 16, 19
apposition
   reflexive pronouns, 54
appositives, 32
   gerund as appositive, 268
   infinitive as appositive, 274
appreciate
   stative verb, 219
are
   form of *be*, 296
   in present progressive, 299
aren't
   form of *be*, 296
   in negative questions, 27
around
   adverbial particle, 130
   preposition of direction/movement, 9
   preposition of movement, 179
   simple preposition, 171
arrange
   followed by gerund *or* infinitive, 278
arrive
   intransitive verb, 222
   linking verb, 221
   stative verb, 219

articles, 108
   as limiting adjectives, 82
as
   conjunction, 190
   conjunction and preposition, 191
   punctuation, 202
   simple preposition, 171
   subordinating conjunction, 195
   subordinator of manner, 196
   subordinator of reason, 196
   subordinator of time, 196
as ... as
   expressing equality, 151
   in comparative structures, 162, 164
as ... so
   conjunction, 191
   correlative conjunction, 8, 192, 194
as a result
   linker, 197
as far as
   conjunction, 190
as if
   conjunction, 190
   subordinator of manner, 196
as long as
   conjunction, 190
   subordinator of condition, 196
   subordinator of time, 196
as soon as
   conjunction, 190
   subordinator of time, 196
as though
   conjunction, 190
   subordinator of manner, 196
As with gerunds, a to-infinitive
   cannot be main verb, 265
aside
   adverbial particle, 130
ask
   followed by indirect object and infinitive, 273
   subordinate clause subjunctive, 228
asleep
   predicative adjective, 87
aspect, 6, 289, 291
   perfect progressive, 292
   perfective, 292
   progressive, 292
   simple, 292
   Table 52 Grammatical aspects of verbs, 292
assume
   infinitive as object complement, 274
assuming
   preposition and participle, 172
   simple preposition, 171
   subordinator of condition, 196
assuming that
   conjunction, 190
assumption
   modality, 250
astonish
   stative verb, 219
astonished
   followed by infinitive, 276
at
   indicating condition, 180
   indicating direction, 180
   indicating reaction, 180
   preposition of direction, 179
   preposition of direction/movement, 9
   preposition of place, 9, 176, 177
   preposition of time, 9, 178
   simple preposition, 171
at that time
   linker, 197
ate
   irregular past form, 8
athletics
   as singular noun, 39, 51
attempt
   followed by infinitive, 277
attributive adjectives, 4, 86, 87
   order in a sentence, 89
   order of adjectives, 88
audience
   as collective noun, 40
auxiliary verbs, 7, 215, 237
   differences from modal verbs, 242, 243
   forms, 242
   in verb phrases, 229
   order in verb phrases, 230
   placement in interrogatives, 63
   pronunciation stress, 258
   similarities with modal verbs, 241
avoid
   verb followed by gerund, 267
aware
   predicative adjective, 87
away
   adverbial particle, 130

back
   adverb of place, 133
   adverbial particle, 130
backward
   adverbial particle, 130
bad
   irregular comparative, 160
bad at
   followed by gerund, 268
badly

irregular comparative, 160
bare infinitive. *See* base form - verbs
base form - comparatives, 151, 152, 154, 155, 156, 157, 158, 159, 160, 164, 166
base form - verbs, 209, 210
   after auxiliary *do*, 239, 242
   after causative verbs, 275
   after modal verbs, 241, 242
   after modals, 230
   after perception verbs, 275
   confusion with simple present tense, 210
   distinction from simple present, 243
   for future time, 289
   in future simple, 319
   in imperative mood, 228
   in past simple, 308
   in present simple, 295
   subjunctive present, 228
   use in imperative sentences, 27
   when connecting infinitives, 273
be
   auxiliary verb, 7, 215, 237, 239
   exception to present simple structure, 295
   in future progressive, 321
   in present progressive, 299
   in semi-modals, 244
   inflections, 213
   linking verb, 16, 221
   main or auxiliary verb, 214
   main verb, 7, 239
   main verb in cleft sentences, 22
   number agreement, 24
   past subjunctive, 228
   stative verb, 219
   subject/verb agreement, 24
   Table 58 Simple present forms of the verb *be*, 296
   Table 63 Simple past forms of the verb *be*, 308
   to test for a linking verb, 220
   verb taking subject complement, 19, 21
be able to
   modal of ability, 246
   semi-modal, 244
be allowed to
   modal of permission/prohibition, 255
   semi-modal, 244
be going to
   semi-modal, 240
   to express future, 258, 320
be likely to
   modal of probability, 251
   semi-modal, 244
be permitted to
   modal of permission/prohibition, 255
   semi-modal, 244
be supposed to
   modal of obligation, 252
   semi-modal, 244
be to
   modal of responsibility, 252
   semi-modal, 244
beautifully
   degrees of comparison, 154
because
   conjunction, 190
   similar to *because of*, 191
   subordinating conjunction, 8, 195
   subordinator of reason, 196
become
   linking verb, 16, 221
   stative verb, 219
   verb taking subject complement, 21
been
   in future perfect progressive, 326
   in past perfect progressive, 316
   in present perfect progressive, 305
before
   adverbial particle, 130
   conjunction, 190
   preposition and conjunction, 172, 191
   preposition of time, 9, 178
   simple preposition, 171
   subordinating conjunction, 8, 195
   subordinator of time, 196
beg
   followed by indirect object and infinitive, 273
   subordinate clause subjunctive, 228
begin
   followed by gerund *or* infinitive, 280
behind
   adverbial particle, 130
   preposition of place, 176
   simple preposition, 171
believe
   infinitive as object complement, 274
   stative verb, 219
belong
   intransitive verb, 222
   stative verb, 219
below
   adverbial particle, 130
   preposition of place, 9, 176
   simple preposition, 171
beneath
   preposition of place, 176
   simple preposition, 171
beside

preposition of place, 9, 176
simple preposition, 171
besides
conjunctive adverb, 197
simple preposition, 171
between
preposition of place, 9, 176
preposition of time, 178
simple preposition, 171
beyond
preposition of time, 178
simple preposition, 171
big
intensifying adjective, 84
bite
monotransitive verb, 223
blame
reflexive verb, 54, 224
bored
participial adjective, 79
boring
participial adjective, 79
both
determiner of magnitude, 104
indefinite pronoun, 56
limiting adjective indicating number, 73
number, 58
predeterminer, 101
quantifier indefinite pronoun, 57
both ... and
conjunction, 191
correlative conjunction, 8, 194
bother
followed by gerund or infinitive, 280
bountiful
degrees of comparison, 152
break
ergative verb, 225
briefly
adverb of time-duration, 137
broken
participial adjective, 78
but
conjunction, 190
coordinating conjunction, 8, 192, 193
infinitive as object, 274
simple preposition, 171
to begin a sentence, 204
buy
as reflexive verb, 54
by
adverbial particle, 130
indicating agent, 180
preposition of direction, 179
preposition of direction/movement, 9
preposition of time, 178

preposition of transport, 179
simple preposition, 171
used with reflexive pronouns, 55
by far
as emphasizing adverbial, 165
call
verb taking object complement, 16
can
modal of ability, 246
modal of offer, 255
modal of permission, 255
modal of possibility, 251
modal of request, 254
modal of suggestion, 249
modal verb, 240, 244
can't
modal of assumption, 250
modal of prohibition, 255
can't help
verb followed by gerund, 267
cannot bear
followed by gerund or infinitive, 280
cannot stand
followed by gerund or infinitive, 280
capital letters, 35
to start a sentence, 13
cardinal numbers
determiner of magnitude, 104
limiting adjectives indicating number, 73
postdeterminer, 101
care about
followed by gerund, 268
case, 41, 47
cataphoric reference, 56, 64
cease
followed by gerund or infinitive, 280
central determiners, 101
certain
specifying adjective, 82
certainty
modality, 250
challenge
followed by indirect object and infinitive, 273
chance
followed by infinitive, 277
chat
intransitive verb, 222
cheap
used as adverb, 155
chiefly
adverb of time-frequency, 136
choose
verb followed by infinitive, 273
class

as collective noun, 40
classifying adjectives, 81, 83
   order in a sentence, 89
   Table 20 Types of classifying adjectives, 84
clauses, 14
   as object of a preposition, 174
   as subject of a sentence, 23
   as subject or object, 22
clean
   dynamic verb, 218
clear
   comparative forms, 156
   used as adverb, 155
cleft sentences, 22
close
   used as adverb, 155
close to
   preposition of place, 176
cold
   degrees of comparison, 152
collective nouns, 2, 40, 51
   British and American English, 40
collide
   intransitive verb, 222
come
   followed by gerund, 270
   intransitive verb, 222
   linking verb, 221
   stative verb, 219
come out
   linking verb, 221
   stative verb, 219
comma splice, 200
command
   followed by indirect object and infinitive, 273
commas
   in tag questions, 27
   linking independent clauses, 200
   linking nouns, verbs, adjectives and adverbs, 199
   use with appositives, 32
   when changing order of adverbs, 141
   with adverbials of place, 134
   with adverbs of assertion, 142
   with adverbs of manner, 133
   with interjections, 338
commence
   followed by gerund *or* infinitive, 280
committed to
   followed by gerund, 268
committee
   as collective noun, 40, 51
common nouns, 2, 34

commonality, 2, 34
commonly
   adverb of time-frequency, 136
company
   as collective noun, 40
comparative adjectives, 105, 151, 152
   finishing the comparison, 165
comparative adverbs, 151
comparative and superlative forms, 154
   adverbial phrases, 159
   adverbs greater than one syllable, 157
   comparing nouns, 163
   comparing verbs, 164
   compound adjectives, 159
   spelling, 157
   Table 29 One-syllable adjectives and adverbs, 155
   Table 30 One-syllable adjectives ending v + c, 155
   Table 31 One-syllable adjective exceptions, 156
   Table 32 Adverbs greater than one syllable, 157
   Table 34 Two-syllable adjectives always taking more-most, 158
   Table 35 Two-syllable adjectives ending -y, 158
   Table 36 Three-syllable adjectives, 159
   Table 37 Irregular comparatives and superlatives, 160
   Table 38 Uses, 161
comparative forms
   comparing two nouns, 162
   Table 33 Two-syllable adjectives stressing first syllable, 158
comparatives, 151
compete
   intransitive verb, 222
complain
   intransitive verb, 222
complements, 16
   distinction from objects, 17
   gerund as subject complement, 267
   infinitive as object complement, 273
   infinitive as subject complement, 272
   locative complement, 21, 223, 347
   object complements, 16, 19
   required with transitive complex verbs, 223
   subject complements, 16, 19
complete
   intensifying adjective, 84
completely
   adverb of quantity, 144

complex conjunctions. *See* conjunction phrases
complex sentences, 14, 130, 193
compound adjectives, 5, 74
   hyphenated, 75
compound adverbial phrases, 129
compound complex sentences, 193
compound conjunctions. *See* conjunction phrases
compound nouns, 2, 31
compound sentences, 14, 192
concentrate on
   followed by gerund, 268
concern
   stative verb, 219
concerning
   preposition and participle, 172
   simple preposition, 171
concrete nouns, 1, 34, 35
concreteness, 1, 34, 35
conditionals. *See* subjunctive mood
confess to
   followed by gerund, 268
confused
   participial adjective, 78, 79
confusing
   participial adjective, 78, 79
conjugation, 212, 289
conjunction forms
   conjunction pairs, 191
   conjunction phrases, 191
   single-word conjunctions, 190
conjunction pairs. *See* correlative conjunctions
   Table 44 Conjunction pairs, 191
conjunction phrases
   Table 43 Conjunction phrases, 190
conjunction types, 193
   coordinating conjunctions, 194
   correlative conjunctions, 195
   subordinating conjunctions, 196
conjunctions, 8, 189
   conjunction types, 193
   coordinating conjunctions, 8, 194
   correlative conjunctions, 8, 195
   distinction from adverbs, 190
   distinction from prepositions, 172, 190
   forms, 189
   placement of punctuation, 203
   punctuation, 199, 202
   same as other parts of speech, 192
   subordinating conjunctions, 8, 196
conjunctive adverbs, 197
   distinction from conjunctions, 197
   in compound complex sentences, 193
   in compound sentences, 192
   placement of punctuation, 203
consequently
   conjunctive adverb, 197
consider
   infinitive as object complement, 274
   transitive complex verb, 224
   verb followed by gerund, 267
   verb taking object complement, 16
considering
   conjunction, 190
   preposition and participle, 172
   simple preposition, 171
   subordinator of contrast, 196
considering that
   conjunction, 190
consist
   stative verb, 219
constantly
   adverb of time-frequency, 136
contain
   stative verb, 219
content words, 10, 182
   pronunciation stress, 11
continue
   followed by gerund *or* infinitive, 280
continuously
   adverb of time-frequency, 136
contracted forms. *See* Tables 57 through 70
   n't, 241
convince
   reflexive verb, 224
coordinating conjunctions, 8, 194
   correlative conjunctions, 194
   in compound complex sentences, 193
   in compound sentences, 192
   in simple sentences, 192
   joining prepositional phrases, 174
   semantics, 194
   syntax, 194
copulae. *See* linking verbs
copular verbs. *See* linking verbs
copulative conjunctions. *See* coordinating conjunctions - semantics
copulative verbs. *See* linking verbs
correlative conjunctions, 8, 194
   in compound sentences, 192
   in simple sentences, 192
   semantics, 194
   syntax, 195
cost
   stative verb, 219
could
   for past ability, 247
   modal of ability, 246
   modal of permission, 255

    modal of possibility, 251
    modal of request, 254
    modal of suggestion, 249
    modal verb, 7, 240, 244
    past form of *can*, 243
couldn't
    modal of assumption, 250
countability, 1, 34, 36
countable nouns, 1, 34, 36
    collective nouns, 40
    inflection for number, 39
    used in an uncountable way, 116
create
    dynamic verb, 218
cumulative conjunctions. *See* coordinating conjunctions - semantics
cut
    irregular verb, 218
    reflexive verb, 54, 224

daily
    as adjective and adverb, 91
    flat adverb, 126
dare
    main verb, 240
    modal verb, 240
darts
    as singular noun, 51
decide
    subordinate clause subjunctive, 228
    verb followed by infinitive, 273
decision
    followed by infinitive, 277
declarative mood, 227
declarative sentences, 25
    affirmative, 25
decree
    subordinate clause subjunctive, 228
dedication to
    followed by gerund, 268
deem
    transitive complex verb, 223
    verb taking object complement, 16
deep
    distinction from *deeply*, 127
    flat adverb, 155
deeply
    distinction from *deep*, 127
definite article
    explicit description, 110
    generic statements of fact, 110
    mutual understanding, 109
    proper place names, 110
    uniqueness, 108
    use with superlative adjectives, 153

degrees of certainty
    modality, 250
degrees of comparison, 151, 152
    comparative, 151
    equality, 151
    superlative, 151
demand
    subordinate clause subjunctive, 228
demonstrative pronouns, 4, 63
demonstratives
    as limiting adjectives, 82
deny
    reflexive verb, 224
    stative verb, 219
    verb followed by gerund, 267
depend
    intransitive verb, 222
    stative verb, 219
dependent clauses, 195, 199, *See* subordinate clauses
    in complex sentences, 192
    in compound complex sentences, 193
    order in a sentence, 201
    placement in a sentence, 203
describe
    monotransitive verb, 223
descriptive adjectives, 4, 81, 82
    classifying adjectives, 81, 83
    intensifying adjectives, 84
    order in a sentence, 88
    order of limiting and descriptive adjectives, 89
    predicative adjectives, 87
    qualifying adjectives, 81, 83
    Table 21 Order of limiting and descriptive adjectives, 89
deserve
    followed by gerund *or* infinitive, 280
    stative verb, 219
    verb followed by infinitive, 273
desire
    subordinate clause subjunctive, 228
despite
    similar to *although*, 191
    simple preposition, 171
determined
    followed by infinitive, 276
determiners, 4, 99
    also indefinite pronouns, 56
    articles, 108
    as limiting adjectives, 82
    central determiners, 101
    comparative quantity, 105
    determiners of definiteness, 102
    determiners of magnitude, 104

functional classification, 102
postdeterminers, 101
predeterminers, 101
quantifiers, 105
structural classification, 101
Table 24 Types of nouns determiners can modify, 100
Table 25 Predeterminers, central determiners and postdeterminers, 101
Table 26 Determiners of definiteness, 103
Table 27 Determiners of magnitude, 104
devoted to
  followed by gerund, 268
devotion to
  followed by gerund, 268
dictate
  subordinate clause subjunctive, 228
did
  in past simple, 308
direct
  as adjective and adverb, 91
  followed by indirect object and infinitive, 273
direct objects, 15, 18
  elision, 16
  interrogative pronouns, 62
  objective pronouns, 49
  possessive pronouns, 52
  reciprocal pronouns, 55
  reflexive pronouns, 54
disagree
  reciprocal verb, 226
  stative verb, 219
disappointed in
  followed by gerund, 268
disapprove of
  followed by gerund, 268
discuss
  verb followed by gerund, 267
disgusting
  participial adjective, 79
disjunctive conjunctions. *See* coordinating conjunctions - semantics
dislike
  followed by gerund *or* infinitive, 280
  stative verb, 219
  verb followed by gerund, 267
  verb followed by infinitive, 273
ditransitive verbs, 223
divorce
  reciprocal verb, 226
do
  auxiliary verb, 7, 215, 238, 239
  in present simple, 295
  in semi-modals, 244
  main or auxiliary verb, 214
  main verb, 7, 239
  negation, interrogation, contradiction, 238
does
  in present simple, 295
double negatives, 57, 65
doubt
  stative verb, 219
down
  adverbial particle, 130
  preposition of direction, 179
  preposition of direction/movement, 9
  simple preposition, 171
downstairs
  adverb of place, 133
down-toners, 143
dread
  followed by gerund *or* infinitive, 278
  verb followed by infinitive, 273
duh
  interjection, 337
dummy subject. *See* non-referential *it*
during
  introducing adverbials of time, 137
  preposition of time, 9, 178
  similar to *while*, 191
  simple preposition, 171
dynamic verbs, 7, 218
  objects, not complements, 16
  sentence structure, 18

each
  determiner of magnitude, 104
  indefinite pronoun, 56
  limiting adjective indicating number, 73
  number, 58
  predeterminer, 101
  quantifier indefinite pronoun, 57
each other
  reciprocal pronoun, 3, 55
each time
  subordinator of time, 196
each/every time
  conjunction, 190
early
  adverb of time-when, 134
  as adjective and adverb, 91
  flat adverb, 126
  gradability, 153
easily
  as emphasizing adverb, 165
easy
  used as adverb, 155
eat

irregular verb, 8, 218
monotransitive verb, 223
transitive verb, 18
used transitively and intransitively, 222, 225
either
   central determiner, 101
   determiner of indefiniteness, 103
   indefinite pronoun, 56
   limiting adjective indicating number, 73
   number, 58
   quantifier indefinite pronoun, 57
either ... or
   conjunction, 191
   correlative conjunction, 8, 194
elect
   infinitive as object complement, 274
eligible
   followed by infinitive, 276
elision of direct object, 16
embarrassed
   participial adjective, 78
embarrassing
   participial adjective, 78
emphasizers, 143
emphasizing adjectives. *See* intensifying adjectives
empty subject. *See* non-referential *it*
encourage
   followed by indirect object and infinitive, 273
   reflexive verb, 224
end focus, 21, 22, 23
end up
   linking verb, 221
   stative verb, 219
enjoy
   reflexive verb, 224
   verb followed by gerund, 267
enough
   adverb of degree, 143
   adverb of quantity, 144
   determiner of magnitude, 104
   number, 58
   placement in a sentence, 145
   quantifier indefinite pronoun, 57
   with infinitive, 276
entwine
   reciprocal verb, 226
equality, 151, 152
equally
   adverb of quantity, 144
equivalence
   conjunctions and linkers, 204
   in conjunction use, 189

ergative verbs, 224
even
   as emphasizing adverb, 165
   in conjunction phrases, 190
even though, 190
   subordinator of contrast, 196
every
   central determiner, 101
   determiner of magnitude, 104
every time
   subordinator of time, 196
everybody
   indefinite pronoun, 56
   number, 57
everyone
   indefinite pronoun, 56
   number, 57
everything
   general indefinite pronoun, 56
   indefinite pronoun, 56
   number, 57
everywhere
   subordinator of place, 196
exactly
   adverb of quantity, 144
except
   infinitive as object, 274
   simple preposition, 171
except that
   conjunction, 190
excepting
   preposition and participle, 172
   simple preposition, 171
excessively
   adverb of quantity, 144
exchange
   reciprocal verb, 226
exciting
   participial adjective, 80
exclamation mark, 13, 337
   in exclamatory sentences, 27
exclamatory sentences, 27
excluding
   preposition and participle, 172
   simple preposition, 171
excuse for
   followed by gerund, 268
exhausted
   participial adjective, 78
exhausting
   participial adjective, 78
existing
   specifying adjective, 82
expect
   infinitive as object complement, 274

    verb followed by infinitive, 273
extreme adjectives
    adverbs to use with, 143

factitive verbs. *See* transitive complex
    verbs
factual moods, 226
fairly
    adverb of degree, 143
fall
    dynamic verb, 218
    linking verb, 221
    stative verb, 219
familiar with
    followed by gerund, 268
family
    as collective noun, 40
famous for
    followed by gerund, 268
far
    as emphasizing adverb, 165
    irregular comparative, 160
fast
    adverb of manner, 132
    as adjective and adverb, 91
    flat adverb, 126, 155
fear of
    followed by gerund, 268
feel
    infinitive as object complement, 274
    linking verb, 16, 221
    stative verb, 219
feel like
    followed by gerund, 268
feminine gender, 41
feud
    reciprocal verb, 226
few
    determiner of magnitude, 104
    gradable limiting adjective, 153
    indefinite pronoun, 56
    limiting adjective indicating number, 73
    number, 58
    postdeterminer, 101
    quantifier indefinite pronoun, 57
fewer
    determiner of magnitude, 104
    number, 58
    postdeterminer, 101
fewest
    determiner of magnitude, 104
    number, 58
    postdeterminer, 101
fight
    reciprocal verb, 226
finally
    conjunctive adverb, 197
find
    irregular verb, 218
finish
    verb followed by gerund, 267
finite verb forms, 212
    in past simple, 308
    in present simple, 295
    Table 46 Example finite verb forms, 212
first
    determiner of definiteness, 103
    postdeterminer, 101
first person, 47, 49, 52, 54
fit
    stative verb, 219
flat adverbs, 126
flock
    as collective noun, 40
follow
    monotransitive verb, 223
following
    determiner of definiteness, 103
    postdeterminer, 101
    simple preposition, 171
for
    complementizer, 197
    conjunction, 190
    coordinating conjunction, 8, 193
    indicating purpose, 180
    introducing adverbials of relative time,
        138
    introducing adverbials of time, 140
    position in a sentence, 139
    preposition and conjunction, 172
    preposition of direction, 179
    preposition of time, 178
    simple preposition, 171
    subordinating conjunction, 195
    subordinator of reason, 196
    with infinitive, 276
for example
    conjunctive adverb, 197
for the time being
    linker, 197
for this reason
    linker, 197
forbid
    followed by gerund *or* infinitive, 278
    followed by indirect object and infinitive,
        273
forever
    adverb of time-duration, 137
forget
    followed by gerund *or* infinitive, 281
    stative verb, 219
forgive for

followed by gerund, 268
forgiven
    participial adjective, 78
forgiving
    participial adjective, 78
former
    determiner of definiteness, 103
    postdeterminer, 101
fortunate
    followed by infinitive, 276
forward
    adverb of place, 133
    adverbial particle, 130
free
    comparative forms, 156
    distinction from *freely*, 127
freely
    distinction from *free*, 127
frequently
    adverb of time-frequency, 135, 136
frightened
    participial adjective, 78
frightened of
    followed by gerund, 268
frightening
    participial adjective, 78
from
    preposition of time, 9, 178
    simple preposition, 171
full infinitive. *See* infinitive
full stop. *See* period
fun
    comparative form exception, 156
function words, 10, 182
furthermore
    conjunctive adverb, 197
future continuous. *See* future progressive
future perfect, 323
    concepts, 324
    Table 69 Forms of the future perfect tense, 324
    use, 324
future perfect continuous. *See* future perfect progressive
future perfect progressive, 238, 325
    concepts, 326
    exception - stative verbs, 326
    Table 70 Forms of the future perfect progressive tense, 326
    use, 326
future progressive, 321
    concepts, 322
    exception - stative verbs, 322
    Table 68 Forms of the future progressive tense, 321
    uses, 322
future simple, 319
    concepts, 320
    Table 67 Forms of the future simple tense, 319
    uses, 319
future tenses, 318
    future perfect, 323
    future perfect progressive, 325
    future progressive, 321
    future simple, 319

gain
    monotransitive verb, 223
gender, 41, 47
    feminine gender, 41
    inflection in determiners, 99, 100
    masculine, 41
    neuter gender, 41
gender-neutral pronoun, 52
general indefinite pronouns, 56
generally
    adverb of time-frequency, 136
genitive case. *See* possessive case
genitive pronouns. *See* possessive pronouns
gerundial phrases, 265
    as subject of a sentence, 23
gerunds, 8, 211, 265, *See* verbs followed by gerunds *or* infinitives
    after possessives, 270
    as appositive, 268
    as nouns related to leisure, hobbies or jobs, 270
    as object of a preposition, 174, 267
    as object of main verb, 267
    as subject complement, 267
    as subject of a sentence, 266
    as subject or object, 22
    cannot be main verb, 265
    distinction from present participle, 271
    forms, 269
    functions in a sentence, 266
    in standard expressions, 270
    infinitive mood, 227
get
    linking verb, 221
    stative verb, 219
get along with
    phrasal prepositional verb, 231
give
    ditransitive verb, 223
    verb taking two objects, 18
give up
    phrasal verb, 231

given that
  conjunction, 190
  subordinator of condition, 196
glad
  followed by infinitive, 276
  predicative adjective, 87
glasses
  as plural noun, 39, 51
glow
  linking verb, 221
  stative verb, 219
go
  followed by gerund, 270
  intransitive verb, 222
  linking verb, 221
  stative verb, 219
goal
  followed by infinitive, 277
going-to future, 320
  uses, 320
good
  irregular comparative, 160
  vs. *well*, 127
gradability, 152
  adjectives, 152
  adverbs, 153
gradable adjectives, 4, 83, 152
grammatical case. *See* case
grammatical number. *See* number
grammatical number agreement, 51
granted
  preposition and participle, 172
  simple preposition, 171
granted that
  conjunction, 190
  subordinator of condition, 196
great
  intensifying adjective, 84
  interjection, 337
group
  as collective noun, 40
grow
  dynamic verb, 218
  linking verb, 221
  stative verb, 219

habitually
  adverb of time-frequency, 136
had
  in past perfect, 314
  in past perfect progressive, 316
had better
  modal of advice, 247
  semi-modal, 240, 244
half
  determiner of magnitude, 104

predeterminer, 101
hankering
  followed by infinitive, 277
happy
  followed by infinitive, 276
hard
  adverb of manner, 132
  as adjective and adverb, 91
  degrees of comparison, 154
  distinction from *hardly*, 127
  flat adverb, 126, 155
hardly
  different from flat adverb form, 155
  distinction from *hard*, 127
hardly ever
  adverbial of time-frequency, 136
  creating negative sentences, 25
has
  in present perfect, 302
  in present perfect progressive, 305
hate
  followed by gerund *or* infinitive, 280
  stative verb, 219
  verb followed by gerund, 267
  verb followed by infinitive, 273
have
  auxiliary verb, 7, 215, 238, 239
  in future perfect, 324
  in future perfect progressive, 326
  in present perfect, 302
  in present perfect progressive, 305
  in semi-modals, 244
  main or auxiliary verb, 214
  main verb, 7, 239
  stative verb, 219
have got to
  modal of advice, 247
  modal of assumption, 250
  modal of necessity, 252
  semi-modal, 240, 244
have to
  modal of advice, 247
  modal of assumption, 250
  modal of obligation, 252
  semi-modal, 240, 244
he
  masculine inflection, 48
  personal subjective pronoun, 3
  subjective pronoun, 49
  third person singular masculine personal
    pronoun, 48
head of the phrase, 14
head of the predicate, 14
hear
  stative verb, 219
help

   as reflexive verb, 54
   infinitive as object complement, 274
   monotransitive verb, 223
   reflexive verb, 224
helping verbs. *See* auxiliary verbs
her
   central determiner, 101
   determiner of definiteness, 103
   determiner with inflection for gender, 100
   objective pronoun, 49
   personal objective pronoun, 3
herd
   as collective noun, 40
hers
   possessive pronoun, 3, 52
herself
   reflexive pronoun, 3, 54
hesitant
   followed by infinitive, 276
hesitate
   verb followed by infinitive, 273
hey
   interjection, 337
high
   as adjective and adverb, 91
   flat adverb, 126, 155
highly
   different from flat adverb form, 155
him
   objective pronoun, 49
   personal objective pronoun, 3
himself
   reflexive pronoun, 3, 54
hire
   infinitive as object complement, 274
his
   central determiner, 101
   determiner of definiteness, 103
   determiner with inflection for gender, 100
   possessive pronoun, 3, 52
hmm
   interjection, 337
home
   adverbial particle, 130
hope
   verb followed by infinitive, 273
how
   in exclamatory sentences, 27
however
   conjunctive adverb, 192, 197
   conjunctive adverb in compound complex sentence, 193
hurt
   as reflexive verb, 54
   participial adjective, 78
   reflexive verb, 224
hurting
   participial adjective, 78
hyphenated compound adjectives, 75

I
   first person singular personal pronoun, 48
   personal subjective pronoun, 3
   subjective pronoun, 49
idiomatic phrasal verbs, 231
if
   complementizer, 197
   conjunction, 190
   elision of subject and *be*, 195
   subordinating conjunction, 8, 195
   subordinator of condition, 196
if ... then
   conjunction, 191
   correlative conjunction, 8, 194
if only
   conjunction, 190
   subordinator of condition, 196
ill
   predicative adjective, 87
illative conjunctions. *See* coordinating conjunctions - semantics
imagine
   stative verb, 219
imperative + and
   conjunction, 190
   subordinator of condition, 196
imperative + or
   conjunction, 190
   subordinator of condition, 196
imperative form
   with conjunctions, 191
imperative mood, 227
imperative sentences, 27
impress
   stative verb, 219
in
   adverbial particle, 130
   preposition of place, 9, 176, 177
   preposition of time, 178
   preposition of transport, 179
   simple preposition, 171
in case, 196
   conjunction, 190
   subordinator of reason, 196
in front of
   preposition of place, 176
in order
   adverbial of purpose, 129
in order + *to-infinitive*

conjunction, 190
   subordinator of purpose, 196
in order for
   conjunction, 190
   subordinator of purpose, 196
in order that
   conjunction, 190
   subordinator of purpose, 196
   subordinator of result, 196
in other words
   linker, 197
in particular
   linker, 197
in that
   conjunction, 190
   subordinator of contrast, 196
   subordinator of manner, 196
in the event that
   conjunction, 190
   subordinator of reason, 196
in the long run
   linker, 197
in the meantime
   linker, 197
in time
   prepositional phrase, 178
inanimate nouns
   how to show possession, 43
inasmuch as
   conjunction, 190
   subordinator of reason, 196
include
   stative verb, 219
indeed
   conjunctive adverb, 197
indefinite articles, 111
   general idea, 112
   not defined, 112
   replacement for *one*, 113
   subject complements, 113
   zero article, 114
indefinite pronouns, 3, 55
   affirmative sentences, 58
   general indefinite pronouns, 56
   interrogative sentences, 58
   negative indefinite pronouns, 56
   negative sentences, 58
   quantifier indefinite pronouns, 57
   Table 14 Indefinite pronouns, 60
independent clauses, 199
   in complex sentences, 192
   in compound complex sentences, 193
   in compound sentences, 192
   linking, 200
   order in a sentence, 201
   placement in a sentence, 203

indicative mood, 6, 227
   declarative, 227
   interrogative, 227
indirect objects, 15, 18
   objective pronouns, 49
   possessive pronouns, 52
   reflexive pronouns, 54
   with infinitive as direct object, 273
infinitival forms. *See* infinitives - forms
infinitival phrase. *See* infinitive phrases
infinitive, 209, 211
infinitive mood, 227
infinitive phrases, 129, 265
   as subject of a sentence, 23
infinitives, 8, 265, *See* verbs followed by gerunds *or* infinitives
   after wh-words, 277
   as adjectives, 277
   as adverbs, 276
   as adverbs of purpose, 277
   as appositive, 274
   as object complement, 273
   as object of a preposition, 274
   as object of main verb, 273
   as subject complement, 272
   as subject of a sentence, 272
   as subject or object, 22
   ellipsis, 278
   forms, 274
   functions in a sentence, 272
   in indirect questions, 277
   infinitive mood, 227
inflection, 38, 47, 212, 213, 289
   case, 41
   determiners, 99
   first person, 47
   gender, 41
   number, 39
   second person, 47
   third person, 47
infrequently
   adverb of time-frequency, 136
inseparable phrasal verbs, 232
inside
   adverb of place, 133
   preposition of place, 176
   simple preposition, 171
insist
   subordinate clause subjunctive, 228
insist on
   followed by gerund, 268
insofar as
   conjunction, 190
instruct
   followed by indirect object and infinitive, 273

intend
    followed by gerund *or* infinitive, 278
    subordinate clause subjunctive, 228
    verb followed by infinitive, 273
intensifiers. *See* adverbs of degree
intensifying a subject
    reflexive pronouns, 54
intensifying adjectives, 84
interest in
    followed by gerund, 268
interested
    participial adjective, 78, 79
interested in
    followed by gerund, 268
interesting
    participial adjective, 79
interjections, 10, 337
    forms, 337
    placement, 338
intermittently
    adverb of time-frequency, 136
interrogation
    auxiliary and modal verbs, 242
    auxiliary and modal verbs - word order, 242
interrogative adjectives, 82, 86
interrogative mood, 6, 227
interrogative pronouns, 3, 61
    as subject or object, 26
    Table 15 Personal and non-personal reference, 61
interrogative sentences, 25
    alternative questions, 26
    negative questions, 27
    tag questions, 26
    wh-questions, 26
    yes/no questions, 26
into
    preposition of direction/movement, 9
    preposition of movement, 179
    preposition of transport, 179
intransitive phrasal verbs, 231
intransitive verbs, 7, 222
    ergative verbs, 224
    intransitive phrasal verbs, 231
    no object, 15
    sentence structure, 18
introduce
    as reflexive verb, 54
    reflexive verb, 224
inversion of order, 137, 142, 194
invite
    infinitive as object complement, 274
involve
    stative verb, 219

    verb followed by gerund, 267
irregular verbs, 7, 217
    Table 48 Spelling rules - present participle and gerund, 217
is
    form of *be*, 296
    in present progressive, 299
isn't
    form of *be*, 296
it, 49
    as subject, 23
    as subject or object, 22, 24
    neuter inflection, 48
    non-referential, 23
    objective pronoun, 49
    personal alternatives, 51
    personal objective pronoun, 3
    personal subjective pronoun, 3
    third person singular neuter personal pronoun, 48
its
    central determiner, 101
    determiner of definiteness, 103
itself
    reflexive pronoun, 3, 54

judge
    infinitive as object complement, 274
    verb taking object complement, 16
just
    adverb of quantity, 144
    in conjunction phrases, 190
just as, 190

keep
    linking verb, 221
    stative verb, 219
    transitive complex verb, 223
kill
    reflexive verb, 54, 224
know
    stative verb, 219
known for
    followed by gerund, 268

lack
    stative verb, 219
largely
    adverb of time-frequency, 136
last
    determiner of definiteness, 103
    postdeterminer, 101
late
    adverb of time-when, 134
    as adjective and adverb, 91

    distinction from *lately*, 127
    flat adverb, 126, 155
lately
    different from flat adverb form, 155
    distinction from *late*, 127
latter
    determiner of definiteness, 103
    postdeterminer, 101
learn
    followed by gerund *or* infinitive, 278
least
    determiner of magnitude, 104
    in superlative forms, 154, 156, 157, 158, 159
    number, 58
    postdeterminer, 101
leave
    linking verb, 221
    stative verb, 219
less
    adverb of quantity, 144
    determiner of magnitude, 104
    in comparative forms, 154, 156, 157, 158, 159
    number, 58
    postdeterminer, 101
lest
    conjunction, 190
    subordinating conjunction, 195
let
    infinitive as object complement, 274
    transitive complex verb, 224
lexical aspect. *See* verb classifications - semantic
lexical verbs. *See* main verbs
liable
    followed by infinitive, 276
lie
    intransitive verb, 222
    linking verb, 221
    stative verb, 219
like
    conjunction, 190
    followed by gerund *or* infinitive, 280
    indicating similarity, 180
    infinitive as object of preposition, 274
    monotransitive verb, 223
    simple preposition, 171
    stative verb, 219
    subordinator of manner, 196
    verb followed by gerund, 267
likely
    followed by infinitive, 276
limiting adjectives, 4, 81
    determiners, 99
    differences from descriptive, 81
    non-gradable, 153
    order in a sentence, 88
    specifying adjectives, 81
    Table 18 Types of limiting adjectives, 82
    Table 21 Order of adjectives, 89
linkers
    placement of punctuation, 203
linkers and transition words, 198
linking verbs, 4, 16, 19, 220
    following with an adverb, 17
listen
    intransitive verb, 222
little
    adverb of quantity, 144
    determiner of magnitude, 104
    gradable limiting adjective, 153
    indefinite pronoun, 56
    irregular comparative, 160
    number, 58
    postdeterminer, 101
    quantifier indefinite pronoun, 57
live up to
    phrasal prepositional verb, 231
loathe
    followed by gerund *or* infinitive, 280
locative complements, 21, 223, 347
long
    as adjective and adverb, 91
    flat adverb, 126, 155
look
    linking verb, 16, 221
    stative verb, 219
lot
    noun in quantifier phrase, 106
loud
    used as adverb, 155
love
    followed by gerund *or* infinitive, 280
    monotransitive verb, 223
    stative verb, 219
    verb followed by gerund, 267
low
    as adjective and adverb, 91
    flat adverb, 126, 155

main
    specifying adjective, 82
main verbs, 7, 214
    forms after auxiliary and modal verbs, 242
    in verb phrases, 229
make
    infinitive as object complement, 274
    verb followed by gerund, 267
    verb taking object complement, 16, 19
make out

phrasal verb, 231
manage
    followed by gerund *or* infinitive, 280
    verb followed by infinitive, 273
mandatory sentence elements, 13
many
    determiner of magnitude, 104
    gradable limiting adjective, 153
    indefinite pronoun, 56
    limiting adjective indicating number, 73
    number, 58
    postdeterminer, 101
    quantifier indefinite pronoun, 57
marking
    for tense, 289
marry
    reciprocal verb, 226
masculine gender, 41
mass nouns. *See* uncountable nouns
mathematics
    as singular noun, 51
matter
    intransitive verb, 222
    stative verb, 219
may
    modal of offer, 255
    modal of permission, 255
    modal of possibility, 251
    modal verb, 240, 244
may not
    modal of prohibition, 255
me
    objective pronoun, 49
    personal objective pronoun, 3
mean
    followed by gerund *or* infinitive, 282
    stative verb, 219
measles
    as singular noun, 39, 51
measure
    stative verb, 219
meet
    monotransitive verb, 223
    reciprocal verb, 226
memory of
    followed by gerund, 268
might
    modal of permission, 255
    modal of possibility, 251
    modal of suggestion, 249
    modal verb, 7, 240, 244
mind
    stative verb, 219
    verb followed by gerund, 267
mine
    possessive pronoun, 3, 52
minus
    simple preposition, 171
modal auxiliary verbs, 7, 215, *See* modal verbs
modal phrases, 240, *See* semi-modals
modal verbs, 237, 240
    differences from auxiliary verbs, 242, 243
    meanings of negative forms, 251
    only one form, 242
    pronunciation stress, 258
    similarities with auxiliary verbs, 241
    structure, 241
modality, 240, 245
    ability, 246
    advice/recommendation, 247
    assumption, 250
    certainty, 250
    necessity/obligation/responsibility, 252
    offers, 255
    permission/prohibition, 255
    possibility, 251
    preference, 256
    probability, 251
    promises, 257
    requests, 254
    suggestion, 249
    Table 51 Summary of modal verbs and modalities, 246
modals. *See* modal verbs
monotransitive verbs, 223
moods, 6, 226
    imperative, 227
    indicative, 6, 227
    infinitive, 227
    interrogative, 6
    subjunctive, 228
more
    adverb of quantity, 144
    determiner of magnitude, 104
    expressing contrast with *less*, 156
    in comparative forms, 154, 156, 157, 158, 159
    number, 58
    postdeterminer, 101
moreover
    conjunctive adverb, 197
most
    determiner of magnitude, 104
    determiner or adverb, 105
    in superlative forms, 154, 156, 157, 158, 159
    number, 58
    postdeterminer, 101

mostly
    adverb of time-frequency, 136
motivation
    followed by infinitive, 277
move
    subordinate clause subjunctive, 228
much
    adverb of quantity, 144
    as emphasizing adverb, 165
    determiner of magnitude, 104
    gradable limiting adjective, 153
    indefinite pronoun, 56
    irregular comparative, 160
    limiting adjective indicating number, 73
    negative quantifier, 107
    postdeterminer, 101
    quantifier indefinite pronoun, 57
much as
    conjunction, 190
    subordinator of contrast, 196
multi-word verbs. See phrasal verbs
mumps
    as singular noun, 39, 51
must
    modal of advice, 247
    modal of assumption, 250
    modal of obligation, 252
    modal verb, 240, 244
mustn't
    modal of prohibition, 255
my
    central determiner, 101
    determiner of definiteness, 103
myself
    reflexive pronoun, 3, 54

name
    verb taking object complement, 16
near
    adverb of place, 133
    adverbial particle, 130
    flat adverb, 155
    preposition of place, 9, 176
    simple preposition, 171
nearly
    adverb of quantity, 144
    as emphasizing adverb, 165
    different from flat adverb form, 155
necessity
    modality, 252
need
    followed by infinitive, 277
    main verb, 240, 253
    modal of necessity, 253
    modal verb, 240
    stative verb, 219

needn't
    modal of necessity, 253
negation, 241
    of modal verbs, 251
negative adverbs, 25
negative declarative sentences, 25
negative indefinite pronouns, 56
negative infinitives, 275
negative questions, 27
    how to answer, 28
neglect
    followed by gerund or infinitive, 278
neither
    central determiner, 101
    conjunction, 190
    determiner of magnitude, 104
    indefinite pronoun, 56
    limiting adjective indicating number, 73
    negative indefinite pronoun, 57
    number, 58
    quantifier indefinite pronoun, 57
neither ... nor
    conjunction, 191
    correlative conjunction, 8, 194
neuter gender, 41
never
    adverb of time-frequency, 136
    creating negative sentences, 25
    negation, 275
nevertheless
    conjunctive adverb, 197
news
    as singular noun, 39
next
    determiner of definiteness, 103
    postdeterminer, 101
next to
    preposition of place, 176
no
    adverb of assertion, 142
    as determiner, 142
    as interjection, 142
    central determiner, 101
    determiner of magnitude, 104
no one
    indefinite pronoun, 56
    negative indefinite pronoun, 57
    number, 57
no sooner ... than
    conjunction, 191
    correlative conjunction, 8, 194
nobody
    general indefinite pronoun, 56
    indefinite pronoun, 56
    negative indefinite pronoun, 57
    number, 57

nominative case. *See* subjective case
nominative pronouns. *See* subjective pronouns
non-count nouns. *See* uncountable nouns
none
   indefinite pronoun, 56
   negative indefinite pronoun, 57
   number, 58
   quantifier indefinite pronoun, 57
non-factual moods, 226
non-finite verb forms, 209
   base form, 210
   gerund, 211
   infinitive, 211
   participle, 211
   Table 45 Examples of non-finite verb forms, 210
non-finite verbs, 227
non-gradable adjectives, 5, 83, 153
non-literal phrasal verbs, 231
non-referential *it*, 23
non-referential *there*, 23
non-separable phrasal verbs. *See* inseparable phrasal verbs
non-tense verbs. *See* non-finite verbs
nor
   conjunction, 190
   coordinating conjunction, 8, 193
   inversion of order, 194
normally
   adverb of time-frequency, 136
not
   adverb of assertion, 142
   contraction with auxiliary, 25
   creating negative sentences, 25
   in negative questions, 27
   negation, 228, 237, 238, 269, 275, 295, 296, 299, 302, 305, 308, 311, 314, 316, 319, 321, 326
   negation - auxiliary and modal verbs, 241
not (only) … but (also)
   conjunction, 191
   correlative conjunction, 8, 194
not always
   adverbial of time-frequency, 136
not ever
   adverbial of time-frequency, 136
not generally
   adverbial of time-frequency, 136
not often
   adverbial of time-frequency, 136
not usually
   adverbial of time-frequency, 136
nothing
   indefinite pronoun, 56
   negative indefinite pronoun, 57
   number, 57
notice
   stative verb, 219
   transitive complex verb, 224
notwithstanding
   preposition and conjunction, 172
   simple preposition, 171
noun forms, 31
   compound nouns, 31
   gerunds, 31
   suffixes, 31
noun phrases, 13, 14
   as object of a preposition, 174
noun types
   Table 6 Noun types, 34
nouns, 1, 31
   as appositive, 32
   as object complement, 32
   as object of a preposition, 33, 174
   as object of the main verb, 32
   as subject, 32
   as subject complement, 32
   case, 2, 41
   commonality, 2, 34
   concreteness, 1, 34, 35
   countability, 1, 34, 36
   functioning as adjective, 33
   gender, 41
   gerunds, 265
   infinitives, 265
   inflection, 38
   number, 2, 34, 39
   placement in a sentence, 33
   possessive, 2
now
   adverb of time-when, 134
   subordinator of reason, 196
now that
   conjunction, 190
   subordinator of reason, 196
nucleus of the phrase. *See* head of the phrase
number, 34, 39, 47
   demonstrative pronouns, 63
   effect on verb form, 39
   in indefinite pronouns, 57
   inflection in determiners, 99
   partitive phrase, 106
numbers
   as limiting adjectives, 82

object complements, 16, 19, 32, 223
   predicative adjectives, 87

required with transitive complex verbs, 223
object of a preposition
  interrogative pronouns, 62
  objective pronouns, 49
  possessive pronouns, 53
  reflexive pronouns, 54
object to
  followed by gerund, 268
objective case, 34, 41, 47
  interrogative pronouns, 62
  relative pronouns, 60
  use in comparatives, 162
objective complements. See object complements
objective pronouns, 3, 49
  as subject complement, 49
  placement in inseparable phrasal verbs, 232
  placement in separable phrasal verbs, 232
  Table 11 Objective pronouns, 49
  use in comparatives, 162
objects, 15, 18, 32
  direct objects, 15, 18
  distinction from complements, 17
  gerund as object of a preposition, 267
  gerund as object of main verb, 267
  in phrasal prepositional verbs, 233
  in separable phrasal verbs, 232
  indirect objects, 15, 18
  infinitive as object of a preposition, 274
  infinitives as object of main verb, 273
  objective pronouns, 49
  of ergative verbs, 225
  placement in interrogative sentences, 61
  placement in phrasal verbs, 232
  required for ditransitive verbs, 223
  required for transitive verbs, 222
  variations, 22
obligation
  modality, 252
occasionally
  adverb of time-frequency, 135, 136
occur
  intransitive verb, 222
oder of adjectives
  Table 23 Full set of adjective categories, 90
of
  indicating possession, 180
  simple preposition, 171
  to show possession, 43, 53
off
  adverbial particle, 130
  preposition of direction/movement, 9

  preposition of movement, 179
  preposition of transport, 179
  simple preposition, 171
offer
  verb followed by infinitive, 273
offers
  modality, 255
often
  adverb of time-frequency, 135, 136
oh
  interjection, 337
oink
  interjection, 338
old
  comparative and superlative forms, 157
  irregular comparative, 160
on
  adverbial particle, 130
  preposition of place, 9, 176, 177
  preposition of time, 9, 178
  preposition of transport, 179
  simple preposition, 171
on condition that
  conjunction, 190
  subordinator of condition, 196
on the contrary
  linker, 197
on the other hand
  linker, 197
on the whole
  linker, 197
on time
  prepositional phrase, 178
once
  conjunction, 190
  subordinating conjunction, 195
  subordinator of time, 196
one
  determiner of magnitude, 104
  general indefinite pronoun, 56
  indefinite pronoun, 56
  number, 58
  postdeterminer, 101
  quantifier indefinite pronoun, 57
one another
  reciprocal pronoun, 3, 55
only
  in conjunction phrases, 190
  specifying adjective, 82
only if, 190
onto
  preposition of direction/movement, 9
  preposition of movement, 179
  preposition of transport, 179
oops
  interjection, 337

opposite
   simple preposition, 171
   specifying adjective, 82
optional sentence elements, 15
or
   conjunction, 190
   connecting infinitives, 273
   coordinating conjunction, 8, 193
   to begin a sentence, 204
   use in alternative questions, 26
order
   followed by indirect object and infinitive, 273
   followed by infinitive, 277
   subordinate clause subjunctive, 228
order of adjectives, 88, 89
   Table 22 Major descriptive categories for ordering, 89
order of adverbs, 141
ordinal numbers
   determiner of definiteness, 103
   postdeterminer, 101
ordinals
   as limiting adjectives, 82
other
   determiner of definiteness, 103
   postdeterminer, 101
   quantifier indefinite pronoun, 57
   specifying adjective, 82
others
   number, 58
   quantifier indefinite pronoun, 57
otherwise
   conjunctive adverb, 197
ouch
   interjection, 337
ought (to)
   modal of advice, 247
   modal of obligation, 253
   modal of probability, 251
   modal verb, 240, 244
our
   central determiner, 101
   determiner of definiteness, 103
ours
   possessive pronoun, 3, 52
ourselves
   reflexive pronoun, 3, 54
out
   adverbial particle, 130
   preposition of movement, 179
   simple preposition, 171
out of
   preposition of transport, 179
outside
   adverb of place, 133
   preposition of place, 176
   simple preposition, 171
over
   adverbial particle, 130
   preposition of direction/movement, 9
   preposition of movement, 179
   preposition of place, 176
   simple preposition, 171
owe
   elision of direct object, 16
   stative verb, 219
own
   as possessive pronoun, 102
   stative verb, 219
Oxford comma. *See* serial comma

paint
   verb taking object complement, 16
pajamas
   as plural noun, 39
pants
   as plural noun, 39
paralanguage, 338
parallelism. *See* equivalence
participial adjectives, 5, 77, 211
   choosing the correct form, 79
   distinction from verbs, 78, 80
   Table 16 Examples describing emotions, 78
participles, 211
   infinitive mood, 227
   participial adjectives, 211
   past participle, 211
   present participle, 211
particles, 231
particular
   specifying adjective, 82
partitives, 37, 38, 106
   using adjectival prepositional phrases, 175
parts of a sentence, 13
   adverbials, 17
   clauses, 14
   complements, 16
   objects, 15
   phrases, 14
   predicate, 13, 14
   subject, 13, 14
parts of speech, 1
   adjectives, 4, 73
   adverbs, 5, 125
   conjunctions, 8, 189
   interjections, 10, 337
   nouns, 1, 31

prepositions, 9, 171
pronouns, 2, 47
verbs, 6, 209
passive constructions, 211, 226, 294
    Table 56 Tenses in active and passive voice, 294
passive gerund, 269
passive infinitive, 275
past
    adverbial particle, 130
    preposition and adverb, 172
    preposition of place, 176
    preposition of time, 178
    simple preposition, 171
past continuous. *See* past progressive
past participles, 78, 211
    after auxiliary *be*, 239
    after auxiliary *have*, 239
    after passive auxiliaries, 230
    after perfective auxiliaries, 230
    in future perfect, 324
    in past perfect, 314
    in present perfect, 302
past perfect, 238, 313
    concepts, 314
    Table 65 Forms of the past perfect tense, 314
    uses, 314
past perfect continuous. *See* past perfect progressive
past perfect progressive, 316
    concepts, 317
    exception - stative verbs, 316
    Table 66 Forms of the past perfect progressive tense, 316
    uses, 316
past progressive, 310
    concepts, 312
    exception - stative verbs, 312
    Table 64 Forms of the past progressive, 311
    uses, 311
past simple, 307
    be-verb exception, 308
    concepts, 309
    Table 62 Forms of the past simple tense, 308
    uses, 309
past tenses, 307
    past perfect, 313
    past perfect progressive, 316
    past progressive, 310
    past simple, 307
pay
    elision of direct object, 16
    reflexive verb, 224
pending
    preposition and participle, 172
    simple preposition, 171
penultimate
    determiner of definiteness, 103
    postdeterminer, 101
per
    simple preposition, 171
percent
    noun in quantifier phrase, 106
perfect
    intensifying adjective, 84
perfect modal structure, 251, 252
perfective aspect, 238
    future perfect, 323
    future perfect progressive, 325
    past perfect, 313
    past perfect progressive, 316
    present perfect, 301
    present perfect progressive, 304
perfective gerund, 269
perfective infinitive, 275
perfective passive gerund, 269
perfective passive infinitive, 275
perfective progressive gerund, 269
perfective progressive infinitive, 275
period
    use in a sentence, 13
permanently
    adverb of time-duration, 137
permission
    followed by infinitive, 277
permission/prohibition
    modality, 255
permit
    infinitive as object complement, 274
person, 47
    first person, 47
    second person, 47
    third person, 47
personal pronouns, 2, 48
    objective pronouns, 3, 49
    possessive pronouns, 3, 52
    reciprocal pronouns, 3, 55
    reflexive pronouns, 3, 53
    subjective pronouns, 3, 48
    Table 1 Personal pronouns, 3
persuade
    followed by indirect object and infinitive, 273
petition
    subordinate clause subjunctive, 228
phrasal prepositional verbs, 231, 232
phrasal verbs, 7, 231
    inseparable, 232
    intransitive phrasal verbs, 231

phrasal prepositional verbs, 231
   separable, 232
   transitive phrasal verbs, 232
phrases, 14
   head of the phrase, 14
physics
   as singular noun, 39, 51
plan
   followed by infinitive, 277
plan on
   followed by gerund, 268
play
   linking verb, 221
   stative verb, 219
plead
   linking verb, 221
   stative verb, 219
please
   stative verb, 219
pleased
   followed by infinitive, 276
plural nouns, 34, 36
   inflection for number, 39
   irregular plurals, 40
   spelling rules, 40
plural subject
   reciprocal pronouns, 55
plus
   simple preposition, 171
police
   as collective noun, 41, 51
positive
   intensifying adjective, 84
possess
   stative verb, 219
possessive adjectives
   followed by gerund, 270
   possessive determiners, 102
possessive case, 34, 42, 47
   interrogative pronouns, 62
possessive nouns
   as limiting adjectives, 82
   central determiner, 101
   determiner of definiteness, 103
   followed by gerund, 270
   placement in a sentence, 86
   structure in a a sentence, 102
possessive pronouns, 3, 52
   confusion with possessive determiners, 53
   Table 12 Possessive pronouns, 52
possibility
   modality, 251
postdeterminers, 101
postmodifying adjectives, 4, 86

attributive, 87
postponed subjects, 23
predeterminers, 101
predicate, 13, 14
predicative adjectives, 4, 86, 87
   placement in a sentence, 87
predominantly
   adverb of time-frequency, 136
prefer
   followed by gerund *or* infinitive, 280
   stative verb, 219
   verb followed by gerund, 267
preference
   modality, 256
preference for
   followed by gerund, 268
prefixes
   associated with adjectives, 74
   associated with verbs, 209
   -self to create reflexive verbs, 224
premodifying adjectives, 4, 86
   order in a sentence, 89
preparatory *it*, 22
   as object, 23
prepare
   reflexive verb, 54, 224
preposition forms
   complex prepositions, 172
   Table 41 Simple prepositions, 171
preposition of direction or movement, 179
preposition types, 9
   prepositions of direction/movement, 9
   prepositions of place, 9
   prepositions of time, 9
   Table 4
      Preposition types, 9
prepositional phrases, 9, 129, 173
   adjectival, 10, 175
   adverbial, 10, 176
   functions, 175
   joined with conjunctions, 174
   order, 176
   structures, 174
prepositions, 9, 171
   distinction from adverbs, 130, 131
   distinction from conjunctions, 172, 190
   meanings, 176, 181
   preposition of direction or movement, 179
   preposition types, 9
   prepositional phrases, 9, 173
   prepositions of place, 177
   prepositions of time, 178
   prepositions of transport, 179
   pronunciation, 183

    same as other parts of speech, 172
    similar to participles, 171
    structural patterns, 182
prepositions of direction / movement, 9
prepositions of place, 9, 177
prepositions of time, 9, 178
prepositions of transport, 179
present
    specifying adjective, 82
present continuous. *See* present progressive
present participles, 78, 211
    after auxiliary *be*, 239
    after progressive auxiliaries, 230
    distinction from gerund, 271
    in future perfect progressive, 326
    in future progressive, 321
    in past perfect progressive, 316
    in past progressive, 311
    in present perfect progressive, 305
    in present progressive, 299
present perfect, 238, 301
    concepts, 303
    Table 60 Forms of the present perfect tense, 302
    uses, 302
present perfect progressive, 238, 304
    concepts, 306
    exception - stative verbs, 306
    Table 61 Forms of the present perfect progressive, 305
    uses, 305
present progressive, 299
    concepts, 300
    exception - stative verbs, 300
    Table 59 Forms of the present progressive tense, 299
    uses, 299
present simple, 295
    concepts, 297
    spelling, 298
    Table 57 Forms of the present simple tense, 295
    uses, 296
present tenses, 295
    present perfect, 301
    present perfect progressive, 304
    present progressive, 299
    present simple, 295
pretend
    verb followed by infinitive, 273
previous
    determiner of definiteness, 103
    postdeterminer, 101
primarily
    adverb of time-frequency, 136

primary
    specifying adjective, 82
principal
    specifying adjective, 82
probability
    modality, 251
progressive aspect, 237
    future perfect progressive, 325
    future progressive, 321
    past perfect progressive, 316
    past progressive, 310
    present perfect progressive, 304
    present progressive, 299
    stative verbs, 220, 221
promise
    elision of direct object, 16
    stative verb, 219
    verb followed by infinitive, 273
promises
    modality, 257
pronominal adjectives. *See* interrogative adjectives
pronominal phrases. *See* reciprocal pronouns
pronoun forms, 47
    Table 9 Example pronoun forms, 48
pronoun types, 48
    demonstrative pronouns, 63
    general indefinite pronouns, 56
    indefinite pronouns, 55
    interrogative pronouns, 61
    negative indefinite pronouns, 56
    objective pronouns, 49
    personal pronouns, 48
    possessive pronouns, 52
    quantifier indefinite pronouns, 57
    reciprocal pronouns, 55
    reflexive pronouns, 53
    relative pronouns, 60
    subjective pronouns, 48
pronouns, 2, 47
    as direct object, 49
    as indirect object, 49
    as object of a preposition, 49, 174
    as subject complement, 48
    as subject of a sentence, 48
    as subject of finite clauses, 48
    case, 47
    demonstrative pronouns, 4, 63
    general indefinite pronouns, 56
    indefinite pronouns, 3, 55
    interrogative pronouns, 3, 61
    negative indefinite pronouns, 56
    objective pronouns, 3, 49
    personal pronouns, 2
    possessive pronouns, 52

quantifier indefinite pronouns, 57
reciprocal pronouns, 3, 55
reflexive pronouns, 3, 53
relative pronouns, 3, 60
subjective pronoun, 3
subjective pronouns, 48
pronunciation stress
   auxiliary and modal verbs, 258
   content words, 11
   noun vs. verb, 213
proper nouns, 2, 34, 35
   zero article, 115
proper place names, 110
   taking the definite article, 110
proposal
   followed by infinitive, 277
propose, 267
   followed by gerund *or* infinitive, 278
   subordinate clause subjunctive, 228
proud of
   followed by gerund, 268
prove
   linking verb, 221
   stative verb, 219
pro-verbs, 242
provided
   conjunction, 190
   subordinating conjunction, 195
   subordinator of condition, 196
provided that
   conjunction, 190
providing
   conjunction, 190
   subordinating conjunction, 195
   subordinator of condition, 196
providing that
   conjunction, 190
pst
   interjection, 338
punctuation
   conjunctions, 199
   linking clauses, 200
   linking nouns, verbs, adjectives and adverbs, 200
punctuation mark
   use in a sentence, 13
put down
   multiple meanings, 181

qualifying adjectives, 81, 83
   order in a sentence, 89
   Table 19 Types of qualifying adjectives, 83
quantifier indefinite pronouns, 57
quantifier phrases, 107

partitives, 106
placement in a sentence, 105
quantifiers, 105
   partitives, 106
   quantifying determiners, 106
question mark
   use in interrogative sentences, 25
questions. *See* interrogative sentences
quick
   used as adverb, 155
quiet
   used as adverb, 155
quite
   adverb of degree, 143
   as emphasizing adverb, 165

rarely
   adverb of time-frequency, 135, 136
   creating negative sentences, 25
rather
   adverb of degree, 143
   as emphasizing adverb, 165
reaction to
   followed by gerund, 268
ready
   followed by infinitive, 276
   predicative adjective, 87
real
   comparative form exception, 156
   intensifying adjective, 84
realia, 35
realize
   stative verb, 219
really
   adverb of degree, 143
reciprocal pronouns, 3, 55
   distinction from reflexive pronouns, 55
   Table 2
      Reflexive and reciprocal pronouns, 3
reciprocal verbs, 225
   reciprocal pronouns as objects, 55
reciprocity, 55
recognize
   stative verb, 219
recommend
   subordinate clause subjunctive, 228
   verb followed by gerund, 267
recommendation
   followed by infinitive, 277
reduced relative clauses, 175
reflexive pronouns, 3, 53
   as intensifiers, 55
   Table 13 Reflexive pronouns, 54
   Table 2 Reflexive and reciprocal pronouns, 3

reflexive verbs, 224
refrain from
   followed by gerund, 268
refusal
   followed by infinitive, 277
refuse
   elision of direct object, 16
   verb followed by infinitive, 273
regarding
   preposition and participle, 172
   simple preposition, 171
regret
   followed by gerund *or* infinitive, 281
   verb followed by gerund, 267
regular verbs, 7, 217
   Table 47 Spelling rules - simple past and past participle, 217
   Table 48 Spelling rules - present participle and gerund, 217
regularly
   adverb of time-frequency, 135, 136
relative clauses, 60
relative pronouns, 3, 60
   in complex sentences, 192
   omission, 61
relieved
   followed by infinitive, 276
reluctant
   followed by infinitive, 276
remain
   linking verb, 221
   stative verb, 219
remaining
   specifying adjective, 82
remember
   followed by gerund *or* infinitive, 281
   stative verb, 219
remind
   followed by indirect object and infinitive, 273
reminder
   followed by infinitive, 277
repeatedly
   adverb of time-frequency, 136
request
   followed by indirect object and infinitive, 273
   followed by infinitive, 277
   subordinate clause subjunctive, 228
requests
   answers, 255
   modality, 254
require
   subordinate clause subjunctive, 228
requirement
   followed by infinitive, 277

resemble
   linking verb, 221
   stative verb, 219
resist
   verb followed by gerund, 267
responsibility
   modality, 252
responsibility for
   followed by gerund, 268
right
   comparative form exception, 156
risk
   verb followed by gerund, 267
round
   adverbial particle, 130
   simple preposition, 171
rule
   verb taking object complement, 16
run
   dynamic verb, 218

safe
   comparative forms, 156
same
   specifying adjective, 82
satisfy
   stative verb, 219
save
   simple preposition, 171
scales
   as plural noun, 39
scarcely ever
   adverbial of time-frequency, 136
schwa, 182
scissors
   as plural noun, 39, 51
score
   dynamic verb, 218
second person, 47, 49, 52, 54
see
   stative verb, 219
seeing
   subordinator of reason, 196
seeing that
   conjunction, 190
seem
   linking verb, 16, 221
   stative verb, 219
   verb taking subject complement, 19
seldom
   adverb of time-frequency, 136
   creating negative sentences, 25
semantic classification, 131
semicolons
   in compound complex sentences, 193
   in compound sentences, 192

  linking clauses, 200
semi-modals, 240, 244
sentence, 13
sentence structure
  simple sentence structure, 18
sentence types, 25, 192
  complex sentences, 193
  compound complex sentences, 193
  compound sentences, 192
  declarative sentences, 25
  interrogative sentences, 25
  simple sentences, 192
serial comma, 200
several
  determiner of magnitude, 104
  indefinite pronoun, 56
  number, 58
  postdeterminer, 101
  quantifier indefinite pronoun, 57
shall
  modal of obligation, 253
  modal of offer, 255
  modal of promise, 257
  modal of suggestion, 249
  modal verb, 7, 240
she
  feminine inflection, 48
  personal subjective pronoun, 3
  subjective pronoun, 49
  third person singular feminine personal pronoun, 48
shhh
  interjection, 338
shine
  linking verb, 221
  stative verb, 219
shingles
  as singular noun, 51
short
  as adjective and adverb, 91
  flat adverb, 126, 155
shortly
  different from flat adverb form, 155
shorts
  as plural noun, 39, 51
should
  modal of advice, 247
  modal of obligation, 253
  modal of probability, 251
  modal of suggestion, 249
  modal verb, 240, 244
show
  elision of direct object, 16
  verb forms, 293
simple aspect
  future simple, 319
  past simple, 307
  present simple, 295
simple gerund, 269
simple infinitive, 275
simple sentence structure, 18, 21
  Table 5 Simple sentence structure, 21
simple sentences, 14, 192
since
  conjunction, 190
  conjunction and preposition, 191
  introducing adverbials of relative time, 138
  introducing adverbials of time, 140
  position in a sentence, 139
  preposition and conjunction, 172
  preposition of time, 9, 178
  punctuation, 202
  simple preposition, 171
  subordinating conjunction, 8, 195
  subordinator of reason, 196
  subordinator of time, 196
single-word conjunctions
  Table 42 Single-word conjunctions, 190
singular nouns, 34, 36
  inflection for number, 39
sit
  linking verb, 221
  stative verb, 219
slightly
  adverb of quantity, 144
slow
  used as adverb, 155
smell
  linking verb, 221
  stative verb, 219
so
  adverb of degree, 143
  conjunction, 190
  coordinating conjunction, 8, 193
  inversion of order, 194
  punctuation, 201
  subordinating conjunction, 195
  subordinator of reason, 196
  subordinator of result, 196
so ... as
  in comparative structures, 164
so as + *to-infinitive*
  conjunction, 190
  subordinator of purpose, 196
so that
  conjunction, 190
  subordinator of purpose, 196
  subordinator of result, 196
some

    central determiner, 101
    determiner of indefiniteness, 103
    determiner of magnitude, 104
    general indefinite pronoun, 56
    indefinite pronoun, 56
    limiting adjective indicating number, 73
    number, 58
    quantifier indefinite pronoun, 57
somebody
    affirmative sentences, 58
    general indefinite pronoun, 56
    indefinite pronoun, 56
    interrogative sentences, 58
    number, 57
someone
    affirmative sentences, 58
    indefinite pronoun, 56
    interrogative sentences, 58
    number, 57
something
    affirmative sentences, 58
    general indefinite pronoun, 56
    indefinite pronoun, 56
    interrogative sentences, 58
    number, 57
sometimes
    adverb of time-frequency, 135, 136
somewhere
    adverb of place, 133
soon
    adverb of time-when, 134
    gradability, 153
sorry
    predicative adjective, 87
sound
    linking verb, 221
    stative verb, 219
spasmodically
    adverb of time-frequency, 136
specific
    specifying adjective, 82
specifying adjectives, 81, 82
    order in a sentence, 88
spelling
    comparative and superlative forms, 155, 157, 158
    gerund and present participle, 217
    -ly adverbs, 128
    plurals - Latin and Greek roots, 40
    plurals - regular, 40
    regular verbs - simple past and past participle forms, 217
spend
    verb followed by gerund, 267
sporadically
    adverb of time-frequency, 136

start
    followed by gerund *or* infinitive, 280
state verbs. *See* stative verbs
statistics
    as singular noun, 39
stative verbs, 7, 219
    future perfect progressive exception, 326
    future progressive exception, 322
    linking verbs, 16
    past perfect progressive exception, 316
    past progressive exception, 312
    present perfect progressive exception, 306
    present progressive exception, 300
stay
    linking verb, 221
    stative verb, 219
still
    adverb of relative time, 138
    position in a sentence, 139
stipulate
    subordinate clause subjunctive, 228
stop
    followed by gerund *or* infinitive, 281
straight
    as adjective and adverb, 91
    flat adverb, 126, 155
stressed form, 182
    auxiliaries and modals, 258
strong form. *See* stressed form
subject complements, 16, 19, 32, 220
    distinction from objects, 18
    interrogative pronouns, 62
    objective pronouns, 48
    possessive pronouns, 53
    subjective pronouns, 48
subject/verb agreement, 39, 64, 227, 230
subjective case, 34, 41, 47
    interrogative pronouns, 61
    relative pronouns, 60
    use in comparatives, 162
subjective complements. *See* subject complement
subjective personal pronouns, 48
    as subject complement, 48
    Table 10 By person and number, 48
subjective pronouns, 3, 48
    use in comparatives, 162
subjects, 13, 14, 32
    elision in imperative mood, 227
    gerund as subject, 266
    infinitive as subject of sentence, 272
    interrogative pronouns, 61
    of ergative verbs, 225
    of reciprocal verbs, 225
    placement in interrogative sentences, 61

possessive pronouns, 52
postponed, 23
subjective pronouns, 48
variations, 22
subjunctive mood, 228
subordinate clauses, 130, *See* dependent clauses
   in subjunctive mood, 228
   taking the role of nouns, 197
subordinate conjunctions. *See* subordinating conjunctions
subordinating clause introducers. *See* subordinating conjunctions
subordinating conjunctions, 8, 195
   complementizers, 197
   in complex sentences, 192
   in compound complex sentences, 193
   introducing adverbial clauses, 130
   placement in a sentence, 199
   semantics, 195, 196
   similarity to adverbs, 195
   syntax, 195
   use in complex sentences, 195
subordinators, 196, *See* subordinating conjunctions
subordinators of concession or contrast, 196
subordinators of condition, 196
subordinators of manner, 196
subordinators of place, 196
subordinators of purpose, 196
subordinators of reason, 196
subordinators of result, 196
subordinators of time, 196
subsequent
   determiner of definiteness, 103
   postdeterminer, 101
succeed in
   followed by gerund, 268
such
   determiner of magnitude, 104
   predeterminer, 101
such that
   conjunction, 190
   subordinator of result, 196
sufficiently
   adverb of quantity, 144
suffix *–er*
   in comparative forms, 154, 155, 158
suffix *–est*
   in superlative forms, 154, 155
suffixes
   associated with adjectives, 74
   associated with adverbs, 126
   associated with nouns, 31
   associated with verbs, 209
   -ed, 308
   -er, 154
   -est, 154
   -ly, 76, 126
   -ly spelling rules, 128
suggest
   subordinate clause subjunctive, 228
   verb followed by gerund, 267
suggestion
   followed by infinitive, 277
   modality, 249
superlative adjectives, 105, 151, 153
superlative adverbs, 151
superlatives, 151
suppose
   stative verb, 219
supposing
   conjunction, 190
   subordinator of condition, 196
supposing that
   conjunction, 190
surprise
   stative verb, 219

tag questions, 26
talent for
   followed by gerund, 268
taste
   linking verb, 16, 221
   stative verb, 219
teach
   as reflexive verb, 54
   elision of direct object, 16
   followed by indirect object and infinitive, 273
   reflexive verb, 224
team
   as collective noun, 40
tell
   elision of direct object, 16
   followed by indirect object and infinitive, 273
temporal noun phrases. *See* adverbials of time
temporarily
   adverb of time-duration, 137
tendency
   followed by infinitive, 277
tense, 6
tense (time), 289
tensed verbs. *See* verb forms - finite
tenses, 289
   aspect, 289
   concept questions, 329

forms, 293
  forms in interrogatives, 294
  future perfect, 323
  future perfect progressive, 325
  future progressive, 321
  future simple, 319
  future tenses, 318
  past perfect, 313
  past perfect progressive, 316
  past progressive, 310
  past simple, 307
  past tenses, 307
  present perfect, 301
  present perfect progressive, 304
  present progressive, 299
  present tenses, 295
  Table 53 Forms in affirmative statements, 293
  Table 54 Forms in negative statements, 293
  tenses tree, 329
  time, 289
tenses tree, 329
terrified of
  followed by gerund, 268
test
  linking verb, 221
  stative verb, 219
than
  in comparative structures, 161, 162, 163, 165, 166
  simple preposition, 171
thank for
  followed by gerund, 268
that
  central determiner, 101
  complementizer, 197
  conjunction, 190
  demonstrative pronoun, 4, 63
  determiner of definiteness, 103
  far proximity, 64
  in conjunction phrases, 190
  limiting adjective indicating number, 73
  relative pronoun, 3, 60
the. *See* definite article
  central determiner, 101
  determiner of definiteness, 103
  in comparative structures, 166
the minute
  conjunction, 190
  subordinator of time, 196
the moment
  conjunction, 190
  subordinator of time, 196
the reason...
  as subject in cleft sentences, 22

the second
  conjunction, 190
  subordinator of time, 196
the thing that...
  as subject in cleft sentences, 22
the way
  conjunction, 190
  subordinator of manner, 196
their
  central determiner, 101
  determiner of definiteness, 103
theirs
  possessive pronoun, 3, 52
them
  objective pronoun, 49
  personal objective pronoun, 3
themselves
  reflexive pronoun, 3, 54
then
  conjunctive adverb, 197
there
  adverb of place, 133
  as subject, 23
  as subject or object, 22, 24
  non-referential, 23
therefore
  conjunctive adverb, 197
these
  central determiner, 101
  demonstrative pronoun, 4, 63
  determiner of definiteness, 103
  determiner of indefiniteness, 103
  limiting adjective indicating number, 73
  near proximity, 64
they
  expressing indefiniteness, 56
  general indefinite pronoun, 56
  personal subjective pronoun, 3
  subjective pronoun, 49
  third person plural personal pronoun, 48
think
  stative verb, 219
  verb taking object complement, 16
third person, 47, 49, 51, 52, 54
  singular pronoun, 51
this
  central determiner, 101
  demonstrative pronoun, 4, 63
  determiner of definiteness, 103
  determiner of indefiniteness, 103
  limiting adjective indicating number, 73
  near proximity, 64
those
  central determiner, 101
  demonstrative pronoun, 4, 63
  determiner of definiteness, 103

far proximity, 64
limiting adjective indicating number, 73
though
   conjunction, 190
   subordinating conjunction, 195
   subordinating conjunction in complex sentence, 193
   subordinator of contrast, 196
threaten
   followed by gerund *or* infinitive, 278
   verb followed by infinitive, 273
three-word phrasals. *See* phrasal prepositonal verbs
through
   adverbial particle, 130
   preposition of time, 178
   simple preposition, 171
throughout
   simple preposition, 171
tights
   as plural noun, 39
till
   conjunction, 190
time
   as an element of tense, 289
   as object of a preposition, 178
   countability and definiteness, 117
   presentation of time in the classroom, 290
to
   ellipsis of verb in infinitives, 278
   introducing indirect object, 180
   preposition of movement, 179
   preposition of time, 178
   simple preposition, 171
to-infinitive. *See* infinitive
tolerate
   followed by gerund *or* infinitive, 280
   verb followed by gerund, 267
tomorrow
   adverb of time-when, 134
too
   adverb of degree, 143
   adverb of quantity, 144
   with infinitive, 276
total
   intensifying adjective, 84
toward
   preposition of movement, 179
toward/towards
   simple preposition, 171
transitive complex verbs, 223
transitive phrasal verbs, 232
   inseparable, 232
   separable, 232

transitive verbs, 7, 222
   ditransitive verbs, 223
   ergative verbs, 224
   monotransitive verbs, 223
   reflexive verbs, 224
   taking of objects, 15
   transitive complex verbs, 223
   transitive phrasal verbs, 232
trousers
   as plural noun, 39
true
   comparative forms, 156
   intensifying adjective, 84
turn
   linking verb, 221
   stative verb, 219
turn up
   linking verb, 221
   stative verb, 219
twice
   determiner of magnitude, 104
   predeterminer, 101
typically
   adverb of time-frequency, 136

ugh
   interjection, 337
ultimate
   determiner of definiteness, 103
   postdeterminer, 101
uncountable nouns, 1, 34, 36
   used in a countable way, 37
   used in plural form, 38
under
   adverbial particle, 130
   preposition of place, 9, 176
   simple preposition, 171
underneath
   preposition and adverb, 172
   simple preposition, 171
understand
   stative verb, 219
unless
   conjunction, 190
   elision of subject and *be*, 195
   subordinating conjunction, 8, 195
unlike
   simple preposition, 171
unquestionably
   as emphasizing adverb, 165
unstressed form, 182
   auxiliaries and modals, 258
until
   conjunction, 190
   conjunction and preposition, 191

preposition of time, 9, 178
simple preposition, 171
subordinating conjunction, 8, 195
subordinator of time, 196
up
   adverbial particle, 130
   preposition of direction, 179
   simple preposition, 171
upon
   simple preposition, 171
upper case. *See* capital letters
upstairs
   adverb of place, 133
urge
   followed by indirect object and infinitive, 273
   subordinate clause subjunctive, 228
us
   objective pronoun, 49
   personal objective pronoun, 3
use
   monotransitive verb, 223
used to
   semi-modal, 244
   to express past time, 258
usually
   adverb of time-frequency, 136
utter
   intensifying adjective, 84

verb classifications, 214
   auxiliary verbs, 215
   ditransitive verbs, 223
   dynamic verbs, 218
   ergative verbs, 224
   general, 214
   intransitive verbs, 222
   irregular verbs, 217
   main verbs, 214
   morphological, 216
   reciprocal verbs, 225
   reflexive verbs, 224
   regular verbs, 217
   semantic, 218
   stative verbs, 219
   syntactic, 222
   transitive complex verbs, 223
   transitive verbs, 223
verb forms, 6, 209
   base form, 6, 210
   finite, 212
   gerund, 211
   infinitive, 211
   non-finite, 210
   perticiple, 211
   phrasal verbs, 7

verb phrases, 229
   order, 230
verbal nouns. *See* infinitives
verbals. *See* non-finite verbs
verbs, 6, 209
   aspect, 289
   auxiliary verbs, 7, 215
   classifications, 214
   ditransitive verbs, 223
   dynamic verbs, 7, 218
   ergative verbs, 224
   followed by gerund, 267
   followed by gerunds *or* infinitives, 278
   followed by infinitive, 273
   gerunds, 8
   head of the predicate, 13
   infinitives, 8
   intransitive phrasal verbs, 231
   intransitive verbs, 7, 222
   irregular verbs, 7, 217
   main verbs, 7, 214
   modal verbs, 7
   monotransitive verbs, 223
   mood, 226
   phrasal verbs, 231
   reciprocal verbs, 225
   reflexive verbs, 224
   regular verbs, 7, 217
   stative verbs, 7, 219
   tenses, 289
   transitive complex verbs, 223
   transitive phrasal verbs, 232
   transitive verbs, 7, 223
   verb phrases, 229
verbs followed by gerunds *or* infinitives, 278
   change in meaning, 281
   little difference in meaning, 279
   no change in meaning, 278
verbs of perception
   followed by infinitive, 272
versus
   simple preposition, 171
very
   adverb of degree, 143
   adverb of quantity, 144
   overuse, 144
   placement in a sentence, 145
very much
   placement in a sentence, 145
via
   preposition of transport, 179
   simple preposition, 171
vote
   subordinate clause subjunctive, 228

walk
    regular verb, 7
want
    stative verb, 219
    verb followed by infinitive, 273
warn
    infinitive as object complement, 274
was
    form of *be*, 308
    in past progressive, 311
wasn't
    form of *be*, 308
way
    as emphasizing adverb, 165
    followed by infinitive, 277
we
    first person plural personal pronoun, 48
    personal subjective pronoun, 3
    subjective pronoun, 49
weak form. *See* unstressed form
weigh
    stative verb, 219
well
    adverb of manner, 132
    interjection, 337
    irregular comparative, 160
    predicative adjective, 87
    vs. *good*, 127
were
    form of *be*, 308
    in past progressive, 311
weren't
    form of *be*, 308
what
    central determiner, 101
    determiner of indefiniteness, 103
    determiner of magnitude, 104
    in exclamatory sentences, 27
    interrogative adjective, 82
    interrogative pronoun, 4, 61, 62, 63
    objective pronoun, 62, 63
    predeterminer, 101
    subjective pronoun, 63
what-clauses
    as subject in cleft sentences, 22
whatever
    central determiner, 101
    determiner of indefiniteness, 103
when
    conjunction, 190
    elision of subject and *be*, 195
    subordinating conjunction, 195
    subordinator of time, 196
whenever
    elision of subject and *be*, 195

where
    conjunction, 190
    subordinating conjunction, 195
    subordinator of place, 196
whereas
    conjunction, 190
    subordinating conjunction, 195
    subordinator of contrast, 196
wherever
    conjunction, 190
    subordinating conjunction, 195
    subordinator of place, 196
whether
    complementizer, 197
    conjunction, 190
    subordinating conjunction, 195
    subordinator of condition, 196
whether ... or
    conjunction, 191
    correlative conjunction, 8, 194
whether or not
    conjunction, 190
    subordinator of condition, 196
which
    central determiner, 101
    complementizer, 197
    determiner of indefiniteness, 103
    interrogative adjective, 82
    interrogative pronoun, 4, 61, 62, 82
    relative pronoun, 3, 60
whichever
    central determiner, 101
    determiner of indefiniteness, 103
while
    conjunction, 190
    elision of subject and *be*, 195
    punctuation, 202
    similar to *during*, 191
    subordinating conjunction, 195
    subordinator of contrast, 196
    subordinator of time, 196
whilst
    conjunction, 190
    subordinator of contrast, 196
    subordinator of time, 196
who
    complementizer, 197
    interrogative pronoun, 4, 61, 63
    relative pronoun, 3, 60
    relative pronoun introducing subordinate clause, 193
    subjective pronoun, 61, 63
whom
    complementizer, 197
    interrogative pronoun, 4, 61, 62, 63

    objective pronoun, 62, 63
    relative pronoun, 3, 60
whoosh
    interjection, 338
whose
    determiner of indefiniteness, 103
    interrogative adjective, 82
    interrogative pronoun, 4, 61, 62
    possessive pronoun, 4, 62
wh-questions, 26
wh-words, 61
    as object of a preposition, 174
will
    auxiliary verb, 216, 237, 239
    in future perfect, 324
    in future perfect progressive, 326
    in future progressive, 321
    in future simple, 319, 320
    modal of ability, 246
    modal of certainty, 250
    modal of necessity, 252
    modal of offer, 255
    modal of promise, 257
    modal of request, 254
    modal verb, 7, 240
    to express future time, 258
wise
    comparative forms, 156
wish
    followed by infinitive, 277
    stative verb, 219
    subordinate clause subjunctive, 228
    verb followed by infinitive, 273
with
    indicating manner, 180
    simple preposition, 171
within
    preposition of time, 178
    simple preposition, 171
without
    simple preposition, 171
without a doubt
    as emphasizing adverbial, 165
won't
    in future perfect, 324
    in future progressive, 321
    in future simple, 319
worried about
    followed by gerund, 268
would
    modal of offer, 255
    modal of request, 254
    modal verb, 240, 244
    to express past time, 258
would like
    semi-modal, 244
would prefer
    modal of preference, 256
    semi-modal, 244
would rather
    modal of preference, 256
    semi-modal, 244
would sooner
    modal of preference, 256
wow
    interjection, 337
write
    elision of direct object, 16
wrong
    as adjective and adverb, 91
    comparative form exception, 156

yearning
    followed by infinitive, 277
yes
    adverb of assertion, 142
    interjection, 142, 337
yes/no questions, 26
yet
    adverb of relative time, 138
    conjunction, 190
    coordinating conjunction, 8, 193
    position in a sentence, 139
yikes
    interjection, 337
you
    expressing indefiniteness, 56
    general indefinite pronoun, 56
    objective pronoun, 49
    personal objective pronoun, 3
    personal subjective pronoun, 3
    second person plural personal pronoun, 48
    second person singular personal pronoun, 48
    subjective pronoun, 49
your
    central determiner, 101
    determiner of definiteness, 103
yours
    possessive pronoun, 3, 52
yourself
    reflexive pronoun, 3, 54
yourselves
    reflexive pronoun, 54

zero article, 108, 114, *See* indefinite articles
    determiner of indefiniteness, 103

www.ingramcontent.com/pod-product-compliance
Lightning Source LLC
Chambersburg PA
CBHW080722300426
44114CB00019B/2466